Rethinking Rights and Responsibilities

Rethinking Rights and Responsibilities

The Moral Bonds of Community

Arthur J. Dyck

The Pilgrim Press   *Cleveland, Ohio*

The Pilgrim Press, Cleveland, Ohio 44115
© 1994 by Arthur J. Dyck

Printed in the United States of America
The paper used in this publication is acid free

99 98 97 96 95 94 5 4 3 2 1

Library of Congress Cataloging-in-Publication Data

Dyck, Arthur J., 1932–
    Rethinking rights and responsibilities : the moral bonds of
community / Arthur J. Dyck.
        p.   cm.
    Includes bibliographical references and index.
    ISBN 0-8298-1002-1 (cloth : acid-free paper). — ISBN
0-8298-1006-4 (pbk. : acid-free paper)
    1. Human rights.   2. Natural law.   3. Individualism.
4. Community.   5. Responsibility.   6. Social justice.   7. Right to
health care.   I. Title.
JC571.D9616   1994
172—dc20   94-3889
                                                                CIP

To the memory of my mother and father and to my grandson, Joseph Arthur, with love and gratitude for all I have learned and now learn of the strength of the moral bonds of community.

Contents

Acknowledgments

This book views the moral bonds of community as sources, standards, and sustenance for our responsibilities and rights as human beings. It is profoundly fitting that I am deeply moved to dedicate this work to the memory of my mother and father, for as a result of these reflections, I have become more aware than ever before of what it means to be lovingly nurtured into life physically, morally, and spiritually. It is equally fitting to dedicate this work to my grandson, my companion for more than six years. Without him, I would not have known firsthand the strong bond awakened by the child of one's child. My first book was dedicated to my children, Sandra and Cynthia, and my wife Sylvia. As the blessed participant in all of these precious bonds, I do not regard the moral bonds of community and our utter dependence upon one another as abstractions or mere conceptual constructs. Mutual love ties me to all of these individuals. These bonds are at once personal and communal. There is no way I could adequately express the joy, fulfillment, and gratitude these ties and this love brings. My hope is that this book worthily expresses our mutual love and the love of the One who makes life and love possible.

This book began with a sabbatical partly funded by the Joseph P. Kennedy, Jr., Foundation. For that, I owe special thanks to Eunice and Sarge Shriver, and to the late Paul Ramsey who commended the project to them. Along the way, it was helpful to try out some of the early thinking in this book in a series of lectures at

Tabor College. I thank Vernon Janzen, then president of Tabor, for the invitation, and both him and professor Wesley Prieb for their helpful and encouraging comments.

I have been blessed to receive instruction from many talented scholars. Some of my debts to the late Roderick Firth and James Luther Adams are quite explicitly referenced in the book. But the inspiration of these exceedingly fine teachers is more than I can know and measure. They have my gratitude.

My colleagues at Harvard Divinity School have been a source of insight and encouragement. On at least two occasions, I had the benefit of open discussions of the manuscript with the faculty. I appreciate especially Dean Ronald Thiemann's critical response to portions of the manuscript and his consistent support. I appreciate as well the insights and comments from colleagues in ethics, some formerly students of mine and some presently; my thanks to Pia Altieri, John Kilner, Robin Lovin, and Nancy Platteborze.

Everyone who aspires to publish a book should have the kind of secretarial assistance I do not take for granted. I appreciate the skills, intellect, counsel, and good-humored wit of Kay Shanahan. That wit has survived many drafts. Thanks also to Bruce Krag and Jenny Song for additional assistance when necessary.

Everyone who aspires to publish a book also needs a press and its editors. I am grateful to have Richard Brown and Marj Pon as editors at Pilgrim Press. Richard has proven to be a genuine scholarly colleague. What a joy it was to me that he had such an immediate and enthusiastic grasp of what this book intends to convey. He strengthened my resolve to share my thoughts in print.

Rethinking Rights and Responsibilities

Introduction

This book surprised me. I began several years ago intending to study contemporary theories of human rights, in part to supplement my own education in the field of ethics, and in part to examine why the language of rights has so largely replaced the language of rules, obligations, and responsibilities. I thought that the language and concepts of rights might be widely shared, especially in light of the claim of the United Nations to universality in matters of rights and the growing tendency to judge nations by international standards of respect for human rights. I thought that such claims and such judgments, and the bases for making them, would receive strong backing in the philosophical literature. But then I began my study. What I soon discovered greatly changed my thinking. I became convinced that human rights must be reconceptualized and urgently so. Reconceptualizing rights is the central task of this book.

Why take on this task and why the urgency about doing so? What I discovered from the very outset of my research can be summarized as follows:

1. Human rights are being seriously violated not only in practice, but in theory.
2. Theories of rights, historically and contemporaneously, foster separation and undermine the human relations that make communities possible.

3. Theories of rights are in serious conflict, but theories that insufficiently protect individual human life appear to be gaining in strength and ascendancy.

Let me now briefly introduce, in a preliminary way, some of the sources for these discoveries. I begin with some skepticism I found about rights and morality itself.

"We have—very largely, if not entirely—lost our comprehension, both theoretical and practical, of morality":[1] this is the central thesis of a recent historical and philosophical study by the contemporary philosopher Alasdair MacIntyre. Sixty-six years before MacIntyre published his study, Sigmund Freud, the founder of psychoanalysis, was sadly expressing his deeply felt lack of comprehension of his own moral life: "When I ask myself why I have always aspired to behave honorably, to spare others and to be kind whenever possible, and why I didn't cease doing so when I realized that in this way one comes to harm and becomes an anvil because other people are brutal and unreliable, then indeed I have no answer."[2] A college undergraduate recently said to me, "It is not possible to make moral judgments, particularly of the behavior of others. Hitler, after all, had his reasons. Everyone can justify what they do and who are we to question their attempts to do what they believe is right? There is no right or wrong—no ethics!"

More than sixty years ago, Freud found his own moral behavior incomprehensible. But, unlike that college student of our own decade, he did not doubt that what he sought to do was morally right, and the brutality he experienced in return, morally wrong. The student I cited, who is not alone, is expressly doubtful that he, or a professor of ethics, can make a moral distinction between the brutalities perpetrated by a Hitler and the kindnesses mentioned by a Freud. Yet the student tries to convince me and others that we should not attempt to distinguish what is moral from what is not. MacIntyre notes that the language and appearance of morality does indeed persist, but, and this is his most devastating claim, "The integral substance of morality has to a large degree been fragmented and then in part destroyed."[3]

MacIntyre expects us to express disbelief about this claim. The disturbing reality, however, is that both theoretically and practically the *substance* of morality is being threatened, if not seriously eroded.

Consider the fact that all of life is held hostage by a proliferation of sophisticated weaponry. Despite recent, hopefully growing efforts to reduce weapons of mass destruction, nuclear weapons still exist and conventional weapons are killing countless human beings, whether two days or ninety years old. Moral innocence or neutrality is no guarantee that human life will be protected. What do human rights amount to in such a situation? The international codes on land warfare declare it criminal to kill deliberately, or even hurt, a single civilian or prisoner of war. Yet the bombardment of cities—whether by air, land, or sea—employing conventional weapons, as in World War II, Vietnam, Afghanistan, Cambodia, Lebanon, and now in former Yugoslavia, although it could be called the moral equivalent of murder and terrorism, is not predictably and universally regarded as such.

Whatever the reader may think about war, conduct in war, and nuclear weaponry, these practices exist and are widely accepted. Western democracies and oppressive regimes alike participate in policies that permit the sacrificing of individuals, even whole classes of people, for the sake of what is calculated to be best for the greatest number, or necessary for the retention of existing governments. This analysis applies as well to the tolerance for enormous economic disparities and poverty.[4]

This actual disregard of human rights and liberties is theoretically sanctioned in philosophy. G. E. M. Anscombe has noted this precisely with regard to the lack of protection of innocent persons in judicial judgments and of noncombatants in war. Anscombe sees all of English moral philosophy since and including Henry Sidgwick in the nineteenth century as similarly flawed in this regard: "Every one of the best known English academic moral philosophers has put out a philosophy according to which, e.g., it is not possible to hold that it cannot be right to kill the innocent as a means to any end whatsoever and that someone who thinks otherwise is in error."[5] They have, she says, constructed "systems according to which the man who says 'We need such-and-such, and will only get it this way' *may* be a virtuous character." And, she complains, this includes the acceptance of circumstances that morally justify what can only be called strictly unjust, "the judicial condemnation of the innocent."[6]

And so individual rights are rendered mute and meaningless in theory and practice. But much is made of rights these days. What is one to think of the rapidly growing lists, codes, and declarations so conscientiously promulgated? One might contend that the significance of human rights and the necessity for their assertion have never been better understood and never been so broadly supported globally. Yet, if a right is to be secured, there must be those who work to make that happen. If a life is to be protected, people must exist who feel that responsibility and who cooperate to foster life and its supporting matrix. Life is brought into being, nurtured, defended, and encouraged to flourish, in communities.

What is happening in theory and practice to communities? As Leo Strauss has so brilliantly shown, there is a radical shift in moral thought and practice when the modern era is ushered in by Hobbes.[7] Traditional theories of natural right included those of Socrates, Plato, the Stoics, Aristotle, Thomas, and Calvin. Despite their differences, all of these earlier thinkers had depicted humans as social beings, desirous of offspring and of forming communities. Hobbes rejected this view. He saw the desire for self-preservation and the freedom to satisfy one's egoistic impulses as characteristic of human beings. Humans seek pleasures and avoid pain for themselves. Previous natural-right thinking viewed virtue, or the good life, as the goal of both individuals and communities. The necessities of life serve as means to this end. Hobbes began, and Locke perpetuated, a theory of rights that makes individual acquisitiveness and the pleasure of having things for oneself primary; the satisfaction of wants is no longer to be limited by the demands of the good life; wants become aimless. Indeed, in Locke, unlimited acquisition, and the protection for the quest, is the reason for forming a society and submitting to a government. "Life," Strauss observes, "is, on this way of thinking, the joyless quest for joy."[8] Locke even claims that "unlimited appropriation without concern for the need of others is true charity."[9] Locke believed that emancipating acquisitiveness increases the total wealth and resources of our world.

If everyone's desire for things is unrestrained, how will such a desire be realized at all? Since Hobbes and Locke, it is commonplace to think of society as formed through a social contract, an invention in order to restrain by means of force the destructive egoistic impulses of individuals and hence make liberty possible. Restraining certain egoistic expressions is no longer thought of as natural and virtuous but as a necessity, forced upon individuals by a sovereign power. Rather, the individual and the ego become the center and origin of the moral world, replacing natural responsibilities.

The desires of the human ego need not be destructive of community and mutual aid, not if human beings are social animals, naturally desiring offspring and practicing mutual aid. But these rights theories broke sharply with such a social conception of individuals. Locke exhibits this break most brazenly when he asserts, "The first and strongest desire God planted in man is not the concern with others, not even concern with one's offspring but the desire for self-preservation."[10] This lack of mutual regard and responsibility permeates familial relations for Locke. For him, children's obligations terminate beyond the age of minority, and in any event, the injunction to honor your father and mother applies only if they, the parents, have deserved it.

At this point, we see in Locke something that is a strong tendency of modern thought: procreation, having offspring and nurturing them, is not viewed as creating moral bonds and mutual responsibilities of a permanent character. I have heard students and others say—I am always astonished by this—"I don't owe my parents anything." (Life, at least, I would have thought, and enough loving care to develop!) One student even declared categorically:

"I don't owe anybody anything." This he said in anger, during a lecture in which I stressed our indebtedness to others for what they have done for us. How will human rights be realized by individuals who owe one another nothing?

Self-preservation does not make a community. Self-preservation occurs only when an individual is brought into being and nurtured by others, and when restraint from harm is observed and effectively enforced, again, by others. Individual life is not actually something that comes solely by having a living body of one's own but is a state of interdependence, maintained by a human network of aid, services, and restraint. Even persons living in isolation on the labor of their own hands exclusively continue to do so only as long as others do not prevent them in any way, and only after they have been brought into being and nurtured by others long enough to be able to sustain themselves. And, of course, the environment—the sources of food, air, and water—must not be destroyed by anyone, as it now so easily can be.

For the most part, contemporary rights theories do indeed justify "separation," as Carol Gilligan has recently maintained, but it is "attachment that creates and sustains the human community."[11] On the basis of her studies of moral development, Gilligan found that women tend to see morality "as arising from the experience of connection and conceived as a problem of inclusion rather than one of balancing claims."[12] This flies in the face of most contemporary rights theories with their stress on achieving autonomy and the satisfaction of one's own desires. It challenges theories of moral and self-development that have followed contemporary rights theory in seeing individual autonomy as the height of maturity. Gilligan presents a concept of maturity that finds its expression in the recognition of our interdependence as human beings and in "taking care."

In one of Gilligan's studies, female subjects were interviewed with regard to their abortion decisions. Their stories include disturbing instances of male disregard for them as individuals and for the responsibilities of procreation and nurture. In one case, it is a lover who makes it clear that the pregnant woman "could not depend on him."[13] In her despair, this woman considers that when she had an abortion, it was not her own wish but an act "commissioned by another." There was also a married woman, pregnant with her second child, who had an abortion "because her husband said he would leave her if she did not."[14] Then there is Lisa, "a fifteen-year-old who, believing in her boyfriend's love, acceded to his wish 'not to murder his child.' But after she decided not to abort the child, he left her and thus 'ruined my life.' Isolated at home taking care of the child, dependent on welfare for support, disowned by her father, and abandoned by her boyfriend, she has become unrecognizable to herself."[15] By Lisa's own account, she once was a happy person but not any more. Despite what her boyfriend has done, she still expresses love for him. This she finds utterly puzzling and a source of confusion and despair.

Although some women continue to develop moral maturity, even building on such crises, there are those who experience a "moral nihilism" as they "seek in having an abortion to cut off their feelings and not care."[16] Concisely and eloquently, Gilligan describes such moral nihilism:

> Translating the language of moral ideology into the vernacular of human relationships, these women ask themselves, "Why care?" in a world where the strong end relationships. Pregnant and wanting to live in an expanding circle of family connection, they encounter in their husbands or lovers an unyielding refusal and rejection. Construing their caring as a weakness and identifying the man's position with strength, they conclude that the strong need not be moral and that only the weak care about relationships. In this construction abortion becomes, for the woman, a test of her strength.[17]

The statistics on adolescent pregnancy, divorce, and single-parent homes indicate that there are many broken relationships being experienced in modern societies such as the United States. The drive for self-preservation and unlimited acquisition for oneself is not a drive for caring relationships in theory or in practice! The ideal of individual autonomy is not the same as the ideal of the interdependence that forms families, makes communities possible, and provides them with a future. Most modern and contemporary rights theory, and moral philosophy generally, have not made much of the indispensable value of procreation and nurturance. And that is a gross understatement. Some moral requisites of families and communities are even attacked directly by someone like Locke. What is more, Gilligan describes several theories of moral and personality development that purport to apply to both men and women and yet depict maturity as the achievement of separation and individualism:

> The models for a healthy life cycle are men who seem distant in their relationships, finding it difficult to describe their wives, whose importance in their lives they nevertheless acknowledge. The same sense of distance between self and others is evident in Levinson's conclusion that, "In our interviews, friendship was largely noticeable by its absence. As a tentative generalization we would say that close friendship with a man or a woman is rarely experienced by American men."[18]

After further analysis Gilligan concludes, "There seems to be a line of development missing from current depictions of adult development, a failure to describe the progression of relationships toward a maturity of interdependence."[19]

Current theory and practice has not generally given positive space to procreation, nurture, and the caring human relationships. Gilligan's work not only provides empirical evidence for the continued existence of a nonviolent caring ethic but shows how this ethic belongs to mature human development. The current neglect of our interdependence is especially grievous because it unfairly denigrates the interdependence more valued by women than men.

Gilligan stresses that this difference between men and women is a present empirical finding. She does not think of an ethic of caring as necessarily "female." Clearly, though, the dominant motif in moral theory and practice is not one of nurture, and nurture has been largely relegated to women, and downgraded.

Theories of rights that are devoid of a responsibility to nurture and a right to be nurtured can and do justify inequalities in the protection of human life. One way in which this occurs is by making the possession of human rights depend upon the degree to which individuals possess certain mental capacities. In an otherwise stout defense of equal rights, Alan Gewirth defines and grounds rights in a way that seriously undercuts his case for equality:

> All humans have the human rights in full to the extent that they are inherently capable of exercising them. This inherent capacity pertains to each human so long as he is a rational agent in the minimal sense of having purposes he wants to fulfill and being able to control his behavior accordingly while knowing the particular circumstances of his action.[20]

Although, as we shall see later, such a view may be unproblematic when applied to limiting a right, such as the right to vote for minors under eighteen years of age, it raises serious doubts about the equality of rights, such as the right to the protection of life for all human beings. Indeed, Michael Tooley has argued for infanticide as a morally justifiable practice on the grounds that infants have no ability to form a conception of themselves and to wish for their future existence, and since infants do not thus have a desire to live in the rational sense, they are not harmed when killed.[21] In this view, infants are denied rights to life and nurture and are not equal with adults in this regard. In the medical context, it is not infanticide in general that some are defending but rather the failure to provide lifesaving intervention for handicapped infants. It was the court in the Baby Doe case in Bloomington, Indiana (1982), that supported the parents' decision, as a right of privacy, to deny lifesaving medical intervention for their mentally impaired infant. Are human rights, particularly the rights to have one's life protected and nurtured, to be considered contingent upon opinions regarding individual life prospects? This question is being raised for individuals who are seriously ill. A number of current rights theories are creating great uncertainties about whether human beings retain their rights by reason of their humanity.

And so I have been moved to reconceptualize human rights. In part because some increasingly powerful modern and contemporary concepts of human rights sanction laws, practices, and policies, sometimes advertently, sometimes inadvertently, bent in the direction of violence and subversive of the strict equality of human rights, especially the rights to have life protected and nurtured. In part because these same theories of rights, and what they sanction, obscure or even undermine the very human bonds that naturally give rise to and sustain families and communities and by means of which human rights are actualized. And in part also because these same theories foster skepticism regarding our natural abilities to know our rights, and the human and cosmic forces by means of which they are actualized.

To whom is this book, this reconceptualization of human rights, addressed? Human rights are surely a concern of every morally conscientious individual and represent significant interests articulated in and protected by laws at all levels of government. But why should those who are not themselves within the field of ethics express their concern for human rights by reading a book in ethics that uses methods developed in philosophy and theology and asks some of the questions characteristic of these pursuits? I could argue that this is a work that is informed also by a wide variety of other fields, such as biology, the physical sciences, psychology, history, the social sciences, medicine, political and social theories, and law, including specific court decisions. I could argue that this work analyzes extremely significant, very important legal and social policies and the competing views of these: the book takes up such issues as physician-assisted suicide, divorce law, the duty to rescue, and alternative plans for universal access to health care.

But I think that what should interest the reader even more is something central to ethics as a disciplined reflection on morality and moral concepts. It is what originally drew me to the field of ethics and fuels my abiding and intense interest in it. I refer to what ethics has to presuppose if it is to have worth, at least for me, as a field of investigation and as a subject to teach. Ethics has to presuppose that people generally can and wish to learn about and act upon what they perceive to be right. What alarms me is that there are so many individuals and groups genuinely concerned about human rights who unwittingly perceive what is right through a screen of philosophical ideas of which they are not aware. And what is more, these ideas include widespread concepts of rights that separate human beings from one another and from communities, from important natural sources of moral knowledge and impulses, and from institutions and institutional arrangements that help to foster self-fulfillment through moral and spiritual development.

This present study has made me aware of how such concepts have influenced me in my thinking, teaching, and actions. It is particularly important to overcome the current skepticism that we can know what rights are due to all human beings as human beings, regardless of age, race, gender, class, ethnicity, culture, nationality, or religious affiliation. For if human rights are not knowable and universal, the quest to reduce the violations of human rights globally is a chimera, or even worse, an arbitrary interference in individual and collective behavior. A major thesis of this book is that human rights can and must be reconceptualized in a way that clarifies, rather than obscures, how we come to know and actualize them.

In order to reconceptualize human rights, I felt compelled to consider a broad range of issues but in a highly selective way to avoid an unduly lengthy treatise. The book is divided into three parts. Part I, chapters 1-4, focuses on the historical origins and current expressions of conceptions of rights that I claim have the effect of severing us from one another and from those relations that sustain individuals, families, and human communities. Only certain highly influential theories are discussed and critically analyzed. This analysis develops the major reasons for reconceptualizing rights and highlights certain problems that need to be addressed. Part II, chapters 5-9, is concerned with reconceptualizing rights and, as the title suggests, grounding rights in the moral requisites of community, in responsibilities, and in what we can know about responsibilities and rights using our natural powers. Part III, chapters 10-11, develops a notion of justice that serves as the name for those basic moral responsibilities including nurture, by means of which rights are actualized. The book ends with an epilogue to highlight what the book wishes to convey. As I now briefly describe specific chapters, I will state some of the major theses, or arguments, of the book.

Chapter 1 compares and contrasts the approach to rights found in Calvin and Hobbes. The significance of Hobbes has already been suggested earlier. Hobbes marks a sharp break with the past by repudiating the idea of Calvin, dominant in the West since Socrates, that human beings are social animals. He also breaks with the past by making rights rather than responsibilities (duties) his primary moral concept. Calvin is chosen for comparison because he represents an influential statement of our social nature as human beings, affirming our natural proclivities for, and our natural knowledge of, both good and evil. As chapter 8 will argue, these ideas from Calvin helped make the case for democratic organizations and governance. Nevertheless, in chapter 1 I contend that neither the views of Calvin nor Hobbes are totally adequate for conceptualizing rights. That human beings are basically social, as Calvin and many others have contended, is retained as a major argument in the concept of rights I defend throughout.

Chapter 2 describes a major shift away from the Hobbesian understanding of rights: Bentham and Mill derive rights from their particular utilitarian calculus, which at the same time provides their conception of what justice requires. But Bentham and Mill continue to uphold the Hobbesian notion that human beings seek pleasure and avoid pain for themselves. Through Mill's influence, this becomes a dominant strain in contemporary concepts of rights and legal decisions. Indeed, in chapter 9, an analysis of a Massachusetts Supreme Court decision reveals that the judges differed in their opinions because, although the majority cited Mill, one dissenting judge cited Hobbes and another reflected views found in Thomas and Calvin. I argue in chapter 2 that Bentham and Mill do not provide a conceptual basis for sufficiently protecting individual life and the right to equal protection of it, and they are part of the problem of eroding the bases we have for being naturally social and responsible. I do appropriate an insight from Mill in chapter 10 when I depict justice as a name for those moral responsibilities that, if not met, can be demanded from others as our human right.

In chapter 3, it is important to see why Marx and Engels reject all previous efforts to appeal to moral concepts at all, including, of course, appeals to justice and human rights. It is equally important to show why their thinking was a major formula for human rights violations and for obscuring our natural sources of moral knowledge.

The attention turns to Alan Gewirth in chapter 4. Why? The contemporary moral philosopher, Gewirth, despite all the criticisms of natural rights that have preceded him, offers a stout defense of such rights. I contend that Gewirth's defense fails. Although Gewirth's theory is individualistic, the method Gewirth has used to justify rights does, I believe, suggest a method by which to uncover the natural human relationships and responsibilities on which human rights are based and by means of which they are actualized. These are the requisites of community identified and discussed in chapter 5.

I argue in chapter 5 that there are human relations or bonds that are logically and functionally necessary to make communities and individuals possible and to sustain them. These relations, brought about by certain of our natural proclivities and inhibitions as human beings, identify basic moral responsibilities. These moral responsibilities are what actualize human rights, and they are what is demanded of human beings when rights are claimed.

Chapter 6 extends the search for what makes human rights possible. It turns out that the whole moral enterprise and its very structure presuppose that human beings act with confidence, or faith, in the power, lasting quality, and ultimate vindication of moral motivations, choices, and actions. Such faith may or may not become explicit; such faith may or may not be expressed religiously. But it is there in any choice to be moral, or to act morally.

Chapter 7 begins to provide reasons why what is identifiably moral inspires confidence, and why the confidence to act on what is identified as moral is knowledge upon which we as human beings can rely. The usual distinctions between "facts" and "values," as well as the usual distinctions between reason and perceptions, are found to be unacceptable. Building on the cognitive model introduced in chapter 7, chapter 8 argues the case for recasting the prevailing philosophical conception of impartiality as a type of individualistic, detached, observational perspective. First, I argue the case for viewing both self-love and the love of particular communities as necessary ingredients of moral cognition. Since, however, self-love and love for particular communities may distort moral perceptions and judgments, the senses in which they aid moral cognition need to be identified. I argue that self-love requires at least two ingredients as an aid to moral knowledge: empathy and wishing the self and others to exist and live. For this same purpose, love of particular communities requires a democratic social context, and one in which intentional moral communities can exist and flourish. Drawing upon what I developed in chapters 5, 6, 7, and 8, chapter 9 proposes a theory of moral cognition. What I am contending in these five chapters is that it is possible to discover those natural moral responsibilities that are requisite for agents and communities to come into being and persist, and that render actual the human rights necessary to our life together in our communities. In short, my contention is that natural rights exist and are knowable. And, for that to be true, moral responsibilities must exist and be knowable.

Chapter 9 ends with an analysis of some current arguments being used by those who propose the legalization of physician-assisted suicide. This analysis serves to apply and clarify the theory of moral cognition in the context of caring for gravely ill individuals, a context in which the appropriateness of "wishing that the self and others live" as an aid to moral cognition is expressly put to the test.

Chapter 10 develops a concept of justice that delineates how rights and responsibilities are related, and the senses in which one can speak of rights as just expectations and claims. I offer reasons for regarding nurture as a requirement of justice and, hence, as both a responsibility and right. The chapter ends with an examination of current divorce laws in the West with a focus on their tendency to undermine the responsibility to nurture children. The purpose is to draw out some of the implications for the policy of viewing nurture as a responsibility and right, and to see what happens as the individualistic view of the self found in Hobbes and Mill becomes increasingly influential within Western legal systems.

In chapter 11, I continue the focus on justice, particularly on nurture as a major expression of what justice demands of us as human beings. There are two areas in which a right to be nurtured is not sufficiently implemented or even recognized as such: in American law, the virtual absence of a "duty to rescue"; in the American health care system, the lack of universal access. These two social policies are assessed from the point of view of what it would mean to try to actualize nurture as a right to have one's life protected, and as a responsibility to rescue and protect human life and agency. At the conclusion of chapter 11, I state the theory of justice, and thus of rights, that this book is advocating, and how it differs from some other current theories. In the Epilogue, I assess briefly what rights I have not discussed and what future research would be helpful and highlight what the book has tried to say about human rights.

The suggestions I am making in this book are put forward with the hope that they will be congenial to those now concerned for human rights, and to those now concerned for mutual, caring relationships. It would be ironic, if not morally irresponsible, to forge a way of thinking about our life together that severs us from our companions in the great journey of life and history, past, present, and yet to come. Ethics, as an endeavor to understand our moral bonds, our ties to one another, must, for reasons that this book will elaborate, be carried on in a way that fosters caring relationships. Just as physics is true to the bonds that hold matter together, ethics must be true to the bonds that hold persons together as friends, families, and communities. We think of science as practical when it makes us aware of bonds that cannot be violated, for example, those that hold up bridges. It is high time once again to rediscover the bonds of community, which, if violated, break the bridges that otherwise link together diverse but fundamentally equal human beings, differing as to race, sex, citizenship, age, and religion. In a word, this book is pleading the case for seeing human caring and interdependence as practical and theoretical necessities for rendering rights actual. And in seeing that, I expect, pursuing virtue rather than joy will bring mutually shared joy.

PART I

Conceptions of Rights Reexamined

Historical and Contemporary Views that Undermine Communal Bonds

ONE

Rights
A Historic Break with the Past

In this chapter, I will focus on a contrast of Thomas Hobbes and Jean Calvin. I have already identified Hobbes as in several respects a significant source of modern, even contemporary, conceptions of rights. As Strauss says of Hobbes, he "originated an entirely new type of political doctrine. . . . He is. . . . the founder of the specifically modern natural law doctrine."[1] But why pick Calvin for comparison? He is an influential representative of the natural law tradition that Hobbes explicitly rejects.

Hobbes and Calvin are nearly contemporaries, but they are very different. Calvin was born in 1509; Hobbes in 1588. Calvin, like Hobbes, is very much ingrained in our modern assumptions and practices, although we are now less aware of what is Calvinist about Western culture than of what is Hobbesian. Nevertheless, Calvin's considerable impact on capitalism, democratic institutions, and Western literature are all well documented.[2] Calvin's thinking, like that of Hobbes, is represented in such significant historical documents as the American Declaration of Independence as noted later in this chapter.

The major break between Hobbes and Calvin lies in the complete rejection by Hobbes of the assumption that human beings are social. For Hobbes that means that no political order is, or can be, actualized by "natural duties" as the tradition represented by Calvin would have us believe. This difference between Calvin and Hobbes is still a major source of contemporary conflicts regarding human rights, law, and social policies, as chapters 9, 10, and 11 will seek to indicate. It is important, therefore, to examine this quarrel between Hobbes and Calvin. Furthermore, in Part II, I will be arguing the case for human beings as naturally social and as exhibiting the kinds of natural responsibilities that dispose humans toward democratic social and political organizations and that make those possible. In that respect, I will be siding with Calvin against Hobbes. In this chapter, however, despite what is insightful in their thinking, I will contend that neither Calvin nor Hobbes provides a fully satisfactory formulation of moral rights and responsibilities.

Hobbes on Rights

Thomas Hobbes (1588–1679), educated at Oxford, studied revolutionary politics and the new sciences. He knew Francis Bacon, Ben Jonson, Galileo, Gassendi, and Harvey. With Descartes he debated metaphysics. A Royalist politically, he sided with King Charles I against Cromwell. Having served as a tutor of Prince Charles, he fared well under royal patronage when monarchy was restored in England and the prince became Charles II.

Hobbes felt strongly compelled to sever himself from past philosophers and theologians. Indeed, he did not even cite them in his works. When challenged about this, he gave as his reason that they had nothing worthwhile to say. Strauss refers to Hobbes as "that imprudent, impish, and iconoclastic extremist, that first plebeian philosopher, who is so enjoyable a writer because of his almost boyish straightforwardness, his never failing humanity, and his marvelous clarity and force."[3] Strauss comments further that for his "recklessness," Hobbes was deservedly punished. Locke, for example, judiciously refrained as much as he could from even mentioning Hobbes in his writings. Yet, for all of this, Hobbes had an enormous influence on all subsequent political thought, Continental and English, and especially on Locke.

Why did Hobbes break so emphatically with traditional natural rights thinking? It was certainly a matter of conviction: He was convinced that "traditional political philosophy 'was rather a dream than science.'"[4] And a science was what Hobbes wanted to make out of political philosophy: "He presents his novel doctrine as the first truly scientific or philosophic treatment of natural law. . . . He means to do adequately what the Socratic tradition did in a wholly inadequate manner."[5] Socrates was regarded as the founder of political philosophy by his contemporaries, but Hobbes regarded himself as that founder.[6] The natural sciences in their modern form had emerged and they were nonteleological. To take purpose out of nature was destructive of the very basis of natural rights theories in the Socratic tradition. Hobbes believed it was necessary to base natural rights thinking on what would stand up to modern scientific scrutiny. He was the first to begin political philosophy on this premise.

Hobbes sees a fundamental mistake in traditional political philosophy: It "assumed that man is by nature a political or social animal."[7] This past error is fatal because no political order can be actualized by an appeal to "natural duty" as traditional views had thought. In other words, traditional political philosophy could not account for, or justify in any convincing way, the existence of governments and societies. They could not because human beings are actually egoistic, seeking pleasure and avoiding pain, and driven by a desire for self-preservation. To be credible and workable, any explanation and justification of government and its powers must begin with such a view of human propensities.

Hobbes, in the spirit of the new geometric applications of his day, looked for conclusions that followed of necessity from premises that could be investigated and substantiated. He was persuaded that he had discovered why governments are necessary: because of human nature. The argument went like this:

1. Human beings by nature seek their own preservation;
2. In the absence of a government with coercive power to curb this self-striving, human beings are in a state of war, living in fear, without assurance of the self-preservation they seek;

3. Out of fear for the safety they seek, human beings submit to a sovereign for the sake of peace and common defense.[8]

Hobbes generates the premises for his conclusion by having us imagine what it would be like in a "state of nature," that is, without a government. He first has us observe how we actually behave. For example, he notes that, even though we have a government and laws against stealing and murder, most of us lock our doors at night, fearful that others will seek gain at our expense and threaten our very lives in the bargain. He notes also how people arm themselves. Secondly, he calls attention to primitive tribes, expecting us to regard them as rather savage and devoid of governments.

A third argument consists in asking us to contrast bees, social insects, and human beings. The harmony reigning among bees is not possible for the very different human beings, unless they have a government. Hobbes asserts that: (1) bees are not competitive; (2) no discrepancy exists between private good and common good among bees; (3) bees are not rational and hence not critical; (4) bees lack rhetoric for stirring up discontent; (5) bees are not offended, and (6) bees are naturally social, while humans are artificially so, only when coerced.

If we grant Hobbes that human beings are by nature selfishly competitive, seeking goods for themselves, fearful of the safety they wish, and out for glory, to gain a reputation, they will, in a state of nature with no government in place, be in a "state of war." What is this "state of war" like? There is no society, that is, no industry, navigation, culture, arts, education, knowledge, and the like. For individuals, living in fear of being killed and robbed, there is only the prospect of a short, poverty-stricken, and brutish life. Furthermore, in this state of nature, that is, a state of war, there is no morality: Nothing is just or unjust; nothing is right or wrong; morality exists only in a society, whereas in a state of war, there is no society, only solitude.[9]

Naturally, then, individuals seek to satisfy their own interests. Left to themselves, they would do only this but not successfully, or so they fear. Individuals, therefore, willingly submit to an agreement, a social contract, to establish a government with the power to restrain individuals who would otherwise harm or impede them in their quest for happiness. With the formation of a government, morality and society are established. Thus, morality and society are not natural occurrences that flow from human nature but artificially created realities that require coercive power to hold together. Hobbes is the first to posit what many now take to be a self-evident and common dilemma, namely, a running conflict between the individual and society. Individual autonomy is seen as independence from society, government, and its demands; this is what individuals crave naturally; the demands of society are artificial impositions but necessary. What enhances this alleged conflict is that the preservation of peace and life requires power to curtail liberty. The legitimacy of a government and the moral obligation to be loyal to it rest on that government's ability to achieve peace and defense. Power to accomplish this is necessary and praiseworthy. Political leadership is shifted from the classical role of education, moral suasion, and the achievement of a virtuous citizenry, to the effective exercise of power to make possible the individual pursuit of pleasure, and the functions of society mentioned above.[10] Governments now are concerned to be powerful and to look out for the "national interest." Power politics and realpolitik are born, or at least given primacy, with Hobbes. Of course, power politics and catering to interests are so familiar to us now that all of history is often interpreted this way as though there is no other way, or even should be, to view things. In order to highlight how radically Hobbes breaks with the past, we will examine Calvin. His views represent the past but also present alternatives to current versions of Hobbes.

Human Rights in Calvin

Calvin's key term for what is moral is law. Morality is characteristic of human communities and these are guided and regulated by laws, general descriptions of standards of conduct for individuals, groups, and governments.

A Frenchman, educated in law and the classics, Calvin defines the term *law* carefully and precisely. *Law* is used in at least three ways by Calvin. *Law* sometimes refers to the whole system and organization of the religion of Moses.[11] Calvin, more than any of the other Protestant reformers, had great regard for Hebrew scripture and institutions and was guided by them. He did not believe, however, that the religious customs and institutions attributed to Moses should, on the whole, be viewed as binding beyond the time of Moses.

One reason not to be fully guided by the "law of Moses" is that *laws,* meaning civil, judicial, and ceremonial statutes, do not and should not conform to the particular political system obtaining under Moses.[12] Laws, in this second sense of *law,* can be expected to vary in accord with changing circumstances and needs as they arise. This variation, then, is necessary if a legal system is to conform to and promote what is moral, as it does, for example, in prohibiting murder and theft.

That brings us to the third meaning of *law* for Calvin, namely, moral law. Moral law is comprised of the Decalogue (Ten Commandments) and its summary, identified with Jesus.[13] That summary calls for love of God and neighbor. The love of neighbor includes the notion of equal regard for all persons; we are to love our neighbors as we love ourselves; this love is to extend to enemies as well.[14]

Like Thomas Aquinas before him, Calvin regarded moral law as *natural law.* It would take us too far afield to debate definitions of natural law. A key element, common to theories of the natural law variety, was a distinction made by Roman lawyers between legislated, customary laws and the higher, universal laws of reason by means of which these legally binding laws were judged and on which they were based.[15] In commerce, for example, an existing rule of exchange might be altered because reasoned deliberation found that rule to be unjust in the sense that one party was not receiving what was their due. To call a law unjust was an appeal to a higher law, or rule of conduct, universally known by reason, expressive of our social nature, and as much a part of the real world as other rules discerned by reason, as in mathematics or as in the regularities of certain casual relations. These characteristics of natural law are descriptive of moral law as Calvin depicted it.

First, Calvin did maintain that "positive law" (or as we would say now, law that has been enacted by governments or determined by courts) finds its basis and sanction in moral law. And, moral law provides what grounds we have for criticizing the laws of our legal system.[16]

Moral law is apprehensible by a person's natural powers.[17] It is also in this respect universal, known by cognitive abilities typically possessed by human beings as such.[18] The moral law is universal also in the sense that it is "implanted" in all human beings.[19] Calvin, in a more theological vein, calls the moral law within us the "image of God." In other words, we are by nature possessed of desires and abilities to will and to do what is required of us in the moral law. It is an aspect of us that equips us to do what is willed by God. In short, we are like God when we live in accord with the moral law, and as humans we normally have that capacity. Moral law is part of nature, human nature.

Furthermore, practicing the moral law is expressive of us as social beings. We are social by nature.[20] To refrain from murder, theft, lying, unfaithfulness to spouses, and envy is to refrain from acts that put us at odds with others. Practicing restraint from harming others in these ways fosters harmony with others but also within ourselves. The more we have such loving regard for others, the more we are actualizing what is distinctively and universally human, that is, love for one's neighbor.[21]

Moral law is also an activity of Being itself—God—the all-powerful force for good in the cosmos, in history, and in all human affairs.[22] The relation between divine activity and the moral law is dynamic and ongoing—not fatalistic.[23] Among the highly significant activities of the power behind the moral law is that rulers or magistrates come under the judgment of, and are responsible to, the moral law.[24] This is a very important difference between "classic natural rights doctrine," as Strauss calls it, and Calvin. Classic natural rights doctrine, both in Plato and Aristotle, "is identical with the doctrine of the best regime."[25] In Calvin, as in Thomas and Augustine before him,

> The notion of God as lawgiver takes on a certainty and definiteness which it never possessed in classical philosophy. Therefore. . . . natural law becomes independent of the best regime and takes precedence over it. The Second Table of the Decalogue and the principles embodied in it are of infinitely higher dignity than the best regime. It is classic natural rights in this profoundly modified form that has exercised the most powerful influence on Western thought almost since the beginnings of the Christian Era.[26]

Bringing governments and government officials under the critical scrutiny of a law—moral law—higher in authority, more universal, and more powerful than any ruler or regime has indeed been of enormous influence, not only on Western thought but also on its practices, institutions, and historical development. A very pertinent example is that of the Puritan revolt in England led by Oliver Cromwell. Calvin taught that unjust rulers, those who deviated from the moral law, ought to be resisted.[27] Although Calvin explicitly considered this the duty of government officials ("lower magistrates"), his general and constant admonitions to all citizens to "obey God" rather than rulers who are violating God's commands appeared to obligate all citizens to resist unjust governments. Puritans, shaped directly by Calvin's thought, did just that under Cromwell's leadership.

Ironically, it was Cromwell's band of Puritans, followers of Calvin, who deposed and executed the patron of Hobbes, Charles I. The differences between Hobbes and Calvin are by no means "academic" or unrelated to events past and present.

Governments, when they are just, serve to carry out one of the general functions of moral law, namely to restrain evil and behavior destructive of communities and the social order.[28] Despite great variation in the laws and customs that obtain among societies, and over time in each society, all communities do in fact frame their laws in accord with the moral law.[29] Calvin, as we previously noted, saw the necessity of adapting the laws to circumstances. Moral law has two more general purposes for Calvin: one, providing the knowledge of right and wrong that makes it inexcusable to be evil; and two, instructing and motivating those who take the moral life seriously, those who are "believers."[30]

You may be wondering when we are going to turn from the "moral law" and say something about rights. From Calvin's perspective, it is the moral law that specifies what actions we should expect from others, and if we are being treated unjustly, what we can rightly claim from others. Calvin urges Christians to be slow to seek redress through the courts but he does accept this as necessary sometimes. He does not generally take a "rights" perspective. For example, instead of speaking as we are prone of an employer's *right* to a day's work for a day's pay, he rather focuses on the employee's obligation not to lie down on the job. If persons fail to do a task that may be reasonably demanded of them, they are stealing. The loss of a fair return on an employee's labor is the moral equivalent of outright theft of the money lost.[31]

If the reader unfamiliar with Calvin's thought thinks Calvin favors the relatively wealthy, another example is in order. Calvin believed that it was right to charge interest on loans where the money borrowed would be used to earn money. But money loaned to persons who need the money for necessities should be interest free.[32] What bank or business would follow such a policy today? We are far from Calvin on this one, and also from his view that we are obligated to share what we have with those in need until we have no more to share.[33] It was frugality, hard work, and a wish to prove their moral worth that first helped make Calvin's followers increasingly prosperous. Philanthropy was part of that whole picture as well, though it was not as generous as the demanding standard espoused by Calvin. Of course, Calvin's partial sanction of interest on loans was not without enormous consequence for the development of capitalism.

Rights, then, were actualized as people faithfully carried out their obligations, and violations of the Decalogue were restrained by governments. On the positive side, governments were to encourage, permit, and safeguard the moral and religious obligations that comprise the Decalogue. Freedom of religion and the separation of church and state are a strong legacy of Calvin's teachings and practices. Churches could exist without any act of government. Where the "Word" was preached and the sacraments celebrated, there was a church. A church was made up of a covenanted community. Churches did not and should not have the power of the sword. Coercion was something exercised by governments. In Calvin's view, however, every individual had the "right" to expect both church and state to be faithful to the same moral law. The church could and should provide moral education to the state and its members. The state should, through the pedagogy of law, instruct its citizenry and restrain them from violations of the law, using sanctions as necessary.

Now let us proceed directly to contrast Calvin and Hobbes as to their understanding of moral obligations and human rights. I am using the term *obligations* for now to cover what in Calvin and Hobbes are also called *duties* and *responsibilities*. Later I will adopt the term *responsibilities* to describe our morally significant relations.

A. The Basis and Nature of Moral Obligations

Calvin	*Hobbes*
1. Moral obligations are natural. They are expressions of our nature as social animals.	1. Moral obligations are artificially realized. They are made possible by a social compact or contract by which a government is formed. By nature we seek to preserve ourselves and to satisfy our own desires.
2. Moral obligations are independent of governments. They are standards on	2. Morality is only made possible when governments exist. There is no right or

which governments should base their policies and by which these can be judged by everyone.

3. Moral obligations are God's will and the image of God in everyone. Rulers and citizens are obligated by the same moral law.

4. Moral obligations are universally known by human cognitive powers apart from any special revelation. The moral law is universally a standard, though policies and judgments based on it vary culturally, and may also be erroneous or ignored.

5. Moral obligations are realized by education in the family and church, self-discipline and self-sacrificial love, and civic laws and their enforcement by rulers.

wrong, justice or injustice, until there is a sovereign with power to enact, administer, and enforce laws.

3. Supreme "law" is obedience to civil law, not moral obligations; to obey the sovereign's commands is what it means to obey God's commands.[34]

4. Moral obligations are not reliably known privately, that is, by individuals on their own, and they are variable. The measure of what is moral is law, that is, what the sovereign commands.[35]

5. Moral obligations are realized, are actualized only by means of a social contract forming a government and by strict fidelity to abide by that contract. (Note: Hobbes creates a circular form of reasoning here; there is no morality without government. Yet, there is no government except by agreements faithfully kept, hence, no government without morality.)

B. The Basis and Nature of Rights
Calvin

1. Human beings have natural rights by reason of what they are owed by others. What people are owed is specified by the content of the moral law—the Decalogue and the love of God and neighbor.

2. Rights are grounded in the *social nature* of human beings. Fulfillment of moral obligations actualizes them. These moral obligations are community forming and sustaining. Naturally, though not perfectly, there is harmony between the individual and society. Governments exist to foster and protect individual rights through legal enforcement of the moral law.

3. Rights are *expectations* we naturally have that others will behave toward us in accord with the moral law. They may justly become claims when violations of the moral law occur: for example, legal redress for recovery of stolen goods. Individuals lacking the necessities of life are owed them by those who are able to share.

Hobbes

1. Human beings have natural rights to self-preservation and liberty (absence of constraint) to pursue their desires. These are specified by the desires people have for their own preservation and pleasure.

2. Rights are grounded in *individual self-interest*. Rights are naturally prior to and independent of society, actualized only by the power of a government. Naturally, then, there is an inherent conflict between the desires of individuals and the demands of society. Peace and protection of individuals are realized through legal enforcement of the sovereign's will.

3. Rights are *claims* and assertions we naturally make on our own behalf. These claims are more securely rendered operative through the social contract that establishes sovereignty, its commands, and the power to maintain peace and the common defense.

Life and Liberty in Calvin and Hobbes

Both Calvin and Hobbes consider life and liberty as basic, natural rights. The affirmation of a natural right to life is highly significant. I say this because of certain contemporary developments. These are to be examined in the next chapter. Liberty is, of course, deeply valued traditionally and now. Calvin and Hobbes are very modern in their stress on freedom. The rights to life and liberty, however, are understood quite differently by Calvin and Hobbes. I think it highly illuminating and worthwhile, therefore, to compare what happens to these rights in Calvin and Hobbes, because what divided them divides us today, and the issues will not go away. What we think and do about life and liberty is a global affair. The loss of life and liberty, like an ominous daily drumbeat, is sounded by the media; the cheerful or indifferent tone of voice newscasters and commentators often adopt makes all the talk of people killed and people deprived of elemental freedoms take on an uncomfortably grotesque, inhuman quality. Calvin and Hobbes were appropriately passionate in their endeavors to see life and liberty flourish.

Beginning with Calvin, let us see how he depicts the moral right to life. Human beings are by nature aware that it is wrong to kill. Governments, informed by that same awareness, make laws that protect human life and punish those who intentionally kill innocent persons. Neither governments nor individuals are ever morally justified in killing persons innocent of any violation of the moral law. Both governments and individuals are under the same obligations to observe the moral law. Governments, but not churches or individuals, however, have the authority to sanction killing under certain limited circumstances: Deviations from the moral and criminal laws, considered grave enough, merit capital punishment; unjust acts of aggression on the part of some group internally, or some government externally, could be repulsed or punished by war.

War, like capital punishment, has to be limited by strict moral considerations. Persons who are not combatants are to be immune from violence of every kind. Calvin included in the moral law love for one's enemies. Toward prisoners of war that means loving them as our own flesh as bearers of the image of God. This reference to the image of God is very important. The natural expression of the image of God is living in accord with the moral law. Calvin expected us to treat others—even our enemies—as we would ourselves and to see every human being as having the same knowledge of the same moral law. War, then, attempts to stop violence with only as much violence as necessary. Prisoners, not capable of violence, have every right to have—that is, every expectation of having, their lives protected.

Calvin, then, limited wars to those waged for a just cause, with just means, under the lawful authority of a just government, publicly declared, and as a last resort, only after a peaceful resolution of potential or actual conflict has been sought.[36]

Lawful government authority should be just. After all, Calvin recognized a right to resist unjust rulers. One would hardly be obligated to engage in violence on behalf of governments that should be resisted from within or stopped from aggression by other governments. War was only morally justified to protect innocent life, and only if that protection was also given within the conduct of war. Loyalty to governments, and of governments, is ultimately owed to the moral law. Loyalty to the moral law is also loyalty to God. But Calvin did not think that we are, by nature, very willing and able to love God. Our natures, as bestowed upon us by God as our Creator, are corrupted by sinful forms of self-love, self-glorification, and false pride in ourselves. Calvin could think of nothing more despicable than our tendency to seek our own advantage, rather than the good of others. The expectation, then, that justice will prevail depends upon seeing God, the omnipotent power for good, as the ultimate ruler of earthly affairs. Governments are not owed ultimate loyalty. That is owed to the moral law and to the author of its power to prevail over evil.

Freedom, for Calvin, is not and cannot be achieved by pursuing one's own desires for self-preservation, glory, and competitive advantages. Freedom occurs when one is liberated from slavery to selfishness and put in touch with that social aspect of our being expressed in love of God and neighbor and in the formation of communities in accord with the Decalogue—that is, in accord with individual and governmental restraints against destructive acts such as killing, stealing, lying, and the rest. Where the Decalogue is not honored, freedom is frustrated; this applies to disorder within individuals as well as to disorder within institutions and communities.

But freedom has a very distinct social dimension as well. We have already noted that the demands of the moral law free one from loyalty to unjust governments. People are free to worship and to form churches—to make agreements with God, as individuals and as groups. No government has any moral authority to prevent or interfere with such individual and social covenants. On the contrary, governments are, under the moral law, obligated to safeguard such covenants with God as are expressed in forming churches and in worshiping God individually or corporately. Furthermore, the church and the family are places for the moral education for all, since they instruct family and church members in the natural obligations known in the moral law and necessary to the formation and nurture of communities.

The family, as well as the church, are directly responsible to God and to the moral law. Obedience to parents and the government is taught by the moral law: Honoring father and mother includes respect for civil authority and the moral law as well. But parents are not to provoke their children to anger, and governments are to be subservient to the demands of the moral law and are never to have final authority.

Hobbes, on liberty, makes a U-turn away from Calvin. Covenants with God are totally forbidden.[37] There is only one valid social contract, and it is with the sovereign. That contract is only good, and only demands obedience, if the sovereign has the power to enforce it, thereby securing the peace and common defense agreed to by all. Only one form of worship is to be permitted by the government. Hobbes places himself here in direct intellectual and political contention with the free church movement of the Calvinist Puritans and one of their leaders at that time, Oliver Cromwell.

For Hobbes, people are naturally striving to preserve themselves as individuals, seeking happiness—that is, pleasure, or the absence of pain. But life is too hazardous as people fight one another for material gain and security in a state of nature. The social contract is an agreement to give up some of one's natural liberty and submit to coercion, forming thereby a government and a society. So liberty is curtailed by government in order to make the right to life (self-preservation) more predictably attainable. There is no right to resist governments, as in Calvin. Private moral judgments are not reliable. It is sovereigns that are beholden to natural law; for citizens, obedience to civil law is the supreme law, and to obey the sovereign's commands is to obey God's commands. This is contrary to Calvin's view of sovereignty. Of course, Calvin does consider all in authority as having it by reason of the providential ordering of God, but one can and ought to challenge authority that is not in accord with moral law, a law belonging to and known by all citizens.

Hobbes does expect considerable spheres of liberty, and he means by liberty absence of constraint. As in Calvin, commerce, vocational choices, private ownership, forming families, and the control of parents over children are part of society and the pursuit of individuals. In Hobbes, however, these are free of government restraint by permission; they are "praetermitted," that is, left free by the silence of the sovereign.[38] Calvin sees these as freedoms under God and the moral law; these are freedoms restrained only by moral law. Whatever obligations governments may have in these areas will be judged by what morality requires, and what therefore enhances human rights. Not so in Hobbes. Since Hobbes has granted great powers to government, all these areas may be judged to be in need of control. By covenant (the social contract), sovereigns have:

1. the power to reduce all citizens to one will and voice insofar as this is necessary to provide and maintain *peace* and *common defense*;
2. the power to make and enforce laws by the use of force;
3. immunity from the law and the law of nature, such as, equality (Hobbes believes citizens should be *equally* free and equally coerced); and
4. absolute liberty to do what is most conducive to the commonwealth (Hobbes warns all would-be rebels that only sovereigns have this freedom and power—there is to be no revolt in the name of liberty).[39]

Now Calvin does not agree with Hobbes on any of this. He would affirm the power of government to make and enforce laws but only with force that is applied in accord with legislation as well as the moral law. Calvin would categorically reject (1), (3), and (4) above and would find them shocking.

Hobbes does reserve an absolute right to individual liberty that never is and never can be handed over to the sovereign: It is the right to life, the right we have by our very nature to preserve ourselves and our powers to seek our own happiness. First, there is the right to self-defense: the right of refusal to kill oneself even when justly condemned to die (Hobbes accepted capital punishment); the right of refusal to testify against oneself. In relation to common defense, there are a number of liberties:

1. exemptions from killing others by sending a substitute, or by refusing to fight because one is naturally timorous—women are excused on this ground—but fright is no excuse once one agrees to fight;

2. banding together for self-defense, unless pardoned, and never offensively in revolt;
3. rights to sue the sovereign for what is one's right by law;
4. freedom from obligation to any sovereign no longer able to maintain peace and common defense;
5. right to accept new sovereignty as a prisoner of war;
6. no loyalty owed during banishment; and
7. defeat in war means subjection to the victor.[40]

The common thread in these liberties, so opposite to Calvin's thinking, is that individual lives depend on power—the power of individuals and of sovereigns. War is a clash of powers, and the legitimacy of sovereignty rests on the power to defend life. Power is associated with the ability to exert physical force successfully.

The ultimate power, for Calvin, belongs to the moral law. The wielding of this power is not only a divine activity, but something humans do as individuals, as corporate bodies, and as government officials. Indeed, a loss of moral legitimacy means a loss of power, for governments, communities, and individuals. People will not, and should not, submit to force that is used unjustly. For Calvin, participation in war is a matter for moral deliberation, not a matter of the material wealth to send substitutes or natural inclinations, such as lack of courage, as in Hobbes.

In Hobbes, the only moral limits placed on war and violence are the right to use force to protect oneself and the right to ally oneself with sovereigns powerful enough to secure peace and defend lives under their jurisdiction. Hobbes expects no mercy for prisoners of war, no general love of the enemy neighbor; the only protection is to submit to the one with power over your life. This view was not popular in Hobbes's day and it is not now. It amounts to treason, except under very extreme circumstances. The practice of Stalin went very far in differing with Hobbes on this. His deviation took the form of punishing his own soldiers who had survived imprisonment— those who had neither escaped nor died fighting.

Hobbes did regard the right to preserve one's life as an absolute liberty. Calvin did also, seeing the preservation of life as an obligation. But Calvin did not think this implied changing political loyalties or resisting punishment. Both Hobbes and Calvin opposed suicide and the killing of innocent life: Capital punishment is only for those who break the law. For Calvin, punishment has to be deserved; for Hobbes punishment has to fit the purpose for which it is deemed necessary. Again, Hobbes has opened up wider latitude for governmental actions and laws. Calvin held government to strict justice in punishment. Some would argue that Calvin, in supplying evidence to the civil authorities who had Servetus burned, was participating in an unjust act; the debate would be over the threat that Servetus posed to the citizens of Geneva. Even framing the issue that way, however, may for some bring Calvin closer to Hobbes in sanctioning something that appeared necessary to peace and order. In any event, their theories are quite distinct.

I wish now to emphasize what I regard as the sharpest dividing line between Calvin and Hobbes on rights, and on the right to life. Calvin has grounded the natural right to life on a universal, natural obligation not to kill; all rights are grounded in and specified by the demands of the moral law, our natural possession (created in the image of God) and guide. Hobbes has grounded the natural right to life on the propensity of all individuals toward self-preservation and seeking pleasure for themselves. For Hobbes, all rights are grounded on our egoistic desires as individuals and belong to us by nature. What Hobbes describes as natural is for Calvin a great evil and destructive of human beings and human communities. Very emphatically, Calvin maintains that there is "nothing more evil than to strive for oneself alone and seek one's own advantage." Hobbes has done something quite unthinkable, certainly utterly unacceptable to Calvin: derived the right to life from the most evil expression of our nature. Calvin, like Hobbes, acknowledges the strength of the quest for pleasure, glory, and goods for oneself, but Calvin believes it is self-destructive and a cause of social disorder to fall under the domination of these impulses. True freedom and self-regard in accord with the nature bestowed by the Creator are under the pull of moral law on us, the image of God in us.

At this juncture a very interesting observation is possible. The American Declaration of Independence treats rights in both a Calvinistic and Hobbesian way. It regards individuals (it says "men") as *equal by birth*. This is what is directly implied by seeing all human beings as bearing the image of God within themselves by nature. This view is not limited to Calvin and was used by many Christian groups and individuals as an argument against slavery;[41] it is no less a basis for opposing sexual inequality.[42] Then, also in Calvinist fashion, the Declaration speaks of persons being *endowed by their Creator* with certain inalienable rights. That rights are grounded in the nature that God gave to us is in keeping with Calvin; rights are owed to us because of what the moral law, with which we are endowed by our Creator, teaches us is due to all human beings.

Hereafter, the language of the Declaration becomes Hobbesian. What humans are endowed with is not the moral law but *rights,* the rights to *life, liberty,* and the pursuit of happiness. And so the Declaration has characterized "rights," as does Webster's dictionary, as powers *belonging* to individuals. This is clearly the Hobbesian framework for rights. The Declaration, however, as distinct from Hobbes and the dictionary but in keeping with Calvin, has God *endow* persons with these rights. With this understanding, the Declaration does not make egoistic striving a basis for rights as did Hobbes; it does, however, incorporate the pursuit of happiness, so basic to Hobbes, but leaves open the question as to how egoistic or how altruistic such a pursuit might be. The Declaration has avoided the great evil, from Calvin's perspective, of expressly sanctioning egoism. As in the dictionary, rights as claims are to be just; they are just, however, because they are bestowed by the Creator.

That Webster's collegiate dictionary does not include the notion that rights are conferred by God is a symbol of a current tension in

American society. Do you base your moral claims on God-given propensities to follow the Decalogue, or on your egoistic strivings for pleasure? The furor over the Moral Majority is partly a failure to see why some might frame these alternatives as the only options. When a court forbids the teaching, even the posting, of the Decalogue in public schools, some people become both angry and frightened, while others are angry and puzzled that people wish to insert religious doctrine into the public sphere. Deeply ingrained in American tradition is a view that regards all human beings as moral in Calvin's sense, guided by the Decalogue as a natural tendency and document, binding on all, governments as well. Also deeply ingrained by now is the legacy of Hobbes in the political arena, basing rights and their assertion on self-interest and on a social contract made out of self-interest. Politicians are supposed to do what is in the interest of their constituents and of the nation. Politics is power exerted on behalf of interests.

That Hobbesian view is in constant tension with the Calvinist view. When former President Carter inserted human rights into politics as a matter of policy in international relations, some regarded this as a salutary sign, others regarded this as utterly inappropriate at best, futile and even morally hypocritical at worst, since everyone "knows" that the President must do what is necessary for the national interest and maintenance of national power. Moral suasion is seen by some as powerful—others as totally ineffective. Calvin versus Hobbes all over again!

But simple reliance on Calvin's teaching is as tenuous as simple reliance on that of Hobbes is dangerous. This is not to say that one cannot, or should not, learn from both. The Declaration of Independence itself is a living witness to what has been learned, and what many affirm as worth retaining, however differently Calvin and Hobbes might understand this worth. As we shall see, however, the rights asserted there are under attack, and I do not mean simply with regard to how they are stated. That is for the next chapter. For this chapter, I want only briefly to signal some reasons why we would not be well served to assert either Calvin or

Hobbes unqualifiedly as a way of grounding and assuring our rights as human beings.

One could peck away at some of the arguments in Hobbes. People are not simply seeking pleasure for themselves or are at least gaining pleasure by pleasing others, not just themselves; primitive tribes are not especially savage nor lacking in governance; and some of what bees have we have, for example, sacrificial mutual aid and organized cooperation. The key problem in Hobbes, however, is that he equates rights with egoistic, asocial, individual wants; and whereas he regards these as primary and natural, he regards obligations and communities as artificial and attained only by force. It is precisely this view of rights and of what is moral that Carol Gilligan opposes. Not only does autonomy as a right and ideal give a false picture of what is moral and of what is the height of maturity, but it downgrades the value of loving, caring relationships. In doing so, it also devalues many human activities, such as nurture and holding together familial and other interpersonal relationships, activities presently more valued by women than men. Hobbes simply does not give moral status to the cultivation of interdependence and of interpersonal relations on which communities are formed and sustained. Autonomy in Hobbes's sense does not make communities possible or viable.

Whereas Calvin does value sharing, interpersonal harmony, and love, even for one's enemies, conceptualizing this as law does create a difficulty. "Law" is like a yardstick or ruler. You can use it to gauge whether behavior measures up to the standard as articulated. And so someone who lies fails to measure up to the standard set in the Decalogue. It misses the mark. But this overlooks the interpersonal element that would make lying the wrong thing to do. When I lie to my friend, I treat him or her as somehow less than a full moral agent, as one not capable of dealing with the fact or truth that I know and he or she doesn't. If my friend discovers that I have lied, our relationship will change as it already did when I lied. My friend trusted me. Does he now? Should she? Does lying or does truth telling bind people to one another? These are, at least, the appropriate questions, I would argue. Certainly all cooperative, joint action relies on faithful communication. Now, once we learn to call lying wrong, we can use it to categorize an act rather than a relationship. But all lying occurs in an interpersonal relationship. (Even self-deceit is one part of the self relating to another part.) Speaking of laws, rules, or duties does not keep the focus where it belongs, namely on the moral significance that attaches to relationships. We can fit two boards together by measuring them separately. We cannot see if two different colors go together well in isolation from one another. Putting them in relation to one another is requisite to seeing how well the colors blend or harmonize. What is fitting morally is what is fitting about human relationships. That is what will be argued more explicitly later in this book.

Calvin has other problems making his way in our contemporary world. There is the question of authority. Calvin saw the Decalogue as containing some universally acknowledged natural standards of right and wrong. Many people today think that the authority of the Decalogue rests on special, even parochial, religious beliefs.

The very idea of any universal, natural moral responsibilities and rights evokes skepticism in our day, despite the affirmation of natural and universal rights in the Declaration of Independence and in the U.N. Universal Declaration of Human Rights. The next two chapters will document two major and influential assaults on the whole concept of natural rights as found not only in Calvin but also in Hobbes. Such assaults, I will try to show, provide significant reason for the reconceptualizing of responsibilities and rights being undertaken in this book.

TWO

From Natural Rights to Utility

The thinking of Bentham and Mill is a very influential part of contemporary concepts of human rights. As chapters 9, 10, and 11 will illustrate, their thinking permeates court decisions and legislation, particularly in the United States. Yet, as the present chapter indicates, Bentham and Mill reject the notion of rights found in Hobbes and articulated by the founders of the United States. In this chapter, I wish to show why I think the conception of rights found in Bentham and Mill is inadequate and tends to lead to public policies that inadequately protect the rights of individuals. That is not to argue that the influence of Bentham and Mill is entirely without merit or without insights. Mill's formal definition of justice will prove useful in clarifying the relationship between rights and responsibilities in chapter 10.

Within less than a century and a half after Hobbes published his *Leviathan*, with its doctrine of natural rights, Jeremy Bentham took aim on them, delivering a blow from which natural rights have never fully recovered: "*Natural rights* is simple nonsense: natural and imprescriptible rights, rhetorical nonsense—nonsense upon stilts." Bentham is not the only one to attack the whole conception of natural rights. As we shall see in the next chapter, Engels, Marx, and Lenin are similarly agitated. While this book was being written, the world became more aware of some of the gross violations of human rights that have occurred in countries dominated by Marxist-Leninist thinking. It is no less important to investigate carefully what is implied by rejecting natural rights in the name of utility.

Bentham, cited above, is thoroughly denouncing *The Declaration of Rights,* published, as Bentham says, "under that name" by the French National Assembly in 1791 (140 years after the *Leviathan*). What is more, his harsh criticisms of that document and its conception of rights apply just as well to the American *Declaration of Independence* and its conception of rights.[1] Bentham, educated as Hobbes was at Oxford, begins the whole line of thinking that culminates in the cool pronouncement of the *Oxford Dictionary of History* that the assertion of self-evident natural rights in the American Declaration is arbitrary and cannot be rationally justified. Undoubtedly Bentham would be delighted to see that his views are enshrined in a weighty publication, appropriately enough, by his alma mater. The heirs of Marx essentially agree with the Oxford Dictionary's assessment.

In no way are we talking about quarrels confined to intellectuals and their writings. The President's Commission for the Study of Ethical Problems in Medicine and Biomedical and Behavior Research took a leaf right out of Bentham in its much cited report, *Deciding to Forego Life-Sustaining Treatment.*[2] This august, policy-recommending body spoke of the "right to life" as "empty rhetoric," the meaning of which is "hopelessly blurred." Again, we have cause for Bentham to celebrate his influence, though he might have wished some acknowledgement that he perceived this almost two hundred years earlier than the commission.

But it is critical to note that the commission members, and many others, are not aware that they no longer have an intellectual and moral rationale for human rights and the modern democratic institutions and states that actualize them. One might well restate the crisis in modern natural rights theory to which Strauss refers, and the crisis of ethics without substance to which MacIntyre refers. Today, the crisis is that there is no rational or moral basis for the affirmation of rights in the American *Declaration of Independence* or in the *Declaration of Rights* of the French Assembly or, for that matter, in the *Universal Declaration of Rights of the United Nations Assembly.* These are arbitrary or ideological claims and cannot be rationally or scientifically defended.

In this chapter, I plan to examine the alternative to natural rights doctrines found in Bentham and Mill. To help draw out the implications of their views, and to illustrate their embodiment, I will examine the Report of the President's Commission noted above. How this report deals with the rights to life and liberty is highly significant and representative of a strong contemporary tendency.

Bentham on Rights

Jeremy Bentham (1748-1832) was born into a well-to-do London family. After studying law, he used his private income to devote himself to his project, to reconstruct and reform the law of England on the basis of a scientific philosophy of morals and jurisprudence. Through his numerous writings and political associations, Bentham's ideas were translated into legislation with enormous impact upon political and social development in nineteenth-century England. It will soon enough become evident that Bentham's mode of thinking is alive and flourishing today.

Bentham embraced certain of Hobbes's most fundamental theses, but he also used those same theses to develop a very different conception of rights. To begin with, Bentham agreed with Hobbes that individuals are motivated by the desires to attain pleasure and avoid pain for themselves.[3] Human beings seek their own pleasure. Any science of morals must start there with what people actually value and disvalue.

But, whereas in Hobbes rights are natural and permanent, in Bentham rights are calculated and changing. First, Bentham identifies what is good with pleasure and what is evil with pain. Then he argues that the way to decide which acts are right is to calculate whether that act or some alternative will produce the most good or the least evil. Those acts are right, then, that produce the best balance of pleasure over pain among the alternatives. This calculus was to bring the greatest happiness for the greatest number. In order to do that, the calculation was to count each person as one, taking the pleasures sought and the pains shunned of all affected by the actions being contemplated. Immediate and remote consequences are to count as having equal value or utility. This is Bentham's utilitarian formula.

Rights, for Bentham, are to be determined by the same formula used to decide what is morally right. What rights persons have, however, is to be decided by governments. All rights vary in accord with the varying needs and interests of all. It is the government that has as its concern and obligation what is best on the whole. Legislators, therefore, create and abolish rights.

Bentham has adopted the Hobbesian idea of the liberty of government to do what is most conducive to the commonwealth and has extended that to granting and withdrawing rights. Adopting this assumption and given the claim that rights are to be calculated by what is productive of the greatest welfare of the greatest number, deciding what rights people should have, then, logically falls to those with the responsibility for the welfare of all. Whether something should be left to the free decisions of individuals depends upon whether the effects of doing so would be best on the whole, that is, realize the most good. If so, it would be proper, morally right, for legislators to *create a legal right* protecting that freedom. Rights are created or abolished, not something discovered to be true, even self-evident. For if better results could be expected by obligating people by law to act in a certain way, then it would be "inefficient" to leave the matter to individual decision.

Bentham, contrary to Hobbes, does make allowance for civil disobedience beyond self-defense. When the suffering caused by the government for the community at large is much greater than the happiness it brings about, then it is more advantageous to overthrow the government than to continue to obey it. There is no natural right to rebellion, or as in Calvin a natural obligation to resist an unjust regime, any more than there is a natural right to property or free speech. Both the content of the legal system and the limits of our obligation to be subservient to it are ascertained by the same method—the utilitarian calculus. There is no other for Bentham.

But why does Bentham reject natural rights and lodge the source of all rights in governmental policy making? There are two aspects of natural rights that are totally unacceptable to Bentham: that rights *belong* to human beings as such; and that rights belong to human beings "imprescriptibly," as the French *Declaration of Rights* claimed. *Imprescriptible* means "cannot be abolished." In rejecting this notion, Bentham rejects also the American *Declaration*'s designation of rights as "inalienable." *Inalienable* means "cannot be taken away." Likewise, Bentham is opposing Hobbes, who saw the right to life as one that could not be contracted away and which governments could not and should not take away.

Bentham's first objection to natural rights doctrine is that it falsely depicts rights as belonging to human beings as such. Rather, Bentham maintains, there are no rights that humans have apart from governments: People have only the rights that are *legally* theirs. Why are people without rights unless there is a government? Because, and here Bentham sides with Hobbes, everyone is egoistically striving to gratify and preserve themselves. Unless this selfish striving is curtailed sufficiently, no one will, in fact, realize any rights whatsoever, and given human selfishness, coercion is necessary to curb this natural, strong drive, as Bentham relates it:

> The great enemies of public peace are the selfish and dissocial passions—necessary as they are—the one to the very existence of each individual, the other to his security. On the part of these affections, a deficiency in point of strength is never to be apprehended: all that is to be apprehended in respect of them is to be apprehended on the side of their excess. Society is held together only by the sacrifices that men can be induced to make of the gratifications they demand; to obtain these sacrifices is the great difficulty, the great task of government.[4]

Bentham's second objection to natural rights is that they are said to belong to individuals in such a way that they cannot be taken away or abolished. For Bentham this is both factually false and morally wrong. The very reason a right is "established and maintained" is that it is advantageous (according to the utilitarian formula) to the society in question to establish and maintain it. But any right should only be retained, and only so long, as it is advantageous to society. And so, says Bentham, "there is no right that, when the abolition of it is advantageous to society, should not be abolished."⁵

The possibility both of limiting and of doing away with rights is a moral imperative: It is the difficult task of government that has the necessary power against the egoistic, asocial passions.

Bentham adopts the Hobbesian notion of egoistic striving as natural. But, unlike Hobbes, he will not make that a basis of rights, or at least, not of rights that cannot and should not be limited or even, at times, taken away. Asserting natural, imprescriptible rights is a prescription for anarchy. Bentham sees all rights, finally, as forms of liberty, allowed or granted. Natural rights are all rights to unbounded liberty and to claim them is an anarchical fallacy for Bentham. Royalists in Hobbes's own times saw this implication of his philosophy and attacked Hobbes with the same furor we see in Bentham. Again, in Bentham's words, "Nature gave—gave to every man a right to everything: be it so true; and hence the necessity of human government and human laws, to give to every man his own right, without which no right to whatsoever would amount to anything."⁶

Bentham embellishes this argument by illustrating what it implies for each of the rights contained in the French *Declaration*— liberty, property, security, and resistance to oppression. In each case, limiting liberty actualizes the right in question. Consider security, for example. Security, Bentham contends, depends upon depriving those people of their freedom who act in ways that rob people of their security. Thus, government declares certain injuries to persons and property to be crimes and curtails the freedom of those who commit such crimes.

Bentham's rhetoric becomes so pungent when he speaks of the right to resist oppression that I wish to quote some of it. Note that he has again reduced the argument to one aimed against the absurdity of unlimited freedom:

> Whenever you are about to be oppressed, you have a right to resist oppression: whenever you conceive yourself to be oppressed, conceive yourself to have a right to make resistance, and act accordingly. . . . Submit not to any decree or other act of power, of the justice of which you are not yourself perfectly convinced. If a constable call upon you to serve in the militia, shoot the constable and not the enemy; if the commander of the press-gang trouble you, push him into the sea, if a bailiff, throw him out of the window. If a judge sentence you to be imprisoned or put to death, have a dagger ready, and take a stroke first at the judge.[7]

Though these verbal barbs were directed at the French *Declaration of Rights,* it could be applied as easily to the absolute character of the right to life, as Hobbes interpreted it, for it did include defending one's life even against one's own government officials.

Bentham altered and rejected some of the thinking of Hobbes but built on some of it as well. Bentham's views of rights and those of Calvin differ radically, though not entirely. More of that later, however, when we come to assess both Bentham and Mill. Just now we focus our attention on Mill and the way he extended Bentham's thought and its implications.

Mill on Rights

Bentham was a close friend of James Mill, the father of John Stuart Mill (1806–1873). John Stuart Mill at an early age took up Bentham's philosophy and cause. The utilitarian formula was assured an even wider circle of influence through its adoption by Mill. In philosophy, Mill receives considerable, continuous attention; in politics, Mill, during his tenure from 1865 to 1868 in the

British House of Commons, helped guide through legislation that reflected the utilitarian perspective. The most notable was the Reform Act of 1867, which extended enormously the number of individuals who could vote, adding 938,000 voters to an electorate of 1,056,000. For the first time working men, who were not landowners, became voters. This act triggered other changes in the distribution of representation in the House of Commons, increasing the effects of the new voters. As K. B. Smellie remarks in his modern history of Britain, "The Conservative principle of representing communities was replaced by the Radical principle of the representation of majorities."[8] "The greatest happiness of the greatest number"; that was the principle of Bentham and Mill and of the Radical party, which they helped found and to which they belonged.

I refer the reader to other sources for Mill's entire moral philosophy. For my purpose, it is sufficient to discuss Mill's accounts of justice and liberty, which contain his understanding of rights. Mill retains the Benthamite calculus, or principle of utility, with certain modifications, as we shall see. He also affirms the proposition, shared by Bentham and Hobbes, that individuals by nature seek pleasure and avoid pain for themselves. Indeed, this human propensity is, Mill contends, the sole proof of the principle of utility.[9]

Mill is aware that the idea of justice has long been one of the strongest sources of opposition to the acceptance of the doctrine that utility or happiness is the criterion of right and wrong. Mill is determined to show that justice, this "powerful sentiment," however natural its origins, is only moral insofar as it is grounded in utility. To do this, he examines the variety of ways we use and apply the concept of justice.

What Mill concludes is that justice is two things: first, a rule of conduct, common to humanity and intended for their good; a sentiment that sanctions the rule. This sentiment is a desire that punishment be suffered by those who infringe the rule. Second, the conception of justice involves the notion of some definite person who suffers by any infringement of the rules. Mill refers to this as the violation of that person's rights. "And," says Mill, the sentiment of justice appears to me to be the animal desire to repel or retaliate a hurt or damage to oneself, or to those with whom one sympathizes, widened so as to include all persons, by the human capacity of enlarged sympathy and the human conception of intelligent self-interest. From the latter elements, the feeling derives its morality; from the former, its peculiar impressiveness and energy of self-assertion.[10]

A right, for Mill, is one of the forms the two elements of justice can take. A person who is a victim of injustice has suffered a hurt, a hurt that occasions a demand for punishment. These two elements compose a violation of a right. On the positive side Mill asserts, "When we call anything a person's right, we mean that he has a valid claim on society to protect him in the possession of it, either by force of law, or by that of education and opinion."[11] If someone were to ask why society ought to comply with such a claim, Mill replies, "I can give him no other reason than general utility."[12] The resort to utility, Mill realizes, may not seem to have the strength that goes with the sentiment of such an obligation. This is because of the animal element, the thirst for retaliation in our rights claims, the intensity of which is enhanced by the important and impressive utility associated with them. The interest involved is security, a security we cannot do without. We are seeking immunity from evil and from the seizing by others of any and all of our goods. The feelings concerned are so powerful and we so count on others to be responsive, to be likewise interested, that *ought* and *should* become a *must* and the recognized indispensability becomes a moral necessity.[13]

If you are wondering what rights Mill would affirm, you need to know what he thinks is just. In Mill's words, "Justice implies something that is not only right to do, and wrong not to do, but that some person can claim from us as his moral right."[14]

But what, for Mill, is the content of justice? "Justice is the name for certain classes of moral rules that concern the essentials of human well-being more nearly, and are therefore of more absolute obligation, than any other rules for the guidance of life; and the notion that we have found to be of the essence of the idea of justice, that of a right residing in an individual, testifies to this more binding obligation."[15]

Characteristic of these moral rules is that they forbid people to hurt one another. Returning good for good is among these moral rules. The failure to return benefits one accepts when those benefits are needed is a real hurt, "a disappointment of expectation," a very great evil present in "such highly immoral acts as a breach of friendship and a breach of promise." Such intense disappointments of expectation, such great hurts, are precisely characteristic of the sentiments aroused by violations of justice. In Mill's words:

> The principle, therefore, of giving to each what they deserve—that is, good for good, as well as evil for evil—is not only included within the idea of justice as we have defined it, but is a proper object of that intensity of sentiment that places the Just, in human estimation, above the simply Expedient.[16]

The observance of these rules preserves peace. For as Mill observes, "If obedience to them were not the rule, and disobedience the exception, everyone would see in everyone else an enemy, against whom he must be perpetually guarding himself."[17] The interests associated with justice have the very highest utility. Observing the rules of justice is a test of one's "fitness to exist as one of the fellowship of human beings."[18]

But Mill does not supply us with a list or summary of what justice requires. Nor does he have a list of inalienable or imprescriptible rights. The reason is evident in his treatment of impartiality as a demand of justice. Impartiality in the utilitarian calculus means counting each person's happiness equally. (Mill explicitly mentions Bentham's dictum everybody is to count for one, nobody for more than one.) But he qualifies equality as follows: "All persons are deemed to have a *right* to equality of treatment, except when some recognized social expediency requires the reverse. And hence all social inequalities that have ceased to be considered expedient, assume the character not of simple inexpediency, but of injustice."[19] Once we consider something that has become inexpedient as unjust, we are amazed that it was once looked upon as just. That, Mill contends, is the history of social improvement. Customs and institutions once supposed to be necessary to social existence come to be viewed as unjust, even tyrannical. Then Mill inserts a prophecy with his comments: "So it has been with the distinctions of slaves and freemen, nobles and serfs, patricians and plebeians; and so it will be, and in part already is, with the aristocracies of color, race, and sex."[20] The reformist thrust of utilitarianism is very evident in those remarks.

Mill, then, has used utility as the moral criterion of the sentiment of justice and of the rights correlative of what justice requires. Someone might claim that justice is a standard per se, independent of utility, which the mind grasps by simple introspection. In other words, are not the demands of justice self-evident? To this Mill has a ready retort. If what justice obligates us to do is self-evident, why are there such very different opinions as to what is just? Mill gives a number of examples. One will suffice. Why punish? Some contend that it is to benefit the offender; others contend that it is wrong to control adults through punishment, so that it is only right if it prevents evil to others; still others contend that punishment is completely unjust because people are not responsible for the evil they do. In this example and in all of those he offers, Mill maintains that one can only decide these debates by deciding what conforms to expedience or social utility.

The Right to Liberty

Earlier we said that Mill gives us no list of inalienable or imprescriptible rights. When it comes to liberty, however, there is one of its expressions that is absolute and should not be curtailed by others or by society. Mill expresses it this way: "The only part of the conduct of any one for which he is amenable to society is that which concerns others. In the part which merely concerns himself, his independence is, of right, absolute. Over himself, over his own body and mind, the individual is sovereign."[21] Explaining this right to freedom in greater detail, Mill asserts that "The only freedom which deserves the name, is that of pursuing our own good in our own way, so long as we do not attempt to deprive others of theirs, or impede their efforts to obtain it. Each is the proper guardian of his own health, whether bodily, or mental, and spiritual."[22] At the very outset of his essay on liberty, Mill states his defense of individual liberty in the form of a principle that is to govern absolutely the dealings of society with the individual in the way of compulsion and control, whether

> by physical force in the form of legal penalties, or [by] the moral coercion of public opinion. That principle is, that the sole end for which mankind are warranted, individually or collectively, in interfering with the liberty of action of any of their number, is self protection. That the only purpose for which power can be rightfully exercised over any member of a civilized community, against his will, is to prevent harm to others. His own good, either physical or moral, is not a sufficient warrant. He cannot rightfully be compelled to do or forebear because it will be better for him to do so, because it will make him happier, because in the opinion of others, to do so would be wise, or even right.[23]

Mill makes it clear that this kind of freedom is not applicable to minors nor to members of "backward states of society." Mill considers despotism legitimate for barbarians, provided that it is exercised for their improvement; any means that actually bring about that end are justified. As Mill says, he is not arguing his case for liberty as an abstract right independent of utility. He regards "utility as the ultimate appeal on all ethical questions; but it must be utility in the largest sense, grounded on the permanent interests of man as a progressive being."[24]

Now when Mill appeals to "permanent interests" and those of a progressive being, he appears to be affirming something like an inalienable or imprescriptible right. It is not one, however, that persons have simply as human beings, certainly not as minors or as so-called barbarians. But Mill considers it a matter of justice to educate and persuade people to "become capable of being improved by free and equal discussion."[25] Persons with this capability are eligible to have liberty in Mill's sense. Furthermore, Mill contends that selling oneself into slavery should be legally prohibited and publicly condemned. He even claims, in apparent defiance of his own notion of freedom, that "it is not freedom to be allowed to alienate [one's] freedom."[26]

Gerald Dworkin maintains that at this point Mill has departed from a strictly utilitarian mode of argument. Choice itself, and not the consequences of choice, is treated as an absolute value.[27] Dworkin's view is plausible, but there is another way to understand Mill that does not interpret Mill as inconsistent or of two minds. Freedom is allowed only to mature adults and to those capable of benefiting from free and equal discussion. Someone in a civilized society desirous of becoming a slave, for whatever reason, has to be saved from regression to the state in which minors or barbarians find themselves. After all, minors and barbarians are deprived of liberty precisely for the sake of becoming capable of benefiting from liberty. I am not arguing for Mill's point of view; I am trying to understand it at this juncture. If one asked Mill how he can decide what is good for someone else, especially since he has excluded doing so even when one believes that it is right to do so, he no doubt would ask you to assume the perspective of a spectator with an enlarged sympathy for all of humanity and intelligent self-interest. From this perspective, we would, on reflection, presumably agree with Mill. This is the perspective Mill employs to distinguish justice from simple expediency as a higher form of utility. And it is on this same basis that Mill speaks of higher and lower pleasures. Indeed, Mill expects us to share his preference for being a Socrates dissatisfied rather than a pig satisfied.

What, more specifically, does Mill see as spheres of liberty for the individual and of authority over the individual by society? With respect to society, Mill prefaces his discussion by asserting that society is not founded on a contract—opposing Hobbes on that—and that no good purpose is served by inventing a contract in order to deduce social obligations from it—opposing contemporary contractarian theories that will occupy us later. By living in a society, however, individuals incur certain obligations: first, an obligation not to injure those interests that ought by law, or tacit consent, to be considered rights; second, an obligation to take on some fair share of the labor and sacrifices necessary for defending the society, or its members, from injury. Whenever people engage in conduct that adversely affects the interests of others, society has the jurisdiction over them, and whether their conduct should, for the sake of the general welfare, be interfered with, is open for discussion. But behavior that does not harm others should be left free, legally and socially.

Mill specifies three areas of individual freedom: (1) the inward domain of consciousness; (2) the liberty of tastes and pursuits; and (3) the liberty of combination among individuals to unite for any purpose provided no harm to others ensues and the union is a voluntary (unforced) union of mature individuals. The liberty of consciousness includes conscience, thought, and feeling on all subjects, practical or speculative, scientific, moral, or theological. This liberty extends to expressing and publishing any and all opinions. For these liberties, Mill gives a series of arguments to show how they contribute to mental well-being and that development of character he associates with increased freedom and participation in democratic institutions.

The liberty of tastes and pursuits is that of framing the plan of our life to suit our own character. It is a matter of doing as we like, subject to the consequences, without being impeded by other people. Again, this liberty holds only so long as our behavior does others no harm, even though others may think our behavior foolish, perverse, or wrong.

The Right to Life

Where, in all of this, is the right to life? Mill does mention that one might kidnap and compel the services of a doctor to save a life. He also advocates that society exact service for common defense and individual acts of saving life. Nevertheless, whereas preventing someone from choosing to be a slave is a strict obligation, legally and socially enforceable, preventing individuals from choosing to kill themselves is not. Here Mill is not on the same wave length with Calvin, nor with Hobbes. What is more, liberty as a form of independence from society, as a form of privacy, has been elevated and spotlighted. This includes a right of individuals to the sole guardianship of their bodily, mental, and spiritual health. Coupled with this absolute freedom is the denial of any such rights to individuals not mature enough to benefit from free and equal discussion, either because of age or membership in a backward society. What happens, under these circumstances, to other rights such as the right to life and to the equality of opportunities and rights? At the very least a cloud hangs over these rights, as well as over all persons handicapped in some way from attaining the maturity that Mill demands of the bearer of rights.

I believe it would be unfair to speculate about how Mill would view certain medical dilemmas. What I think is more appropriate and illuminating to do is to examine some contemporary policy suggestions for medical practice that are based on the kind of thinking about rights we have discovered in Mill. I refer to the policies and the rationale for them put forth in *Deciding to Forego Life-Sustaining Treatment*, a report issued in March 1983 by the President's Commission for the Study of Ethical Problems in Medicine and Biomedical and Behavioral Research. For the sake of brevity and convenience, I shall refer to this commission simply as the Medical Ethics Commission, or sometimes just the commission.

The Medical Ethics Commission and the Right to Life

As we have observed from examining Mill's conception of rights, no list of rights is given or sanctioned, but the liberty of a mature person is absolute in some of its expressions. All rights, however, are decided on the basis of the well-being or welfare they produce. Similarly, the Medical Ethics Commission singles out self-determination and well-being as dominant values.[28] Equity is the third value considered dominant by this commission, but as we shall see, it is limited to equal access to health care and does not guide the nature of the care given. The question I have for the commission, as I do for Mill, is: What status do you give to the right to life? How do you view this right, regarded as self-evident and as belonging to all human beings in the American *Declaration of Independence*? The commission deals with other types of medical situations but I wish to focus on their discussion of care for seriously ill infants where conceptions both of the right to life and the right to self-determination are explicitly involved under circumstances of great ambiguity—where, as some like to say, everything looks gray. To put our question in its bluntest form: Does the commission sometimes favor infanticide in the context of caring for seriously ill infants?

If by infanticide we mean killing directly, with measures known to be lethal, newborns or very young children classified as infants, the Medical Ethics Commission should be viewed as totally opposed to infanticide for the following reasons:

1. "A physician's shooting or poisoning of a dying patient, even at the patient's request and from merciful motives falls within the definition of murder."[29]

2. The omission of lifesaving is to be regarded in the same way as murder if the result is the same.
3. "Society seems well served by retaining the prohibition on killing."[30]
4. The traditional prohibition of the Hippocratic Oath is to be retained: "Neither will I administer a poison to anybody when asked to do so, nor will I suggest such a course."[31] The reasons for following the Oath in this respect is that to do otherwise would risk loss of patient trust, damage the professional's self-image, and undermine the wholehearted treatment of gravely ill patients. (There is no mention here of violating a right to life and we will see why momentarily.)
5. Physicians are to favor life.[32]
6. Early intervention for infants, seriously ill, is cost effective.[33]

The Medical Ethics Commission has apparently rejected infanticide for physicians and other health care providers. They also reject certain acts of omission that result in death as akin to murder. This does not end the matter, however. They suggest policies that have heretofore resulted in the deaths of *handicapped* infants by omitting lifesaving intervention, including instances where the intervention would be considered routine for nonhandicapped infants. By the commission's own reasoning, one would think these should be reckoned as cases of infanticide and murder. Let us carefully trace the commission's position on this.

First of all, recall that life is not a basic or "dominant" value for the commission; self-determination, well-being, and equity are. The commission explicitly lists the "right to life" as among the phrases that constitute "empty rhetoric" and that "have been used in such conflicting ways that their meanings, if they ever were clear, have become hopelessly blurred."[34] No self-evident affirmation here of the idea that persons are endowed with an inalienable right to life! No assurance is given that people who spoke this way knew what they were saying. Like Mill, the commission believes that self-determination and well-being are clearly values that create obligations and are the basis of rights.

One very pertinent example illustrating this occurs in the context of the commission's commentary on the commitment of acute care hospitals to the extension of life. This commitment, the commission maintains, is an important source of trust and an endorsement of the value of persons, both medical necessities. Nevertheless, the commission admonishes these hospitals by asserting, "Patients should not face such marked resistance to a decision to forego life-sustaining treatment as to either rob them of the right to self-determination or damage their mental, or physical health."[35] The commission is not limiting its remarks to those who are terminally ill but is concerned with all patients and their surrogates, that is, those authorized to choose for patients who are judged not to have sufficient ability to choose for themselves.

For newborns, the commission generally favors parents, where available, as surrogate decision-makers. The decisions of surrogates should be guided by two principles: respect for self-determination; and the welfare or well-being of the patient in question. Equity or equality is not invoked at this point. The apparent reason is that it does not apply to decisions regarding care, only to decisions regarding *access* to care as we noted earlier. For infants, only the principle of well-being applies. I remind the reader that the infants we are talking about are *seriously ill*; only some of them may be correctly, though with difficulty, judged to be *terminally* ill; some of them may be treated with the prospect of a normal life span, or in the case of certain handicaps, a life span typical of that handicap. Where then in the case of handicapped infants is their right to live, and where is their right to equal treatment, that is, to have the same life-sustaining treatment afforded normal infants with similar ailments, such as a bowel obstruction? Perhaps these are implicitly recognized by the commission though not mentioned. Perhaps they are not regarded as rights. The answers to these questions require a further probe into the exact advice the commission gives to surrogate decision-makers.

The surrogate should, in the judgment of the Medical Ethics Commission, decide whether the continued existence of the seriously ill infant would or would not be "a net benefit to the infant." This, for the sake of the self-determination that the infant lacks, should be done from the infant's perspective. In the commission's words, "The Commission is concerned with the value of the patient's life for the patient."[36] It is this value to which the commission refers when it speaks of judging what is for the patient's well-being or best interests. The commission, however, is concerned at the same time that enormous resources may be spent, for little benefit, to sustain "a painful and burdened life for an individual who has little or no capacity to enjoy it." How much is a little in benefit, or a little in capacity? Aware that many do not think it beneficial to sustain infants with Down's syndrome, the commission categorically suggests that the lives of persons with this degree and range of mental handicaps should be saved, when possible, because their lives are generally meaningful in the commission's judgment, a judgment shared by some but not all persons.

From the standpoint of equality then, lives are not clearly seen as equally worthwhile, and some lives may not be deemed worth sustaining. From the standpoint of the value of life, its worth depends upon the worth assigned it by the patient, or in the case of infants, whether handicapped or not, by what is thought to be the worth that would or should be given it. An individual's life is a right only insofar as it is claimed as such, or when it cannot be claimed by that individual, insofar as it is judged by someone else to have sufficient worth for that individual.

But if physicians and health professionals are to favor life, and hospitals are committed to extending it, would not there still in fact be a functioning right to life, even for handicapped infants? There are two aspects to care for handicapped infants that militate against this.

First, the commission recommends that parents generally be the surrogates for their own infants whenever possible. The commission is fully aware of the well-publicized data on parental choices not to treat their seriously ill newborns even in instances where their lives could clearly be sustained and their illnesses were not terminal. These instances included failure to save the lives of infants with Down's syndrome, whose lives the commission thinks should be saved. The Baby Doe case in Bloomington, Indiana, is only one case in addition to the many reported in medical journals. The Baby Doe case is especially notable because it was a state supreme court that sanctioned a parental decision not to feed and not to operate on their infant child. By the commission's own standards, not feeding an infant would qualify as murder, as a failure to act that leads to death.

The commission depicts the relation between parents and physicians with regard to treating seriously ill newborns in the table below.[37]

Physician's Assessment of Treatment Options	Parents Prefer to Accept Treatment	Parents Prefer to Forego Treatment
Clearly beneficial	Provide treatment	Provide treatment during review process
Ambiguous or uncertain	Provide treatment	Forego treatment
Futile	Provide treatment unless provider declines to do so	Forego treatment

The physician strives with the parents only when parents refuse clearly beneficial treatment, and/or in the case of futile treatment, when parents want treatment that the provider is unwilling to offer. If life were a dominant value, one would expect that ambiguous or uncertain cases would be decided on the side of maintaining life. Such is not the recommendation of the commission, and this certainly qualifies what they say about physicians favoring life.

Not just parental attitudes but also those of physicians affect the care seriously ill infants will receive, and it is physicians who make the assessments of how beneficial treatment will be. They tend to see treatment for mentally handicapped infants as futile. The commission is willing to see infants with Down's syndrome treated; these are infants who are usually moderately retarded. But many physicians take issue with this, and the decisions of parents will be based on their assessments. Physicians often use the term "hopeless," for example, to describe a condition of terminal illness, and also one of a permanent mental handicap. As many as 61 percent of the physicians surveyed in California in 1975 would, with parental consent, fail to provide lifesaving treatment for a Down's syndrome infant. In a national survey, 85 percent of the pediatric surgeons in 1977 said they would acquiesce in parental wishes not to treat an infant with Down's who also had congenital heart disease; 65 percent of the pediatricians would do likewise. Another study found that 51 percent of the pediatricians surveyed in Massachusetts would not recommend surgery for a Down's syndrome infant with intestinal blockage. The commission cites these three studies.[38] Hence, the commission is aware that by their own formulations what could be interpreted as murder or infanticide will take place unless some protection, not now in place, is provided and enforced. The commission explicitly rejects legal and governmental interference in these decisions. Self-determination both of health professionals and of patients or their surrogates is a right not to be interfered with.

One might well ask how the value of life can be subordinate to the value of self-determination. The value of life is to be judged by the individual, and when it is judged by another person, it is done on the basis of the well-being of that life, particularly whether that life will still allow the individual to be at least somewhat self-determining. Self-determination, for the commission, consists in "a person forming, revising over time, and pursuing his or her own particular plan of life."[39]

During the time the commission was preparing the final draft of its report, I had the opportunity to read and comment on a draft that closely resembled the final one—the one I have been describing. I noticed and commented in a letter that "life" was not treated as a dominant value. In reply, Dr. Joanne Lynn wrote a cordial letter, dated 1 November 1982, in which she said, "The Report does not list life as a 'dominant value' because, for the purposes of this Report, the value of life is included in the other categories, especially well-being and self-determination." The commission also saw fit not to change their minds or their report in this respect.

Now, regardless of how the reader may think or feel about the commission's conception of rights, it should be evident that it is not making a separate right out of the right to life. The claim to life is a matter of self-determination as to what others are obligated to secure and protect. The value of life is to be determined by reference to its value for each individual; and for individuals deemed incapable of judging the value of their lives, what value life has is based on an assessment of their best interests or well-being. Of course, we are talking about the value of an individual's life in the context of health care decisions. And this is a sphere of individual liberty for the commission and for Mill. Neither Mill nor the commission work with the assertion in the American *Declaration of Independence* that each individual has an inalienable right to life. Unlike that declaration, for Mill and the commission, every judgment with regard to the value of individual life is either a self-assessment of its utility or an assessment of its utility by someone else. Liberty is presumed to have very high utility. Certainly any loss in the capacity to be self-determining is deemed a loss in the utility of one's life to oneself and to others. Equality is always tempered, therefore, for Mill and for the commission, by differences in utility, and a great deal of utility is tied to the abilities necessary for being self-determining. Therefore, as we shall now argue, the high value Mill places on life and its protection is undermined by his resort to utility for assessing the right to it and the responsibility to protect it.

Rights and Utility: An Assessment

If, then, we have no specific rights that we can claim as natural endowments and as powers or possessions no one can justly take away from us, what do we have left in the way of rights? We certainly have a natural desire for liberty, but it is a desire that requires some curtailment and educating. What rights would anyone have if governments did not curtail the liberty of those who would otherwise harm others and deprive them of their liberty? Mill would add an enlightened public, tolerant of a wide range of personal liberties, as another source of rights.

But why should we expect governments to be concerned with any rights except possibly their own? Why wouldn't governments simply act on what is their own self-interest, especially since all people are doing this anyway? Bentham and Mill would grant us that governments would act out of self-interest, but it *should be* the *rational* self-interest and wide sympathies consonant with utility, that is, "the greatest good for the greatest number." This is the moral standard to which we should hold all governments, and though democracy is best because it increases freedom and the participation that develops character, legitimate despots should use this standard to curtail liberty sufficiently to bring a backward people to the point where greater liberty has utility for them.

This sounds fine, unless we are considered members of a backward group. Hobbes at least grants us by nature our own right to seek our own survival, no matter what a government thinks of us. Bentham and Mill grant us no such "abstract" right to life or liberty. If a government is not acting in a way that maximizes welfare, we have a right to resist it, they would say. If we are part of a minority, however, and our rights are being denied or less fully recognized, how can we argue with assurance that everyone would be better off if we were? The society might be better off without us.

Mill believes he has protected minorities and individuals with his doctrine of liberty. People are "sovereign" over their own bodies and minds and are free to pursue their own plans, so long as they harm no one. But, this is no right independent of utility, and everything hinges on what behavior is considered by the government and public to be harmful to others. Is there any standard they would or should use besides their own opinions as to what is conducive to the general welfare? Mill can reply that there are many varied opinions about what is considered just, but utility at least engages our self-interest. Mill proposes that utility be judged from the standpoint of an intelligent self-interest, one that is "grounded in the permanent interests of man as a progressive being."

If we ask Mill to explain "permanent interests" and "progressive being," he has two possible replies at hand. He can cite the perspective of an "ideal spectator"—this is the perspective of one who sympathizes with everyone's interests and possesses an intelligent, consistent self-interest. He can point also to his insistence on free and equal discussion, formation of groups, participation in government, and education as processes that help people achieve this standpoint. Given, however, that Mill believes all of us to be driven by the desire for pleasure for ourselves, what hope is there that these processes will take place and that they result in closer approximation of utility grounded on permanent interests of a progressive being? Mill has looked at changing conceptions of the powers of government and of equality; and he sees governments as increasingly democratic and freedom as increasingly expanded, such as the abolition of slavery and the extension of the vote, the latter being something he had a hand in helping along.

Finally, Mill's conception of utility and of the rights it undergirds rests on metaphysical or theological assumptions concerning the nature of the human self, its historical destiny, and of the powers shaping and moving it. That is true of Hobbes and Calvin as well. Mill rests the right to liberty on the faith and the hope that the powers that help shape people and events will move toward actualizing his own conception of utility. Calvin sees that power in goodness personified (God) and in people themselves (the image of God). This means that people are able to see what the moral law requires and know what rights they can expect to have through its fulfillment and what governments are supposed to do. Bentham and Mill, like Calvin, are resting their case on the confidence that what is right triumphs or is at least more powerful than evil. We will say more about such confidence in chapter 6. Bentham and

Mill, however, have no confidence that human beings as human beings know what is right. Despotism and government enforcement of "enlightened views" of utility may be expedient and right to actualize the level of enlightenment needed for free and equal discussion in a world where no rights are self-evident and no rights exist in nature to be discovered. Rights are created and abolished by human decisions, largely governmental decisions, say Bentham and Mill. Widespread education makes democratic governments possible; widespread lack of education makes despotism necessary.

That brings us to the serious difficulties for Mill's notion of utility resulting from his adherence to a doctrine of psychological egoistic hedonism. In the context of providing a proof for utility as the standard for identifying moral rules, Mill states, "No reason can be given why the general happiness is desirable, except that each person, so far as he believes it to be attainable, desires his own happiness."[40] The quest for "general happiness" is a quest for pleasure and the avoidance of pain. Mill is well aware that human beings desire things besides pleasure, such as virtue, for example. As Mill carefully points out, however, "Virtue is not naturally and originally part of the end," but it can come to be desired as a part of an individual's happiness.[41]

Mill's assumption that all of us pursue happiness for ourselves means that the achievement of general happiness, the best balance of pleasure over pain, depends upon finding ways to restrain the individual's pursuit of happiness. Force is necessary to gain compliance with moral rules forbidding individuals from hurting one another, and education is preferred to legal coercion, if and when it suffices. Individuals, Mill maintains, need education to develop social feelings. At the same time, the concern of government to use force to attain general happiness and prevent threats to it can lead to ever-increasing power over the lives of individuals. To counteract excessive use of governmental force and power, Mill seeks to define a sphere of privacy, a sphere that government (and other individuals) should not enter unless permitted. It is a sphere of individual sovereignty over one's own body, health, and thoughts; it is a sphere not to be interfered with unless the behavior of the individual demonstrably harms others. Mill, like Hobbes and Bentham, has accepted a view of basic human striving that sets up an antagonistic relation between the individual and the larger community; there is no natural harmony between the end for individuals, their own happiness, and the end for government, the general happiness. The utilitarian principle of the greatest good for the greatest number is not necessarily the greatest good for any one individual.[42] Individuals have no natural inhibitions and proclivities to be morally responsible and virtuous. They do not naturally exhibit and pursue the requisites of community. The problem for Hobbes, Bentham, and Mill is that of transforming egoistic hedonists into morally responsible and law-abiding members of communities.

Hobbes prefers to have egoistic persons to strike a bargain and obtain that government power to have some liberty when no one can have it all. At the same time, he does not believe anyone can or will give up their own preservation. He will hold governments to that. In the cruelest world and under the greatest tyranny, people still have rights that others will simply have to reckon with. People will defend themselves and have a moral right to do it. What Hobbes has to have faith in is the moral law, those impulses to keep faith and cooperate that he denies exist without governments. The success of contracting depends on the power of the moral law to move people to keep their bargains. Were this not so, that chaotic state of nature that is the war of all against all would be what takes place, even among contracted parties. At this point, Hobbes might claim that a sovereign simply has to be powerful enough to put down those who welsh on their contractual agreements. Yet, why wouldn't Hobbes expect a constant power struggle? Only because he really does believe in that same rational self-interest invoked by Bentham and Mill. And though he denies all morality prior to the contract, he believes that self-interest will take the form of promise keeping. Calvin would be smiling by now and tempted to chide Hobbes, as well as Bentham and Mill, for thinking societies could exist if human beings were not naturally social enough, and knowledgeable enough, to see and to do what the moral law demands. Fidelity is one of those demands.

Beyond fidelity, there is the moral requirement not to kill. Hobbes, like Calvin, promotes a clear right to life. People are not to kill themselves or others. In Bentham and Mill, killing is judged expedient or inexpedient like everything else. Shouldn't an infant, innocent of all harm to others, be absolutely protected? Mature adults, not minors, have control of their own bodies and minds in a civilized society, Mill assures us, but there is no right to liberty or life independent of utility. There is no way in advance to reject the proposition that it is sometimes expedient to fail to save the life of, or even to kill, an infant.

This it seems to me is a tragic flaw in using utility as a basis of rights. It is the prohibition of killing innocent people that specifies the wrong in terrorism, the bombing of cities, and the nuclear targeting of whole populations. Again and again, representatives of democracies as well as of dictatorships argue the expediency of killing innocent people. In the movie houses of Harvard Square, terrorists have been sometimes cheered. How can this be? Terrorists presumably represent liberation, freedom from oppressive governments: The high utility of freedom for intelligent and mature adults has become, well, self-evident. Independence from what society or establishments dictate, even from what moral demands dictate, are noble and a mark of maturity. Mill explicitly links freedom with independence from society, while Calvin links it with conformity to the moral law. Terrorists in our day can qualify as heroes when they fight established power. The terrorist element in a strategy of nuclear deterrence is only now more generally being recognized. Some basis, however, has to be found for asserting the wrong in killing each individual innocent life. That basis is not in Bentham and Mill, and so we will look elsewhere.

To say that Bentham and Mill do not provide an adequate basis for human rights is not to say that their thinking has not and does not contribute to furthering human rights. Indeed, many since Bentham and Mill have used their way of thinking to champion individual and civil rights. There is power in the appeal to utility and its maximization. Morally significant relations that build and sustain our human communities have enormous utility, as Mill perceived. But, familial ties, friendships, fairness, and restraint from harm cannot be reduced to utility, or to a utility that is not differentiated from nonmoral and immoral forms of utility. As with interests, utility comes in moral, nonmoral, and immoral expressions. Failure to make these distinctions and failure to defend a basis for doing so, robs morality and ethics of all their substance; and, above all, robs us of our rights, in theory and in practice. Bentham and Mill sincerely believed that their calculus of utility identified and differentiated the more moral from the less moral, and good from evil. What I wish to contend later is that their partial success and positive political contributions rested on the actual, high utility their contemporaries placed on justice. If people are not convinced of the utility of the rights to life and liberty, and of their equal realization, then the status of rights for some may depend on a power struggle to be among those who do the calculations of utility for society. That the actualization of rights will come only with a power struggle is exactly what the theory of rights we will next consider is contending.

THREE

From Natural Rights to Class Consciousness

Scarcely a century had passed until another mighty salvo was fired at the much embattled idea of natural rights:

> We ... reject every attempt to impose on us any moral dogmas whatsoever as an eternal, ultimate and forever immutable moral law on the pretext that the moral world too has its permanent principles which transcend history and the differences between nations. ... we have not yet passed beyond class morality, a really human morality which transcends class antagonisms and their legacies in thought becomes possible only at a stage in society which has not only overcome class contradictions but has even forgotten them in practical life.[1]

Thus, in no uncertain terms, morality is linked to the classes and class conflicts existing in particular stages of history, which stages are economically determined.

Friedrich Engels explains why all moral dogmas claiming to be permanent are to be opposed:

> All former moral theories are the product in the last analysis, of the economic stage which society had reached at that particular epoch. And as society has hitherto moved in class antagonisms, morality was always a class morality; it has either justified the domination and the interests of the ruling class,

or, as soon as the oppressed class has become powerful
enough, it has represented the revolt against this domination
and the future interests of the oppressed.[2]

Engels sees progress in this history, but class moralities still prevail. That is what is wrong with Bentham and Mill: Governments
under the dominance of the bourgeois profess to calculate what is
best on the whole, but what they actually do is oppress the masses,
the proletariat. When justice prevails in a classless society, the
state, that instrument of oppression, will wither away.

Once again, we are confronted with an alternative conception of
rights. Rights will be assured only by the abolition of all classes.
Once again, the past and all past moral conceptions are given totally failing grades. This includes the work of Hobbes, who had
flunked his predecessors and presumably given a scientific grounding to rights. And Calvin, well, he is at the bottom of the class. For
as Engels asserts, in a tone of mocking condescension, "In a society in which the motive for stealing has been done away with...
how the teacher of morals would be laughed at who tried solemnly
to proclaim the eternal truth: Thou shalt not steal!"[3] Let us turn,
then, to the new chapter in the story of human rights.

Engels and Marx on Rights

Although it was Engels who explicitly wrote on human rights,
he did so on the basis of premises developed and published by
Marx. Therefore, the account given by Engels requires prefacing
with a sketch of its Marxist premises. Marx and Engels were
friends who worked closely together, jointly publishing the *Communist Manifesto* in 1847 and cooperating to organize The First International in 1864. It is not totally clear how exact was their agreement about what Engels wrote on morality and rights. Some are
content to treat what Engels says as the Marxist view;[4] others wish
more specifically to separate certain claims of Engels from Marx
and not assume that Marx's silent acceptance implied complete as-

sent to what his friend and benefactor wrote.[5] I shall not try to resolve what may not even be a resolvable issue. Here, it is sufficient
simply to refrain from imputing to Marx anything he did not either
explicitly say or logically imply.

Friedrich Engels (1820–1895) and Karl Marx (1818–1883) were
both Germans who spent a considerable portion of their lives in
England. They were contemporaries of Mill. In fact, volume 1 of
Das Capital was published in the year Mill helped pass the Reform
Act of 1867. While Marx criticized the oppressive conditions of the
working class at that time, Mill worked successfully at extending
the vote to them. This was ironic, because in Marxist theory, bourgeois governments were instruments for oppressing the working
class, the proletariat. Engels was a businessman, though he was
also a political activist and writer, retiring in 1869 to devote all his
time to literary and political activities. He edited the second and
third volumes of *Das Capital* after Marx's death. Engels gave Marx
financial aid to enable him to write. Engels had no university education but Marx had studied at Bonn and Berlin, switching from
law to philosophy. Marx opposed the Hegelianism of his day and
there was no place for him in philosophy at the German universities. In life, judged by ordinary standards, Marx was unhappy, unsuccessful, and largely unknown. In death, he is undoubtedly a
major shaper of our modern outlook. One need only think of the
concept of class and the weight given to economic conditions and
analyses of them. Politically, his name and thinking have until recently been favorably embraced by a significant portion of the
world's governments, in various degrees.

Marx put forward a theory of history known as dialectical or
historical materialism, or simply, the economic interpretation of
history. This was proposed as an alternative to Hegel's idealism
and as a statement of the principles implicit in the revolutionary
movements of that time. In this theory, the law-making substance,
the state, is distinguished from the economic associations of a society. The economy is a society organized to make possible production by a division of labor and distribution by exchange. An eco-

nomic interpretation of political history is one that traces the events and changes in polity to the events and changes in the economy. Within the economy, the most fundamental principle is the way production takes place. An economy is defined by its method of production. Capitalism is one type of economy analyzed in *Das Capital*. Marx's central thesis covering capitalism is that the capitalist economy evolved out of the feudal economy, and it will evolve into the communist economy.

The driving force of social change is class struggle and the determining power is economic rather than political. Political power is a consequence of economic position. Those who control the mode of production have political control. In capitalism, Marx saw the government as controlled by those who own the means of production and as a tool for exploiting the masses, the wage laborers. Thus, capitalism, Marx contended, contains within it the seeds of its own destruction. It provides its own grave diggers. Communism is inevitable. Why? The arguments may be outlined in three steps.

1. Productivity is increased by means of technical improvements as well as the increasing accumulation of the means of production. This means more wealth for the few; more misery for the many. And the few will decrease whereas the many will increase.
2. All classes will disappear except a small ruling class, the bourgeoisie, and a large exploited working class. This will heighten tension between the two classes and will lead to a social revolution.
3. After the victory of the workers over the bourgeoisie, there will be a society consisting of one class only; the society will be classless and without exploitation. A classless society is also one in which the state will wither away. The state is a tool of the "haves" to repress the "have nots"; remove this distinction and you remove the necessity of the state. Justifications for the state are bourgeois propaganda to retain their control over the workers.

Marx has abolished the moral purpose of the state accepted by Calvin, Hobbes, Bentham, and Mill, namely, to protect human rights and enhance their attainment. In Bentham's case, governments are the source of all rights worthy of the name. The pre-Hobbesian traditional view, shared by Calvin, saw the state as an expression of the social nature of human beings and as an enforcer of the moral obligations that individuals and communities require to exist and flourish. Marx has developed a very different notion of where power lies. The real power is in the evolving ownership of the modes of production. These, in turn, generate class struggle, the driving force of history. Out of class struggles, ideology, politics, law, morals, and religion are produced. Morality is not a force; it is a product ultimately of economic forces.

Is there then a morality, and are there human rights for which humans should work to realize? In Marx, there is the constant theme of the oppressed, the exploited laborer, whose cause is the goal of history. The moral appeal of Marx is in his portrayal of inhumane working conditions. One case, for example, is quite illustrative. In England, there was equality and freedom before the law, but what did it look like in practice? There were six-year-old children working fifteen hours a day. One girl died after working twenty-six and a half hours in a row with sixty other girls, thirty of them in one room. The medical doctor testified at an enquiry that the death was caused by overwork and overcrowding. The coroner's jury called it apoplexy (stroke), and the doctor was given a lecture in good manners. Occurrences like these confirmed Marx in his contentions that politics is impotent, reflecting economic realities rather than altering them; and that all governments, even democratic ones, are dictatorships of the ruling economic class over those ruled. The great achievement of the revolution against capitalism is that the dictatorship of the proletariat will prevail and then, since no other class will exist, there is no class to dominate. This means real freedom: complete liberation from government; and real equality, everyone in control of the means of production.

It was Engels who expressly conceptualized these implications of the Marxist interpretation of history for human rights. The first striking and radical conclusion to be drawn from Marxist premises is that all previous theories of rights are incorrect and to be totally rejected; rights and their proper understanding belong to the future, when the requisite economic conditions have been attained, as they inexorably will be. The problem with the utilitarians, as we have already indicated above, is that they have put rights in the hands of governments and bourgeois calculations, and so, only the rulers will have rights, and not the ruled—only the few, and not the masses. People are under the power of economic forces, and so what they allege to be general interests are actually the interests that are economically advantageous to them.

We have alluded also to the crux of Marxist objections to natural rights and the natural law tradition: There are no "permanent principles which transcend history and the differences among nations."[6] For this view, Engels offers two closely related arguments. First, very different, historically conditioned moralities persist and compete with each other, and natural rights theories are simply one alternative among others; and second, natural rights theories have no future, since history is not going their way.

Engels describes three types of morality present in his day: Christian-feudal morality, inherited from past periods of faith; modern bourgeois morality; and the proletarian morality of the future. These, Engels says, are present simultaneously in "advanced European countries" and represent the past, present, and future.[7] Then Engels asks, "Which one is the true one? Not one of them, in the sense of having absolute validity; but certainly that morality which contains the maximum durable elements is the one which, in the present represents the overthrow of the present, represents the future: that is, the proletarian."[8] From the observation that "the three classes of modern society, the feudal aristocracy, the bourgeoisie and the proletariat, each have their special morality, we can only draw the conclusion, that men, consciously or unconsciously, derive their moral ideas in the last resort from the practical relations in which they carry on production and exchange."[9]

Engels turns explicitly to his own interpretation of the history of human rights doctrines. Equality is the key term. It is a primeval notion that humans have something in common as humans and are equal in this respect. The modern demand for equality is totally different; it deduces from the common characteristics of humanity, "a claim to equal political or social status for all human beings, or at least for all citizens of a state or all members of a society.... Before this conclusion could appear to be something even natural and self-evident, however, thousands of years had to pass and did pass."[10] The Greeks and Romans distinguished the freemen and slaves, and thus limited the notion of human equality. Christianity saw all persons as equally born in sin and equals as members of the elect. That is what Engels alleges, and he also alleges that once priests and laymen were distinguished, even the tendency to Christian equality was at an end. The Germans, Engels claims, abolished for centuries all ideals of equality and built up a social and political hierarchy without precedent. But in the feudal middle ages, the standard bearer of the modern demand for equality evolved—the bourgeoisie.

Engels sees the development of industry, especially the passage to industry employing workers, as making more freedom and equality economically necessary. And unconsciously, the equal status of all human labor, because and insofar as it is human, was expressed in bourgeois economics: "The value of a commodity is measured by the socially necessary labor embodied in it."[11] The bourgeois demand was a demand for the abolition of all feudal class privileges. Equality and freedom came to be proclaimed as *human rights*. Engels comments, "It is significant of the specifically bourgeois character of these human rights that the American Constitution, the first to recognize the rights of man, in the same breath confirmed the slavery of the colored races in America: class privileges were proscribed, race privileges sanctified."[12]

Alongside the bourgeois, there appeared the proletarian demand for equality: "Equality must not be merely apparent, must not apply merely to the sphere of the state, but must also be real, must be extended to the social and economic sphere."[13] Equality, for the proletariat, has what Engels calls "a double meaning." One of its expressions is the revolutionary instinct, as at its start in the peasants' war, to react "against the crying social inequalities, against the contrast of rich and poor, the feudal lords and their serfs, surfeit and starvation."[14] Its justification is found in that revolutionary instinct, and only in that, according to Engels. The other expression of the proletarian demand for equality is as a reaction against the bourgeois demand for equality. What it does is deduce from the bourgeois demands what workers should also have, and that pits workers against capitalists. In both of these embodiments of the proletarian quest for equality, Engels tells us, "is the demand for the *abolition of classes*. Any demand for equality which goes beyond that, of necessity passes into absurdity."[15]

Why are alternatives to the proletarian demands an absurdity? One line of argumentation in Engels is consistent and clear: The proletarian class represents the next stage of economic history; this class and its morality will endure into the future; the other class moralities will disappear with changing economic conditions. This is an historicist argument. It is a theory of what will in fact be produced by changing historical circumstances. No moral judgment need be involved or logically implied.

The other line of argument in Engels is not so clear and is inconsistent with the purely historicist view of morality held by Engels and Marx. Engels states that as a consequence of the historical process of class antagonisms, "There has on the whole been progress in morality, as in all other branches of human knowledge," and this "cannot be doubted."[16] The future interests of the oppressed keep asserting themselves. "A really human morality" is one that "transcends class antagonisms."[17] According to the Marxist understanding of history, the proletariat will at some stage usher in a classless society. Therefore it is the proletarian morality that is "a really human morality" and that spells "progress" even now in the present. And that means an increase in "knowledge" as well. Engels and Marx, however, have argued that moralities are ideologies, effects of economic forces, and reflections of class interests. Why any particular class interests or economic stage of history that causes them should represent moral progress, increased knowledge, and interests that are "truly human" is not evident from a totally materialist interpretation of historical forces that do not include morality or moral conceptions as powers or as sources of knowledge. Furthermore, since all moralities are class moralities, Engels and everyone else is seeing what is moral from the perspective of their class membership. Engels has, from the historical perspective, denied absolute validity to all the existing class moralities and has denied that there are "permanent principles which transcend history." He has not provided a way of knowing that one should affirm or prefer proletarian morality.

Marx was fully aware of the kind of difficulty Engels created by making normative claims about the superiority, in some sense, of proletarian rights claims. In the *German Ideology* Marx wrote, "Communists preach no morality at all. They do not put to people the moral demand: Love one another, be not egoists, etc.; on the contrary, they know very well that egoism, like sacrifice, is under specific conditions a necessary [inevitable] form of the individual's struggle for survival."[18] Eugene Kamenka describes this consistent element in Marx concisely and accurately:

> Throughout the remainder of his life Marx would object bitterly to any attempt to base a socialist programme on "abstract" moral demands embodied in such terms as "justice," "equality," etc. Marxism was a science; it did not advocate socialism, it showed that socialism was inevitable. It did not ask for a "just" wage, it showed that the wage-system was self-destructive. Marxism did not confront society with moral principles, but studied the laws of motion that governed social change. It did not tell the proletariat what it ought to do, but showed the proletariat what it would be forced to do, by its own character, and situation, by its position in "history."[19]

Marx, like Engels, allied himself with the self-conscious struggle to bring about the inevitable. Is not such a preference or commitment in some sense a moral one? Karl Popper has developed a very interesting thesis on this question. He imagines himself in a conversation with Marx in which he has managed to elicit from Marx an answer to the question of why he is actively engaged to help the oppressed. Here are some excerpts from the reply Popper constructs as the one consistent with the thinking of Marx:

> As a social scientist...I am able to see that the bourgeoisie, with its system of morals, is bound to disappear, and that the proletariat, and with it a new system of morals, is bound to win. I see that this development is inevitable. It would be madness to attempt to resist it, just as it would be madness to attempt to resist the law of gravity. That is why my fundamental decision is in favor of the proletariat and its morality. And this decision is based only on scientific foresight.... Although itself not a moral decision, since it is not based on any system of morality, it leads to the adoption of a certain system of morality.... My fundamental decision is not (as you suspected) the sentimental decision to help the oppressed, but the scientific and rational decision not to offer vain resistance to the developmental laws of society.... I adopt the facts of the coming period as the standards of my morality. And in this way, I solve the apparent paradox that a more reasonable world will come without being planned by reason; for according to my moral standards now adopted, the future world must be better, and therefore more reasonable. And I also bridge the gap between my activism and my historicism.... I cannot shuffle the natural phases of its [society's] evolution out of the world by a stroke of the pen. But... I can actively assist in shortening and lessening its birth-pangs.[20]

Then Popper comments that this "reply" of Marx to his question "represents the most important form of what I have called 'historicist moral theory'."[21]

This last statement attributed to Marx by Popper does not make sense to me. It is plausible for Marx to say that he cannot halt certain inevitable social changes; but it is not plausible at the same time for Marx to claim that he *can* assist or shorten these changes. If Marx can affect history at all by his decisions, he *can* decide whether to delay the coming changes, or whether to speed them up. Also, he can do nothing. Marx would only reasonably decide to help speed up the course of history if he favored it. He does not have to favor what is coming even if he believes it senseless to oppose it. Also, he can favor social change yet do nothing because he does not enjoy the activities necessary to try to change things. And why bother? The changes will come without him. But Marx advocates revolution, and he believes in freedom, a freedom, however, that requires certain economic conditions. These conditions he considers worth struggling for. Needless to say, so does Engels.

In the *Communist Manifesto* Marx and Engels were clearly advocating revolution, and they did so in the name of freedom. They argued as follows: "Political power, properly so called, is merely the organized power of one class for oppressing another." Should one favor the use of such power, then? Marx and Engels do not directly ask or answer the question in that form. Rather, they say:

If the proletariat during its contest with the bourgeoisie is compelled, by the force of circumstances, to organize itself as a class; if by means of a revolution it makes itself the ruling class, and as such sweeps away by force the old conditions of production, then it will, along with these conditions, have swept away the conditions for the existence of class antagonism, and of classes generally, and will thereby have abolished its supremacy as a class.[22]

Note what is happening as the argument unfolds. If the proletariat organizes itself as a class, and if it gains power, by revolution over the bourgeoisie, do not think of this as oppression because, when the proletariat takes over it will also abolish itself as an oppressor class. Therefore, there is no reason to hold back from engaging in force. This particular revolution and any violence that might be involved will do away with antagonisms and conflict: "In place of the old bourgeois society, with its classes and class antagonisms, we shall have an association in which the free development of each is the condition for the free development of all."[23]

The argument is a consequentialist one, like utilitarianism in that respect, but the criteria for it are more exacting. For Marx and Engels, it is not enough to have the "greatest good for the greatest number." Each person is to have the freedom to develop under circumstances where the development of each person is mutually reinforcing in some way. Strict equality of liberty and the opportunity to develop oneself is being posited as the outcome necessary to justify the use of class power and force on a temporary basis. Given the goals, and given that the more permanent and long-term consequences of revolution are equal liberty and opportunities for development, Engels and Marx consider themselves justified in concluding the *Manifesto* with a summons to revolution: "Let the ruling classes tremble at a Communist revolution. The proletarians have nothing to lose but their chains. They have a world to win. Workingmen of all countries, unite!"[24] How quickly and by the use of how much force the nonproletarian classes will cease to be sources of class conflict is not at all made explicit. The *Manifesto* concentrates on overcoming inhibitions to engage in class conflict, using force if necessary, in the name of eliminating all class conflict and exchanging for it a truly universal freedom, free of the present chains for the working class. As we shall see shortly, Lenin transforms this into a purely utilitarian argument for the use of violence against all of his opponents.

Any call for revolution and force cannot be claimed as necessary logically or factually, even if one could know absolutely that these will inevitably take place. Anyone, on moral grounds, and if moral grounds are denied, on grounds of preferences, may elect to abstain from or even oppose revolution and/or violence. One could, from a Marxist perspective, be accused of being bourgeois or sympathetic to the bourgeois. But from a Hobbesian perspective, one might well hold back from any fighting either because one is cowardly or because one is justified in giving loyalty only to those with enough power to protect one's life. Why not wait until the proletariat is powerful enough to justify loyalty and bring peace? Hence, even if Hobbes believed every claim of Engels and Marx about the inevitable outcome of history, he could offer reasons for rejecting the behavior exhibited and advocated by Engels and Marx in their activities and writings on behalf of revolution and the organizing of the proletariat. What is at stake involves more than class interests: Hobbes would assert a right to an interest in his own life and ground this on what he considers the relevant scientific facts about human beings.

Now we have come to the crux of the matter. Marx, especially in his earlier writings, has a very different conception of what is human and *truly* human, as he often puts it. His moral criticism of capitalism and what he expects from its overthrow appear to be based on his view of human nature and its potentialities. More explicitly, he is choosing the morality of the proletariat because he believes it will actualize what he most values among our human potentialities.

Kamenka has characterized this aspect of Marx's thought succinctly:

> Underlying the whole of his work, providing the ethical
> impulse that guided his hopes and his studies, was a vision
> and a theory of human freedom, of man as master of himself,
> of nature and of history. It was a vision of the fully social
> man who has developed all his potentialities, made himself the
> aim and measure of all things, subsumed them to his human
> needs and purposes.[25]

This is what is often called Marx's "humanism" or "Promethean ethic." Dignity consists in independence and mastery over obstacles; the most detested vice is servility. In Kamenka's words:

The servitude of man in all past human societies and the coming liberation from this servitude provide the basic plot of the Marxian conception of history which is a moral drama (though it is not only that). Those things which Marx sees as enslaving man are the primary targets of Marx's criticism and the main object of his study.[26]

One way that Marx expresses what he means by servitude is in the concept of alienation. Alienation occurs when human beings are not self-determining and their needs are not being met. This can happen in at least four ways: (l) The things human beings produce dominate them instead of meeting their needs, as in creating consumer desires for things not needed; (2) people in competition in a system based on private property and classes with irreconcilable interests, hostile to one another and limiting, rather than extending one another's capacities; (3) nature limiting people rather than providing a field for creative use of our powers, is alienating; (4) humans are alienated from society when in a capitalist or any class society, state interest is distinguished from and conflicts with private interests.

In this last point, the criticism of any economic system in which private and public interests conflict, we see an important difference between Marx and Mill as contemporaries, both actively concerned to increase human freedom. Mill seeks to do two things: one, increase the sphere of freedom to pursue one's own interests without interference; and two, increase the opportunities to participate in and influence the nature and expression of public interests. When Marx looks at this, he sees a bourgeois morality. Why? Well, consider how it is for a worker. Laborers have to sell themselves, their energies, for wages. And the work they do is not a source of contentment:

It does not belong to his essential being. . . . He is at home when he is not working and when he works he is not at home. His work is not voluntary but coerced; it is *forced* labor. It is, therefore, not the satisfaction of a need, but only a means for satisfying needs external to it.[27]

Mill is proposing to make certain the law permits workers to vote and does not interfere with the pursuit of their own plans, provided they harm no one in these pursuits. From Marx's perspective, all four kinds of alienation are left untouched because the economic system that breeds them is untouched. In a communist society there would be harmony. People would be caught up in productive labor, in socially cooperative creation. There would be no state, no criminals, no conflicts, no need for punishment and coercive rules. Mill accepts the economic system in which people assert their rights and have duties required of them and enforced by legal authority, so that these rights are actualized. Mill has, from Marx's vantage point, an impoverished view of human potential and a false picture of what is *truly* human. In *German Ideology*, Marx takes aim at the kind of outlook represented in Mill (and in Bentham and Hobbes, for that matter): "Rights and duties are the two complementary sides of a contradiction which belongs only to civil society."[28] Marx means by "civil society" one in which individuals pursue interests in conflict with one another and have not internalized the concept of community, and have not yet brought about the economic conditions for such a community. What human dignity requires is an overcoming of those situations in which interests conflict and the creation of a society in which individuals have common purposes and agree with one another on what is to be done. Morality is not a question of rules, such as those Bentham and Mill suggest, but of habits. Truly moral habits can only arise when human beings are free—free of superstition, free of external compulsion, free of divisive classes and interests, free of property, and free of compelling need or fear of need. True morality is what free, rational, self-determined individuals, acting without external compulsion would do. Kamenka has summarized concisely and accurately the presuppositions of Marx's moral advocacy:

(1) Man, when truly and fully human, when conscious of his nature, his potentialities and his relations to other men, is naturally cooperative. . . . (2) Man, in becoming truly human, is able to exercise untrammelled rationality. . . . (3) All social conflicts can ultimately be derived from the institution of private property and the class structures created by it.[29]

Abolish this whole system of private property, and the realities of propositions (1) and (2) will become realities, and the state, the law, and the criminal will disappear. Marx has a social conception of liberty; Mill, and Bentham and Hobbes as well, has an individual conception of liberty. Marx expands greatly the expectations human beings should have for the realization of their potentialities.

Not everyone shares these expectations or considers them realistic. This fact of life was directly confronted by Lenin as he sought to bring about the communist world, envisioned by Marx, in czarist Russia of 1917.

Marxism-Leninism on Rights

Nicolai Lenin (born Vladimir Ilich Ulyanov in 1870) was premier of the Soviet Union from 1918 until his death in 1924. He was the Russian revolutionary leader of the Communist (Bolshevik) party who directed the Revolution of 1917. As is well known, his mausoleum in the Red Square of Moscow became a national shrine. After studying law at Kazan and St. Petersburg, he gave up legal practice to study Marx and was twice exiled to Siberia for revolutionary activities.

Like Marx and Engels, he held that the state is a tool for repression and that it will cease once the bourgeois are eliminated because everyone will be a wage earner. Lenin, however, expressly endorsed the necessity of violently repressing and doing away with the bourgeois. For Lenin, this included the forceful elimination of all noncommunist parties, something he accomplished by 1921. Whereas Marx had believed in majority rule, Lenin formed a party of disciplined shock troops, a definite minority, comprised of the most class conscious, and hence, the most revolutionary, of the working class. Majority rule, Lenin claimed, would come once the revolutionary party had power: People, after all, know what they ought to want. Unlike democratic socialist parties, Lenin's party had no legal status until it seized and exercised the controlling power of government. In order to accomplish this, he won the help of peasants by giving them land, while he bought time to swell the ranks of industrial workers. Once securely in power, the land was controlled by the Communist party.

Lenin applied Marx's reasoning to international relations, speaking of "have and have-not nations" in conflict, until by international revolutionary activity, the "imperialism" and "colonialism" of the have nations, and this distinction of the "haves" and "have-nots," could be abolished. Kamenka speaks of "the notoriously end-directed ethic of Leninism," as though Lenin had, as it were, an ethic of his own.[30] It is true that Lenin had introduced a new element into the revolution sought by Marx, Engels, and now their followers. Lenin organized the Communist party as a group of revolutionaries to be the mouthpiece of history and the representatives of the class consciousness of the proletariat. And so Lenin could portray the good as that which promotes the power of the Party and, hence, the revolution. Good is what is on the side of history. Or as he expressed it, "Our morality is wholly subordinated to the interests of the class struggle of the proletariat."[31] This took a rather crude form in some of Trotsky's formulations: "A gun is good in the hands of a proletarian fighting for the Revolution and evil in the hands of a *bourgeois* opposing it."[32] Or again, later, Trotsky, in remarks related to terrorism and the struggle of the Party to establish its power, denounced "the Kantian-clerical, vegetarian- Quaker chatter about the 'sanctity of human life.'"[33]

It is true also that an ethic that began with a vision of a society as composed solely of workers, and in which classes, property, the state, police forces, the bourgeois family, crime, and self-seeking have all vanished, became an ethic that was increasingly a call to obey the Party and work loyally for the former Soviet Union and against its enemies.

The courts also, as Solzhenitsyn has so graphically depicted them, under Lenin, did what was expedient: A defendant was to be evaluated "from the point of view of class expediency."[34] In intent and spirit, Lenin is at this point rather far from Marx and Engels. But we would miss the whole point of discussing Marx and Engels on rights if we failed to see the connections between their thinking and the subsequent Leninist expressions of it, with its blatant denials of any rights to life and liberty for their enemies, and even for their own comrades, when expedient.

Rights and Class Consciousness: An Assessment

In pointing to a link between Lenin and Marx and Engels, I am not making judgments about what Marx and Engels might have done in Lenin's circumstances; nor am I speculating about their reactions, favorable or unfavorable, to Lenin's thinking and behavior. Rather, I wish to make explicit what Lenin could draw upon in Marx and Engels for support. First, they urged the workers to organize themselves as a class and to use this power to revolt if necessary to win out over the bourgeoisie. Lenin applied this idea to the Party as a revolutionary vanguard of the revolution. Second, Marx and Engels considered all previous moralities passé and appeals to what they taught, futile. It is quite in keeping with this outlook to deride those who would appeal to these outworn moral demands. Note Trotsky's sarcastic dismissal, for example, of any appeal to the sanctity of life as "Kantian-clerical" and "vegetarian-Quaker." It is also consonant with Marx and Engels not to be guided by "rights" and "duties" that Marx said were products of a society in conflict and its members alienated, with no proper sense of community. This can be seen as a third source in Marx and Engels to use as a justification for disregarding elemental rights to life and liberty to those seen as opponents of the revolution.

Sharing the ideals of the communist revolution did not, and does not, commit one to the tactics and methods of Lenin. Petr Kropotkin, like Lenin, Marx, and Engels, looked for the "elimination of the state and all governmental processes, and their replacement by a free and spontaneous cooperation among individuals, groups, regions, and nations."[35] Kropotkin had been imprisoned both in Russia, his native land, and in France, for revolutionary activity. He returned eagerly to Russia in 1917 as the revolution started. His meetings with Lenin were unsatisfactory. He was dismayed by the activities of the Bolsheviks under Lenin's direction. Several times he wrote Lenin. The one letter from which I will quote protests the Party's practice of taking hostages to protect themselves against possible violence from their opponents. He wrote in 1920, on the very day he learned of the use of hostages. The following are excerpts:

> Vladimir Ilyich, your concrete actions are completely unworthy of the ideas you pretend to hold.

> Is it possible that you do not know what a hostage really is— a man imprisoned not because of a crime he has committed, but only because it suits his enemies to exert blackmail on his companions? These men must feel very much like men who are condemned to death, and whose inhuman executioners announce every day at noon that the execution has been postponed until the next day. If you admit such methods, one can foresee that one day you will use torture as was done in the Middle Ages.

> I hope you will not answer me that power is for political men a professional duty, and that any attack against that power must be considered as a threat against which one must guard oneself at any price. This opinion is no longer held even by kings.

> How can you, Vladimir Ilyich, you who want to be the apostle of new truths and the builder of a new State, give your consent to the use of such repulsive conduct, of such

unacceptable methods? Such a measure is tantamount to confessing publicly that you adhere to the ideas of yesterday.

Being at the head of European communism you have no right to soil the ideas which you defend by shameful methods, methods which are not only the proof of a monstrous error, but of an unjustifiable fear for your own life? What future lies in store for communism when one of its most important defenders tramples in this way on every honest feeling?[36]

We can see the sheer anguish of Kropotkin. He wishes so much that the ideas Lenin professed would be realized, but Kropotkin, unlike Lenin, linked those ideas to the methods used, not just the ends. And, Kropotkin was not shy about using an expression like "you have no right." In no way did he believe that the ideals of communism would ever come about through behavior he considered incompatible with them. Clearly, Lenin disagreed, and it would be easy for him to dismiss Kropotkin as still under the influence of his aristocratic heritage.

Kropotkin was exhibiting a moral mode of reasoning that is not characteristic of Marx and Engels. Indeed, it was something Marx and Engels directly attacked. I am speaking here of treating certain responsibilities and rights as inviolable. Kropotkin was arguing that the denial of liberty to an innocent person cannot be justified by an appeal to the necessities of power or safety, public or personal. It is this kind of reasoning that is absent from Marx and Engels as they suggest that circumstances may make it necessary to organize the proletariat as a class and by revolutionary force use the power necessary to win the contest with the bourgeoisie. Lenin, it could be argued, did what was necessary in forging a party of class-conscious followers. That he had no majority following, would "have to" use the peasants under false pretense, and would "have to" use considerable violence to crush his opposition, were "reasons" he could give. My point is that Marx and Lenin argued from circumstantial necessity as guides to policies designed to gain the victory of the proletariat, and that they did so without setting moral limits. They did not posit inalienable rights to life and liberty and responsibilities to secure them for all persons as guides and limits for policy.

In fairness to Marx and Engels, they favored majority rule, and they did not give any express sanction to a permanent communist party, particularly one that functions as a new class. At the very least, the party should be temporary, in their view. And they were outspoken in their rejection of imposed morality, and surely they would have reason to see Lenin's party and the whole "party" concept, since it does not include all workers, as an imposition on those excluded. This rule of the party is not the classless situation of spontaneous freedom and harmony, the self-determination of each an aid to the self-determination of all.

That the Communist party constitutes a new class, denying elemental liberty to all outside it, is exactly how Milovan Djilas, then a Yugoslavian communist, argued from his own Marxist perspective. Once vice president under the late Marshal Tito, Djilas has been in and out of jail for speaking out, an ironic example of the denial of liberty he sees as characteristic of the Communist party, Lenin's creation.

Marx and Engels taught that all class moralities were relative and the morality of a dominant class—in their day, the capitalist owners of the means of production—was imposed on other classes. They absolutized the proletariat ethic because to it they attributed both the most permanent elements (Engels) and because it would be the only class, the owner of all modes of production, and in this situation no one would be oppressed, all would be equally free. Now that is the theory, according to Djilas, but it is not the reality under communism. In practice, a new class of owners, the Communist party, exploits wage earners who are under compulsory employment, earning lower wages and having fewer privileges than their owners.[37] Furthermore, the Party claims to speak and act for the proletariat; hence, they assimilate to themselves the authority Marx and Engels attributed to the proletariat, once classlessness had been achieved.

But classlessness is not a reality wherever the Communist party owns and manages all the means of production in Marxist nations. This means that there is no separation of powers in theory or in practice. The courts and laws are all partial to the new class, favoring the owners and managers who constitute at the same time the government and the Party.[38] Wage earners, Djilas contends, do not have their interests represented. The Party manages, makes laws, and enforces these laws in ways that assure the retention of party power and privileges.[39] Djilas sees no impartiality, no justice, in the courts or in the economy.[40] In a passionate critique, Djilas says that the Communist party cannot claim any of the noble ends they profess: "By justifying the means because of the end, the end itself becomes increasingly more distant and unrealistic, while the frightful reality of the means becomes increasingly obvious and intolerable."[41] These were prophetic insights indeed!

But it is one thing, important as it is, to recognize that under the influence of the Leninist version of Marx, otherwise laudable goals were corrupted by the means used to attain them, and that what was attained were the cruelties and injustices of those policies; it is quite another thing, equally as important, to recognize that the allegedly laudable goals were stated and conceived in a form that makes them at best morally debatable, and at worst, quite immoral. I do not wish to be misunderstood. I am not speaking in opposition to the ideas of freedom and self development. Rather, what I believe needs to be questioned is the particular way in which these ideas are conceptualized by Marx and Engels.

The emphasis in Marx and Engels was upon creating an economic situation in which people's most basic needs were equally met. Stated abstractly in that way, without indicating how this was to be accomplished, and how extensive are the needs to be satisfied, everyone, or virtually everyone, finds here a goal consonant with the affirmation of the inalienable rights to life, liberty, and the pursuit of happiness for people considered in some sense equal at birth. But Marx and Engels do not affirm these rights as natural birthrights. Any appeal to these rights, further, is but a sign that the economic situation that leads to freedom from the fears and competitiveness that characterize a capitalist economy and a bourgeois morality has not been realized.

Appeals to rights, and the obligations to protect and realize them, occur in economic conditions in which people are not yet spontaneously free, and one class tries to impose its morality on another. They include moral rules among the obstacles to freedom, along with the class conflicts that they reflect. Marx and Engels call upon one class, the proletariat, by force, if necessary, to do away with all the obstacles that stand in the way of freedom and self-determination. That they put no limit on the force to be used, we have noted earlier. They also put no limit on the expression of freedom and the quest for self-determination. Indeed, when freedom comes and we are self-determining, we will also be free of the external compulsions of moral rules and rights claims. "True morality, in fact, is what free, rational, self-determined men acting without external compulsions would do. If there has been no true, spontaneous, natural morality in the past, this is only because men have never been able to realize themselves in free, rational, uncompelled social activity."[42]

To be fair to Marx and Engels: They contended that the kind of egoistic individualism interpreted as freedom by Hobbes, Bentham, and Mill only reflected and aided the alienation of human beings from their social and communal impulses. But Marx and Engels thought that alienation could be overcome only by the removal of all the external impediments to the free expression of our communal natures. They had no place in their theories for self-restraint. In Plato and Aristotle, rational self-determination meant an internal victory of the rational self over the self of unlimited desires. Virtue consisted in cultivating and controlling the right desires, and doing so to the right degree. The Jewish and Christian traditions also posit an internal war within persons. Freedom consists in overcoming slavery to evil and choosing what is right. One major expression both of our social nature and of becoming what we were created to be lies in refraining from evil and not giving in to impulses to do evil. These impulses to harm one another are strong and governments are ordained to enforce curbs to the evil that people are prone to perpetrate.

Return, now, to Calvin's version of this. Our moral and social natures are among our endowments as individuals. But all individuals struggle internally with their propensities to seek their own good and to do so even when this may harm their neighbors. These harms are specified in the Mosaic Covenant (The Decalogue), and we have the abilities and inclinations to recognize and refrain from the evils specified there. Calvin did believe that it is possible to live freely, spontaneously, and without any sense of being constrained in accord with The Decalogue. But this kind of freedom is possible only because of the cosmic force for good that is at work in the world (God). God is also at work in keeping alive the churches and governments. Churches and governments both facilitate the self-restraint and unselfishness necessary to freedom, but only governments should use force to deal with those who harm others in grievous ways. Government has a clear moral purpose, but it also is to be restrained by the requirements of the same moral rules that everyone naturally recognizes. In contrast to Marx and Engels, Calvin distinguishes evil forms of self-determination and expression from the kind of freedom and self-realization that consist in overcoming evil, egoistic desires, and actions. In a word, Calvin believed that only people who are moral are free; and people who do what is right spontaneously and willingly cannot claim that they have accomplished this on their own.

I cite Calvin to draw out two starkly contrasting views of freedom. I do so also to call attention to a very modern, rather pervasive phenomenon, namely the tendency to think of morality as imposed on us by laws or rules or even by a nasty conscience that forbids what we want. We have seen in Hobbes, Bentham, Mill, and now Marx and Engels different versions of this same idea. As one who teaches ethics at a university, I often, and increasingly so, am asked how one can teach ethics at all. Am I not, by so doing, imposing, or trying to impose, my own morality or moral opinions on others? Of course, there is such a thing as imposing, or seeking to impose, our own moral opinions and attitudes on others. But, morality as such, I would maintain, is not something any of us do or can impose on one another, any more than I can make a moral agent out of a rabbit. I can only teach ethics if I am dealing with recognizable, shared human realities and impulses. To put the matter very simply, I am dealing with our deepest values as human beings, those which, if we violate them, and know we have violated them, have the potential to create in us terrible regrets and conflicts, even a sense of tragedy. In ethics, we reflect on these values. Not all of our strongly held values are moral values, and not all of our preferences are values we should seek to realize.

Now that last statement sounds dangerously like an imposition—there are values that should not be sought.

Consider the injunction not to steal. Engels specifically took this to be an example of a class morality, taught as dogma because considered "eternal," that is, considered to be a valid moral claim, always and universally. That is how Calvin would see it, not as the view of a class but as something human beings as such normally recognize as true. Engels argues that in a classless society, where all our material needs are met, the motive for stealing is gone, and so the restraint has no relevance or validity. People would simply laugh at a teacher like myself calling attention to it at all. But Engels is closer to Calvin than he thinks. Like Calvin, he opposes stealing and passionately prefers a society in which even the impulse would be bizarre, literal madness, since unnecessary. Calvin believes, however, that no society composed of and governed by human beings will ever eliminate this impulse. The power to abolish that impulse is not a human power. As human beings and as free moral agents, according to Calvin, we are desirous of what others have, as well as capable of sharing what we have with others. In our struggles, we need help to curb our desire to take what is not ours. Governments will be necessary for this purpose.

Engels might counter by saying that once private property has been done away with what is there to steal? If Calvin were living today, he might well reply, "Your kidney or your liver, Engels, should mine fail. Of course, I shouldn't take it unless you offer it, and of course, it would be good to have a law that doesn't allow me to do it. Wouldn't you agree?" I confess I am not sure how Marx and Engels thought on such subjects. At this juncture, I am simply questioning whether they have given us sufficient reasons to discard our strongly held value that people are not to take things from others without permission or without a justifiable claim, and that concern is important enough that, if they do, they should not expect immunity from being forced to rehabilitate or make amends in some way. Later in this book, I shall discuss what reasons there are for considering prohibitions of stealing and other harms, as moral imperatives and expressive of the sociality and desire for community that Marx and Engels valued as well.

There is at least one more very troublesome aspect of the thought of Marx and Engels in its implications for human rights. It is the certitude and scientific basis they claim for their predictions regarding the direction and outcome of history. Furthermore, they had such confidence in their prophecies that they were willing to urge all workers to join them in the use of force to make the inevitable changes of the future come sooner.

I am not criticizing them for believing that "justice" or what they considered right will ultimately triumph. I will examine in chapter 6 the sense in which all morally conscientious individuals, by their decisions and actions, presuppose something akin to this belief. I will not repeat the various criticisms that have been made of their actual predictions. Economic classes are probably more numerous now than ever before, and classlessness and freedom from governments are not realities. One could argue that the bourgeoisie became ever more numerous, long before the widespread defection from communism.

I am not so much concerned with the mistakes I think Marx and Engels made in their predictions, though I believe that the truth of their predictions should be carefully analyzed, as they have been by others. My focus now is on the whole form of reasoning that bases the *actuality* and realization of our moral rights to life and liberty on what is yet to come and claims to know for certain what is coming. Our moral aspirations, any rights we may claim to life, liberty, and the pursuit of happiness, are, as it were, held hostage to the future. Small wonder that it appears intolerable to Marx and Engels to do anything but revolt. Theoretically, they had nothing we could call rights, nor did anyone else, until the bourgeois class was eliminated! That's a powerful argument for revolution and violence. It does not auger well for the life and liberty of anyone who could be regarded as a bourgeoisie, or who took a different view of history. Indeed, Djilas complains bitterly of communist tyranny over the mind.

Leo Strauss has noted the moral impact of the belief that one knows how events are ordered and can be guided by this knowledge:

> The secularization of the understanding of Providence culminates in the view that the ways of God are scrutable to sufficiently enlightened men. The theological tradition recognized the mysterious character of Providence especially by the fact that God uses or permits evil for his good ends. It asserted therefore that man cannot take his bearings by God's providence but only by God's law, which simply forbids man to do evil. In proportion as the providential order came to be regarded as intelligible to man, and therefore evil came to be regarded as evidently necessary or useful, the prohibition against doing evil lost its evidence. Hence various ways of action that were previously condemned as evil could now be regarded as good.[43]

Strauss believes that this characterizes all modern political philosophy, the beginning of which he traces to Hobbes. His analysis characterizes Bentham, Mill, Marx, and Engels as well. For the utilitarians, it was the best balance of good over evil consequences anticipated or predicted that should determine human rights; for Marx and Engels, it was the future freedom and equity of classlessness certain to come that could make revolutionary violence and oppression of the bourgeoisie necessary temporarily until the victory is won. Of course, crusades and holy wars have not been limited to nontheological traditions. When religious persons or organizations profess to know what Providence ordained, the same "best consequence" arguments or arguments from necessity have sometimes emerged.

It is incredible to me that moral choices are constantly made to do evil on the basis of a professed knowledge of good to come. It is on this basis that it becomes necessary, for example, to use torture, hold hostages, bomb cities, or fail to save the life of a handicapped or elderly person. Why is it, for example, that in deciding the treatment of handicapped infants, future events are projected for them, virtually none of which could be known? In cases where lifesaving intervention is available but not used, it is claimed that the future of that handicapped infant is "known" to be totally or mostly bad. It is not the life of Helen Keller that is projected when people are uncertain whether they should save the life of a handicapped infant whose life can be saved. Nor should one do so. One should not project any particular life for any infant handicapped or normal. Why should one even have to raise such an issue? Isn't it evident that no one is omniscient and no one has knowledge of this kind? So ingrained is this form of reasoning that we are supposed to take for granted that physicians, presidents, and others play "god." We have perfected this reasoning to the point where we are unaware that all rights to life and liberty are presently held hostage to our weaponry and a way of thinking that has made it acceptable to kill and threaten to kill, anyone or everyone, but of course, only if necessary or better than the projected alternatives.

I am not suggesting that there is no need to employ force by duly constituted, democratic governments. I am suggesting that we have been willing to think of international uses of force in ways totally inappropriate to police behavior. Police are to use just means, not only have just ends. For the sake of capturing an armed person, one does not drive through a crowd. Governments we otherwise respect, however, have tried to "clean out" snipers by bombing apartments and whole city blocks. How we can be even remotely convinced of the good outcome of this I do not know. All I know is that doing this is a violation of the human rights to life and liberty of innocent persons. What will come of crossing those lines I cannot predict. What I wish to suggest later are some grounds on which such community-destructive acts, such as killing innocent persons, are to be considered wrong. The argument will not be based on a claim to omniscience about the future. Marx and Engels have not supplied us with the conceptual foundations needed to protect innocent life, freedom, and equality of basic rights.

FOUR

Natural Rights
Autonomy versus Interdependence

As the past two chapters have indicated, natural, inalienable rights were rejected by the founding representatives of utilitarianism and Marxism. What then is the fate of natural rights today?

In his carefully documented study, Max Stackhouse describes the "Liberal-Puritan Synthesis" that provides the rationale for modern Western democratic institutions and practices.[1] Natural, inalienable rights were seen as rationally self-evident by liberals, and as divinely and rationally revealed truths by Puritans. Looking at our contemporary situation, Stackhouse notes that almost imperceptibly this synthesis has largely been replaced by appeals to utility as a basis for justifying policy.

But what about the formal endorsement of universal human rights by the United Nations? Is not this strong evidence, or at least some evidence, that natural rights have not been rejected by the world's governments? The United Nations has, indeed, claimed universality for "human rights" as recognizable characteristics of "all members of the human family."[2] Furthermore, the recognition that all human beings as human beings have an "inherent dignity" and possess "equal and inalienable rights" is for the United Nations "the foundation of freedom, justice, and peace in the world."[3] In the immediate aftermath of World War II, the United Nations' affirmation, in 1949, of the link between regard for human rights and the existence of freedom, justice, and peace for the whole world is neither implausible nor gratuitous: Human rights of the kind declared by the United Nations as universal had been grossly violated, and to defend their human rights, a great many nations had been drawn into a war itself conducted in ways destructive of human rights. The language of rights was chosen as the vehicle for asserting universal standards of conduct for all nations and peoples: All achievements of nations and peoples are to be gauged by how well human rights are taught, respected, and effectively recognized and observed in the actual policies of nations and peoples toward their own members and toward other nations and peoples.

The first article of the *Universal Declaration of Human Rights* does equate human rights with what is a natural, common event, shared by all human beings: "All human beings are born free and equal in dignity and rights."[4] And as noted above, these "natural" rights, Bentham notwithstanding, are considered to be "inalienable." For the United Nations, there is a great deal at stake if these claims are without foundation or treated as such: nothing less than the existence of freedom, justice, and peace in the world. We remind the reader, therefore, of the seriousness of MacIntyre's terse and biting observation: "In the United Nations declaration on human rights of 1949 what has since become the normal United Nations' practice of not giving good reasons for *any* assertions whatsoever is followed with great rigour."[5] If the world were not plagued, as it is, with widespread and numerous violations of equal dignity and rights, some of them episodic, some long institutionalized, the lack of good reasons might well seem utterly insignificant. But, as things now stand, it is extremely important to determine whether Alasdair MacIntyre is correct when he says of all natural or human rights: "Every attempt to give good reasons for believing that there *are* such rights has failed."[6] Appeals to self-evident truths in the eighteenth century, and to self-evident intuitions in the twentieth century, are tersely dismissed by MacIntyre: "We know that there are no self-evident truths," he says, and furthermore, when a philosopher resorts to "intuition," it "is always a signal that something has gone badly wrong with the argument."[7]

MacIntyre's account of rights is part of his general assessment of the failure of philosophy, or any other discipline, to provide a persuasive account of what is moral. This failure is exemplified by all theories that base morality on rights and all that base morality on utility: "Natural or human rights then are fictions—just as is utility."[8] Utility is a fiction because the interests or desires on which its calculation depends are "irreducibly heterogeneous."[9] And what does it mean to call rights and utility moral fictions? "They purport to provide us with an objective and impersonal criterion, but they do not."[10]

MacIntyre is by no means alone in discounting all theories that try to ground rights on intuitions or calculations of utility. Others see as well that when policy has no more to justify it than someone's idea of what is obviously right, or what yields the best cost/benefit ratio, then we are back in a situation in which "might makes right." Trying to provide an alternative to that view was the vocation chosen by Socrates, a task that helped launch Western moral and political philosophy. But MacIntyre rejects all current efforts to provide alternatives to utilitarianism and Marxism and to the political traditions they underlie, traditions MacIntyre regards as "exhausted."[11]

Among the conceptions of rights MacIntyre regards as unsatisfactory are those of Alan Gewirth, a moral philosopher presently at the University of Chicago. Like MacIntyre, Gewirth believes that substantive moral principles and rights *must be demonstrated.* But, unlike MacIntyre, Gewirth believes that they *can be demonstrated.* Furthermore, Gewirth is convinced that he has made a case for the logical necessity of universal and natural rights.[12] MacIntyre accepts Gewirth's criticisms of previous and contemporary efforts to provide rational grounds for the existence of human rights; he does not accept Gewirth's own efforts to provide such rational grounds. In our quest for finding a basis for human rights, however, it will turn out to be helpful to examine with some care Gewirth's thoughtful and stout defense of natural rights, as well as MacIntyre's specific comments on its flaws.

Universally Necessary Rights: Alan Gewirth

Alan Gewirth is not content with those who would base rights on utility or historical contingencies. For him, human rights are natural. Human rights are "natural" because they pertain to all human beings insofar as they are by nature actual or prospective agents.[13] For Gewirth, "Human rights are a species of moral rights; they are moral rights which all persons equally have simply because they are human."[14] Rights, furthermore, are "moral" in the sense that they are "based upon" or "justifiable" through a valid moral principle; a principle is "moral" in that it identifies the categorically obligatory nature of certain requirements for action.[15] These requirements apply equally to all actual or prospective agents; they serve the important interests, equally shared by all persons or recipients.[16]

Gewirth views rights as claim-rights. A claim-right is a right of one person that "entails a correlative duty of some other person or persons to act or to refrain from acting in ways required for the first person's having that to which he has a right."[17] Gewirth states his primary thesis regarding the nature and basis of human rights as follows:

> Human rights are of supreme importance, and are central to all other moral considerations, because they are rights of every human being to the necessary conditions of human action, i.e., those conditions that must be fulfilled if human action is to be possible either at all or with general chances of success in achieving the purposes for which humans act.[18]

Rights, because they have this character, "must" be respected by every human being and governments are primarily justified in so far as they secure these rights.

Gewirth believes that the equality and necessity of certain human rights must be demonstrated. The flaw he sees in contemporary social contract theories is that they begin with the assumption that the contractors are equal moral agents, motivated by rational self-interest. Furthermore, assumptions are made that these agents will choose to be impartial, that is, will choose with the proviso that all principles chosen apply to each contractor alike in some way. This "egalitarian universalism," Gewirth argues, is assumed by other theories but not proved, is advocated but not made part of the very conception of rights as such. Gewirth's "Justifying Basis" for rights is what he terms the "Principle of Generic Consistency." "Addressed to every actual or prospective agent, it says: act in accord with the generic rights of your recipients as well as of yourself."[19] And, as Gewirth explains, "generic rights" are rights to the "generic features of action-freedom and well-being."[20] Freedom and well-being, in turn, are what Gewirth calls the "objects" of rights, that is, what one has a right to.[21] Freedom and well-being "are, respectively, the procedural and substantive necessary conditions of acting for any purposes either at all or with general chances of success."[22] It is this connection of the "objects" of rights with necessary conditions of purposive action that provides the justification of the moral principle that, in turn, is the "justifying basis" for moral rights, namely the Principle of Generic Consistency. Let us examine Gewirth's line of reasoning.

The generic purposive feature of human action is, for Gewirth, that persons act for purposes they consider good. But the "objects" of rights are not these particular, apparent goods purposively sought, but rather the necessary conditions of acting for any of these purposes: These necessary conditions are freedom and well-being. To deny the necessity of freedom and well-being for action would involve an agent in a logical contradiction. Having argued that the "objects" of human rights are the necessary conditions of human action, Gewirth believes he has a proof that it is freedom and well-being that are claimed as human rights. The proof consists in showing why it would be a contradiction for *any* agent to deny that they have rights of freedom and well-being as the necessary conditions of their actions.[23]

Gewirth offers four other major reasons for basing human rights

on the necessary conditions of human action. First, these are unde-
niably conditions of supreme importance. At the same time, they
indicate why actual and prospective agents are concerned with
human rights and why these rights must take precedence over all
other practical criteria or requirements. Second, action is the common subject matter of all moralities. And so, by connecting rights
and the necessary conditions of actions, rights have been directly
tied to morality. Third, the necessary conditions for action have
more specific and less disputable contents than other concepts like
"dignity" and "flourishing." Fourth, grounding human rights in
the necessary conditions of human action emphasizes that

> all the human rights, those of well-being as well as of free-
> dom, have as their aim that each person have rational auton-
> omy in the sense of being a self-controlling, self-developing
> agent who can relate to other persons on a basis of mutual re-
> spect and cooperation, in contrast to being a dependent pas-
> sive recipient of the agency of others.[24]

Gewirth is aware that rights sometimes require assistance from
others. On his view this is not for the purpose of reinforcing or increasing dependence, however, but rather for supporting persons
in the "control of their own lives" and in the pursuit and sustenance of their own purposes without being dominated or harmed
by others. "In this way," he says, "agency is both the metaphysical and moral basis of human dignity."[25]

Gewirth makes a very strong case for the rights not to be harmed
and not to have one's freedom curtailed by others. Although these
rights are not, as such, absolute, there are nevertheless some absolute prohibitions against killing and interfering with freedom.

Life as a Right

Taking up first Gewirth's view of life as a right, we note that it
is a "basic right," a necessary condition for action of purposive

agents, actual and prospective.[26] It is not absolute for Gewirth because there are circumstances, such as self-defense and the use of violence against oppression, that justify killing. In both of these instances, Gewirth carefully limits the use of deadly force.[27] Certain limits to killing are absolute rights not to be harmed, in Gewirth's view. By describing a right as absolute, he means that it cannot be "overridden" in any circumstances and so can never be justifiably "infringed" and must be "fulfilled" without any exceptions.[28] One of the most important, Gewirth claims, is that "all innocent persons have an absolute right not to be the intended victims of a homicidal project."[29] His absolute prohibition applies to infants but not to fetuses.[30]

Gewirth makes it very clear that there are absolute rights in addition to the right not to be made the intended victim of a homicidal project. What underlies all absolute rights he states as follows: "Agents and institutions are absolutely prohibited from degrading persons, treating them as if they had no rights or dignity."[31] The benefit of this prohibition extends to all persons innocent or guilty: Criminals who are justly punished should still be treated as moral agents, and hence, punishment should be neither cruel nor arbitrary. Another absolute right delineated by Gewirth is what he calls "The Right to the Non-Infliction of Cancer."[32] The reasons why this species of the right not to be killed or severely injured is absolute, occupy a whole chapter of Gewirth's volume *Human Rights*.[33] He is concerned here with working conditions, pollution, food additives, and the like and does not assimilate to this absolute right instances where, in his view, people harm only themselves, for example, by smoking. Smokers, however, may be liable in certain ways for any harm their smoking may cause others.

Protecting the individual's right to life does not, for Gewirth, consist only in refraining from homicidal projects; he also argues for what he calls a duty to rescue others when they are in danger.[34] Gewirth discusses at considerable length a set of circumstances in which one individual (Carr) is in a position, with little effort and no apparent risk, to save an individual (Davis) who will surely drown if not helped. (In this case Carr has a rope and it is all that is needed; he can pull Davis from the shore and he, Carr, is strong and in good health.) Gewirth argues that Carr, and anyone else in a similar situation, has a strict duty to rescue Davis; doing so is not to be construed as an act of supererogation, and why is that? It is because the harm to Davis is basic, a good necessary to him as an agent, and because Carr is in a position to ward off this harm at no comparable cost to himself. This duty to rescue others is one example of the moral duties required by the Principle of Generic Consistency to engage in positive actions to defend the rights of others to basic goods when the actions necessary for such defense bring no comparable harm to their agents.[35] Gewirth notes that this drowning case can be extended to cases of starvation, alerting the police to criminal attacks, and other threats to basic goods, such as life. These are instances in which the basic goods necessary to our purposive actions as agents are equally goods necessary to the purposive actions of others as agents, and it is as rationally (logically) contradictory to deny the necessity of these goods for others as purposive agents as it is to deny their necessity for ourselves as purposive agents. Life, one of these necessary goods, is therefore equally a right for all prospective and actual agents.

Freedom as a Right

But freedom is another basic right for Gewirth. And, as he understands freedom, it qualifies the value life is given and the extent to which life can and should be protected. This aspect of Gewirth's thought surfaces most explicitly in his understanding of suicide. First, however, we will examine his portrayal of freedom as a right.

In Gewirth's view, freedom, like life, is a basic good: "It has its own independent value as a necessary condition of action."[36] Is it, as such, an unlimited or absolute right? No, says Gewirth:

An agent should be free to perform any action, to engage in any transaction, if and only if the recipients are left free,

through their voluntary consent, to participate or not participate in that transaction and if and only if he does not inflict
basic or specific harm on them.[37]

Clearly, therefore, one limit to an agent's freedom occurs when
coercion or harm is necessary to prevent the agent from inflicting
harm on others or from violating the freedom of persons other
than themselves. A person's freedom may also be restricted for the
sake of preventing them from inflicting on themselves a basic harm
or from giving up their own dispositional freedom; coercion or interference for this purpose, however, should be temporary.[38]

The right to freedom of a recipient of action is, first of all, "a
right to be let alone by others until and unless he unforcedly con-
sents to undergo their action."[39] Thus people have what Gewirth
calls "a sphere of personal autonomy and privacy."[40] Agents have
this as well. From this right to freedom, within the limits set by the
right to well-being as described above, it follows that "prospective
agents have rights to a vast area of protected actions of their own,
including physical movement, speech and other forms of expression, assembly, religion, and sexual conduct."[41] How this protection is obtained and sustained, and how these rights and others are
related to legal rights and governmental policies will not occupy us
in this chapter. It should be noted, in addition, that Gewirth does
not overlook the freedom agents enjoy and have because of their
rights to well-being; these are rights to the nonperformance of actions by others in the form of restraints against killing, physical
maiming, libeling, and the like.

The freedom of agents is an egalitarian, universal right. But, tied
as it is to agency, there are those who do not enjoy fully this right:
Some agents do not fully have the abilities to attain their purposes
without being a danger to themselves or others. Children, persons
who are mentally deficient, and fetuses are prime examples for
Gewirth. These individuals come under what Gewirth refers to as
the "Principle of Proportionality."[42] This principle requires the
limitation of the generic or basic rights, particularly freedom, but
only to the extent needed to protect the right to well-being. Per-

sons also have rights to certain assistance in the development of their abilities and opportunities to be agents and successful in realizing their purposes. Education would be a case in point. An example of a freedom not permitted children is the right to vote. Old age and physical hardships are not reasons for denying full basic rights. Brain damage is not either, provided that a recovery sufficient for normal agency is possible.

There is some ambiguity about how stringently the right to life of those with irrecoverable, severe brain damage is considered equal to that of all purposive agents. Clearly, they do not have the opportunity to have fully their right to freedom, and perhaps not at all those rights that depend on their own activities. Is their right to life, however, to be compared with fetuses—who do not, according to Gewirth, possess it equally with other agents? Or, is their right to life on a par with infants, who are protected in this respect like all other agents? Infants, in Gewirth's account, do express purposive behavior, and he uses this to distinguish infants from fetuses. A question mark, therefore, hangs over the status of the rights of some people who are not expected to recover and who are not considered capable of some requisite degree of purposiveness. Criminals, another group with diminished rights to freedom and well-being, are punished for the sake of making it possible to restore them to the moral community; punishment respects the criminal as a responsible agent and makes up for the inequality of rights created by the criminal behavior being punished.[43]

Autonomy versus Interdependence: An Assessment

MacIntyre does not regard as successful any of the attempts to provide autonomous moral agents with a secular, rational justification for their moral allegiances. For MacIntyre, Gewirth is the latest, albeit carefully argued, failure of that "Enlightenment project." It is in Gewirth's treatment of suicide that we can see most graphically the peculiar difficulties of basing all rights claims on rational autonomy, or at least on rational autonomy as Gewirth understands it: His alleged right to commit suicide does not fit into the logic of rights claims as he has so carefully crafted them.

Gewirth asserts that agents act in accord with their own generic rights by maintaining their own freedom and well-being in ways that avoid any interference from other persons to which they do not consent.[44] The would-be suicide is no exception to this generalization, Gewirth argues. Such individuals seek to be in control of their behavior, and to prevent others from interfering with their freedom and well-being without their consent. But do they not, in their intention to commit suicide and in the very act, relinquish both freedom and well-being, doing so irrevocably?

With regard to the right to well-being, Gewirth contends that there are circumstances when the act of suicide is purely an act of harming the one who does it. To qualify as such, the person committing suicide must have no dependents for whom suicide would mean a loss of economic or other support.

What about the freedom of a would-be suicide? Do not others have a responsibility to rescue them and hence, to interfere with their freedom? Gewirth suggests that in cases of a would-be suicide, other persons should express concern to such individuals over the contemplated act. Second, persons should interfere with the project temporarily to test whether the would-be actor has met the conditions of a voluntary undertaking. The third step in relating to a self-harmer, however, is to discontinue interference if the conditions for voluntariness have been met. Gewirth argues that if one interferes with the would-be suicide's action, then that individual will not be able to act; and if that individual does carry out the act of self-destruction, the ability to act is also ended. It follows, for Gewirth, that there is, in such an instance, no justification for interference with freedom. You should not be the one who ends a person's freedom. Those who commit suicide voluntarily do not violate their own generic rights, says Gewirth, since they do not allow other persons to interfere with their freedom or well-being without their consent.[45]

But if I am morally forbidden to prevent individuals from committing suicide, what happens to my "duty to rescue," a duty Gewirth has strongly endorsed? Clearly Gewirth has qualified the duty to rescue: You rescue only those who consent under certain specified circumstances.

Suppose someone, Cal, who meets Gewirth's criteria for noninterference from others, has just turned on the gas jets in his locked apartment for the purpose of committing suicide. Gewirth, who approves of what Cal is doing, has said goodbye to him, and is about to leave for home. When, however, he notices me breaking the basement window, Gewirth grabs me and demands to know what I am doing. I explain that I am going to turn off the gas for Cal's apartment. I know from a neighbor's call what Cal is trying to do and I am going to try to save his life. What now, should Gewirth do? If he permits me to shut off the gas, he has, in effect, deprived Cal of his right to noninterference. (I am assuming that Gewirth has the karate skills to stop me with a minimum of force, and that he risks nothing, except a few moments of time for this purpose.) If, however, he does forcibly stop me, and it would take force, he has deprived me of the freedom to carry out what I consider to be a strict moral responsibility. Whose freedom should be respected in this instance? Frankly, I am not certain what Gewirth would do, nor do I find guidance from his thinking on rights and duties as to what he should do. I would expect Gewirth to try to persuade me not to turn off the gas, but why should I listen until I have made certain that, for the time being, Cal would continue to live, and would enjoy the freedom to consider again the value of his life. After all, in this case, the infringement of Cal's freedom is temporary; its purpose is like any other rescue, namely to save his life. The complexities of determining when people with suicidal tendencies are to be hospitalized, or otherwise recommended for treatment, is not at issue in this example. The issue under discussion is that for many individuals, the duty to rescue includes the prevention of death from suicide, even suicides in some sense voluntarily chosen and intended to harm no one. To prevent a suicide is, after all, to prevent a killing and save a life.

So far then, Gewirth's own thinking has generated certain questions he has not explicitly addressed nor resolved, given his premises. First of all, Gewirth gives us no explicit basis for choosing between Cal's freedom to commit suicide and anyone's perceived responsibility to prevent it episodically whenever possible. If Gewirth chooses forcibly to block someone's efforts to stop Cal's suicide, the loss of freedom of the person blocked, in cases of this kind, is permanent: One can never again prevent Cal's death. (The example assumes that Cal will die unless the gas jets are turned off by someone other than Cal.) Second, why should not Gewirth consider the freedom of all agents in this example as equal? All agents require freedom to carry out their purposes and, in this example, these are aimed at preserving life, which is among what Gewirth calls "genuine rights." Strictly, then, is there any logical reason for Gewirth, given his own premises, to prefer Cal's suicide, someone's prevention of it, or someone's prevention of interference with Cal's actions?

Gewirth could well accuse me of a strange inability to grasp his thinking: "Have you forgotten," he might say, "that individuals have a right to freedom when they are engaged in activity that harms no one but themselves? If you can show that Cal is harming someone other than Cal, then you have a duty to rescue him, but otherwise you deny his right to freedom, provided, of course, he is acting voluntarily."

I think I am beginning to see why Gewirth and I are talking past one another. We have a different view of the relations individuals have a responsibility to cultivate toward others, and toward themselves. Gewirth believes that Cal can achieve, and has a right to achieve, a detachment from all other persons, such that no one *should* be harmed by his death. But Cal cannot achieve such a detachment if I, or anyone else, wish him to live, something he is powerless to suppress in me or others. Furthermore, Gewirth has to show that my desire to see Cal live is morally irresponsible, given Cal's desire to detach himself from all relations to others and to do so irrevocably. Gewirth does not recognize as explicit moral responsibilities seeking to preserve one's own life to its natural end and seeking to do that for the lives of others as well. Nor does Gewirth recognize life-long responsibilities to improve one's own moral character and to cultivate mutually beneficial relationships as long as life permits such efforts. Freedom, then, for Gewirth is a moral right that includes a right to detach oneself completely and permanently from all relations and responsibilities to oneself and others at a time of one's own choosing. And Gewirth believes this can and should be done without harming anyone but oneself.

In order to arrive at this view, Gewirth has to grant to individuals a right to make one's own self the intended victim of a homicidal project; no one has a right to act this way toward others, only toward oneself. That is why I said above that Gewirth does not explicitly formulate, or otherwise recognize, a responsibility to preserve one's own life, except insofar as someone else might be harmed by the failure to do so. Life is treated here as a private possession, say like a house one has built. If the person who has built the house does not make it available to anyone and creates a situation in which no one else could reasonably expect to gain anything by the continued existence of the house, since the owner chooses not to sell, rent, or share it, no one is harmed by its complete destruction by the owner. Others may complain that the house, if not desired by the owner, should have been used by needy persons or used to generate revenue for needy persons or communities. Analogously, people may well complain that a life taken should rather have been a life put at grave risk or simply sustained for the sake of others. And Gewirth would be among those who would try to persuade someone to consider the needs of others. But at some point, he regards it as morally wrong to interfere with someone's right to dispose of themselves, if they have appropriately severed themselves from others, which is also their right.

In all of this, Gewirth is making some implicit assumptions about what kinds of selves we are and ought to be. First of all, we are selves who seek goods for ourselves in accord with what we regard as good and choose as goods. Life is necessary for this pursuit; but whether we regard it as good for us is a choice we are able to make, and we ought to be free to make, for ourselves. If we are not allowed to choose whether to be or not to be, our dignity as human beings is violated. He has assimilated into the private sphere the choice as to how and whether to value one's life and whether to pursue any goals or goods at all; how one pursues goals and goods is limited by restraints upon harming others. The freedom not to be interfered with is the moral right that no persons should give up and no person presumably would want to give up; the right to live one may reasonably give up.

Gewirth has dropped the view that Hobbes espoused regarding our natural inclinations. Hobbes regarded every human being as inclined toward self-preservation and that meant the preservation of one's own life. For Hobbes, it was irrational to destroy one's own life; it was rational to give up freedom to preserve it. In short, Gewirth does not tie human dignity to the preservation of one's own life. Instead, Gewirth regards being an agent as the fundamental moral status human rights secure for each person; and agents, says Gewirth, "control their own lives and effectively pursue and sustain their own purposes without being subjected to domination and harms from others. In this way, agency is both the metaphysical and moral basis of human dignity."[46] But the German philosopher Immanuel Kant (1724–1804) would reject Gewirth's reasoning with regard to suicide. Kant would do so because he would see Gewirth as condoning a self-contradictory and irrational act, one in which our dignity as human beings is lost not preserved.

In his discussion of suicide, Kant first of all observes that the body is a necessary condition for *both life and freedom*. To destroy one's body is to destroy one's life by the use of one's will, which is thereby itself destroyed. And so Kant concludes that it is self-contradictory to use the power of a free will for its own destruction.[47] Kant is not, here, opposing surgery or otherwise risking our lives in order to preserve our own lives or those of others. And he recognizes that there may be other moral values worth defending by risking one's life. Morally motivated acts of putting one's life on the line are not regarded as suicide by Kant. (I suspect he is aware that the line is sometimes hard to draw, when for example, people take risks that others might deem "suicidal.") But he explicitly rejects as a reason for suicide that in so doing a person "need not submit to anyone." This, Kant notes, seems to have a moral aspect to it but it vanishes once the necessity of life for freedom is recognized. Kant makes the further claim that someone "who does not respect his life even in principle cannot be restrained from the most dreadful vices."[48]

Kant does not rest his case against suicide solely on the self-contradiction he sees involved: "We shrink in horror from suicide because all nature seeks its own preservation."[49] One's nature as a human being, one's humanity, is expressed in acts of self-preservation. Thus, humanity in one's own person is inviolable; it is never, for Kant, permissible to commit suicide. What one is setting out to do in an act of suicide is to make a thing of oneself, to cease to be human. Kant does not regard the inadvisability of suicide to rest on any of our opinions as to how highly we should prize life. Rather, as he says, "The role of morality does not admit of it under any conditions because it degrades human nature below the level of animal nature and so destroys it."[50]

Whereas Gewirth proclaims a moral right to commit suicide and sees human dignity attained by not letting anyone rob an agent of the freedom to exercise this right freely claimed, Kant sees suicide, under all circumstances, as a paradigm case of completely losing one's dignity as a human being. When Kant looks at what conditions are necessary for human agency, freedom and well-being are necessary but not sufficient; to be a *human* agent one must also be self-preserving and respect that aspect of oneself and others. In the end, Gewirth does not consistently base human rights on necessary conditions for human agency but rather on being able to control one's own life, free of attachments and of interference from them, if one so chooses, and free also to destroy one's life and freedom—all that is necessary for agency—if one so chooses.

Now we have come full circle. Gewirth does not, and cannot, base his judgments as to what is moral on what is logically necessary for human agency. The conditions under which we do and can perceive what morality demands of us are not sufficiently specified by what is necessary to make choices, nor by what is logically consistent.[51] With different images or conceptions of our humanity and of our natural human qualities, we make different choices about what is moral and what is logical. And so what is rational and dignified for Gewirth is both irrational and undignified for Hobbes and Kant when it comes to suicide. This means also that Gewirth is not consistently carrying out his enterprise. He is not deriving moral claims from a morally neutral notion of agency and what is necessary for its exercise. Gewirth, of course, believes that he has based moral claims on neutral premises. After all, the basic moral rights of freedom and well-being are logically necessary conditions for whatever actions are being sought by agents without presupposing anything about the perspectives of agents, not even their abilities or willingness to be impartial. That moral rights have their justifying basis in what is logically necessary and universal is what provides a neutral, impartial basis for them. But what we have seen is a quarrel as to whether or not suicide can, or ought to be, morally justified. What is logically necessary for action does not settle the dispute. For Kant, what is logically necessary for action is denied and contradicted by successfully committing suicide; for Gewirth, what is logically necessary for action is neither denied nor contradicted provided that agents freely decide how to regard their freedom and well-being and freely decide what to do about these logical necessities for action. How to choose between Kant and Gewirth and how to regard suicide requires something more than an appeal to logic. And so the quest for the possibility of some cognitive perspective to shed light on such decisions remains open at this point. This quest we will pursue in subsequent chapters.

But Gewirth's conception of selfhood not only affects what he regards as human rights but also what he regards as the structure of our moral life. Gewirth depicts the self in a way that supposes that each of us as individual agents can logically and experientially choose whether and to what degree we are connected to others. Gewirth even supposes that individuals can achieve a form of isolation or disconnectedness such that harms we do to ourselves, including self-destruction, are not harmful to others or at least should not be so regarded. This view of how human beings are related to one another is very different from that of the English poet John Donne (1573–1631), who in one of his *Devotions* maintains that no one is an island and that every person's death diminishes him. So close is this tie to another person's death that Donne concludes his portrayal of it with these much quoted lines: "And therefore never send to know for whom the bell tolls. It tolls for thee."

Curiously enough, had Gewirth completely and consistently followed his own method of explicating the logically necessary universal conditions for human agency, he would have had to change his picture of how we are related to one another. Indeed, as I will argue, he would also have had to change his depiction of the relationship between rights and responsibilities. It is his view of individual autonomy and how it is expressed that thwarts him and leads him to be less than faithful to his methods.

Gewirth takes autonomous individuals as his starting point: The necessary goods for achieving an individual's purposes as an agent identify our moral rights; each individual needs well-being, including life and freedom, to accomplish their purposes. But Gewirth has not at all considered what is necessary for there to be agents at all; he simply assumes their existence. He portrays agents without regard to the fact that they cease and come to be. Yet, agents cannot come to be, nor can they persist on their own.

To begin with, human agents only exist because other human agents cooperated to conceive, nurture, love, and instruct them— and further cooperated to prevent and rectify potential and actual harm to them. The lives of all individual human beings are gifts bestowed and sustained by others. The gift of life is daily reaffirmed and rendered possible by the responsible behavior of all those who refrain from killing us, who protect us from those who would harm us, and who stand ready to save our lives whenever it is necessary and possible. Even the remotest hermit is not without a history of parental love, for without love in the form of some attention and fondling no human will live and grow in infancy; food is not sufficient. And no hermit can live alone and have the space and resources to do so unless others permit it. Hermits are also here at everyone's mercy and, like others, share the responsibility to ask themselves how to use the gift of life in ways that honor and express gratitude to those who nurtured them, both family members and that larger protective and sustaining community and communities. At the very least, one may reasonably exact from hermits that they value their lives to some degree commensurate with the restraint, protection, and institutional aid, such as health facilities, fire-fighting equipment, and police forces, with which we in the surrounding community envelope them. When a hermit commits suicide, it negates the efforts expended to protect that life by a number of individuals, groups, and social institutions. In turn, to ask all those persons to experience no harm whatsoever to their well-being is itself a repudiation of the attachments, the moral bonds that make communities and the freedom of their members possible.

Gewirth has not been very thorough in his investigation of the necessary conditions of individual agency; like so many of his contemporaries and predecessors, he has not taken into account the agent's dependence upon communities and the actions that made, and make them, possible. Life is, to be sure, a necessary good for actual and prospective agents. But life as a right cannot be attained simply by the claims of individual agents on others; life as a right cannot be attained simply by claims on others to avoid killing, to rescue and heal, and to provide legal protection and enforcement agencies; the right to life cannot simply come to be as a claim of an individual agent at all. For human life to be, survive, and flourish there must be, as necessary requisites, some procreation, some nurture, and some sharing of time, resources, and energy. Every living human being is a recipient of these activities on the part of others. Nor does one outgrow any of these efforts of others, except, of course, the necessity to be conceived and live for some time in someone's womb.

Freedom, like life, is a necessary good for actual and prospective agents. But, as in the case of a right to life, a right to freedom does not come to be, nor is it attained, simply by individual claims to it. Necessary conditions for the freedom of agents presuppose that other human beings behave in ways that make freedom possible. Fundamentally, this means on the one hand that human beings, to a high degree, refrain from various forms of harm to one another, such as lying, killing, and stealing; and on the other hand that human beings foster ways to enhance their capacities and opportunities to act. These requisites of freedom, if freedom is to be an actual condition existing for individual agents, are characteristics of communities and their institutions.

Freedom and life may be necessary conditions for agency. But what is necessary for agency does not end there. Life, a necessary condition for agency, only comes to be, and only persists, if people cooperate in ways that are at once forms of community and also the necessary conditions for community. The same is true of freedom. What is requisite for agency and for agents to exist is requisite for the existence of communities. And what is requisite for communities to exist is that individuals act in morally responsible ways, or as some other formulations have it, in accord with moral law. To argue, then, that requisites of agency are requisites of community is to argue also that responsibilities are prior to rights. Indeed, I will argue that the reality and actualization of human rights depends upon the reality and actualization of human responsibilities. These human responsibilities consist in the formation, sustenance, and protection of certain human relationships or bonds that are regarded as morally significant. Chapter 5 begins the identification of these moral bonds.

Before taking up the subject of these moral bonds, I wish to keep my promise, made near the beginning of this chapter, to discuss MacIntyre's criticism of Gewirth's theory of human rights.

Trying to ground morality in individual purposive behavior underlies what MacIntyre regards as the fundamental flaw in Gewirth's whole conception of rights. Recall that Gewirth argues that basic rights, well-being, and freedom are logically necessary goods for successfully attaining the purposes of actual and potential agents. But MacIntyre counters that although these goods are universally necessary for accomplishing the purposes of agents, what agents desire for their own purposes are not "rights." Rights, MacIntyre asserts, are unlike goods universally necessary for rational agency: Rights presuppose "the existence of a socially established set of rules. Such sets of rules only come into existence at particular historical periods under particular social circumstances. They are in no way universal features of the human condition."[52]

MacIntyre is saying Gewirth's assertion of a right, such as the right to commit suicide, presupposes some rule or set of rules that provide a ground for claiming it, and this rule or set of rules is of a "highly specific" and "socially local character." Furthermore, MacIntyre contends that claiming a right is unintelligible unless the necessary social institutions or practices exist; it is unintelligible in the same way that presenting a check for monetary payment would be in a society that lacked the institutions of money. The social institutions and practices that render rights claims intelligible have never, MacIntyre says, existed universally in human societies.

I agree with MacIntyre that giving an intelligible account of rights requires a reference to what behavior is expected by communities of their members. Anything we would call a legal right, that is, a claim defined and enforced by the governing authority within a community, is grounded on a social rule or regulation that we call a "law" or its equivalent, that is, a custom de facto as binding and uniformly enforceable in practice as a "law." Moral rights, however, are something more than historically and culturally variable social inventions. Not all rights are legal and customary. Moral claims are, as Gewirth has noted, universal and necessary claims. At the same time, there is no quarrel in general with the proposition that "social rules" may refer to rules, practices, guidelines, laws, and the like, which are anything but universal and necessary to either individual purposive action or the existence of communities.

But some social rules are moral responsibilities that ground universal, basic rights, and just as some things are universally and necessarily requisite to succeeding in purposive activity, some things are requisite to making communities and its practices possible. If there are to be social rules at all, certain human relationships are necessary and universally so. That is what I intend to argue. In effect, there are rules without which there are no rules. More precisely, there are human relationships without which there are no communities and no social institutions. Certain human relationships, such as procreation, nurture, and caring for human life, are relationships without which none of the relationships characteristic of and requisite to individual and communal life can and do exist. The next chapter seeks to identify those human relations that are universal and necessary requisites of community. Rights are to be grounded on these expressions of our interdependence and sociality as human beings.

PART II

Rights Reconceptualized

Grounding Rights in Responsibilities, Communities, and Moral Knowledge

FIVE

Moral Bonds as Requisites
of Community

What makes human communities possible? For Hobbes, and for many in our time, the question of what makes a community possible is a question of what it takes to achieve and maintain one. This way of asking the question posits a problematic relation between individuals and communities. In Hobbes this problem is very acute, for individuals are seen as naturally in pursuit of their own self-preservation, not the preservation of communities or other individuals.

But I am proposing that the question of what makes communities possible is a question of what is logically and functionally necessary, and universally so, for the existence and sustenance of communities. The presupposition is that human communities exist and always have, at the very least, in the form of kinship and familial groupings. People do procreate, nurture, aid, and protect offspring, exhibiting and fostering the requisite behavior for doing all of these things. Humans are more like bees than Hobbes was willing to concede; but unlike bees, people do make various choices to be cooperative or uncooperative, helpful or harmful. Hobbes cannot be faulted for noting our antisocial behavior, but it is no more natural than some of our social behavior. Whatever our destructive proclivities, our lives are socially spawned and sustained. How reasonable it is to spawn and sustain life, however, depends in part on whether we have some basis for believing in the strength of these tendencies in us and in the forces that shape them in us.

Hobbes cannot account for community unless these tendencies and these forces necessary for spawning and sustaining life and cooperative behavior are real and strong enough to prevail sufficiently. These tendencies and forces are requisites of community.

When Mill speaks of basing morality on the "permanent interests" of humans as "progressive" beings, the requisites of such permanent interests and progress, I wish to contend, are the requisites of life itself, and these are requisites of community. Communities persist so long as individuals are able and willing to express their "interests" in the existence and progression into the future of other individuals and communities. Whatever else may be said for the permanence and progressive nature of our human interests, they have a destiny if, and only if, life making and life sustaining have a future.

That is what I would say also to Engels when he speaks of a true morality as the one that contains the "maximum durable elements" and represents the future. That morality, whatever else it may contain, will contain what is logically and functionally necessary (requisite) for community.

Over against any suggestion that all of morality and its elements are invented, I am prepared to argue in this chapter that it is possible to discover by conscious reflection, by participation in communal structures and traditions, and in conversation with others, the logically and functionally necessary ingredients of our actual behavior and existence in communities. Of course, not all characteristics of human communities are moral and not all aspects of a developed morality are uninvented. For purposes of this chapter and for launching a search for grounding human rights, I will regard as moral requisites of community those requisites that in a preliminary way, may be described as the rules without which there are no rules. In other words, I will make a beginning of identifying the requisites of moral and legal rule making. I do not deny thereby that we invent moral and legal policies or guidelines; I simply deny that we could do so at all if there were not within us certain powers and tendencies that help make such rule making, communities themselves, and their cooperative behavior possible. So to the social contractarians I am proposing what it is they have to presuppose morally if there are to be actual contracts, constitutions, and declarations of rights—and actual fidelity to what these exact of us.

The method I will use to identify moral elements is very similar to that adopted by Gewirth. There are important differences, however. Gewirth wishes to ground rights on the necessary conditions for realizing our purposes as individual and rational agents. It turns out that these will have to include more than well-being, life, and freedom: They will have to include the procreative, nurturant, and protective behavior of others as necessary presuppositions of there being an agent, and of there being an agent who can pursue and achieve purposes for which life and freedom are requisite or necessary conditions.

The failure of Gewirth to see these requisites of community as requisites of individual moral agency is related to what he conceives as "moral." In specifying the identifying characteristics of morality, he leaves out, I have suggested in the previous chapter, an essential element. Every moral decision contains within it some attention to the ways in which the alternatives being decided for and against relate to the kind of "self" reflected in the choice being made. What kind of self am I if I choose to kill someone or to take my own life? Is that the self consistent with the self I profess and aspire to be? Often these questions are couched as well or alternatively as questions about what others will think of us if we do or fail to do one or the other of the actions we are choosing between or among. Our moral choices are much more relational than Gewirth would have us believe, and relational in ways he does not mention. We respond to one another constantly, and we are in a network of relations with one another. Our responses include what I wish to call moral responsibilities; these are relations or bonds between individuals and groups; moral responsibilities are moral bonds. At their most basic level, these responsibilities and bonds are what I am calling requisites of community. To identify those responsibilities or bonds that are to be regarded as moral requisites of community is the task of this chapter. The meaning of the term *moral* and the distinction between moral and nonmoral requisites of community will occupy us in subsequent chapters.

Before we can intelligibly proceed, it is necessary to offer a definition of *community*. A community is *an affiliated and mutually beneficial network of interdependent human beings who, as human beings, share what is requisite for forming and sustaining such a network.* A "network" of individuals and/or groups may be connected or affiliated in a variety of ways, including ties created and/or sustained by procreation, nurture, affection, culture, religion, politics, or economic exchange—or some combinations of these. These affiliations are characteristically mediated by language, symbols, and artifacts. Individuals may be affiliated in their capacities as moral agents or as recipients of human agency, for example, infants or seriously incapacitated individuals. This means that affiliated individuals may not always perceive the benefits of affiliation or actively assure the mutuality of such benefits. These benefits are not always moral, but each affiliative relation is sustained by moral elements.[1]

By itself, this definition is morally neutral in certain respects even though it contains moral elements. Thus, for example, a criminal group like the Mafia is a community by this definition, though it may be regarded as an evil one in its parasitic relations to the larger community that it uses and abuses for its own purposes. Yet, members of the Mafia share the requisites for being a community, and this means they observe certain moral restraints such as not deceiving one another. Indeed, deceit can bring the death penalty in this community.

Our definition of community is neutral as well with respect to size: A community may be a group as small as a married couple or two friends, or a nation as large as the largest nations of the world. Some speak of the world as a community and it is possible to do that within this definition.

Although this definition is morally neutral as a description of what communities are when they exist, actually existing communities are not morally neutral entities. Their purposes, behavior, and structures may be moral and immoral in various ways and to various degrees.[2]

Of course, this definition is not theoretically neutral. In particular, that human beings as human beings share what is requisite for forming or sustaining the network that makes up a community is a claim that moral behavior is not entirely learned nor entirely procured by socially invented rules and laws. One could leave this claim out of the definition and argue for the existence of requisites for community defined apart from these requisites. That, however, leads to a paradox: How can one describe a community in its essential aspects without including what is essential to its existing at all? Be that as it may, I turn now to consider what at least some of these requisites are and how it is possible to argue their universal necessity for making communities possible.

A Thought Experiment

I have found it helpful, particularly for students with no previous preparation in ethics, to introduce them to the following thought experiment.

Imagine you are among a band of recently escaped slaves. You are located in a vast barren land. Now try to imagine what this is really like! None of these slaves have had their own social institutions, such as governments, schools, unions, businesses, armies, and police forces. Nor have they been entirely free to associate, whether as friends, kinfolk, immediate families, or as religious celebrants. As slaves, this present group in the barren wilderness have not previously been free to say publicly what they think and have not had opportunities to express themselves in public meetings or publications. In none of the usual significant ways have these slaves functioned as a "people" or community. They have been in a state of relatively enforced isolation, even at times from family members and relatives.

So this group of previously brutalized individuals are thrown together, by circumstances and some charismatic leaders, into the new harsh realities of a far-reaching, barren wilderness, one that they wish mainly to traverse, not inhabit indefinitely. They are face to face with the possibility that their impossible dream of freedom may become a nightmare that ends in defeat and death for everyone. Why might you and the other slaves die?

Well, a barren land can do that to people. When a wilderness is barren, resources are obviously scarce. Also, and more importantly, scarce resources can lead to quarrels, and quarrels can lead to death or handicaps. Weakened or otherwise sickly persons may lose out in the struggle. And sickness, after all, is something all, or virtually all, individuals experience at some time or other. Yes, life hangs in the balance for this band, despite its newly found freedom from organized violence. What would you advise this collection of past slaves—you and the others—to do?

First, I think it is important to note that no one, in several large classes, has ever proposed that individuals simply go their way alone. Hypothetically that is a genuine option, especially if one were to believe strongly that people do not, and/or will not, refrain from robbing one another blind and killing one another whenever necessary or whenever it is in one's self interest. One could argue, like Hobbes, that people are in a state of war, literally at one another's throats, unless constrained by a government powerful enough to do the job.

Also like Hobbes, however, the classes exhibit a strong belief in the necessity and efficacy of force and in the acceptance by others of an armed force as needed and efficacious. Students, therefore, do not hesitate to suggest as the very first step for forming and sustaining a community among these former slaves that they organize armed forces, including a police force, to provide for safety and order. Often, this is the first proposal made.

At first glance, this has the ring of common sense about it. The call for the necessity of force to resolve conflict or dampen deviation from moral and legal standards has strong and wide endorsement as a place to begin. But I am not satisfied. Consider what it means that these escaped slaves have no existing institutions. Who among them will function as members of police forces and of the other armed services? Who will serve as officers at various ranks? How will persons be chosen? Who will make these choices and on what basis? Should questions of age or sex count and if so, to what degree and in what ways? Only a few such questions suffice to turn the class to what is then seen as the obvious retort.

The retort is: "They (the band of exslaves) will have to organize a government for these purposes." And when I ask how that is supposed to happen, the usual reply is: "Of course, they will have to agree to a contract or a constitution that spells out the nature, functions, and selection of a government and its agencies."

But this suggestion is still not one I am prepared to accept. On what grounds does one expect this whole process to occur? Why would any of us be convinced that there would not be endless wrangling and fighting over how to do this and what the content will be? And if by any chance leaders are somehow selected to govern in some way, why would it not or could it not be the case that such leaders are murdered, threatened, or bribed by others equally or more ambitious to assume leadership? What is to stop this kind of intrigue?

So far, then, the class has offered Hobbesian solutions to a problem interpreted in a Hobbesian way: How do we form societies? The question and its formulation, in my experience with students, graduates, and undergraduates with little or no formal education in ethics, is not challenged. And, as one would expect, my challenges to each suggestion made to this point are also not questioned. I have so far made no appeal to morality as something possessed by or known to the individuals comprising this band of former slaves. That is Hobbesian too!

Once this impasse in the discussion has been reached, the contract idea is reasserted, but it takes on a new form and purpose. Someone proposes that, "People must have rules if they are to accomplish anything at all. To make it as a group, we will need to draw up some rules and have people agree to them."

At this point, there is a shift away from agreeing to a government first in order to achieve the power necessary for there to be constraints; the shift is to a recognition that rules to guide procedures and conduct are necessary both for the selection and acceptance of leadership—otherwise there will be no followers for these would-be leaders. The appeal to armed force will not do because there are the prior considerations of who commands these arms, for what purposes, and on the basis of what constraints. Without limits on the use of force by leaders, why would anyone yield their arms or power to command them to any other person? This is essentially the contemporary use of social contract thinking: Generate what moral rules underlie our social institutions and structure by imagining what we would agree to in a situation of drawing up a contract on which to base behavior in the society in which we will be members.[3]

But I am not satisfied yet. Nothing has been put forward that gives me any reason to believe that these individuals in the wilderness or any other set of individuals will agree to any rules sufficient to elicit compliance and terminate conflicts. What, in short, leads one to believe that there will not be interminable quarrels, verbal or even physical, over what the rules should be?

The frustrated reply, most often, is a direct appeal to rational self-interest: "They will all die if they do not get along with one another! They will see, out of sheer fear for themselves and for their lives, that they must agree on some things. It is a matter of life or death!"

This particular assertion of rational self-interest is couched in the framework of Hobbes. It presupposes the desire to preserve one's own life as the shared, most powerful drive behind everything we do; the "buck stops there." However plausible this may sound, it is not the whole truth about us as self-interested individuals. To elicit a more convincing account of how communities are possible, I feel compelled to ask: "Would you actually argue that persons who murder, steal, lie, and rape others in no sense act out of their particular self-interest? And isn't it possible, since it did actually occur, that a Hitler, in what he believed were his interests, could convince many Germans that it was in their interest as individuals and as Germans to exterminate a whole group of people, in this instance Jews? We prefer to think of these occurrences as monstrous and irrational expressions of self-interest, or even as not "really" self-interested behavior. When we think that way, however, we are begging the question: What is the "rational" or persuasive argument for agreeing on rules, that we know some people do not see as in their interest to act in accord with, or even to acknowledge as binding on them? And if you now tell me that for a case like Hitler's you need armies to stop irrational, not really rationally self-interested behavior, we are back where we started. Why should you not expect among this band of exslaves at least some of Hitler's tendencies, or failing that, at least some very different, perhaps uniquely different, interests? And, there exists no government, court, or armed force to achieve enforced arbitration of conflict.

At this juncture, the class is quite puzzled and becoming rather wary of continuing the exchange. That in itself is very interesting, because as I see it, I have been using Hobbesian notions to counter Hobbesian notions. We find ourselves spinning around in the circle largely created by Hobbesian assumptions: No morality without a government, and, at the same time, no government is created or sustained without morality. The twentieth-century contractarians have to presuppose that individuals are moral in some sense. John Rawls explicitly does so by characterizing each person who is deciding on moral rules in a hypothetical situation of agreeing to a contract as possessed of a sense of justice; Robert Veatch explicitly assumes that every individual accepts and understands the necessity of being impartial.[4] In short, both start with people who are moral. Gewirth questions the whole idea that the morality of individuals can be presupposed. Potentially, then, that band of exslaves in the wilderness may not have a basis for forming a community. Whether they do has to be demonstrated. Is it possible to form a community? That is a question for all of these contractarians and for Gewirth. They need to answer the prior question as to whether there are bases for forming and sustaining communities.

If we respond to this question, not with theories however "scientific" they claim to be but rather with observations well known to us all, the fact is that every individual was conceived, born, and nurtured in a community. Human beings owe their existence and development to sufficiently loving though imperfect relationships. Even someone conceived by rape can only survive and become a functioning individual with the aid of some persons caring enough to provide more than mere food and a minimum of sanitation. Infants require some warm, reassuring contact for sheer sustenance and growth. The first sign of infant or child neglect is lack of normal growth or development, mentally and physically.

In the light of what we know from observation and not speculation, however specific, about our prehistorical origins, all individuals requiring care by their biological or social parents only live and flourish because other persons permit all of this to unfold. Every individual has life and protection from injury and death only within some group that functions to assure such protection and prevention of killing. What is more, individuals live and develop only because they are rescued, healed, or otherwise kept from fatal diseases and injuries by instruction, supervision, and regulation. At the same time, individuals live and develop only because what resources they need are not seized by others but rather shared.

It is possible to claim that having and rearing children and maintaining a protective, sharing social environment is a matter of self-interest. There is no necessity at this juncture to carry on a debate over whether altruism is partly, or even entirely, self-interested in some sense. I wish only to draw attention to certain specific facts; in particular, I wish to emphasize that individuals cannot begin themselves without the existence of some caring community, however small; nor can they mature and sustain themselves in the absence of mutual aid, restraint, and protection from others. The real world is like that, whatever else the real world may be like.

So what follows from calling attention to something so obvious and so well known? What I would recommend for this band of escaped slaves is that they engage in a process of consciousness raising: They exist only because of the mercy of others previously and now. If they forget that and think of themselves as self-constituted individuals with no known or knowably continuous ties to others, they may indeed consider it impossible to be together, stay together, or cooperate at all in any way sufficient to sustain life and limb for very long in a relatively desolate land. If they are unmindful of the caring that brought each of them into being and has sustained them so far, they may not accept anything but self-referential behavior devoid of all regard for the lives, property, and well being of others. But whatever the state of their awareness of other-regarding behavior, I would contend that the harsh realities of their circumstances require consciousness raising or a heightened consciousness of the requisites of community. They will require knowledge of what makes communities possible. What do they need to bring to consciousness? What do they know already about the requisites of community if they think about it?

Known Requisites of Community

They certainly know that they have not chosen to be slaves, neither to be born into slavery, nor to remain in it. They have not regarded themselves as slaves by nature. And, they know, as they think about it, that no power on earth is predictably able to force them to be slaves, for they remember that they escaped despite the wealth, armed might, and spy system of their masters. Indeed, all the powers within them have moved them to risk death and deprivation in the quest for freedom from oppression rather than remain chained to deprivation and constantly at risk of being victims of cruelty and death at the whim of their oppressors. They know what it is to be exploited; they have chosen against it. (Interestingly, classes confronted with this thought experiment did not ask about how they escaped and whether they cooperated to do so.) The community they seek and strive for is not one in which some exploit and some are exploited; indeed, they recognize that the relation they had as slaves to their masters was not and cannot hold them together in a community, for they seek a future community in which each member has some responsibilities for every other member, a responsibility, for example, not to torture others. As slaves they were subject to torture with no defense or recourse against their tormentors.

You might be thinking by now that I am belaboring the obvious: No one wants to be a slave! People will always choose freedom rather than oppression; they choose to be moral agents. But if that were so obvious, why is it that we heard so many media commentators and experts telling us that the Shah of Iran was too powerful to be overthrown by the opposition against him? After all, I recall being told over and over again, the Shah had control of the armed forces, police, and wealth of the country. No relatively unarmed religious leaders or other dissidents could possibly prevail against the armed might of the Shah. These pundits did not give weight to the perceptions of the people who saw themselves as oppressed and many of their deepest values in utter jeopardy. Nor did these same pundits give weight to the arbitrary arrests, killings, and misuse of public funds daily visited upon the people. If people will choose freedom rather than yield to enslavement, then the Shah cannot win. Who will serve in his army, police force, and administration on behalf of exploitation?

The media almost without exception were taking the view that power belongs to those who have the arms to obtain what they will; power in this view does not belong to the forces that strongly incline us against being exploited or otherwise arbitrarily mistreated. The media largely forgot that weapons are ultimately subject to the purposes of those who possess them. The Shah discovered, as have so many other ruthless tyrants, that they can be defeated by the very people they supposedly command. The weapons amassed by the Shah were largely, in the end, not used on behalf of his purposes but took the direction of what most of the people perceived as liberation from oppressive policies. The media and many others have largely learned nothing from this insofar as they continue to measure the power of nations mostly by the size and firepower of weaponry and the forces possessing them. The collapse of the Berlin Wall was also largely discussed as a surprise, something unexpected. These attitudes prevail despite the historical and current reminders of how seemingly invincible empires and military dictatorships have fallen and fall. This is not to say that arms make no difference: They are not in themselves decisive.

Individuals who have been in slavery and have made the choice to do what it takes to be free of it know, if they reflect on it, that within them is a powerful force rejecting enslavement and yearning for fair, equitable, and nonexploitative human relations. This force has in the past and can in the future overcome the evil forces mobilized to oppose and suppress it. There is a future in working with others to form and sustain a community without slavery and slaves; it is a genuine, human possibility. First of all, then, these former slaves will be a community only to the extent that they remember that they were once slaves in the past, that they are not slaves now, and that the powers that move human beings and help shape their destiny are not on the side of slavery and exploitative relations. With those presuppositions of their past actions firmly in mind, they have one of the requisite reasons for being a community.

But these escaped slaves will not even come to a meeting to remember their past and organize for the future unless they are confident that each one of them has the knowledge and disposition to avoiding killing human beings; individuals recognize that killing is wrong and are inhibited sufficiently from initiating actions that endanger the lives of others. It is this set of presuppositions that make it feasible to call a meeting and have people attend. How would students be able to come to classes and other meetings if even small gatherings usually include one or more persons who have either no inhibitions about killing or have an intense love for doing so? In California, when someone walked into a McDonald's restaurant and opened fire, gunning down people who had done nothing to provoke it, no one was prepared for it. Utter shock was the reaction to something so rare and so inhuman, that is, so uncharacteristic of human beings.

A student in class once ventured the opinion that we think killing is wrong because most of us oppose it. Can you imagine the constant terror we would be in if all that prevents killing is majority sentiment and enacted legislation? No one is safe and no law efficacious if human beings, as human beings, are incapable of inhibiting any urges in them toward killing. It is the very essence of terrorist tactics to try to shake us loose from our reliance on the inhibitions against killing. And how does the terrorist seek to move us toward a state of terror in the presence of others? Precisely by slaughtering persons they have no specific reason to kill in places where individuals feel utterly safe. Even then, terrorism fights a powerful force in all of us. The outrage against the Irish Republican Army (IRA) for the bomb that killed children and shoppers in England was so strong from every direction that even the IRA leadership, honestly or dishonestly, felt compelled to disavow having authorized any of their number to carry out this particular bombing. Apparently, they feared losing some or all of their support. After all, who would fight under the command of persons who have no inhibitions whatsoever about killing anyone, even babes in the arms of their totally unprotected, unsuspecting, and unprepared parents? Even the IRA has to depend upon a membership composed of persons who have some inhibitions about killing lest members fear for their own safety or that of friends and relatives.

It is easy to forget how much we depend upon one another to place a very high value on human life and not just our own. One reason is that at the conscious level many of us espouse views that belie what we functionally presuppose in ourselves and others. Thus, for example, it is rather common to hear it said that all values vary over time and circumstances, across cultures, and among individuals. Values vary indeed along all these dimensions, but do they vary so completely that cooperative activity and communities are impossible? Whatever people profess, they do not tend to act as if life, for example, is a value that some do not recognize at all or that some value only at times or only as it suits them.

Consider that individuals from very different cultures, religious backgrounds, and national origins, climb high dangerous mountains roped together. Suppose I were slated to go mountain climbing with you. I know nothing about you, not even what country you are from and where you were born and raised. Ordinarily, this does not bother people very much, if at all. That is an amazing fact in itself. I have been studying ethics, however, for a number of years and that means learning about the potential for evil as well as good in people. And in ethics you also learn something about the power of theories and ideologies to warp otherwise natural inhibitions against doing evil, such as killing persons. To be a terrorist, for example, requires enormous resolve to overcome the pervasively human reluctance to kill and be killed. Because I have learned to respect people's thinking about values and how different that thinking may be from mine, I have a strong urge to talk with you before we begin climbing tomorrow, especially before we find ourselves roped together.

And so, on the night before the scheduled climb, I ask you: "What do you think about the value of human life?" Suppose you are steeped in some of the conceptions of our day and you reply quite casually: "Oh, that depends. How much people value their lives and those of others depends on how they are raised and on circumstances at the time they have to make choices about the value of life."

Such an answer would not help me in the least. In fact, it would raise in me serious doubts about you. I would need to ask you: "About these circumstances that shape how much we value human life, tell me more. Would there ever be circumstances in which my life would have less value than yours?"

Imagine that you regard this question as hopelessly naïve. "Come on," you say, "how can I decide in advance that our lives are equally valuable; that depends, as I said before, on the circumstances. Besides, I know nothing about your worth. Without more knowledge, I cannot reasonably answer your question."

This reply would increase my anxiety about you considerably: "What I want to know from you is very simple and requires no special knowledge on your part. I want to know what you would do if I slipped while roped to you! Would you make every reasonable effort to save my life and yours?"

What if you became incensed at this point. What if you now shouted at me in no uncertain terms: "Look, leave me alone. I have tried to tell you that I have no answer to such questions and no one should expect me or anyone else to come up with an answer to moral questions. There aren't any answers, only personal opinions. Of one thing I am sure! Nobody is going to impose their values on me; I have a right to my own opinions and to be left alone, too! I am not going to sit here and have you put a value on my life. My life has the value I give it, and if I choose, I have a right to commit suicide without any interference from the likes of you. Now, either we change the subject, or I'll hit the sack; we have a hard day ahead of us!"

Do you think for a moment that I would go mountain climbing with you? Certainly not! If I suspect that you may believe what you have said and may act on that basis, I would be a fool to be roped together with you. Although I doubt that your actions are as extreme as the views you have expressed, I would take no chances. I do value my life dearly and my responsibilities to others as well.

Of course this whole exchange on the night before a climb is most unusual. Much more common is the implicit trust we have for one another as we climb, drive automobiles, ride elevators, and share the highways at high speeds with complete strangers.

Indeed, one kind of training now being undertaken for young executives includes climbing and being roped to one another. As they climb together, they become conscious of their dependence on one another and of the implicit trust within themselves for one another. In short, this is consciousness raising of precisely the kind this group in the wilderness must experience to form and sustain a community. They will need to remind each other and confirm openly that they as human beings are not killers by nature and inclination. But, note, they will attend an assembly for that purpose if, and only if, they are sufficiently implicitly or explicitly convinced beforehand that human beings are not born killers, for whom killing one another is as natural as hunting and gathering food and just as driven by physical appetites and needs. No community could exist without inner restraints against killing, whatever external restraints may also be necessary. Just as requisite are restraints against stealing those goods necessary for life and self-respect, such as food and clothing.

Something else has to be remembered and raised to consciousness by this band in the wilderness. They would not attempt to discuss and agree on anything unless they could expect people to speak truthfully. No one would attend a meeting or endeavor to agree on how to organize and institute rules, governance, services, and enforcement agencies unless promises are understood and kept, at least as a general practice. Why would you read this or any book purporting to be a work of nonfiction if you believed that authors are devoid of any responsibility to be honest and reliable in conveying what they believe and know to be true? As an author, I might say something that turns out to be false on reflection or investigation, but if you were to expect me to say something is true that I know to be false, you would see no point in wasting your time to read this book. To check out all the references and research alone would be an enormous effort, requiring years for even the most rapid reader.

No knowledge of any kind could be learned or communicated if lying were to be one of the accepted forms of behavior for those who conduct and report research. The waste of time and resources and the sheer chaos created by the discovery of one deceptive researcher at Harvard was enormous, involving as it did numerous institutions, published data, and a highly important inquiry into the treatment of cancer.[5] What that researcher did cannot be called science, and he could not remain a member of the cooperative research efforts. Indeed, in one sense, he never did become a member of that or any other community of scholarship; he could only do that by being completely honest as an observer and reporter.[6]

Thus it comes as no surprise that the avoidance of lying, like the avoidance of killing, is a requisite of community; it is a rule without which there are no rules. When we draw up and write down the rules of baseball, they would be meaningless if sprinkled with deceptions or if the implementation of them were to be unfaithfully or inconsistently carried out. We cannot imagine that the rule requiring first base to be ninety feet from home plate is neither equally binding nor equally enforced for all teams playing the game of baseball. Were any team to lengthen this distance for the opposition, playing in their park, they would, upon discovery, not only forfeit the game but no doubt would place their whole future in jeopardy. Truthful compliance is absolutely demanded.

You might seize on this example and claim that it illustrates precisely that moral rules are invented as the rules of baseball surely have been: To play a game, we invent the rules and enforce honest and equal compliance, for if we do not, we cannot attain our purposes in playing the game and in making skill a decisive factor in the outcome.

But the ability and willingness to contract together to make and enforce rules and laws, social and legislative, presuppose, factually and logically that people have fairly strong inhibitions about killing, lying, stealing, and cheating.[7] Though it is helpful to become conscious of this, it is not necessary when these inhibitions may be assumed to be deeply, virtually habitually, at work, as in a well-established, small community in which people know one another well. Even before a community such as a town is formally organized or incorporated, the benefits of working together may rise to consciousness first, without much apparent attention to what is being presupposed about the tendencies to help rather than to harm one another. We can illustrate this in an account given of the history of Alton, New Hampshire, a small town of approximately four thousand year-long residents.

The first settlers came in the summer of 1770, twenty-five families in the first ten to twenty years. *The History of Alton* describes
the founding: "Each, an entity unto himself, cleared his own land
and built his own home in the wilderness."[8] Though each was an
"entity unto himself," the history notes how people banded
together: "One family might perish alone but never two standing
together."[9] In the earliest days when there were only four or five
families, "there were no roads or even as much as a cart path.
These self-sufficient souls usually marked trees to find their way
about and to procure what supplies they needed for their homes."[10]
It is explicitly stated that "the family was a very important unit to
every man, whether seventeen or sixty-seven and he was intent
first and foremost on keeping his family healthy."[11] But these "self-
sufficient" family-oriented pioneers "felt the need of banding together in mutual protection and self-preservation, TO FORM A
COMMUNITY."[12]

The author, Barton Griffin, gives as the reasons for forming a
community the need for travel and supplies. Meetings were held in
1777, before the United States had a national government, and
town leaders were elected, including a constable. Taxes were col-
lected and roads built before the town was officially incorporated
by the state of New Hampshire in 1797. All through this historical
account by Griffin, people are depicted as helping themselves and
one another; cooperation is viewed as not only mutually beneficial
but as the basis for progress. Griffin's portrait of a human community in the making exhibits what Kropotkin expects of human behavior. Human beings survive and thrive as a species characterized
by mutual aid.[13] Forming a community is a natural expectation for
Griffin, and clearly possible. Griffin never sees the families in their
early isolation and without a government as a danger to one another; danger exists for a family that tries to stand alone. Griffin
assumes, however, that no one tried to "go it alone," and Kropotkin believes that no one is naturally inclined to do so.

The premises in Hobbes, on human nature, are so different from
those of Griffin and Kropotkin. Neither fear of violence nor violence is mentioned in this history of Alton. Hobbes has us at one

another's throats and afraid of each other even once governments exist. But the earliest settlers of Alton, the band of escaped slaves in the wilderness, and all of us have to various degrees experienced the community of the family and its relations of mutual aid. The escaped slaves may need to remember these exhibits of mutual aid and sharing because they are all too aware of the human potential for exploitative and brutal relations in social and political situations of great inequality in power. They may need to raise consciousness again about the fact that human beings are not by nature killers, liars, stealers, and cheaters, seeking only their own advantage over others. If it were the case, however, that individuals uniformly derive intense pleasure from harming others and intense pain from refraining from such harm, it is difficult, if not impossible, to imagine families and larger communities existing at all. Students often worry that as an ethics professor I will impose my values on them. Indeed, some believe that teaching ethics can be only that. But you and I can no more impose the moral requisites of community on one another than we can make vegetarians out of lions.

Communities in the form of kinship relations are a given for those who are thinking about beginning a community beyond the family. Everyone has or has had parents; everyone has been procreated and nurtured by others. For a community to be, mothers and fathers have to be remembered and when necessary, cared for. If there is to be a future for a community, it must of necessity have continuity with its past. No community exists and persists without an honored, recognized past. Honoring one's parents is particularly critical ,because it is a positive affirmation of procreation and nurture, indeed, of life itself. Those people who repudiate their ancestors can continue the species through their own procreation but not the particular community to which they have belonged and might have continued to belong. These escaped slaves will forge a specific community to the extent that they take responsibility for and affirm their parents, as well as parenting itself. Once more, this requisite of community is part of their experience: It is an inclination they feel and share as human beings.

But communities require not only that there be parents and children. It is certainly possible to bear children without accepting responsibility for nurturing and rearing them. It is also possible that those who unite sexually to begin a human life will not remain faithful to one another nor stay together to share in seeing through the life they began together. If this group of escaped slaves is to form a community, it will have to be true that they are not without inhibitions about unfaithfulness in sexual relations, particularly in the context of becoming or being a family. Children will not be predictably cared for where their parents do not predictably and faithfully share their lives with those children and one another. Escaped slaves will be particularly conscious of the destructiveness that imposed separations of families and rape bring in their wake. Certainly those who use their political and social power to separate families and force sexual relations are not forming community with their victims. And for the victims, maintaining community will require enormous efforts and sacrifices. Indeed, this collection of escaped slaves have good reason to become conscious of the faithfulness, sexual and otherwise, without which they would not be alive and would not enjoy the capacity for organizing themselves.

By now, if not from the outset, you may be fully aware of an historical example that suggests a situation like the one I have relied upon to pose the question about what is necessary, logically and functionally, to presuppose as requisite for beginning and sustaining a community. Our thought experiment is suggested by what we know historically about the experiences in the wilderness of the Hebrew people. These experiences are formative for Jewish people; they are part of the Christian tradition as well; I speak of the Mosaic Covenant, or Ten Commandments. However else this covenant may be seen, it does constitute a critical historical moment of heightened awareness of what is required for the existence and maintenance of a community. The fuller impact of the Mosaic Covenant for the Jewish and Christian communities, however, is not at all addressed by the simple thought experiment I have been discussing. Readers would do well to consult some excellent recent studies that place the Mosaic Covenant in its historical and religious context and pay attention to its religious as well as moral significance at the time and now.[14] At this juncture, I wish to examine some of what has been gained so far by shifting from the necessary conditions of individual actions, Gewirth's basis for rights, to the necessary conditions for forming and maintaining communities.

Requisites of Community and Rights

Recall the words of Alasdair MacIntyre, cited at the very outset of this book: "The integral substance of morality has to a large degree been fragmented and then in part destroyed."[15] Now if we actually lived solely in accord with the modern and contemporary conceptions of rights we have reviewed, what MacIntyre is saying would be totally true. As we have discovered, however, by reflecting upon the logically and functionally necessary requisites of community, we as human beings have deep propensities to support human life by means of our procreative and nurturant behavior; we wish human lives into existence and nurture them. We have identified as well deep aversions to killing, deceiving, stealing, and infidelity. These restraints make cooperative behavior possible. And what we tend even more to forget, all of these propensities and restraints make it possible for there to be individual moral agents and for them to have the freedom to function as moral agents. Only if and when other persons observe the community-sustaining restraints and, as necessary, sustain and aid us, are any of us as individuals free to pursue our individual and social purposes.

MacIntyre is aware that rights to life and freedom cannot be actualized and meaningfully conceptualized unless communities exist with their social rules and institutions obligating individuals to honor or make good particular claims to life and freedom. But MacIntyre treats all social rules as inventions of historically and uniquely differing communities. Although there are rules, customs, and laws that vary with time, place, and circumstances, communities in all their variations, nevertheless, share certain forms of human relatedness—moral bonds. These are universally necessary for there to be communities with their customs, rules, and laws. Using MacIntyre's language of "rules" one could call these moral bonds the rules without which there are no social rules.[16]

These moral bonds, then, provide a basis for there being rights and for making it both possible and meaningful to claim them, if and when that becomes necessary. In a relatively well-ordered community in which these moral bonds are largely strong and intact, rights are expectations, mostly below the threshold of awareness, that individuals and groups will not be destructive of existing moral bonds. If and when, however, given moral bonds are threatened or destroyed, rights may take the form of claims. These claims may be solely moral or both moral and legal.

For example, in an instance of fraudulent business behavior, those who have been cheated may morally request or demand to be compensated. If this compensation is not forthcoming on an informal, interpersonal basis, it is generally possible to seek the remedies available in courts of law.

The right not to be deceived, in a community where a high degree of honesty and trustworthiness prevails, will take the form of a mostly implicit expectation that others will be responsible, that is, will be trustworthy. Honest transactions are moral claims on each and every participant; rights as claims that exact honesty from others only function as such claims when one or more participants in a business deal engage, or threaten to engage, in acts of lying and/or stealing. Refraining from lying and stealing preserve basic moral bonds that make it possible to do business. Given these moral bonds and the responsibilities they entail, rights are the expectations or claims that no individual or group will be harmed by fraud and theft. In this sense, we may speak of individuals and groups as "having these rights"; or, similarly, we may say that these rights "belong to" individuals and groups. These two ways of characterizing rights, however, are slightly misleading because it is the ability and willingness not to lie and not to steal that function as the ground of any rights not to be harmed in these ways. Only if the will and ability to avoid lying and stealing are powers that "belong to" individuals and groups does it become possible and comprehensible to think of individuals and groups as being able, and justifiably so, to expect and lay claim to the exercise of such powers from other individuals and groups.

So far, then, our analysis has identified certain forms of human relatedness (moral bonds), each of which is the basis for a correlative human right and each of which is logically and functionally requisite for the existence of communities and their social rules. We have thereby related rights to social rules, and this, MacIntyre correctly insists, is essential if human rights are to have substance and comprehensibility. But we have done more. These moral bonds are universal and logically necessary elements within social rules and communities; they include the requisites of individual, purposive actions as well. But these moral bonds and the rights based on them give a fuller picture of moral life than we find in the modern and contemporary rights theories reviewed in previous chapters.

In the first place, these rights theories do not identify nor recognize the very special, morally significant relations of spouses to one another, of parents to children, and of children to parents. In these theories, the objects of rights are not human relationships but interests or desires of individuals regarded as naturally detached, or rationally detachable, from communities and other individuals. For example, the right to life is based on self-preservation, for Hobbes; on the freedom to pursue happiness, without interference, for Bentham and Mill; and on its necessity for individually preferred action in Gewirth. But such a right fails to materialize and sustain itself unless there is procreating, nurturing, and faithful parenting taking place generally.

In the second place, rights cannot be seen simply as individual claims, as some modern and contemporary rights theorists see them, if one is to recognize what is absolutely requisite to the very existence and maintenance of individual rights. There is no individual to claim a right to be and to be nurtured before procreation and the generating of individual life takes place. Indeed, any rights attributable to an individual only come to be for that individual by the prior procreation and nurture of others in cooperative relations and activities and by the dependable network of protection characteristic of communal life.

In the third place, the moral responsibilities parents and children have for one another, and the expectations (rights) based on them, are rendered problematic in modern and contemporary rights theories insofar as individual agents, actions, and claims are identified as the units of morality and the bases of moral rights. When the relationships of parents to their children and of children to their parents are viewed as moral bonds, the breaking of these bonds requires some kind of moral justification.[17] When these relationships also flow from natural inclinations to form and sustain communities, their personal and life-long character is an understandable, predictable characteristic of our moral and communal life. If, however, self-preservation as in Hobbes, or pleasure for oneself as in Bentham and Mill, or individual self-development and self-control as in Gewirth constitute the natural bases of our moral rights, the parent-child relationship becomes a social custom, institution, or invention that requires justification. For such relationships to be life-long becomes much more decidedly dependent upon such variables as contractual arrangements, personal commitments, emotional attachments, and articulated social goals and laws.

At this point, we have come full circle, returning to the issue enjoined by Hobbes in launching modern rights theories. He rejected all previous theories of morality and rights because they made what he regarded as a fundamental error: to view human beings as social animals. Hobbes explicitly rejected any notion that we were naturally inclined to form communities and be morally responsible in the ways required to make this possible. By nature, Hobbes argued, we seek to preserve ourselves, not others. But clearly we also procreate and nurture other selves. Even if these acts are seen as somehow self-preserving, they are social, requiring cooperation, and they do bring into being and preserve selves other than ourselves. Why not regard this behavior as natural and our behavior in a state of nature as social?

Before we can address any quarrel over what is natural, we have to clarify how the word *natural* is being used. *Natural* has a number of uses. Something natural is something real. Nonsocial and social behavior are both real enough phenomena. There is no issue worth disputing there. Natural when applied in the context of human nature, refers to some power or ability that human beings have by reason of being members of the human species; what is natural in this sense is something that has not been invented, imposed, or learned, though it may be influenced by inventions, impositions, and learning. This is an issue as to how to understand our moral nature.

Sometimes the natural has been identified with the moral. Indeed, virtue for Plato and Aristotle, and the cardinal virtues—courage, prudence, wisdom, and justice—for Thomas Aquinas, were viewed as perfections of our natural powers as human beings. In a sense, all modern rights theories are trying to make a case for the realization and flourishing of certain human powers. But at issue here is that to call the realization, perfection, or flourishing of any human power a moral responsibility or a moral right to which one is entitled, it is not enough to call it natural. Self-preservation, pleasure, or self-development may all be sought in ways that are destructive of the life, pleasure, or self-development of others or even of oneself. "Natural" in the sense of "real," and "nature" in the sense of an unlearned, unimposed, and uninvented ability or power can sometimes refer to what is immoral rather than what is moral or worthy of development.

It is not enough to demonstrate that communities are real phenomena, that is, natural phenomena and something we by our natures as human beings have the power and inclination to bring about. Nor is it enough to identify what is logically and functionally necessary in the way of human behavior and relationships to bring agents and communities into being and allow them to actualize their natural potentials. We still have not indicated why these human relationships, and not others, are among those that should be considered as morally significant, nor what is requisite if these relationships are to be formed, sustained, and perfected. These questions about moral knowledge and its foundations occupy us in chapters 7, 8, and 9. In chapter 6, we will consider certain requisites of community not yet considered.

SIX

Requisites of Morality, Freedom, and Community

Moral rights are only possible, logically and functionally, because individuals and groups relate to one another in the ways exhibited by the moral bonds of community. But communities and these moral bonds would not exist if there were not the forces or powers, necessary and sufficient, to bring about and sustain these bonds and communities. Human beings are moved to procreate, nurture, care for one another, and refrain from injuring themselves and others. If they were not so moved, individual rights to life and freedom would not be actualized; there would be no bearer of these rights and no effective power to expect or claim them from anyone.

The forces that move us in the ways just described are sometimes thought of as motives. As such, they are part of our human propensities observed and analyzed within the various sciences in accord with their methods and concepts. From a psychological perspective, one may speak of traits or drives of a self or personality, conscious or unconscious. From a sociological perspective, one may speak of roles and mores of a culture or class. From a biological perspective, one may speak of the adaptation or evolution of a species and its genes. Each of these perspectives looks at the forces that move us as human beings to form and sustain those relationships we are calling moral bonds. All of these perspectives, however, simply begin and end with manifestations of the forces that form and sustain moral bonds. Before there are selves, there is that which makes it possible for selves to be; before there are cultures, there is that which makes it possible for cultures to be—selves and self-creating forces; before there are genes, there are the forces that make selves and communities possible so that genes may be transmitted and protected.

So, whatever light the sciences may shed on motivation, the powers that form and sustain moral bonds are not simply forces of selves, or groups, or biological entities: These powers are prior to and external to the self in certain respects, and self-initiated and internal to the self in other respects. The powers that make morality possible are at once powers *beyond* each individual self and also powers *of* the self that move that self and other selves affected by that self. What are these powers or forces that move us toward being morally responsible and hence toward meeting those expectations and claims we entertain as rights? Those powers identifiably functioning within us as individual selves are manifest in: (1) moral development; (2) cognition; and (3) moral agency or freedom. All of these aspects of human selfhood are powers requisite to being morally responsible and having moral rights. But these powers cannot be properly understood and assessed apart from the power on which they depend and that they partly represent. What power is this and how does awareness of it arise?

Grounding Moral Behavior: A Conversation

I begin with a conversation I once had with a biologist, a practicing psychiatrist. This biologist was interested in having me participate in a conference he was planning on medical ethics, but he was worried about asking me. What was the problem? What I gathered from our conversation was that he wondered what to expect from someone who teaches at a divinity school. What does one encounter from someone who has studied and taught religious as well as philosophical ethics? And so it was that he invited me to his office in order to become better acquainted.

I prefer not to identify the biologist in question: I will simply refer to him as Hal. After exchanging some remarks about the hot weather, Hal bore right in by asking me point-blank, "How do you ground ethics?"

"Well," I said, "we begin by reflecting on our experiences as selves and as selves in relation to others." "What kind of experiences?" Hal wanted to know. In response, I began by giving a version of the moral bonds of community. But Hal soon grew impatient and interrupted me: "I'm a biologist," he said emphatically. "I think ethics is grounded in biology. Do you believe in evolution? Do you think we're making progress ethically?"

The gist of my reply was as follows: "I believe there is change in nature, and I believe that our knowledge of nature and of ethics has, in some respects, progressed. And, when you say that you ground ethics on biological evolution, you are pointing to forces that are very much a source of our moral and intellectual development.

"One of the most amazing and wonderful forces pulsing through us as human beings is our desire to unite with one another, male and female. We do so not only to have sex and companionship with one another, but we conspire also to have children. And though all of us appear in so many ways selfish and out for ourselves, we nevertheless go through a long period of nine months of waiting for a child to be born—much longer than most animals; then we endure, with surprising good humor at times, the sleepless nights, the incessant demands, and the less than pleasant habits of our infants; then we struggle to protect, discipline, and educate our increasingly independent, intelligent, and strong-willed children as they turn into adolescents and adults. Sometimes we have to deal with almost daily declarations of independence, each seeming like a declaration of impending battle. But we hang in there, and most of our adult children, though we could scarcely have realistically expected it, become quite moral and even friendly.

"This whole incredible period of altruism, of living mostly for others, occurs despite all of the strong impulses in us to the contrary. And what is gained by such a long period of gestation, nurture, and growth? Human beings develop a brain much superior to all other animals and are much more conscious of their tendencies to be altruistic, and of the necessity of these altruistic tendencies for attaining freedom and some of our greatest accomplishments.

"When I contemplate the forces that move us to practice such altruism despite our egoistic tendencies to the contrary, I am led to feel awe and gratitude. When I am so moved, I think of that force as 'God,' that is, as a force more powerful and more permanent than myself or any other human being. And moved as I am by awe and gratitude, I am led to express those emotions in what we call worship. That is why on a Sunday morning driving by my church, you might be able to catch a glimpse of me singing 'Now Thank We All Our God' with conviction and enthusiasm.[1]

"Some people, observing these forces toward the altruistic nurture and instruction of offspring, experience no emotions of awe, humility, and gratitude. In the absence of these emotions, they are not religious, or do not think of themselves as such."

By now Hal had relaxed a great deal, and the last statement brought a warm smile: "That's why I'm not religious. I have no feelings about these biological forces you describe. But I certainly agree with you about these grounds of our progress as humans: Progress does stem from our altruistic behavior."

At this point, and in all our subsequent collaboration in medical ethics, Hal exhibited complete confidence in me and in what I had to say. Whatever our differences, and we clearly knew what some of these were, the explicit agreement we had about what grounds "ethics," that is, about what grounds our morally responsible behavior, was apparently what Hal needed to be able to treat me as a reliable person and scholar of ethics with whom he could form community and from whom he could learn. As the reader might suspect, I had been, and continued to be, willing to presuppose that I could form community and learn from Hal unless and until Hal acted in ways to make this presupposition untenable. What are the beliefs about the necessary conditions for morality that Hal and I shared? Why is sharing these so important that people like Hal, in at least some situations, cannot trust others to be intellectually and morally responsible until they have some confidence that these beliefs are actually shared?

Essentially, the requisites of morality acknowledged by Hal and me are that: (1) a cosmic moral power exists; (2) goodness is more powerful than evil; and (3) morally responsible behavior is ultimately vindicated. I will discuss each of these in turn.

A Cosmic Moral Power Exists

Hal believes that there are forces—he considers them to be biological and evolutionary—that produce the human behavior necessary for the survival of the species. This behavior is altruistic; it is at least as cooperative, procreative, nurturant, and noninjurious as survival demands. Though the forces driving persons and all living creatures toward survival are within them, the power these forces represent is in certain respects prior to each individual and more powerful than each of them. In human beings, the power to assure the behavior needed to spawn and sustain life is strong enough to overcome the impulses to the contrary in most individuals. People inherit this power working in them genetically and culturally; they do not and cannot choose to forego its presence in them, though they may struggle against it. In short, the power to be altruistic exists; it is not something individuals have created, nor something that they can destroy, for it is cosmic in extent and species-wide in its effectiveness.

What Hal calls altruism is his term for the much more specific kinds of moral bonds I have described earlier. Altruism, therefore, is functionally and logically required for the forming and sustaining of communities, the survival network of the human species. Given the existence of what can only be attained by the forms of altruism I have been calling moral bonds, it is illogical to deny the existence of the power to bring these about and to deny that this power is prior to what it has brought about and currently sustains.

What accounts for altruism is one basis for the belief Hal and I share in a power that gives rise to and sustains morality. But there are other experiential bases for this belief.

When it comes to our experiences of cosmic moral power, Hal and I agree in some respects but differ in others. Both of us have an implicit confidence that this power is at work. We choose to be morally responsible without even thinking about whether or not it is possible. Of course, we know that there are situations in which we cannot choose to carry out responsibilities; we cannot keep our promise to be somewhere if sickness prevents us from the necessary travel. When I say we rely on the power to be moral without giving it a thought, I refer to what is analogous to our reliance upon the power of gravity. Our cumulative experiences are such that we move our legs in walking with the confidence, usually implicit and functional but not conscious, that they will keep coming up and down in the appropriate, necessary way. I make a promise without wondering whether the powers that move me—my impulses, interests, motivations—will continue and be strong enough to maintain the bond my promise has established with someone else.

Hal wanted to know what I believed regarding the power to be moral. In some ways, the question seems as unnecessary as wanting to know what I believe with respect to gravitational force. Does it really make any difference? Both of these forces are at work in the cosmos whatever we believe about them. Even if anyone would consciously deny moral and gravitational powers, their actions would betray an implicit trust in them. Hal's reliance on what I would say is a reliance that truth-telling would take place and that I, whatever my beliefs, would be dominated by an inclination to tell the truth and by an inhibition to lie. So what is the problem?

Hal is a nontheist. He suspects that I am a theist. What if I believe that cosmic moral power is God? What if God is a being known only to those who are believers in God? And what if being a believer in God equips one with special, perhaps even superior knowledge of what is moral? Furthermore, what if such knowledge is unavailable, or unacceptable, to those who are nontheistic or atheistic in their beliefs? For Hal, the power to be moral is a natural phenomenon, a force he as a biologist characterizes as evolution. Do I as a religious person acknowledge and believe that Hal, without professing to be religious, knows and exhibits the power to be moral, and that this power is as accessible to him as it is to me? In short, can we, and should we be able to learn from one another; are we fundamentally moral equals, whatever my expertise as an "ethicist?"

And so Hal relaxed once he found out what he wanted to know: My religious beliefs in no way denied the possibility of shared knowledge of the forces that make morality possible. The altruism necessary for survival and progress is fueled by a power that may be observed and characterized by biologists as well as by ethicists, including religious ethicists. The key to agreement was that access to moral experience and knowledge was not made conditional upon explicitly religious belief. Faith (meaning confidence) that a cosmic moral power exists and is exhibited in the altruism that sustains our species does not also have to be a professed faith in God and God's existence. The emotions of awe and gratitude I mentioned to Hal are not emotions he has relative to his faith in a cosmic moral power; his faith in that power is not experienced as a faith in a being but rather in an impersonal, causal force observed and described by biologists studying natural evolution. In other words, he professes to have no experiences that would provide a basis for personalizing cosmic power or for relating to it as though it were a person. Being grateful is something he reserves for human beings. As long as the beliefs I have, however, do not deny that the bases and manifestations of morality are accessible to him as a biologist, and as long as I do not require him to have experiences he genuinely lacks or repudiates, we are and remain members of a common universe of faith and belief in the power that makes morality possible. And, as a psychiatrist, he feels no need to consider my emotions as utterly without foundation or as indications of insanity. After all, the feeling of gratitude is at least an understandable reaction to the very powerful cosmic force pulsing through human beings in a way that favors their existence and makes their own existence possible as well. That this power is so pervasive and effective can also surely evoke awe. And a belief regarding the extent of that power is another of the beliefs Hal and I hold in common.

Goodness Is More Powerful Than Evil

The term *goodness* here refers not only to what is being accomplished by morally responsible activities but also to positive dispositions toward morally responsible actions and toward the powers necessary to carry them out. In our conversation, Hal was thinking of goodness as survival of the human species and the altruistic behavior necessary to actualize it. Evil would constitute maladaptive behavior, relative to survival; such behavior would be non-altruistic or contrary to what altruism would demand of us. Hal believed that in the struggle for survival, altruistic behavior has been powerful enough to produce progress; increased altruism not only makes survival more likely but also leads to increased self-consciousness and knowledge and hence greater ability to adapt to our environment. This is one way to frame the greater relative power of goodness over evil.

As noted earlier, I am willing to affirm that we do attain a higher degree of self-consciousness and intelligence relative to other animals by means of the long period of altruistic nurture and education we provide for our young. Also, we have made progress, if that means self-consciousness and knowledge have increased over time. More theoretical and technical knowledge, however, brings with it a greater capacity for evil as well as good. Tragically, the twentieth century has been the arena for massive destruction of life and the enormous increase in firepower that makes such destruction quickly and efficiently possible. But that is not all. So many of the lives being destroyed, or maimed, are unarmed and helpless innocent persons, victims of genocide, terrorism, or torture. My confidence that good is superior in power relative to evil is not based on any calculus that in the world as we know it, the amount of good is increasing. I do not even know how to make such a quantitative assessment. Who does?

How then is it possible to have the faith (confidence) that goodness is more powerful than evil? There are at least two considerations that uncover the bases we have in experience for faith in the power of goodness despite the evil in our world: (1) each evil act depends for its existence on the existence of a sufficient degree of goodness; (2) whenever evil is a choice, goodness is also.

To begin with, what does it mean to say that evil depends upon goodness for its existence? Suppose I wish to obtain some money. Suppose also that I believe I can only attain it by a lying promise, or that I wish to attain it that way. In other words, I expect to achieve some goal of mine by borrowing money I promise to repay but with no intention of paying it back. To borrow this money I must find someone who will take my word for it, and this is true regardless of how many guarantees I offer. Even if I prove I have the assets to repay and sign a witnessed agreement, the one who hands over the money still has decided to rely on my word as a bond I do not intend to destroy. If no promises were ever kept, no one would be able to convince anyone else to do anything that depends upon a promise. Conversely, if promises had been always kept prior to my attempt to procure money by a lying promise, it is virtually certain that I would succeed.

Kant (1724–1804) used this very example to illustrate why it is contrary to reason to approve of lying. He argued that it is logically contradictory to will the goal of this lying promise, that is to obtain money, while at the same time willing that the maxim of this action (obtain money by a lying promise) be a universal law of nature, that is, something everyone acts upon. It is, in short, illogical to expect the goal to be met if lying promises were to be a universal practice rather than a deviation being contemplated.[2]

Although Kant did not draw this inference, the logical and actual possibility of lying exists only if and when truth-telling is sufficiently practiced and sufficiently recognized as the standard. Once, for example, people have written enough fraudulent checks, this use of personal checks, and the use of checks generally, becomes extremely difficult, and special devices, such as driver's licenses displaying the owner's photograph, are instituted to make deceptions more difficult.

Consider another example: Suppose it takes three persons to rob a particular bank—the driver of a getaway car, a person to collect the money, and someone armed to cover the person collecting the money. To choose to carry out this evil deed, to execute it, and to succeed in carrying it out, all require faithful communication, and all the responsible behavior among these three persons needed to engender trust and cooperation at every stage of the project. Augustine (354–430 A.D.) long ago observed that a band of thieves was not without honor. Such a band required sufficient morally responsible behavior from its members to be able to engage in the evil of thievery. Indeed, Augustine maintained that only good exists in the world; evil is the absence of good. Expressing this in relation to moral bonds, evil lies in the destruction of a moral bond. In other words, there exist moral bonds in the world, and when any one of them is destroyed, that is, rendered absent, we call that evil.

It is possible to accept Augustine's view if we think of it as a claim that evil can only be defined by reference to some good it is directed against or eliminates. Moral evil, however, does consist in the intentions and actions of actual human agents. And both of these forces, against what is good or different from it, are present in the world and the whole cosmos. What Hitler was doing through his SS troops amounted to great evil and the exercise of enormous power. It is too paradoxical to think of the vast destruction of human life involved as the absence of good only. Nevertheless, Hitler's power to do evil was no greater than the trustworthiness and reliability of his whole chain of command. And his power was also limited by the revulsion of many throughout the world to the evils he was perpetrating. Indeed, he was finally rendered powerless by the opposition from within and without Germany.

And so, paradoxically enough, goodness is prior to and requisite to evil as a viable option for human conduct. No person can ever exist and flourish enough to choose and perpetuate evil without being procreated, nurtured, and protected from the evil inclinations of others. And evil on a large scale requires the cooperative and reliable behavior of others to plan and effect. We tend to regard the sustenance of our moral bonds as a constant struggle. Doing evil, however, is normally a much greater struggle against greater odds. After all, the percentage of people in communities around the world who actually murder others is a relatively small minority. And communities are organized to render criminal behavior quite risky to one's life and reputation despite any imperfections in police protection, courts, and legislation.

The power of evil is limited in still another way: Whenever evil is a genuine option, goodness is also. In one sense, this is an obvious tautology. A genuine option is one that involves at least two practically possible alternative dispositions and/or actions that it is within the power of the chooser to set in motion, neither one of which alternatives is so absurd or crazy that no "normal" person would consider choosing it. So it is possible to dismiss the point that goodness may always be chosen if evil may by calling this a tautology inherent in the logic of morality: Logically, people can only be moral if they can be moral. This is surely not the point we wish to make, however logical it may be. Rather, the point is that when people choose to do what is morally wrong, we hold them responsible for not choosing to do what is morally right.

This is what we do when we convict someone of murder and submit them to punishment. We assume that the person who chose to kill someone had the power to choose otherwise. Even in an accidental death, we tend to hold someone responsible for knowingly having faulty brakes, if faulty brakes are considered the proximate cause of that death. Whenever people are exercising their powers to choose, goodness is possible and evil need never be chosen. That is the basis on which SS troops, who participated in the killing of obvious noncombatants, such as children, the aged, and the infirm, were convicted of crimes against humanity. Even the possibility that a Nazi would himself be killed for failing to carry out orders did not suffice by itself as a defense.

The fact that we do punish people for failing to reject evil when they chose it only shows, to begin with, that we have the confidence (faith) that people capable of choosing what they think or do are capable of choosing what is morally responsible to think or do. The question I have posed for us is whether there is some basis in reality for such a faith.

Consider again that human beings live in communities. This means that the dominant pattern of human existence is that of observing the restraints against killing, lying, stealing, and the like and exhibiting the proclivities for procreation, nurture, education, and mutual protection to the extent necessary for communities to be and for many to flourish. The expectation that people may choose to behave in these ways is no more startling than the fact that they do by and large choose to do so. Choosing to behave otherwise is a form of deviance. If such deviance is due to a failure of a person's capacity to choose through some loss of brain function, some overpowering uncontrollable emotion or mental state, or some insurmountable force exerted over the deviating person by another person, object, chemical or whatever, then we do not, of course, hold that person responsible for their thoughts or actions while under such influences. If these extenuating circumstances and conditions were themselves dominant forces in the world, we would not be the species that we are, a species not only surviving but growing. Whatever limits there may be to growth, the fact of growth represents a triumph of procreative, nurturant, protective, life-affirming and community-affirming forces over the many potential and actual life-destructive and community-destructive forces present in us and in our cosmos.

Upon reflection, then, it is not surprising, nor is it arbitrary, that we expect those capable of choice to be capable of choosing good rather than evil, and that we will, under a variety of circumstances, punish them or deprive them of choice, if they choose to do or even to threaten evil.

But some might say that doing evil is sometimes unavoidable. Thus, some might describe killing in self-defense as a necessary, lesser evil. Others might say that self-defense as a morally responsible act should not be regarded as in any sense evil, or at least not an evil perpetrated by those persons trying to save their own lives. In either case, any loss of life is a tragic, evil outcome. Those who oppose taking life under any circumstances do not avoid such tragedies; despite all of the restraint against killing exercised by literally billions of people in the world each day, some killing, intentional or otherwise, persists and has persisted throughout human history as we know it. Some of our morally responsible actions will only mitigate or lessen evil, not completely prevent it or its harmful effects.

Some reader may be willing to grant that so far the human species has been dominated by life-affirming and community-affirming powers of cosmic proportions but momentous decisions for destroying lives and communities are surely possible. What is to prevent decisions that would bring about a nuclear holocaust? What is to prevent decisions that would, more slowly, irreversibly fill our environment with toxic substances? Decisions that would destroy our species and most or all others with it are hypothetically possible. Yet at the same time, worldwide, there are strenuous efforts to avoid any such decisions. These efforts would be senseless if based on the assumption that they are futile. But might it not be false in fact to assume that our efforts on behalf of the survival of our species are anything but futile?

With regard to the degree of certainty that attaches to choices for evil, we can only go by the long history of the dominant pattern of behavior that has issued in the survival and growth of our species and communities. In this respect, we have a situation comparable to other patterns we live with and study. For example, we expect gravitational forces to continue roughly as they are, based only on the fact that they do and have done so as long as we are able to trace these back in time. This is true also of the actions of bodies such as the sun and the moon. People would be regarded as quite unusually skeptical, if not beyond sanity, to act on the hypothetical possibility that gravitational forces or the sun's energy will fail imminently or in the clearly foreseeable future. Our confidence is based on their record so far and the probabilities this generates in our mathematical mode of thinking. That is true also for the forces generating and sustaining our moral bonds; so far, they support our moral choices in much the same way as gravity supports walking and the sun supports the life on which we feed.

The biologist E. O. Wilson has also been inexorably drawn into this mode of thinking. He is uneasy about what will happen as the rapidly growing science of genetics provides us with the knowledge to change our own human nature. After suggesting a range of choices that might be made, such as choices to breed more intelligence and/or more sociality, he remarks that "Perhaps there is something already present in our nature that will prevent us from ever making such changes. In any case, and fortunately, this... dilemma belongs to later generations."[3] Isn't it curious? He is explicitly uncertain about what choices will be made but he expresses no explicit uncertainty about the existence of future generations. And the whole evolutionary epic, an explanation of the tenacious forces that make for our survival, he regards as a mythic epic, the best myth available, since the belief in the continuity of evolutionary laws, in a cause-and-effect continuum from this world to all visible worlds and backward through time to the beginning of the universe, cannot be proved with finality. In effect, he banks on what has fueled survival so far and unself-consciously projects that survival into an indefinite future. More recently, Wilson posits that there is within us a deep love of life and of what supports it and expresses confidence that we will neither wage a totally destructive nuclear war nor destroy the ecosystem upon which our survival depends.[4] His hope is fixed on an ever-increased understanding of the powers that have so far sustained our species, and he has the confidence that these powers and such understanding will be indefinitely available to us. What a deep faith! But it is based, as is the faith we have described, on the long history and prehistory of the very forces existing in our world that affirm life, whether described from a biological or moral perspective.

What of the future of the powers that be? How can Wilson or anyone else treat them as somehow indefinitely there?

Morally Responsible Behavior Is Ultimately Vindicated

Human behavior both presupposes and works for the continuation of the powers that be. E. O. Wilson, like Hal, believes that evolution, as a process of an ever-increasing human ability to survive and flourish, is a fact of life. The moral behavior that makes this possible is also a fact of life. Wilson expresses it this way:

> If human existence has any verifiable meaning, it is that our passions and toil are enabling mechanisms to continue that existence unbroken, unsullied, and progressively secure.... For if the whole process of our life is directed toward preserving our species and our personal genes, preparing for future generations is an expression of the highest morality of which human beings are capable.[5]

Specifically, Wilson says this in the context of a plea to preserve genetic and species diversity by limiting our destruction of natural habitats. And he does believe that "the whole process of our life is directed toward preserving our species and our personal genes." This belief he bases on biological knowledge, and he expects that knowledge to increase. With more biological knowledge, an ethic that puts very little value on the fauna and flora of a country will change to an ethic that regards these as a part of one's national heritage no less important than one's language and art. This shift in ethics will occur "for reasons that have to do with the very fiber of the brain."[6] He suggests: "The more the mind is fathomed in its own right, as an organ of survival, the greater will be the reverence for life for purely rational reasons."[7] As this occurs, he expects we will shed the now prevalent myths concerning our predatory actions toward other organisms and our environment that are, says Wilson, "obsolete, unreliable, and destructive."[8] "Ultimate survival" or "protection of the human spirit" is what a conservation ethic will bring about as our biological knowledge grows. This ultimate survival will bring together our drive toward perpetual expansion—personal freedom—and the delicate, knowledgeable stewardship of the living world needed to sustain that drive.

In effect, as a biologist, Wilson cannot see any empirical basis for an end to the whole life-affirming evolutionary process. Procreation, nurture, and education are *ultimately* vindicated by Wilson. By that I mean that these activities do not occur in vain, and their immediate goals are part of a continuous, indefinite future for what is being realized in these goals—life and life in community, not only with human beings but with all living organisms. Whatever their express beliefs, the confidence, conscious or unconscious, that there is a future for children and grandchildren is functionally present in the vast numbers of actual and aspiring parents and grandparents active on a global scale. Some even think that procreative and nurturant behavior is too prolific; governments in Asian countries, notably China, are strenuously trying to limit family size. But procreative forces are powerful. In democratic India there were riots and electoral defeat for Indira Gandhi's government after a brief attempt at state-legislated, mandatory sterilization to enforce population goals.

So far I have taken no issue with Wilson's way of voicing confidence in the continuity of forces that sustain our lives and communities. Wilson, however, quite arbitrarily reduces the scope and nature of these forces. This is seen most clearly in his response to the biblical story of Job, a portion of which he cites, including the following questions God is described as asking Job: "Have the gates of death been revealed to you? Have you ever seen the doorkeepers of the place of darkness? Have you comprehended the vast expense of the world? Come, tell me all this, if you know." Wilson's immediate response is, "We *do* know and we have told."[9] And he alleges that we know more than the biblical writers even imagined in their questions. What he claims is that we know the physical basis of life and approximately how and when it started. We can create new species in the laboratory and splice genes from one kind of organism onto another. These are marvelous discoveries indeed, and they were not anticipated in the scriptures of Jews and Christians. They fall short, however, of answering the questions posed in these scriptures.

To begin with, Wilson himself has noted that the big bang theory of the world's origins to which he and others subscribe does not account for there being something rather than nothing. The scientific method demands an antecedent for every consequent, and for life, all that we know allows us to derive life from existing living matter. Strictly speaking, we cannot create life in the laboratory; we can only create with it and from it; in a word, we procreate. And that is the point: human beings have not called life into being and do not understand the basis of physical life sufficiently to see or close the "gates of death." Whatever our understanding, what is procreated dies, and we remain powerless to prevent death. At the same time, we do not know whether the powers of life, the sources of our procreative power, are eternal. To posit some beginning in time to life sets up an infinite regress as to what is there to make the beginning possible. As an avowed materialist, Wilson, to be consistent, has to posit some type of material power to start that big bang and has no basis on which to conclude that this same power will ever end.

Of course, Wilson does not assert the end to life-sustaining powers in the world; evolution is described as an indefinitely self-perpetuating pattern. The mechanism for it is the human brain and its striving to extend genetically into the future. It is no accident that Wilson has affectionate regard for Marcus Aurelius; they are both Stoics. Wilson wonders if Marcus Aurelius shares his hope that human beings will love life enough to save it. Marcus Aurelius had observed the transitory nature of biographical and political events. For Wilson, these events are but a tick in the ultimate history of Surinam, a South American country he calls "eternal"; its people, he says, will survive its current political tragedy to witness ecological and evolutionary change; for such change, Wilson neither posits nor foresees any limit of time. Wilson, like the Stoics of ancient times, has located the powerful energy that originates, sustains, and extends life in the human mind. But, as we have seen, the scientific method logically demands that mind, as a consequent of life-creating forces, originates in powers beyond it as well as in it; and these powers, or some one or more powers among them, are without origin, as Plato, Aristotle, and religious traditions generally understood so well. From our limited perspective, all of our analogies with what we do know incline us to think of what is without beginning as something without end. That is a function of the logic of our scientific thought; it can never be a direct observation for any being that is not itself eternal. The Stoics felt compelled to posit an eternal mind to account for our finite mind, an eternal mind found both within and beyond human minds. Logically and functionally, Wilson works with similar presuppositions.

Whereas Wilson speaks of reverence for life, and whereas he believes that our knowledge of the human mind as an organ of survival will increase such reverence, the vast majority of people, presently and historically, have experienced reverence as they become aware of the power of survival as a power no human mind could ever invent and as a power that courses through us mightily. They realize that before human beings can experience love of life, the powers that be had to "love" life enough to multiply it and endow it with the power to multiply itself. This occasions awe; this occasions gratitude; this occasions humility. Now awe, gratitude, and feeling loved are what we experience most intensely and meaningfully in relation to other persons. When our awareness of eternal forces favoring life evoke such emotions, we tend to associate those forces with a super person; it would take a denial of what we experience in the presence of eternal forces to depersonalize ultimate life-affirming forces. Wilson denies the existence of any such being, not so much because he lacks awe but because he insists that the human brain's drive to survive is explanation enough for our survival—and the "big bang" enough for its origin. Yet, Wilson explicitly acknowledges that he cannot answer the question as to why there is something rather than nothing. But more important, Wilson, as we noted earlier, cannot avoid an infinite regress, given his commitment to find an antecedent for every event.

There is another aspect to the story of Job. Wilson does not consider it. In this story, Job loses all of his children. A key part of Job's story unfolds when he realizes his comparative powerlessness relative to the power that originates, sustains, and designs the whole cosmos. He repents of any pretensions he has had regarding his understanding of this mighty power. After experiencing forgiveness, Job does have another family and regains his health.[10] But not everyone will live to have children nor be capable of having them. And some will lose all of their offspring and have no more; still others will have offspring who will not have offspring. Wilson recognizes that some people can contribute to future generations by way of living the conservation ethic and helping to achieve its aims. That does not give meaning to the lives of those who die early, of those who never are mentally capable of making the requisite vocational choices, and of those who are physically unable to accomplish their goals. In short, human survival and flourishing can be the dominant reality while, at the same time, some individuals die prematurely or otherwise fail to reach their potential as human beings. What is more, some survive and flourish only because others take risks for them, whether in childbirth, or in the line of duty as members of fire or police departments or the armed forces.

Until now, we have provided some vindication for being moral, procreative, nurturant, and the like, based on some of our inferences regarding the eternal character of life-sustaining forces. But why should individuals be moral? Why should I be the one to risk or lose life or limb so that my family, or my neighbor, or a stranger I could protect or rescue may live? Why should I be the one to care? Isn't it better to depend on the care of others rather than offer it in situations where caring may cost me dearly?

Again, it is necessary to recognize that people do care in circumstances in which their own lives may be lost or their own welfare seriously jeopardized. Indeed, being a parent is a great risk if one is seeking specific rewards or trying to avoid tragic disappointments or losses; not all of our children will live long or successful or healthy lives. And there are many occupations, some noted above, fraught with danger; yet these responsibilities are being fulfilled by countless people throughout the world. Even on an individual level, doing what is right, or even intending it, is the pattern, despite the fact that individuals may lack the power to succeed or may be defeated in the act.

Throughout history, religious thought has been aware that if individuals live only one life, a finite one on this earth, the cosmos is filled with injustices. Some die prematurely, some suffer greatly, and some are senselessly killed whether by someone's intentions or by accident. And so it is that various religions have, each in their own way, indicated how individuals can become in death a part of the life-affirming cosmic forces, part of God or Being, and participate in the life that is eternal, without beginning or end.

In a recent book, Ronald Green, professor of religious ethics at Dartmouth College, discusses how a number of major religions make their case.[11] Religion offers reasons why we are moral, despite the apparent unreasonableness of being moral in a wide variety of individual cases. Without adopting a more than individual and finite perspective, our persistent willingness to be moral does indeed make no sense. Wilson and other biologists tend to find that meaning in being part of the human effort to survive. But if these efforts are ultimately futile, they can be regarded as both pathetic and irrational.

Although religious thought has as one of its most important functions providing cogent reasons for us to be moral, even against odds that are insurmountable for us or that appear ultimately insurmountable for anyone, some people are moral who reject religions and their reasoning about such matters. There are clearly people who insist on doing right even if and when they believe it highly probable that the cause for which they strive is a lost one. Indeed, one professor I engaged on the subject expressed his willingness to be a nuclear pacifist while thinking it highly likely that the whole species will perish soon in a nuclear war; and he would continue his efforts against nuclear war even if he knew it was coming despite all attempts to prevent it, his included. His idea is that we do what is right because it is right and need no other reason.

Kant, like Green who draws on Kant, believed that reason demanded more. Doing right takes place in a cosmos presupposing freedom, God, and immortality. Imagining it to be otherwise made no sense to Kant. After all, we are hardly free, and it is not a moral choice if choosing to do what is right has no future. I am not free to hold a job if I can never find one. If life is doomed, soon or eventually, how free are we to choose its course?

Nevertheless, people do not have to be religious believers or Kantian in order to be conscientiously moral. People have faith in the power of morality in the sense that they actually choose to do what is right. Countless people are parents; they exhibit the requisite confidence in life's continuities by being nurturant and a similar confidence in gravity by walking. This confidence need not be conscious to be exhibited in these ways. If this confidence or faith becomes conscious, as it does for Wilson and Hal, it need not issue in consciously religious belief. It does not for Wilson and Hal; they offer nonreligious, or at least nontheistic, reasons for their confidence in morality. The power of morality is simply such that it operates without conscious faith in it and without beliefs to lend it support.

Human history, however, is largely a story of giving reasons and fostering beliefs supportive of morality. Whatever the ultimate strength of beliefs that condone the killing of innocent lives, the struggle against such beliefs continues. This book is part of the struggle against killing innocent lives. Those who have read this chapter now know that my commitment to this struggle is, at least in part, driven by my gratitude for all the love, human and super-human, that spawned, nurtured, and now sustains my life and yours.

But whether or not you, the reader, regard yourself as in any sense possessed of religious belief, I have endeavored to make a case for the kind of implicit confidence shared by all who strive to be moral: It is the confidence—faith—in a power at work of suffi-cient magnitude to impel us toward doing good rather than evil. And if this confidence becomes explicit, it may become the basis for a belief in the indefinite continuity of altruistic forces favoring life and the continuation of the human species; it may also induce some people to adopt worshipful attitudes toward the Power or powers favoring life. Some such power favoring life is a requisite of community and the moral bonds that make community and indi-viduals and their freedom possible.

In the chapter that follows, we will begin a discussion of how it is possible to distinguish the moral from the nonmoral and to iden-tify the requisites of community as moral bonds. This discussion of the nature and extent of our moral cognition, that is, of the cog-nitive bases we have for affirming certain moral responsibilities and rights, will extend throughout the next three chapters.

SEVEN

Moral Knowledge
Experiential Bases of Responsibilities and Rights

In chapter 5, I identified certain naturally occurring human relationships. They are relationships that are functionally and logically necessary if there are to be human agents and communities, and if there are to be freely chosen human actions, both individual and corporate. I called these relationships "moral bonds." These moral bonds include procreating, nurturing, protecting, and not killing human beings. To render actual a right to life of any given individual, the behavior creating and sustaining these bonds must be exhibited. These ways of behaving toward ourselves and other human beings are ways of being morally responsible. Unless people are willing and able to act in these ways, there will be no human agents and no freedom of human agents to be and to act. The actualization of rights to life and freedom rest on the existence of the requisite morally responsible behavior.

It may seem evident that the term *moral* applies to a responsibility to refrain from killing. Though the actual rules, customs, and laws that limit killing vary over time for a given culture, and vary as well across cultures, limits to killing are part of the moral life of every human community. But what does it mean to call certain aspects of our individual and corporate lives *moral*? How do those aspects of our individual and corporate lives designated as *moral* differ from those designated as *nonmoral* and *immoral*?

To try to answer those questions it would help if we could count on agreement that some acts of killing are morally wrong for any one and for any community and its individual members. But that is where our whole exploration of moral rights began. Although it is true that actions with the express intent of killing innocent persons are generally, perhaps universally, regarded as morally wrong, punishable actions, it is also true that contemporary national governments have defense policies that sanction attacks and threatened attacks on populated areas and hence sanction the killing of innocent defenseless individuals, such as infants. Indeed, in discussions of terrorism in the United States media, I have heard it said that "one person's terrorist is another person's freedom fighter." In the context, I took this to mean that people use the word *terrorist* to condemn their enemies by accusing them of killing innocent persons. But those who do so are themselves engaged in or lend support to terrorist acts. In short, in any conflict, the protagonists use and justify violence against innocent individuals and against their institutions and communities.

Refreshingly, Gewirth has opposed this conceptual and practical erosion of individual human rights. He has painstakingly defended the absolute right of an innocent person not to be the victim of an intentional homicidal project. This is indeed a key right. Lose it and you lose all others.

Gewirth's philosophical reasoning is impressive. This right, as well as the generic rights to well-being (including life) and to freedom are universal and necessary claims. As such, they are founded on the logical relation between our choices as agents seeking what we perceive as good and the conditions necessary for making these choices and actualizing them. But some demands of logic are not considered to be moral demands. It will still be necessary, even when moral demands are demands of logic or have the same felt necessity, to indicate why some such experiences are called *moral* rather than *logical*. Furthermore, it is not presently common to think of moral judgments as having the force of logic or of being at all within that realm. It is conventional wisdom to separate facts and values, regarding values neither as facts of logic nor as facts based on perceptions of reality: Whereas facts are objects of knowledge, values are objects of interests, preferences, and desires.

G. P. Adams traces this contemporary outlook to the assumptions contained within modern science and its rejection of medieval ways of thinking about value:

> The world of nature, life, and mind was discovered to contain an infinite wealth of facts which could no longer be pressed into the older, simple teleological framework of values and of the Good. The inevitable and fruitful result was the growth of the physical, biological, and historical sciences bent solely upon the discovery and mastery of the facts of nature and of life, a cognitive enterprise which would have been impossible had it been guided by the older traditional assumptions of the fusion of reality and value. But there resulted as well just that insistent dilemma with respect to the basis of our practical interests and our judgments of value, a dilemma which has its roots in the assumption that orderly knowledge and science deal only with matter of fact, which is *wertfrei*, stripped of all . . . value, and that the world of our practical interests and values has its roots in will—attitudes, desire, and feelings totally distinct from our cognitive apprehension of the real. On these premises values . . . belong to a dimension and realm apart from that order of facts which may be known by scientific and theoretical inquiry.[1]

Bertrand Russell, the noted twentieth-century British philosopher, shared the scientific view of the relation between facts and values depicted by Adams above. He expressed this view in his understanding of the subject matter and cognitive status of ethics:

> Ethics differs from science in the fact that its fundamental data are feelings and emotions, not percepts. This is to be understood strictly; that is to say the data are the feelings and emotions themselves, not the fact that we have them. The fact

that we have them is a scientific fact like any other and we become aware of it by perception, in the usual scientific way. But an ethical judgment does not state a fact; it states, though often in a disguised form, some hope or fear, some desire or aversion, some love or hate. It should be enunciated in the optative or imperative mood, not in the indicative.[2]

But is it correct to separate facts and values, and to do it in such a way that the data of ethics are, as Adams expresses it, "totally distinct from our cognitive apprehension of the real"? Is it possible that the uniqueness of moral phenomena may be expressed by distinguishing moral facts from nonmoral facts? I believe it is. Why?

To begin with, how is a *fact* defined? *Webster's Ninth New Collegiate Dictionary* includes the following entries: (1) "the quality of being actual"; (2) "something that has actual existence"; (3) "a piece of information presented as having objective reality"; and (4) "*in fact*: in Truth." Russell, quoted above, regards the data of ethics as factual only in the sense that persons do in fact have the feelings and emotions that constitute moral phenomena (the data of ethics). Moral (ethical) judgments, however, according to Russell, do not state facts. In other words, the feelings and emotions that make up moral experience, such as our desires or aversions, loves or hates, do not provide any basis for asserting a fact, for providing a piece of information that can be presented as having objective reality. Ethical or moral assertions are not assertions of fact but expressions of our wishes or desires or demands of others. So, for Russell, and for many others, moral experiences as such do not, like percepts, count as evidence for factual or scientific claims about what is true of our world.[3]

If our moral choices consist of or are based upon our interests or desires, there would seem to be no reason, except our own individual or collective preferences, to question actions based on national interests. The widespread resort to practices in which innocent persons are knowingly killed are expressions of national interests, or in other instances of groups seeking what they regard to be national interests, as they seek to remove or destroy an existing government or political group. Indeed, this is the situation we described at the outset of our book. I do not think this situation is intractable. The conceptual framework on which it rests, I will now argue, does not yield an accurate picture of the realm of morality nor of the cognitive status of our moral observations and evaluations. The stakes are high as I undertake to present an alternative to the widespread tendency to take our moral convictions out of the realm of knowledge. We are at a critical juncture in history, and I need not remind the reader that history is replete with tragically inhumane behavior perpetrated in the name of false beliefs. What we believe to be true and what we think we know with some certainty are what we are most likely to act upon.

I intend to argue that there are moral facts. These moral facts are, like nonmoral facts, pieces of information about reality: *moral facts are truths, identifying something that is true of reality.* Pursuing this argument will require attention, not only to the convention of dividing facts and values, but also to the convention of dividing nonmoral facts into contingent and necessary truths.

Consider the claim: "Sally's height is three feet." To call this a factual statement is not controversial. The existence of Sally may be checked by the senses and so by the kind of perceptual data commonly used to yield scientific facts and claims based on them. Height, in this case "three feet," is the type of datum science favors. Being three feet is a quality that earns the title of being "objective," that is, of belonging to objects and of being verifiable, of being observable by visual inspection of the lines on a ruler. That Sally is three feet in height is a contingent fact, that is, true by reason of observation and not logically necessary. No one has to be three feet tall at Sally's age—she is exactly three years old; it is not a deficiency or a necessary quality of someone to be exactly three feet at three years of age.

"The height of Sally is one yard" is a necessary truth that follows from the statement Sally is three feet tall; three feet equals one yard (by definition); hence, Sally is one yard tall. It would be inconsistent and contradictory to claim that Sally is three feet but not one yard tall. This is a fact of logic and of mathematics.

Let us now compare these two examples of factual assertions with what Gewirth considers to be an absolute moral claim: "All innocent persons have an absolute right not to be made the intended victims of a homicidal project."[4] Consider then this statement: "It is morally wrong intentionally to kill Sally." Assuming now that I am making this claim, you might ask me: "To what does 'morally wrong' refer? In what sense is this a moral wrong? In what sense is this *wrong*?"

The "wrong" in this instance may be called a "moral" wrong because of a failure to be responsible; a requisite of community has not been faithfully maintained. Some would prefer to say that a moral norm or principle is being violated. Intentionally killing, or even trying to kill, Sally breaks the moral bond otherwise implicitly present in the inhibition against killing. One could add also that any intentional homicidal project against Sally would violate our responsibilities to nurture and protect human life, particularly the lives of those who are by reason of age in special ways dependent on such nurture and protection.

To assert that making Sally a victim of an intentional homicidal act is morally wrong is to assert not only that certain responsibilities have not been met; it is also to assert that such a project is morally *unjustifiable*, that it is, morally *incorrect* both to carry out the project and to approve of it.

When we speak of intentions or actions as *morally* right or wrong, we make two kinds of references: (1) references to certain experienced "ought" or "ought nots," demands on us to act or not to act in certain ways; (2) references to judgments we form or make as to the reliability of given, experienced demands to inform us of what "actually" or "in fact" ought or ought not to be approved or done. Russell, as we noted earlier, focuses on the reference to experiences and identifies those with feelings, desires, or aversions and the like. But Gewirth, as we have seen, focuses on the reference to judgments and identifies these with the universal and necessary claims of logic. The truth of the matter is that we make both kinds of references in our moral assertions and evaluations. And I will not agree with either Russell or Gewirth in their characterizations of them. Gewirth, however, is closer to the view I am taking in leaning toward moral facts as necessary truths, even though they cannot be identified with facts of logic.

Moral Demands versus the Demands of Logic

Recall that for Gewirth, a right is "moral" if it is a universally necessary claim, that is, a claim logically demanding recognition from all agents: "Moral" claims are experienced as universal and necessary demands on agents to act in a certain way. They are impartial claims to objectively impartial needs. The needs met by moral claims are impartial in the sense that they are equally needs of all human agents. Furthermore, moral claims and the responses to them are only "moral" if they represent unforced or voluntary choices of human agents. Moral claims and logical claims do not differ in these respects.

Consider the logical and universal necessity of a mathematical claim. For example, given our definitions of "plus" and "equals" and our conceptions of "2" and "4," the expression "2 plus 2" *must* equal 4, we say: 4 is universally and necessarily demanded by the expression "$2 + 2 = .$" The demand or "logic" of the expression "$2 + 2 = $" is not only experienced as a universal and necessary demand for the completion "4," but this demand is not simply our own desire or interest; it is an objective, impartial demand on us and others, like a moral demand. And like a moral demand, the expression as such does not force or coerce us to act; the answer mathematically *must* be "4," but the answer we give need not be; indeed, if we do not feel like it, we may not answer the question with "$2 + 2 = $" in it. The demand for the answer may remain one of perceiving the logic of the expression and nothing more. Now, notice that the expression "$2 + 2 = $" does have all the characteristics of a moral claim as Gewirth has depicted them. His analysis, therefore, cannot be complete. A mathematical claim is not, as such, a moral claim. Taken by itself, the expression "2 + 2 = " demands "4" as its completion; we say, 4 must be the right (correct) answer. The "must be" refers to a mathematical or logical necessity. If as a freely acting agent, I simply perceive this universal, impartial necessity and note it to myself, or verbally relate this experience to someone else, what I do is not moral or immoral; it is, as such, a morally neutral act describing what I perceive and judge to be a fact, namely that 2 plus 2 equals 4.

What is missing from a nonmoral mathematical claim upon us that is present in a moral claim? It is a reference to our ideal self-image, that is, a reference to the self we aspire to be and to have others see us as being. As I have already indicated, whether or not I accept or reject what is universally and necessarily demanded by a mathematical expression such as "2 + 2 = " is a matter of choice. I am not apt to reject this demand, however, because my ideal self-image includes being logical and also includes an unwillingness to deny as logically demanded what I perceive and judge to be logically demanded. Ideally, I see myself and present myself to others as able to perceive what is true and as one who tells the truth, neither deceiving myself nor others about what I actually judge to be true. Insofar as I experience a demand on me to give the "right" mathematical answer, however, one that deceives no one, and I do so because of my conception of who I am ideally, the demand on me becomes also a moral ought, the morally right thing to do, and not only a universal and necessary demand of mathematical logic. "Four" *must* be the "right answer" is a demand of logic for the expression "2 + 2 = "; "4 is the answer I *ought* to give" is a demand flowing not only from mathematical logic but also from my thinking about the self I am and aspire to be; as the psychologist Gordon Allport has observed, "I experience 'ought' whenever I pause to relate a choice that lies before me to my ideal self image."[5]

Perhaps you, the reader, find it puzzling to speak of accepting or rejecting what is universally and necessarily demanded, especially something as simple to grasp as the answer to "2 + 2 = ," and equally puzzling may be the very idea of raising any question as to whether giving the answer "4" "squares" with my ideal self-image. It is true that the "logic" of mathematics is so compelling, and the simpler answers are so self-evident, that it does seem strange to regard the act of giving correct answers in mathematics as a matter of choice, and even stranger to regard that act as a moral "ought" or responsibility. Nevertheless, although "4" is the logical, not moral, equal of "2 + 2," responding that this is the case may be experienced as a moral, as well as, logical demand. Indeed, in one sense, whether or not I give true or logically correct answers is not only a matter of my intelligence but also of my truthfulness, trustworthiness, and identity as a morally responsible person.

Is there any empirical evidence that we are disposed to report accurately and faithfully what we regard as factually correct or true? And is there any evidence that we not only generally choose to do so but also under some circumstances choose not to do so; and in both instances that we relate those choices to our ideal self-image? Solomon Asch, a social psychologist, conducted a controlled experiment in which the task of subjects, in a series of trials, was to identify which two lines, of four presented, were equal in length.[6] The task was perceptually clear enough that subjects, individually presented with these lines, reported the correct answers 92.6 percent of the time. But when individual subjects were given this same simple series of trials in the presence of seven to nine persons of the same age group (college students) who were instructed by Asch to give some wrong answers, and to do so unanimously, the rate of correct responses offered went from 92.6 percent to 66.8 percent. Indeed, Asch discovered that among the subjects responding naïvely to the experimental trials in the presence of a group instructed to give a certain number of incorrect responses, 58 percent were definitely influenced to offer as correct some or all of these same erroneous responses. When Asch interviewed these subjects, each was aware of the contradiction between what each, at the outset, regarded as correct perceptions and appropriate reports, and what this group was sometimes unanimously reporting. This contradiction was very troubling and led each to raise questions about their own abilities, and what answer they "ought" to report. These subjects were also aware that what was at issue were perceptions of fact; that each of them and the group were oriented to and reporting about the same objectively given relations; that only one result was correct; and that the group was at certain points in unanimous opposition. Despite their perplexity and doubts about themselves, those subjects who refused to report the errors being offered by the group with which they were "paired," explicitly told Asch that they had been determined to say what they saw. Subjects who did this were also pleased to learn that they had been correct in their responses, and pleased that they had been true to their convictions. Some of those who began to give the same erroneous reports of the instructed group, once apprised of what had actually happened, did feel some guilt or regret that they capitulated and reported as correct what they believed to be incorrect. They had worried about how they would be seen by others and were not afterwards indifferent as to what kind of person the experimenter thought they were.

This experiment does provide some evidence that our ideal image of ourselves, the self we esteem, is a truth teller, not a liar. And, under less social pressure to doubt our abilities, we are prone to be truthful. Asch tested this by giving some other subjects the same experimental task in the presence of one other subject instructed to give the same erroneous responses given by groups of seven to nine in the previous experiment: Not a single naïve subject gave erroneous responses; they neither made errors nor reported any. They faithfully reported what they saw, despite their astonishment at the other person's "errors."[7] This is what they expected of themselves and this is how they wished to be seen.

That human beings are inclined toward truth telling and persist in the face of circumstances unfavorable to being truthful should not surprise us unduly. Our daily lives depend upon this requisite of individual and communal achievements. And this inclination to truth telling is rendered more predictable because it is a source of self-esteem. As Asch's experiments and our own experiences confirm, we aspire to be truthful persons and tend to feel guilty when we fall short of this ideal.

One can imagine Gewirth growing impatient by now and asking, "What is your point?" Gewirth might well mount the following argument. "I have depicted a moral claim as a necessary condition for realizing our aims as purposive agents. Certainly, if I were in one of Asch's experiments I would seek faithfully to say what I see because this is the 'right' claimed by the experimenter; it would be inconsistent of me to deny him that right when faithful communication of facts is a necessary condition of my purposive behavior as it is of his. Is there really any reason to incorporate something like an 'ideal self-image' into our understanding of this moral demand on me to observe Asch's right to honest responses? If you want to say that I make an implicit assumption that being consistent is a vital ideal for every self striving to be moral, go ahead. Being logical is a morally neutral, universally necessary demand and it serves as the objective and impersonal criterion by which to judge rights claims. MacIntyre thinks no one has successfully provided such a criterion. Well, I have done it!"

It is true that the experiments by Asch and our own experience exhibit, as we noted earlier, a strong tendency within us to ascertain what is correct and to report this faithfully. And this strong tendency extends to being consistently correct and honest about communicating what is correct. But, the demand of the nonmoral facts, as in the case of which two lines of four are equal, and the demands of mathematical logic, as in "2 + 2 = 4," are not identical with the demands to be factually and logically accurate and to be truthful. These latter two demands, unlike the demands of nonmoral facts and logic, are demands to be a certain kind of person: (1) a person who is motivated neither to deceive nor to be deceived; and (2) a person who possesses and cultivates the abilities necessary to overcome obstacles both to discovering what is true and to telling the truth.

Reflect again on the experiment in which persons are to judge which two of four lines are equal. Confronted by an opposing group of seven to nine persons unanimously reporting erroneous answers, some people keep on seeing and saying what is true. But some people do not. In most instances, these people saw what was factually correct, but decided to report as correct what they believed was incorrect. They gave at least two reasons: They began to doubt their abilities, and they began to worry about how they would be viewed by the opposing group. Confidence in one's abilities can be lost so that in the given situation, those abilities do not function. A few persons in this situation did virtually lose their ability to perceive correctly, thinking that some of the erroneous responses that brought them into agreement with the group instructed to make errors were not erroneous but correct. Also, the concern about how they would be seen by the group giving erroneous responses led some to lose their motivation to be truthful, or at least led them to be insufficiently motivated to be truthful and hence, knowingly make false statements about what they perceived.

And so I am saying to Gewirth: that our perceptions of what is a moral right and our moral decisions to respect human rights, such as the right not to be deceived, are based, in part, on the image we have and hope others will have of ourselves; and that the universal and necessary demands of nonmoral facts and logic are, in this respect, to be distinguished from moral demands.

The failure to distinguish the demand-quality of nonmoral facts from the demand to be factual, that is to be faithful in the seeing and/or relaying of facts, is of great consequence. Cheating in science illustrates this rather dramatically. When a scientist manufactures data he or she is neither sufficiently influenced by the demand-quality of nonmoral facts nor by the demand-quality of the rights of others not to be deceived. The right not to be deceived should be quite obvious, particularly when the fraudulent research is federally funded and concerns cancer treatment, as it has![8] Science as an enterprise is not morally neutral.

At a college in the Boston area, I spoke on cheating in science.

Afterwards, I was challenged to respond to the observation that persons vary with regard to their tendencies to be truthful, coming as they do from various backgrounds. The commentator asked me to acknowledge that science, like other activities, would involve a certain amount of dishonesty. In reply, I did not argue against the proposition that people differ in the strength of their dispositions to be honest. Since it is not only the discovery of what is truth that constitutes science, however, but also the faithful sharing of discoveries and how they are made, those who are unfaithful in conveying what they discover are as unqualified to be scientists as those who are unable or unwilling to make discoveries.

But what qualities of intellect and emotional sensitivity will help a person become a "good scientist," that is, a person with the perception and will to do what is right? Are these qualities simply drawn from the contingencies of biological inheritance and environmental shaping? Gewirth understandably seeks to avoid such contingencies by grounding the universal, necessary, and objective or impartial character of moral judgments in logical judgments consistently made. As we noted in chapter 4, however, the claim that under some circumstances, it is possible to take one's life and harm no one other than oneself is "logical" for Gewirth, but this logic is contingent upon a particular view of the self in its relations to others. One may seek to be detached spatially, socially, and emotionally from all other persons, but does one ever succeed? Not if, as I contended in chapter 5, each of us is bound to one another by natural and "moral bonds," and these not only make communities possible but our lives and our freedom to act as well.

The quarrel I have with Gewirth cannot be resolved simply by an appeal to our abilities and propensities to be logical and consistent, though these qualities are relevant. Moral perceptions and judgments involve a whole range of shared sensitivities and abilities. To discover the relevant conditions for perceiving and judging what is morally right is an open-ended process and takes place in changing historical and cultural conditions. What is at stake here is of enormous significance.

Black civil rights leaders in the United States realized that not only whites but also African Americans had to develop positive emotions about being black. The will and the ability to see equality as a right depends in part on seeing oneself and feeling oneself to be no less a self than others. Women struggling for equality also seek to raise consciousness, their own as well as those of men, about who they are as women and what potentials of theirs are as yet less than fully acknowledged and given space to develop in our communities. What each of us will acknowledge as rights and as moral claims will depend, in part, on who we envision ourselves and others to be and to be capable of becoming. In turn, these perceptions and conceptions of selfhood will depend, in part, on who we are and on the forces that shape us: our gender, our racial or ethnic identity, our families, and our communities. And our function and standing in them will, in various ways and to various degrees, be among these forces. That moral knowledge partly depends on such factors should not surprise us. We have just noted above that people may err in making simple judgments about the length of lines and may falsely report what they correctly see when they interact with a sufficient number of people who make these same false statements.

This last observation has important implications. The conditions for knowing something include not only the data to be perceived and judged but also certain characteristics of the perceivers and the context, social and otherwise, in which the necessary perceptions are being made. In simple judgments regarding the length of lines that clearly appear to be equal, we do not usually think about our judgments as based on anything but the actual appearance of the two lines. When confronted by a group of persons who differ with our judgments, however, we become aware that the claim to know that the two lines are equal is also a claim that other people, otherwise of normal eyesight, in similar light, at a similar distance, and so on, will see what we see and judge as we judge. Indeed, as in Asch's experiment, when one person differs from us, we do tend to think that something is wrong with that person, since the environment is otherwise similar; when several persons differ with us, we may shift our focus from the datum—what we perceive—to what kind of perceivers we are, a clear indication that both considerations are critical to knowing whether the lines are truly equal, or simply appear that way to us.

Again, Gewirth may be growing impatient, perhaps even astonished, that I am not distinguishing contingent truths from those that are necessary. That "4" equals "2 + 2" is necessarily true; that two of four lines are equal is contingently true—it could be otherwise. Furthermore, the concern with observers, and the conditions for making observations, applies to perceptions of the length of lines. After all, appearances may be deceiving and any subject in Asch's experiments is reasonably led to question what appears to them to be equal when a whole group directly reports otherwise. But that "2 + 2" equals "4" is not subject to the influences of observers on the observed; equality here is a logically necessary relation of the numbers as expressed and defined; necessity characterizes that relationship, independently of anyone perceiving or reporting it. Moral claims are not based on perceptual data; rather they are based on necessary truths. This is Gewirth's position and I suspect he may not, as yet, be persuaded to relinquish it.

But Gewirth is following a convention that I think should be rejected, or at least significantly modified. How do we know that "2 + 2" equals "4"? I think certain observations by the English moral philosopher W. D. Ross are very helpful in reflecting on this.

Ross, like Gewirth, rejects perceptions as the basis of our moral knowledge. Rather, the data of ethics are our moral convictions.[9] Some of our moral convictions are self-evident. If we ask how they come to be self-evident, the answer for Ross is that they come to be so just as mathematical axioms do:

We find by experience this couple of matches and that couple make four matches, that this couple of balls on a wire and that couple make four balls: and by reflection on these and similar discoveries we come to see that it is of the nature of two and two to make four.[10]

Similarly, Ross argues, we see rightness as belonging to the nature of promise keeping, after apprehending the self-evident rightness of individual acts of promise keeping and reaching sufficient maturity to generalize from these particular experiences of rightness.

Notice that the "felt necessity" that "2 + 2" equals "4" is something that is built up over time and based upon certain human abilities that need to develop and mature. Ross is calling our attention to the phenomenon of counting. Even more basic than counting is the fact that our environment is experienced as differentiated into figure-ground relations, such that certain figures, objects, or units are separated within the total perceptual field we are able to observe or imagine. If our perceived world were undifferentiated, we would not see individual units or objects and there would be nothing to count. What necessity would attach to "2 + 2" making "4," if we could not even imagine such concepts, in a world in which no discrete units and no counting ever occurred? Mathematics is indeed genuinely abstract and its extraction from its experiential basis in reality fools us into talking about it in ways that do not presuppose our actual world and our actual perceptions of it. But numbers would be as fanciful as unicorns in a world that would never be perceptually unitized and would never be susceptible to counting.

Inadvertently, Ross has uncovered the perceptual basis of what he otherwise regards as a self-evident conviction of reason. Perceptual experience is composed of a great range and variety of relations observed and/or felt to be necessary. The experience of a necessary relationship may arise in all three kinds of factual judgments about Sally mentioned above: those based on observations of height, logical deductions, and moral evaluations. Gestalt psychologists have described these experiences of necessary relationships.

They refer to these as experiences of requiredness that arise within our perceptual world.

Moral Demands as Felt Necessities

In dealing with cases of specific perceptual organization or gestalt, Gestalt psychologists have distinguished the following major traits, conspicuous in all such cases:

> Phenomenally the world... exhibits definite segregated units or contexts in all degrees of complexity, articulation, and clearness. Secondly, such units show properties belonging to them as contexts or systems. Again, the parts of such units or contexts exhibit dependent properties in the sense that, given the place of a part in the context, its dependent properties are determined by this position.... A melody is such a context. If it is in *a*-minor, for instance, minor is a property belonging to the system, not to any note as such. In this system, the note *a* has the dependent trait of being the tonic with its static quality.[11]

Among the dependent properties of perceptually organized contexts is requiredness. Requiredness is a consequential attribute, a quality of some gestalt that results from the manner in which the parts of the gestalt in question stand in relation to one another. The notes of a melody, for example, fit together in such a way that a given note will be heard as a "right" or "wrong" part of the melody; a certain note is heard as a right or wrong part of a harmonic. Melodies and harmonics form a context for requiredness such that specific tones sound acceptable or unacceptable as completions of the auditory context formed.

Köhler offers the following summary of the essential features of requiredness: (1) It takes place *within* a definite perceptually organized *context*. In instances where such a context is itself experienced as required, that context is then being cognized as a part of a larger context into which it does or does not fit. (2) Requiredness is a *dependent* quality of a perceptually organized context and does not occur in the perceptual world apart from entities that are seen to fit or not to fit each other within a given context. (3) Like all other kinds of reference, requiredness exhibits *transcendence* insofar as it is experienced in the form of a vector directed from certain segments of its context to other segments of that same context. (4) Requiredness has a *demanding* character. This demand-quality is experienced as the acceptance or rejection of one "thing" by another "thing" or by a configuration of other "things." That which is accepted or rejected *fits* or *fails to fit* given conditions as experienced in the perceptual world. Furthermore, this demanding character has degrees of intensity.

This demand-quality or requiredness is a very common perceptual experience. Gestalt psychologists have noted our tendencies to smooth out curves so the lines of curves are continuous, to straighten pictures on the wall, to close curved lines we perceive as circles with gaps to be filled, and the like. These tendencies toward "good continuation" and "closure" have been expressed as the Gestalt principle of "prägnanz," which states that percepts always tend toward as "good a figure" as the circumstances, that is, the stimulus pattern, will permit.[12] Experiences of a demand toward completion of percepts that are in violation of "good form," or have not yet attained them, have been experimentally demonstrated. It was found that incomplete tasks are remembered better than tasks considered to be complete; a gap-induced tension toward closure was interpreted as the explanation.[13] These experienced tensions toward completion are the data on which the "necessary truths" of logic and mathematics rely for their confirmation. Facts, such as the height of Sally, are also confirmed by obtaining data that yield the perception that the distance from the top surface of Sally's head to the surface on which she stands "fits" exactly with the distance of all the points on a ruler that add up to three feet. In such matters of logic and observations of height, we expect others to see these facts as we do.

What about the claim that it is wrong to kill Sally? How might this demand not to kill be experienced? Normally, it is an inhibition that is dormant. It could be aroused, however, in a situation where we saw someone about to push Sally off a bridge above a swiftly flowing stream. This is where we would expect that everyone, ourselves included, would experience a demand to act to prevent this, provided of course that this was perceived as possible and not so risky as to be suicidal. If Sally is our child, we may experience a demand to intervene even at great risk to ourselves, whereas a stranger may feel a similar demand only if little risk is involved. There would, for example, be little risk to someone who is a big and strong adult if the individual pushing Sally is a small and weak child.

This seemingly simple example of moral requiredness illustrates the complex character of moral facts. The felt necessities attaching to a three-year-old like Sally interact with the kinds of relations obtaining between the perceivers and the perceived. Nevertheless, this is not unique to moral requiredness. All experiences of requiredness have this quality to a greater or less degree. The fact that Sally is three feet tall will be unavailable to persons who are not old enough, disciplined enough, or sufficiently motivated. Although measurements used in a laboratory or a clinic can be made by any sufficiently normal and mature person, there are individuals who have to be fired from such jobs for making too many mistakes. Logic, with its universal necessities, still is not uniformly experienced by all, and as the "necessities" become more refined and complex, only logicians work to discover and communicate what they perceive as universal and necessary relations.

But moral demands do differ from logical demands. As we already saw from our earlier discussion of the differences, what is perceived as morally required is in the context of a demand on us as agents to act or make judgments.[14] What is seen as required is not simply a relation in which some number or entity is seen as completed by some other number or entity, as in the perceived requirements of "4" as a completion of "2 + 2 =." Furthermore, what will be experienced as morally required is experienced in a perceptual context that includes the self and the self in relation to oneself and others. In a quick act to rescue Sally at the very moment she is about to be pushed, there may be no awareness of the self-image that would emerge either if we later contemplated the act or if the circumstances permitted time to reflect on why we ought or ought not to try to rescue Sally, as might be the case if an individual is threatening to push Sally from the bridge, and at the same time, has a gun pointed at us. If, for example, we have been trained in an appropriate martial art, it may occur to us, even if only in a flash, that we and others may regard it as cowardly or uncaring or both if we do not employ obvious skills in which we have excelled but never before used in "real life." And, if Sally is our daughter, our anticipation of shame or guilt at failing to act may be heightened or we may act so quickly that no such awareness has time to arise. Moreover, our love for Sally and our desire to be perceived as loving would almost certainly surface in later reflections or conversations about our responses to Sally's would-be killer.

Notice how moral requiredness attaches to a relation that is both interpersonal and intrapersonal, the self in relation to others and in relation to itself. As we shall see, however, moral demands are not located only in oneself and another person or persons being immediately experienced. We shall come to that in a moment. Notice also that the arousal and perception of a moral demand to rescue Sally entails certain emotional capacities and propensities such as caring whether individuals live and caring that particular individuals live. The intensity of a capacity and propensity to care may vary. They will be stronger in relationships involving parental love, marital love, other forms of friendships, or care that has been explicitly promised; the experienced moral requiredness to act in accord with such bonds will be correspondingly a more strongly felt "necessity."

The psychologist Fritz Heider has provided a very careful analysis of the perceptual experiences of ought and value within his study of the psychology of interpersonal relations.[15] He has noted, as we have: "There may be many occasions in which the person may experience the tension of incompleteness in the situation, without at the same time experiencing the tension of an ought."[16] A person, for example, may be aware that they desire *X*, view the situation as incomplete in that their wish is unrealized, and yet sense no obligation to seek *X* or even sense that they *ought not* to have it. Again turning to interpersonal relations, a person may recognize that someone else wants *X* but unlike the case in which this other person stands in need of rescue, filling in the perceived gap by satisfying the other person's longing does not necessarily coincide with what is seen to be morally required.

To distinguish the experiences of "ought" from other species of genuine requiredness, Heider depicts the perception of ought as the perception of "a vector that is like a wish or a demand or a requirement on the part of some suprapersonal order and that has the validity of objective existence." Such a suprapersonal order is objective in the sense that its demands have interpersonal validity and people generally concur in its demands. This suprapersonal order "may also be experienced as a supernatural being who personifies this objective order."[17] Heider readily acknowledges that when persons have the conviction that some other person or group of persons wants them to do *X*, such persons also recognize a vector in the environment and feel that the desire of the other person or group is objectively existent. But under those circumstances, the desire originates from, or is located in, only part of the environment, that is, the part consisting of some other person or group, and no ought is generated by it unless we see it as a fitting or unfitting part of the whole suprapersonal objective order as it exists in our perceptual world. To specify further what he means by a "suprapersonal objective order," Heider characterizes the wish of that order as impersonal. Heider regards such wishes as impersonal in the sense that they appear to issue from standards independent of our own wishes, or the wishes of others, whether individuals or groups. Heider quotes Asch with approval when he says, "We distinguish between personal preferences or aversions and right and wrong. It is one thing to desire an object and quite another to have the experience of should."[18]

Although it is true that as Sally's parent I may not wish to tangle with some strong or armed person threatening to kill Sally, I will undoubtedly experience a demand on me to do something to try to prevent her death, if even only to plead for her life and warn the would-be assailant of the bad consequences of killing someone. There may be no other actions remotely feasible. Furthermore, I might even wish I could be free of any felt requiredness to do anything that risks my own life. In these ways, actions I ought to try may be independent of certain desires to avoid them. But this independence is not total as Heider and Asch imply. When I choose to intervene, despite my desire not to do so, I am then in some sense asserting a personal preference, and in some sense intervening is acting in accord with a personal wish. And this wish to intervene, once decided and acted upon, is, or becomes, a wish not to allow any contrary wishes to prevent such intervention. Thus, what is morally required, when chosen and/or acted upon, does express personal wishes or preferences. But what is morally required is never *just* a personal wish or a preference; what ought to be moral is not *just* any of our personal desires or preferences. Clearly, we are depicting a desire to kill Sally as morally wrong, as a wish that does not square with the wish Heider tells us to expect from the "suprapersonal objective order." Calling the wish that Sally not be killed "impersonal" or independent of personal preference does not sufficiently clarify the special character of an ought, although it does point to the inadequacy of viewing the moral data *solely* as personal desires, and *solely* as personal preferences and aversions, and as nothing more. Oughts are not merely personal wishes or preferences, but they are not impersonal demands like those of logic either.

But Heider has provided two clues to the special nature of moral demands that differentiate them from the necessities of logic and other perceived necessities providing data for factual claims: First, that moral demands are experienced as requirements of the *whole* objective order, that is, of all that exists; second, that moral demands are sometimes experienced as a wish or demand of a supernatural being that *personifies* the whole objective order. If, then, we think of moral demands we choose to act on as moral preferences, they are clearly not only personal preferences and requirements of our own: The whole world, including all of its people and peoples, potentially or actually share or favor these preferences; a supernatural being, a being of much greater power, knowledge, and merit than human beings, yet having some personlike characteristics, shares or favors these preferences. In our perception that we ought to try to rescue Sally, whatever we may otherwise prefer doing, the weighty wishes of all humanity or of a mighty self even more powerful and knowledgeable than all humanity, either courses through us almost automatically, or comes to our awareness; and we will, either in anticipation or upon later reflection, judge what we believed was demanded of us, and what we chose to do, by reference to what we perceive humanity, and/or a supernatural being, wished or would have wished us to do; or we may refer not so much to all of humanity or a supernatural being but to some ideal self we aspire to be, given our propensities and capacities. This comparison of the self we are and the self we could or should be is not incompatible with comparing ourselves with our humanity and/or with a supernatural self.

Gap-induced moral requiredness then is experienced within a perceptual field of intrapersonal and interpersonal relations. When I feel responsible (morally required) to rescue Sally, I as a self am relating to Sally, to her would-be assailant, and to some more generalized self representing all of humanity, and/or representing the superior power, knowledge, and dispositions of a deity, and/or representing my ideal self.

There are numerous conceptions of a generalized or ideal self as an element in moral perception and our inner deliberations over

what is morally right or wrong. Kant speaks of the business of conscience transacted "as if at the command of *another* person . . . this
other may be an actual or a merely ideal person which reason
frames to itself."[19] Adam Smith describes as an actual, empirical
disposition that we judge our actions with "the eyes of other
people or as other people are likely to view them. . . . We endeavor
to examine our own conduct as we imagine any other fair and impartial spectator would examine it."[20] Westermarck regards as "in-
separable from the judgment that we pass on our own conduct . . . the image of an impartial outsider who acts as our judge."[21]
G. H. Mead suggests a similar phenomenon with his notion of a
"generalized other."[22]

It is important to emphasize that these references to ideal selfhood as "impartial" and as "spectators" are in certain ways misleading. They do express important aspects of experienced moral
demands: These demands are not only demands on us; they are not
merely personal; they do not, if accurate, reflect only our own personal preferences. But the notion of a spectator, if it suggests that
our moral perceptions are to be judged from a totally detached perspective, loses sight of the involvement of will and of emotional
sensitivities that are requisite for experiencing, making, and validating moral decisions. Similarly, "impartiality" as a concept may
lead people away from these same elements in moral experience.
Furthermore, attaining interpersonal validity requires an ideal process that is, in fact, interpersonal. "Impartiality," in the sense of
correcting distortions of the truth, is needed in gathering knowledge; but, as I shall argue in the next two chapters, impartiality
cannot be attained by glossing over differences in perspective, such
as those that may be linked with gender, race, and social location.
Nor can impartiality be attained by a detached perspective devoid
of our emotions.

H. Richard Niebuhr is a theologian who has suggested an inclusive community as one of the ways to characterize the perceived
source of our moral responsibilities. Like the Gestalt psychologists, he describes moral demands as a species of fittingness, informing us of our responsibilities. In one passage he depicts the

moral fittingness or gap-induced requiredness of the moral life as "a life of response to actions which is always qualified by our interpretation of these actions as taking place in a *universe* and by further understanding that there will be a response to our actions by representatives of universal community."[23] Niebuhr does not believe that this aspect of moral experience is something to which theists like himself are uniquely attuned. He contends that the very structure of the moral demand is such that nontheists and theists alike will, in the conscientious pursuit of a responsible way of life, "interpret all events and their reactions as occurrences in universe."[24] And this universe will be representing to us, as human beings, a universal community. For Niebuhr, a universal community is one inclusive of the total community of being and beings. This is Heider's "suprapersonal objective order," but with people in it—all people.

That we as human beings judge our actions by seeing how they fit into the whole universe is not a speculative or merely introspective hypothesis. This same experiential element as described by Niebuhr is evident in psychiatrist Robert Jay Lifton's study of Vietnam veterans.[25] The Vietnam veterans in question were experiencing profound psychological disturbances, including enormous guilt precisely over their involvement in situations where innocent civilians were killed, including children. As a survivor of My Lai portrays it:

> Here in Vietnam they're actually shooting people for no reason. . . . Any other time you think, it's such an extreme. Here you can . . . shoot them for nothing . . . it's even smiled upon.

> Good for you. Everything is backwards. That's part of the kind of unreality of the thing. . . . Something [at My Lai] was missing . . . that made it seem like it really wasn't happening.[26]

Lifton mentions two recurring images present in the struggle of these veterans with their guilt, some over having killed innocent persons, some over having been unable to stop such killing: The first was that their transgressions caused "a wound in the order of being"; the second was "an image of a world beyond the transgression itself." This image of a world beyond meant to these veterans that in order "to transcend the conditions of the transgressions (the atrocity producing situation) one had to open oneself up to the larger 'order of being' one had injured."[27] In fact, these veterans spoke of psychiatrists and chaplains who sought to assuage their guilt over the killing of innocent civilians—including children—as representing to them a "counterfeit universe," the title of chapter 6 of Lifton's book. They had an intense anger for those chaplains and psychiatrists who "blessed" what they called murders and atrocities.

Even in the midst of war, the deep inhibitions surfaced not to kill or fail to rescue anyone innocent of wrongdoing or threat of harm, like Sally in the example we have pursued in this chapter. What needs to be explained, as we turn to our next chapter, are: (1) the conditions under which some at the level of policy, some at the level of practice, though scarred by it, are able to justify the killing of innocent individuals; and (2) the processes requisite to creating the conditions in which such policies and practices may be persuasively called into question.

In summary, then, how far have we come in our quest for moral data on which to base judgments as to what is, in truth, moral or immoral, moral or nonmoral? We have observed that felt necessities are experienced in sensory perceptions, such as those of determining height; in perceptions of logical relations, such as those between precisely defined expressions containing numbers; and in perceptions of what is moral. Factual claims in all three of these instances are based on those felt necessities as data. Also, in all three instances, it is the expectation that any person, under specific conditions, should be able to have the experiences on which to make the relevant factual claims. These experiences of necessity are often, for this reason, described as objective and universal. Many, though not all, felt necessities in corroborating sensory observations, like pointer readings and logical relations, command a fairly high degree of consensus—almost universally at simpler levels and almost universally among experts at more complex levels. Felt necessities in the moral sphere vary enough that it is possible to deny that moral demands are experienced as required of us and as data for judgments of what is in fact the case. One source of variation is probably a unique feature of what is a moral demand, as contrasted with demands that are nonmoral; I refer to the intrapersonal and interpersonal character of the relational context in which moral demands arise. When I decide that it is right to prevent someone from killing three-year-old Sally, I either anticipate or later profess that this demand is not only the one I would or did prefer, but it is the preference of a self and community of selves having the power, knowledge, and disposition to perceive the preference that in fact is morally right. The characteristics of such a self and community of selves will occupy our attention in chapters 8 and 9 following. There too we will examine the cognitive place and the significance of emotions or feelings. After all, I have been using the language of "felt necessities" even in the realms of sensory perception and logic. That requires some explanation.

Some readers may be suspicious by now of this effort to specify characteristics of "ideal selves," whether "observers" or "participants" or whatever. If you have to do this, you must be leaving the realm of knowledge, someone might argue. I will later join that argument. I do want to say one word, however, about the importance of making a case for the possibility of attaining some degree of knowledge that some choices are right and some choices are wrong, and for the possibility of seeing moral demands as more weighty than purely individual, personal desires. All knowledge in all the sciences depends upon fidelity to the truth as perceived, as judged, and as communicated. No claims have interpersonal validity unless they are based not only on nonmoral facts, sensory and logical, but also on successful efforts by those who collect those data and make the claims, to avoid deceiving themselves and deceiving others. If the demand to avoid these deceptions is a personal preference of no more discernible weight than other personal preferences, a person trained to be a scientist could have a whole set of preferences that would be satisfied by falsifying data: advancing to a higher rank, higher pay, greater prestige—and all at a faster rate. It has been done. Were such behavior to be the norm, science would be a name for an unachievable ideal. Being moral is an absolute requisite of any knowledge whatsoever. Need I add that lives depend on knowledge and its moral requisites.

EIGHT

Moral Knowledge
Loving Impartiality

In the previous chapter, we depicted moral demands as a species of gap-induced fittingness or requiredness. Perceptual experiences of requiredness are very common occurrences, illustrations of which include: observations, such as those needed to verify a person's height; logical inferences, such as the equality of "2 + 2 = " and "4"; moral responsibilities, such as trying to prevent the killing of an innocent three-year-old child.

So clear and certain do we often regard these particular kinds of felt necessities to be that we treat them as self-evident facts. Often when we do that, we also make no conscious distinction between the perceived necessities that serve as evidence for our belief in their facticity and the assumptions, or assertions, of their facticity. Nevertheless, all felt necessities, whether obtained by visual inspection, logical inference, or feelings of responsibility, may be inaccurate or illusory and, hence, claims based on them factually false. Our concern in this chapter and the next is to investigate and clarify what conditions are requisite for experiencing a felt necessity as a moral demand and for checking the veracity of what we perceive as morally demanded. It will be the case that these same conditions provide reasons for asserting that what we perceive as morally required is in fact morally required. It will also be the case that these same conditions will help explain why people's moral perceptions can and do differ, and why uncertainty about the veracity of some of our particular moral judgments is a reasonable expectation. At the same time, the premise being defended in this and the next chapter is that perceptions of moral demands do, under some conditions, yield knowledge of the moral responsibilities on which the expectations and claims of human rights are realistically to be based.

In chapter 7, I cited and developed the observation of the psychologist Gordon Allport that a demand is experienced as moral when we relate a choice before us to our "ideal self-image."[1] I also took note of a number of moral philosophers who described the kind of self necessary for perceiving and verifying what is moral as an "ideal" or "impartial" spectator or observer.[2] In this chapter, I wish to begin with a discussion of an ideal observer theory delineated by the late Roderick Firth of Harvard.[3] Firth's ideal observer theory is the most complete and precise one of its kind, and it is compatible with the psychological description of the moral data presented in chapter 7.

Although Firth's theory will provide a solid beginning for understanding moral cognition, the theory as a whole will not prove to be satisfactory. At issue especially is Firth's account of impartiality. Firth's view of impartiality is very common, certainly dominant, in the philosophical literature, and he has defended that view very clearly and skillfully. The clarity of Firth's portrait of impartiality facilitates what this chapter seeks to accomplish, which is to work with but change that portrait. The reasons for the changes will emerge.

Impartiality as a Characteristic of an Ideal Observer

Firth understands impartiality as a characteristic of an ideal observer. An ideal observer, in turn, is a hypothetical being used as a device to describe what characteristics someone would have to possess for "reacting in a manner that will determine by definition whether an ethical judgment is true or false."[4] Firth's theory provides a definition of the moral terms that are used in moral assertions or judgments. According to Firth, "X is right" means "X would be approved by an ideal observer who is omniscient, omnipercipient, disinterested, dispassionate, and otherwise a normal human being."[5] These characteristics of an ideal observer, then, identify the conditions requisite for making factually true judgments of what is morally right or wrong.

In what sense is this observer, or these conditions, "ideal"? Firth uses "ideal" simply to suggest that our ideal observer is "conceivable" and has "certain characteristics to an extreme degree," in the same sense in which "we speak of a perfect vacuum or a frictionless machine as ideal things."[6] It should also be explained that Firth's use of the term *approved by* to describe the morally significant reactions of the ideal observer is not intended to rule out descriptions such as "perceives as morally required." Firth explicitly discusses that at some length.[7] How to characterize the morally significant responses of the ideal observer is a question about how to characterize "the moral data" on which our moral judgments are based and to which we refer, for example, when we doubt our moral judgments. Firth is defining moral judgments for purposes of the essay under review; for these purposes he was content to note the compatibility of his theory with differing psychological formulations of the moral data.

Readers may wonder how Firth came up with these particular conditions for veridical experiences of the moral data. Firth would ask such readers to reflect on the very processes they would use to resolve doubts about their moral judgments or resolve conflicts with others. If a moral judgment turned out to be based on incomplete knowledge, would we not have a reason to seek more knowledge or ask someone who differs with us to consider knowledge that individual is lacking? Is it not also the case that our moral judgments hinge on whether or not we have sufficiently imagined how our action we call right or wrong would affect someone? Our decision not to give any money for hunger relief can certainly be called into question by viewing actual pictures of starving individuals and of the dwindling supplies left to save those individuals.

Consider also how much more readily we would share our resources were we to experience a starving child left on our own doorstep. This is very different from reading a statistical account of how many children die of malnutrition in some region of the world on a given day so far as what moral demand that may or may not arouse in us.

It is not surprising that knowledge of nonmoral facts and vividly imagining how individuals would be affected by our actions have been widely recognized as part of the very logic of moral assertions, or of the impartial perspective characteristic of the "moral point of view."[8] But the typical view of impartiality found in Firth and so many moral philosophers does present a problem. Before I am willing to argue the case for an impartial perspective, therefore, I find it necessary to develop one I can defend. Questions about Firth's use of "omniscience" and "omnipercipience" to describe the degree of knowledge and imagination necessary for true judgments will come up in chapter 10. There, also, questions about what Firth means by "otherwise normal" will be considered. The remainder of this chapter concerns impartiality.

Impartiality for Firth has two aspects: It must be achieved in regard both to interests and passions. Impartiality is an attribute of an ideal observer insofar as such an observer is both disinterested and dispassionate. Firth makes a distinction between general and particular interests. The ideal observer is not lacking in general interests but is a being uninfluenced by particular interests. Firth very carefully distinguishes between "essentially general properties" of X and "essentially particular properties" of X:

> The properties of x which are essentially particular are those properties which cannot be defined without the use of proper names (which we may understand, for present purposes, to include egocentric particulars such as "I," "here," "now," and "this"); thus one of the essentially particular properties of x might be its tendency to increase the happiness of the citizens of the U.S.A. All other properties are essentially general;

thus one of the essentially general properties of x might be its tendency to increase happiness. We may then say that a person has a positive particular interest in x if (1) he desires x, (2) he believes that x has a certain essentially particular property P, and (3) he would not desire x, or would desire it less intensely, if, his other beliefs remaining constant, he did not believe that x had this property P.[9]

Firth believes it is important to single out the influence of emotions in addition to the influence of interests in an adequate account of what it takes to be impartial. An ideal observer, therefore, is a being that is not only disinterested but also dispassionate. Firth's understanding of dispassionateness directly parallels his understanding of disinterestedness. An ideal observer would not be devoid of general passions but would not be influenced by "particular emotions." A "particular emotion" is defined as one that is directed toward an object only because the object is thought to have one or more essentially particular properties. And we can say that an ideal observer is dispassionate in the sense of being incapable of experiencing emotions such as jealousy, self-love, personal hatred, and others that are directed towards particular individuals as such.[10] Firth is contending that all particular interests and emotions distort moral cognition. This means that the ideal form of impartiality is attained by a perspective detached from and uninfluenced by the specific affection individuals have for their particular friends and kin. Notice that self-love also is explicitly cited as an emotion that must be absent if the ideal conditions for cognition are to be actualized.

In this view, the distorting influence of all particular emotions and interests definitely encompasses the loyalties individuals exhibit toward groups, such as love for their own countries or for their own religious communities. Indeed, insofar as an individual is deeply identified with particular groups, love for such groups is, in part, the form love of self takes in that individual's life. The theologian Reinhold Niebuhr has argued that our attachments to particular groups, even more than our attachments to ourselves as individuals, undermine our abilities to perceive correctly what is right or wrong. Reinhold Niebuhr quite explicitly maintained that as members of groups relating to other groups, individuals are less well informed, less able to imagine how it is for others, less disinterested, and less dispassionate, and hence, less morally perceptive and more immoral, than they are as individuals relating to other individuals who are their near-neighbors.[11]

It is difficult to quarrel with the view that our emotional attachments to ourselves and others can and do distort moral judgments. Individuals can and do pursue desires destructive to themselves, desires that do not provide clues as to how they ought to behave toward themselves or others. And groups can and do stir up emotions that blind its members to significant facts about themselves and others. One need only think of the use of propaganda and how effective it sometimes is in skewing perceptions, moral and otherwise. But, however difficult it may be to quarrel with the view shared by Firth, Niebuhr, and many others, quarrel I must.

My contention is that emotions, self-love and love for particular groups, are essential to moral cognition and to achieving an impartial perspective. Put very simply, individuals cannot know how to behave toward themselves and others unless they have positive affection for themselves and others. And if they do not have the appropriate feelings, how will they be able vividly to imagine how it will feel to be on the receiving end of a particular action or policy? Since, however, emotions and emotional attachments distort as well as clarify moral cognition, it will be necessary to indicate how to identify conditions in which emotions and emotional attachments aid, rather than hinder, moral perception. In the process, impartiality will be defined in a way that identifies at least some of the emotions and emotional attachments necessary to its actualization within moral cognition. The present chapter will argue the case for emotions and emotional attachments within moral cognition and redefine impartiality; chapter 10 will discuss additional ideal conditions for attaining moral knowledge.

Self-Love as Necessary for Moral Cognition

Self-love has been recognized in the literature of ethics as a guide to moral cognition and behavior. One of the clearest expressions of this has come from the pen of the eighteenth-century Anglican bishop Joseph Butler.

Among the published sermons that established Butler's renown as a moral philosopher are two, sermons 11 and 12, "Upon the love of our neighbour."[12] These are both based on the biblical text Romans 13:9 (King James Version): "Thou shalt love thy neighbour as thyself." With his focus on the meaning of "as thyself," Butler explains "this precept" to "love thy neighbor" as follows:

> The precept may be understood as requiring only that we have the *same* kind of affection to our fellow creatures as to ourselves; that as every man has the principle of self-love, which disposes him to avoid misery, and consult his own happiness; so we should cultivate the affection of good-will to our neighbour, and that it should influence us to have the same kind of regard to him . . . and this will not only prevent our being injurious to him but will also put us upon promoting the good.[13]

Butler then observes that self-love is the source of our notion of "private good." The problem is that we have a tendency to exclude the good of others from our notion of private good. For this he offers us the following remedy:

> Thus, as the private affections make us in a peculiar manner sensible of humanity, justice or injustice, when exercised towards ourselves, love of our neighbour would give us the same kind of sensibility in his behalf. This would be the greatest security of our uniform obedience to that most equitable rule; *Whatever ye would that men should do unto you, do ye even so unto them.*[14]

Butler is portraying self-love as an essential ingredient in our "sensibility," our cognitive apprehension, of what is moral: Having a positive affection for ourselves helps reveal to us what is moral, what is just or unjust about actions affecting us, whether our own actions or those of others; having this same positive affection for our neighbors, for others, helps reveal what is moral, what is just or unjust about actions affecting others. Knowing how actions affect us because of the love we bear to ourselves, we have a basis for imagining how others are affected by our actions. An impartial cognitive perspective is achieved when the same love we have for ourselves is felt toward others: What is just or unjust about actions directed toward us is just or unjust about actions directed toward others. In Butler's view, it is not our emotional attachment to ourselves (self-love) as such that introduces the partiality (bias or favoritism) that distorts moral cognition. Rather, impartiality in moral cognition is thwarted when our actions toward others are not informed by the same kind of love we have for ourselves. Impartiality is not dispassionate; it is loving. Butler is well aware that individuals have desires that cannot properly be characterized as instances of a positive affection for oneself and hence such desires can conflict with, inhibit, or distort the self's empathic basis for moral cognition and an impartial perspective. This problem will occupy us later.

What needs emphasis at this point is that our empathic emotions illumine our moral perceptions. Indeed, being detached from those emotions, which as Butler puts it makes us "sensible of humanity," can lead to tragic failures in moral sensitivity and behavior.

The psychiatrist Robert Jay Lifton studied and counseled veterans of the war in Vietnam.[15] In his study, Lifton takes note of a phenomenon he calls "numbed warfare," a mode of combat in which participants have psychological contacts only with their military cohorts and their own equipment. This kind of warfare occurs when technology allows killing to take place in a hidden and distant way. High-altitude bombing is a case in point. Those in the air force who participated in bombing raids from high altitudes did not "experience the searing inner conflicts of ground troops."[16] As Lifton observes, "avoidance of guilt is built into the technology."[17] Lifton describes research that found a striking negative correlation between altitude and potential for guilt:

> B-52 pilots and crews bombing at high altitudes saw nothing of their victims and spoke exclusively of professional skill and performance; those on fighter-bomber missions had glimpses of people below and tended to have an inclination to explain or rationalize what they did; those who flew helicopter gunships saw everything and experienced the kinds of emotions we have described in ground personnel.[18]

Lifton calls these B-52 pilots "numbed warriors." What has been numbed are their empathic emotions: "Lacking emotional relations with his victims, the numbed warrior receives from them very little of the kind of feedback that could permit at least one layer of his mind to perceive them as human."[19] These numbed warriors are able to kill and mutilate people with no regard to their innocence whether by reason of age or conviction or pursuit, and to do so without emotional turmoil and guilt. The emotions that would make them "sensible of humanity" have not been aroused. They are devoid of all particular emotional ties to their victims, and without these ties, do not even imagine their victims as fellow humans.

In sharp contrast, ground troops experienced enormous inner conflicts as a result of the feelings aroused by what they saw in combat. Even those who had not knowingly killed innocent individuals felt guilty because they had not prevented such killing by others around them. They had terrible feelings about themselves. But when such veterans were able to acknowledge openly their profound feelings of guilt, they spoke of feeling "human" again. Guilt, they could see, was the morally appropriate response to being implicated in the death of innocent human beings: Guilt was evidence within them that they were, as Butler would have it, "sensible of humanity"; guilt was evidence that they had a shared human capacity for empathic emotions.

The very different experiences of high-altitude bombing crews, as compared with ground troops, illustrate the necessary roles of particular emotions within moral cognition. Having no emotional contact with their victims, bombing crews had no vivid images of their fate and of who they were; without these particular emotional ties to their victims, bombing crews did not attain an impartial perspective. In their total emotional detachment from those they killed, bombing crews did not "see" those killed as human like themselves, and the love they had for themselves was not aroused and felt toward their victims. Ground troops, however, were emotionally tied to those killed. They saw the innocence of these victims and saw what they suffered. Ground troops experienced the particular emotions that allowed them to attain an impartial perspective; they experienced the emotions that allowed them to see their victims as human like themselves. This impartial perspective enabled them to experience the wrongfulness of being implicated in the death of innocent human beings; enabled them to experience the "demand" on them to feel and acknowledge guilt as the morally correct response; and enabled them to feel positive affect for themselves.

Readers may well be asking themselves why these ground troops were not prevented, by their capacity for empathy, from killing innocent individuals. A great many were. Many of these veterans described by Lifton were feeling guilty that they did not, in some instances, prevent the deaths of noncombatants. For example, some of these veterans feeling guilty had been at My Lai. None of them obeyed Lt. Calley's order to shoot down a row of unarmed women, men, and children, some of them mere babes in the arms of their mothers. But they realized, in retrospect, that Calley could and should have been prevented from carrying out the unjust and illegal order he had issued.[20]

The arousal of the particular emotions necessary for feeling the empathy for others we are capable of feeling toward ourselves will not by itself guarantee an impartial perspective, nor the behavior that should follow from it. But Lifton's data do suggest that detachment from such emotions, or otherwise being devoid of them, make it extremely difficult, perhaps impossible, for an impartial perspective to emerge. At the very least, our particular emotional attachments to ourselves and others do have a positive role to play in moral cognition. Is that true also of the loyalties we have to groups and communities? That is the question to which we now turn.

Social Attachments and Love of Communities as Necessary for Moral Cognition

As we noted earlier, Firth regards all particular emotions, as well as all particular interests, as distortions of moral cognition. Not only self-love but all of our particular attachments block the attainment of moral knowledge and the impartial perspective essential to that attainment.

Ruth Smith, a contemporary feminist ethicist, rejects the notion of cognition she finds in moral theories that depict particular relations to ourselves and others as impediments to rational processes.[21] She decries such theories for finding objectivity in nonparticularity and in the detached perspective of an observer or spectator. In her view, moral knowledge is gained from our specific attachments, natural and historical. She is especially concerned to take issue with Reinhold Niebuhr's contention that human groups are less moral than individuals in their more private, intimate relations to others. Smith is explicit about the positive contribution of groups and communities to moral cognition and to moral development. Feminism as a movement is a "unit of consciousness raising and speaking a new self-relation to others into being."[22] Indeed, she asserts that "this group is not just an association" but "a community" of shared goals and experiences.[23]

Michael Polanyi, himself a chemist, has described science as a community of shared goals and experiences.[24] Like Smith, Polanyi sees membership in a community as a source of knowledge. In fact, Polanyi defends the view that communities are necessary for the whole process of attaining knowledge. Through a discussion of Polanyi, it will be possible to illustrate why this is so and why communities are necessary for moral knowledge as well. In assessing Polanyi, we will make use of certain of Ruth Smith's insights to illumine the ways in which communities are dependent on one another in the quest for knowledge, moral knowledge especially.

Science: A Community of Consciences

Polanyi begins his account of science by examining its relation to reality. The guesses that fuel an experiment and yield new observations depend on the clues provided by "an intuitive perception of the real structure of natural phenomena." What Polanyi is calling "intuition," I would prefer to call "felt necessities," as described in chapter 7, and emphasize that such "felt necessities" are also experienced in the kind of imagined relations that will lead to new experiences of felt necessities, confirmed as new facts. Polanyi considers the role of imaginative guesses in scientific discovery as more important than observations and experiments. There are no explicit rules by which to glean scientific propositions from observational data and none as well for deciding when to abandon a scientific proposition in the face of any new observation. What observation does is to supply clues for apprehending reality, and that process underlies scientific discovery.

Polanyi wants to make clear that he is not denying the existence of rules in science to guide verification,

> but only that there are none which can be relied on in the last resort. Take the most important rules of experimental verification: reproducibility of results; agreement between determinations made by different and independent methods; fulfillment of predictions. These are powerful criteria; but I

could give you examples in which they were fulfilled and yet the statement which they seemed to confirm later turned out to be false.[25]

"The rules of science cannot be codified," according to Polanyi; rather, "they are embodied in practice alone."[26] Scientists are of two minds in the process of discovery: One part of their minds bubble with new, imaginative claims; another part opposes them. Science could rely too much on intuitive speculations, reaching to wish-fulfillments; or too much on rules, reaching to the paralysis of discovery. This conflict between "intuitive speculation" and "critical rules" requires "a judicial decision by a third party standing above the contestants." That third party transcending impulse and caution within a scientist's mind is a "scientific conscience." Scientists take personal responsibility for their ultimate claims. This, says Polanyi, "indicates the presence of a moral element in the foundations of science."[27]

How then is this scientific conscience formed, and of what is it composed? How, in short, does one become a scientist? This requires exposure to the premises of science. These include general assumptions about our common experiences, constituting a "naturalistic" outlook, as contrasted with one that is magical; and more particular assumptions that ground processes of scientific discovery and verification.

The naturalistic view held by modern scientists now is introduced in their primary education. There are roughly three stages in the contemporary teaching of science's premises: school science imparts scientific terms, revealing thereby established doctrine; the university opens up possible implications of established doctrine and imparts intimations of scientific judgment through some exposure to scientific practices; the personal association with a distinguished practitioner by those sufficiently gifted provides a full initiation into the premises of science. This apprenticeship provides a simplified repetition of the discoveries that have established the science in question. Throughout this process, the soundness of scientific doctrine and method are presumed and their ultimate premises unquestionably accepted. Polanyi regards this whole process of becoming and being a scientist as an instance of what forbearers of the Christian church called "faith in search of understanding." The place of faith in moral cognition has already been suggested in chapter 6 and will be pursued further.

In discussing apprenticeship, Polanyi is aware that he has touched upon one of the institutionalized structures within science as a community for fostering its practices and premises. There is a whole domain administered by scientists.

First, there are periodicals. Scientists serve as referees and editors, excluding from publication whatever is considered unsound or irrelevant. Once published, each article receives further scrutiny and reactions. What gains acceptance is still further evaluated for incorporation into textbooks and/or standard books of reference. With this seal of approval, a discovery is taught at schools and universities and disseminated to the public at large.

Second, there are scientific posts. These are mainly at universities and other endowed institutions with their extensive facilities, salaries, and increasing independence for senior scientists. Authority and its influence in obtaining grants, choosing personnel, and advising government and other donors about the money needed for research, as well as public policy, is hierarchical. Exceptional authority, however, attaches more to persons than offices. Influence largely goes to those whose opinions are valued and sought.

This "government," Polanyi says, "is indispensable to the continued existence of science."[28] By such governance the qualifications of teachers and researchers are assured. Cranks, plodders, self-deceivers, and those prone to deception for the sake of honor or advancement are essentially screened out of the publications and posts.

Polanyi considers unanimity to be another major characteristic of science as a community. The origin of coherence among scientists, manifest even in its conflicts over what is scientifically valid, valuable, and interesting, lies in its common tradition. The teacher-student apprentice system is an important part of that. But this relationship and all relationships among scientists require an ultimate arbiter. This arbiter is scientific conscience. Such a conscience is comprised of loyalty to the ideals of science, which can then function critically and in independence from all efforts merely to conform to scientific opinion, or otherwise please other scientists.

It is very important to clarify the kind of authority exerted by a tradition. The authority of science, based as it is on a community of consciences, demands freedom. Scientific tradition is subject to constant reinterpretation. Polanyi compares the scientist's relation to scientific tradition to the Protestant's relation to Christian scripture; scripture serves as a creative tradition because it is constantly reinterpreted in new situations by individual consciences. Conscience can be used to oppose scripture where it is found to be spiritually weak, yet without renouncing its general authority. In short, says Polanyi, both science and Protestantism nurture processes of creative renewal based on "an appeal from a tradition as it is to a tradition as it *ought to be*."[29] In other words, conscience is informed both by devotion to a specific community and by its devotion to ideals for that community.

Now we are at a critical juncture in Polanyi's account of science, particularly of its moral element. Devotion to the traditions of science—its methods and premises—is necessary but not sufficient to gain and support an effort that requires mutual cooperation; devotion to an ideal community is also required. If Polanyi is to argue successfully that cognition in science depends, in part, on moral judgments, the ideal community for cognition within the scientific community will have to include the ideal conditions for moral cognition as well. What ideals does Polanyi recognize and espouse for informing scientific consciences?

Polanyi is aware that the ideal conditions for cognition within science cannot be actualized in isolation from the existing conditions within the particular societies to which particular scientific communities belong. Of necessity then, ideals requisite for communities more inclusive than those of science are essential to achieving and sustaining the cognitive gains of the scientific community. In exploring this, Polanyi considers national societies. The nub of the relationship between scientific communities and their national affiliations is, for Polanyi, found by examining the conditions necessary for free discussions, a sine qua non both of science and of democratic societies.

Polanyi identifies two conditions as essential for the existence of free discussion: (1) commitments to fairness and tolerance; and (2) institutions that shelter free discussion. By fairness he means making an effort at laying out the whole of one's position to an opponent, including known biases and limitations, at the same time acknowledging true points in the position of an opponent. By tolerance he means a capacity to listen to an opponent's unfair and hostile statement, looking for any sound points as well as sources of error. Note that Polanyi does not describe the basis of free discussion as demands or claims one participant makes on another but rather as responsibilities in our relations to one another.

As for the institutions that sustain free discussion, Polanyi cites examples in Britain, such as its Houses of Parliament; courts of law; churches; press, theater, and radio; the local governments; and many private committees of diverse organizations. Custom and law enforce the rules of fairness and tolerance found throughout these bodies. Again, Polanyi does not use the language of claims and demands but of responsible and legally enforced freedom of opinion and participation in social structures. Relative to those modern rights theories that stress individual claims on our neighbors and freedom from interference, Polanyi instead stresses individual and communal responsibilities to be fair to and tolerant of one another. Indeed, the actualization of such attitudes and behavior, and of a free society, presupposes specific commitments. Instead of depicting free discussion as a right of individuals and groups, he ferrets out the requisites for its realization and sustenance.

Those who are willing to argue, and to do so fairly and tolerantly, presuppose a disposition towards truth in others such as they find in themselves. More specifically, Polanyi sums up the requisites of this kind of free discussion:

> A community which effectively practices free discussion is therefore, dedicated to the fourfold proposition (1) that there is such a thing as truth; (2) that all members love it; (3) that they feel obliged and (4) are in fact capable of pursuing it.[30]

Polanyi does not claim that the communities behaving in accord with love of truth and confidence in the love of truth of their fellow citizens do so in theory; rather, they do so in practice. This love of truth and confidence that others share it are embodied in free discussion as premises of its practice. Free societies have traditions and institutions in which these premises, and the free discussion embodying them, are practiced and taught. Confidence that the truth exists is, for Polanyi, a faith: it is a faith that is being expressed when we "accord validity to science—or to any other of the great domains of the mind"; it is "a faith which can be upheld only within a community."[31]

Since this faith on which science depends requires democratic societies for its nurture, Polanyi is understandably deeply concerned about what it is that undermines democratic societies and institutions. Although skepticism and false theories may in theory deny the premises of science, the practices in which they are deeply embedded have so far survived.

Polanyi regards false doctrines of liberty as serious threats to science as well as democracy. Both the Nazi and Marxist movements are, for Polanyi, examples of such threats, denying as they did the reality of equity and reason. But these movements did not and could not succeed on the basis of their false views but rather on the basis of hidden spiritual resources. How does Polanyi argue that? Logically it is false to deny the existence of truth since that assertion could only be true if truth exists. But truth, as well as justice and charity and the aspiration to attain them, are imperishable realities. What happens when these ideals are said to have no reality, whereas the interests and power of particular groups are considered real, is that the aspiration for truth, justice, and love are attached to the struggle of a particular party for power: ultimate reliance and all love and devotion are attached to the power of the chosen party.[32] From this analysis, Polanyi derives a theory of totalitarian government.[33]

Although every society requires competent forces to resolve disputes, it is possible to leave a great deal for individual consciences to decide,

> if the citizens are dedicated to certain transcendent obligations and particularly to such general ideals as truth, justice, charity, and these are embodied in the tradition of the community to which allegiance is maintained.[34]

Polanyi does not believe that totalitarianism is inevitable. In fact, it has, in his view, "never been fully established in any place; as in fact no society could continue to exist for one day if the radical denial of spiritual reality were actually put into effect."[35] People can live only what Polanyi calls "an intellectually and morally acceptable life" in a society dedicated to truth, justice, and charity. And, he suggests, the whole purpose of society lies in enabling its members to pursue these transcendent obligations to truth, justice, and charity. The burden of his whole book is to show that the pursuit of any major intellectual process requires such a society. Otherwise, it fails.

In the last paragraph of his book, Polanyi expresses his belief that societies that rest on free consciences fulfilling their purposes and adding to our spiritual heritage are thereby "in continuous communication with the...source...of their society-forming knowledge of abiding things." Polanyi does not wish to conjecture as to how near that source is to God, but "knowledge of reality and the acceptance of obligations that guide our consciences, once firmly realized, will reveal to us God.[36]

Love of Community: A Preliminary Analysis

I wish now to assess what Polanyi has contributed to an understanding of the ideal conditions for moral cognition. First of all, Polanyi has done something very significant. His description of science provides a living example of a particular group, represented throughout the world, that pursues truth and can only do so as a community. Scientists constitute a community characterized by (1) a common tradition; (2) a common purpose; (3) an apprentice system of education; and (4) a network of publications, appointments, and research, all subject to peer review and well-represented in societally supported educational and research institutions. As noted earlier, Ruth Smith complained that there was generally insufficient recognition of the positive cognitive contribution of particular groups and membership in them. Polanyi has not only acknowledged that a particular group contributes to our knowledge of truth but has argued that the pursuit of truth requires embodiment in a community with established institutional arrangements and a common tradition. The scientific community, its organizational structures, and its achievements constitute additional strong evidence that loyal membership in a particular group is not necessarily a bar to discovering truth; indeed, under properly defined conditions, it is indispensable to discovering truth.

Polanyi has shed some light on "conditions indispensable to discovering truth." Distinguishing truth from falsity requires "a community of consciences." Science and any other serious intellectual pursuit of truth cannot be successfully carried on and sustained without making explicitly moral judgments based on specific and transcendent ideals by which consciences are guided. The rules that are embodied in scientific traditions inevitably clash with new perceptions or "intuitions," Polanyi's term. Resolutions of these conflicts are moral decisions, that is, decisions made by the individual consciences of scientists. Conscience is the devotion to transcendent ideals that make such decisions possible. Science constitutes a whole community of consciences.

The successful pursuit of truth requires freedom for individual consciences and the freedom to carry on fair and tolerant discussions. Such freedom can be found only in democratic societies with their many institutional means of protecting and fostering free discussion: and democratic societies, like the scientific community, can only exist and function if its members believe in and love the ideals of truth, justice, and charity. Discovering truth and distinguishing it from falsity is, then, a communal process, and the moral requisites of community are requisites of this cognitive process.

Polanyi has articulated not only the necessity of particular communities but also the necessity of moral ideals for validating our perceptions of reality. This means that the possibility of knowledge is dependent, logically and functionally, on the possibility of moral knowledge. He has argued for the logical and functional necessity of certain moral ideals. And these ideals, when functioning in a democratic setting, correct the distorting influence that would result from mere loyalty to the communal traditions; loyalty to transcendent ideals moves traditions as they are toward traditions as they ought to be.

But what corrects our grasp of these ideals? Polanyi is aware of the distorting influence of denying that these ideals can ever be known. Polanyi is correct about the need for "faith" in these ideals; the need for that "faith," what I describe as confidence and its essential content, was described in chapter 6. But totalitarianism and the justification of violence do not occur only because of the skepticism and false theories described by Polanyi. Ideals not only become attached to parties seeking power; they are also often attached to nations seeking power, including democracies like England, to justify overstepping internationally recognized protection of innocent individuals. Furthermore, just as scientific communities require a communal context in which citizens are devoted to democratic ideals, so, too, democratic societies require a larger communal context in which the specific traditions shaping these ideals, and their attachment to specific groups and nations, come under corrective scrutiny. In other words, Polanyi has argued for an ideal community, national democracies, for seeking knowledge in general; he has not argued the case explicitly for an ideal community seeking knowledge of the ideals essential to democracy. Nor has he identified what particular communities might assist us in gaining such knowledge.

Polanyi has, perhaps, intended an answer in the stress he puts upon creating those communal conditions embodying the requisite ideals—requisites of community—that permit the sovereignty of individual consciences to discuss and judge freely the validity of our cognitive apprehensions of reality. I have no quarrel with that answer as far as it goes. It presupposes, however, what cannot be taken for granted, namely, that the ideal conditions for validating moral decisions are assured by the very conditions that encourage freedom of individual consciences. That is indeed a necessary condition for knowledge generally and hence for moral knowledge as well. But moral knowledge demands its specific communal context; communities that shape consciences require corrective conditions beyond those discussed by Polanyi. Consider the fact that Polanyi is devoted to free, fair, and tolerant discussion within the scientific community and within the civic communities in which science is housed. Consider also that the ideals presupposed by such discussion are truth, justice, and charity. Then consider that Polanyi does not mention the possibility that there are individuals talented enough to be full participants in science, but they are almost totally unrepresented, certainly underrepresented in the scientific community. I speak of women, blacks, and other minorities. The question I have is this: What would have helped to sensitize Polanyi to a situation that does not sufficiently actualize free, fair, and tolerant discussions or the ideals presupposed by them?

Someone may be thinking by now that it is unfair to raise this issue with Polanyi. After all, he cannot deal with everything in his little book. That is true enough. And, furthermore, he did not have the benefit of the current level of consciousness in the women's movement. That is true also. Now if we agree that he would have a more expanded, more correct understanding of fairness and tolerance in scientific and public discussion if he had been experiencing the heightened consciousness of the women's movement (and other civil rights movements), then we have found a beginning clue to the larger communal context for consciences missing in Polanyi's ground-breaking book.

Taking the women's movement as an initial clue to some pieces missing in Polanyi's picture, recall that Ruth Smith, cited above, referred to the feminist movement as a community: it is a unit for consciousness raising. Indeed, the book in which Smith's essay occurs bears an astutely apt title: *Women's Consciousness, Women's Conscience.* Clearly, Smith is thinking of feminism as an international movement, critical of all traditions, cultures, and nations that would ignore or repress freedom of the consciences of women. Furthermore, the specific experiences of women, in their diversity and commonality, are to help form and shape consciences, and these in turn aspire to new societal structures for women and for societies.

What is happening in all of this? First of all, an international community of women drawing upon their perceptions of reality is a more inclusive community than that of science or a democratic nation. And, from this perspective of greater inclusiveness, societies with democratic traditions have in the past, as well as in the present, been greatly altered toward fuller participation of its members. Those who experience exclusion from a particular political act, like voting, or a particular vocation, like being a scientist, are certainly in a position to be aware of not only the fact of exclusion but also its unfairness. Those excluded are also in a position to ferret out the false theories of sexual differences behind such exclusion, as well as to jog the complacency of those who are favored by traditions as they are. Parallel observations could be made with respect to black civil rights movements in the United States, exposing exclusions and moving the society toward greater racial inclusiveness in its domestic and foreign policies.[37] Because of their particular experiences and love for their particular group, these consciousness-raising communities can embody and illumine the moral demands of truth, justice, and love. Attachment to their particular communities is a requisite for increasing moral understanding, on the part of their own members and on the part of other groups as well.

Polanyi recognized that the pursuit of truth in science required the embodiment of truth in a particular community dedicated to that pursuit and loved by its members. He recognized also that this community requires illumination from the ideals of truth, justice, and love. What he did not explicitly recognize is that the knowledge of these ideals requires their own embodiment in particular communities dedicated to their pursuit. It is not disembodied ideals that illumine science as a community of consciences. Rather, it is particular communities seeking to know what these ideals demand of any community. A scientific claim is not accepted as knowledge until it is confirmed within a specific communal context. The same is true for moral claims.

As in the case of self-love, love of particular communities is necessary for attaining moral knowledge. Again, as in the case of self-love, positive affections for particular groups can serve as impediments to an impartial perspective. Indeed, as noted previously, Firth, Reinhold Niebuhr, and many others simply regard such particular emotions and loyalties as partial and, by definition, as cognitively distorting. But since self-love and love of community are necessary bases for moral insight, the task is to indicate how their distorting influences can be reduced and their illuminating influence enhanced. That is the task with which the next part of this chapter begins.

Self-Love and Loving Impartiality

Recall our discussion of Bishop Butler's concept of self-love and its relation to moral cognition. Self-love is the source of our knowledge of what actions directed toward us are perceived as just or unjust, that is, as right or wrong. An impartial perspective is achieved when the same empathic love we have for ourselves is felt toward our neighbors, toward all other human beings. That is an expression of what I am calling "loving impartiality." And as Butler observes, it is the attainment of that perspective that makes it possible to comply with the Golden Rule.

The Golden Rule, based on self-love, is, I would contend, one of the significant ways in which the quest for impartial moral knowledge has been acknowledged and expressed. It is intended to give guidance to those who are seeking to know and to do what is morally right and to know and avoid doing what is morally wrong. It is found in some version within all known religious traditions; however, how the Golden Rule is characterized is not a matter of indifference.

Gewirth is among those who have recognized the intended cogency of the Golden Rule for ethics, and he has sought to state it in such a way that its cogency is secured. He takes up this task by noting certain ambiguities in the account of the Golden Rule found in the Gospel of Matthew: "Do unto others as you would have them do unto you."[38] He notes that the Greek word *thelete* (translated "would have") has a very general desiderative sense. For Gewirth this means that what agents wish for themselves may not accord with how recipients might wish to be treated. He cites Bernard Shaw's famous quip, "Do not do unto others as you would they should do unto you. Their tastes may not be the same."[39] He cites as well Henry Sidgwick's observation, "One might wish for another's cooperation in sin and be willing to reciprocate it."[40]

Gewirth concludes quite correctly, "If the Golden Rule is to be saved, then, its criterion of rightness must be separated from the contingency and potential arbitrariness that attaches to desires taken without qualification."⁴¹ Gewirth's solution is to limit the Golden Rule to *rational* desires for oneself and others, and to use rational in a morally neutral, strictly logical sense.

To argue for a "Rational Golden Rule," Gewirth draws upon his Principle of Generic Consistency with which the reader is by now familiar: Freedom and well-being are generic rights; they are necessary, generic conditions of our purposive activity. It is contradictory to deny that one has such rights. To do so is to affirm, on the one hand, that freedom and well-being are necessary goods as the conditions of my acting for the sake of any other goods, and on the other hand, that people may be permitted to stop me from having these necessary goods. To be rationally consistent, then, agents must "Act in accord with the generic rights of your recipients as well as of yourself."⁴² Because, logically, every person who is a purposive agent has these same rights and to deny any purposive agent these rights is to deny them for oneself as a purposive agent. The Golden Rule, as Gewirth has formulated it, is a call for rational consistency, the content of which is a demand that each agent refrain from coercing and harming other persons and "preserve a rationally grounded mutuality or equality between his generic rights and those of his recipients."⁴³

In spelling out the content of the right to well-being enjoined in the Golden Rule, Gewirth includes the following prohibitions: interference with basic goods through killing and physical assault (except in self-defense), lying, stealing, and promise breaking. These are prohibited because they diminish one's level of purpose fulfillment, those of children, for example.

We can see from this that Gewirth affirms, albeit in his own language, a number of the requisites of community and that portion of the Mosaic Covenant (the Second Table of the Law) summarized as love of neighbor within Jewish and Christian traditions. But Gewirth's concept of the self as agent is not morally neutral, and the supreme value he puts on being free from interference and human attachments undermines self-love and love of neighbor alike. Indeed, he has no explicit concept of self-love and love of others and does not appear to see them as necessary for impartiality, though he does see impartiality as a necessary aspect of moral cognition. Gewirth, however, cannot claim to have a consistent notion of impartiality. Persons have an absolute right not to be an innocent victim of an intentional homicidal project. Yet the self committing suicide is immune from this absolute prohibition, provided that the self in question is so detached from others that no other individual would presumably be harmed by such an act. Thus, in Gewirth's notion of impartiality, it is not violated by wishing oneself dead and friendless. This is certainly not a morally neutral view of how impartiality is achieved and maintained. It is a view that contradicts impartiality in the form of positive regard for all human beings. And, it is equal love of all particular human beings that maintains the moral bonds requisite for community and for individual human agency, both for agents to be and for them to attain their purposes.

As noted in chapter 4, Kant perceived clearly the contradiction involved in using one's freedom to destroy, by a voluntary act, what is necessary for that freedom, but he also perceived clearly that persons ready to die at their own hands undermine an important basis for decent behavior toward others. He saw the clear link between self-love and love toward others.

Aristotle saw this same link in the relations characteristic of friendship: friendly relations with our neighbors and the defining qualities of friendships are knowable and attainable because of the relations persons have to themselves.[44] That good we desire and do for ourselves, we do also for our friends. And that wish we have to exist and live, we wish for our friends. Aristotle identifies mothers as exemplary in this respect. Friends also grieve and rejoice with one another: Aristotle cites mothers as exemplary in this respect as well.

These relations that persons have to themselves and to their friends are characteristic of a good or virtuous person, so far as Aristotle is concerned.[45] They are forms of love we have to ourselves and to a friend. As Aristotle says of love, it is "ideally a sort of excess of friendship."[46] And this love is the kind of emotion exhibited by parents, particularly mothers, for their children. Our wish that someone else exist and live is what mothers wish in wishing to have and nurture children, and it is what we wish for ourselves and others if we love ourselves and others. Grieving and rejoicing with others is what mothers do with their children and what we do if we love ourselves and others.

Gewirth not only has failed to see the cognitive role of love for ourselves and others, particularly wishing ourselves and others to exist and come into existence, but also would have us regard it as rational to pursue extinction and friendlessness as goals. By contrast, Aristotle has made love of our own lives one of the bases for knowing how to behave toward ourselves and others. If we were to ask Aristotle how we could know whether our behavior to another is moral, he could point to the kind of parental love a mother expresses in yearning to have and sustain a child, and to see that child live a long, healthy life.[47] And he could remind us that we surely know that others wish to exist; that, for example, they do not wish to be killed by us. How do we *know*? We know that if we love ourselves, we do not want to be killed either.

But Gewirth and others might object strenuously at this point: "You are making our knowledge of right and wrong contingent on whether we love ourselves, and whether we love ourselves in a particular way." To this it is necessary to reply: No more than you do, Gewirth. The love of self that gives you the knowledge of what to do about suicide is the wish for yourself and others to be in control and free of interference from others; the freedom you wish for yourself, you wish for others. Of course, some might say that it is not self-love but self-hatred and hatred of others that is often expressed in a voluntary suicide. Be that as it may, our particular feelings about ourselves and others are part of what we draw upon to determine what we "ought" to do. The question for you, Gewirth, as well as for me, is not whether self-love is essential to impartiality but rather in which of its expressions does self-love help us to achieve impartiality?

Reflect again on Aristotle's reference to parental love. Surely parental love is the opposite of impartiality. Is not my love for my own child such that I might in a wide range of circumstances give my child favored treatment over others? That is indeed true, and in some circumstances morally justifiable. But what if the love I have for all human beings, including myself, were to be informed by the kind of love I have for my own child, or that parents generally have for their children? That expression and use of parental love, a wish that all live and a sympathy for how they feel, could be deemed impartial.

Firth might well ask whether self-love in the special sense that I am using it is a particular, that is, a self-referential emotion. After all, the love for the self of which I am speaking is an instance of love for *every self* and includes *my self*. That is a point I will not dispute. I have however, incorporated the concept of love into what it means to be impartial in our moral perceptions and judgments. Firth has rejected the notion that love is required in any specification of the ideal conditions for moral cognition. Clearly Firth and I are at odds in that regard. I am interpreting self-love, when it takes on certain concerns for oneself and others as exhibited by caring parents for their children, as one source of moral knowledge. It is this kind of self-love that makes sense out of the Golden Rule and saves it from the potential flaws of any rule that would unqualifiedly base what we wish for others on whatever we wish for ourselves. That could entail wishing them ill, even wishing them death.

Gewirth's discussion of the version of the Golden Rule found in Matthew paid no attention to the context in which the rule is stated. The Golden Rule as stated in both the Gospels of Matthew and Luke occurs within the context of the Sermon on the Mount and an affirmation of the law and the prophets. One important theme in this context is that of loving every individual, friend and foe alike. The model for such love is God as a parent to every human being. This is clearest in Matthew's account (7:7–12). At this point in the sermon, the audience is being invited to ask things of

God and to expect to receive them (Matt. 7:7–8). Then the Golden Rule is put into its context of divine and human parenthood as follows:

> Is there anyone among you who, if your child asks for bread, will give a stone? Or if the child asks for a fish, will give a snake? If you then, who are evil, know how to give good gifts to your children, how much more will your Father in heaven give good things to those who ask him! In everything do to others as you would have them do to you; for this is the law and the prophets. (Matt 7:9–12; NRSV)[48]

Matthew links the Golden Rule to the law and the prophets. (The "law" includes what I call the moral requisites of community.) The knowledge of how we are to behave in accord with the law and prophets is knowledge we have about how parents ought to behave toward their children. Furthermore, Matthew portrays God as our parent and us as children of God who, as parents ourselves, "know" what we can expect from our more perfectly loving parent when we ask for things. We know what is good; hence we know what to wish for ourselves from others and what it is they wish from us. The examples given of the good things that loving parents know enough to give their children are foods, namely, bread and fish: the focus is on what is requisite for life. At the core, then, of what we wish from others and for others are those things requisite for life. Moreover, parental love symbolizes not only the love that will nourish life but also bring it into being. In this scripture, human beings are seen as having the same parent, the author of life itself. God as that parent wishes every human being to have life and, even more than human parents, those things necessary to life.

The reader should note that it is only certain qualities of love characteristic of parental love that assist us in clarifying the ideal conditions for moral cognition. It is not the actual parent-child relation on the whole that provides a model. That relation includes many special factors, such as those associated with the dependency of the child on the one hand, and particular kinds of authority and legal obligations for parents on the other. Indeed, the moral responsibilities of parents to their children are illuminated and guided by the very qualities of love to which Aristotle and Matthew have pointed; those qualities are both empirically anticipated to be present to some degree and regarded as ideals to be attained. I mention ideals in this context because child abuse is a reality and it is defined, in part, by using as standards what are the otherwise normal or typical expressions of parental love now under discussion and which I will now summarize.

Drawing upon Aristotle and the context for the Golden Rule in Matthew, the first morally instructive things we know from or about parental love is that it is life giving and life sustaining. Without parental love there would be no continuation and development of human agents and communities. Self-love instructed by this parental emotion takes the form of wishing oneself and others to exist and live.

Another thing we know from or about parental love is that it is empathic. Parental love can be intensely willing and able to perceive and share times of grief and joy. Self-love instructed by this parental emotion is willing and able vividly to imagine and anticipate how the self and others will be affected by a particular action.

The Golden Rule, then, can serve as a guide to moral cognition if it calls upon moral agents to be loving in these two ways, with the same kind of love for others they have for themselves. This is loving and impartial—loving impartiality—in the sense that I love others with the same love I have for myself. The ideal of moral cognition is an impartial perspective that is all-loving. In other words, complete or perfect knowledge depends upon loving all particular individuals, regarding them as equally worthy of love. Buddhism includes the idea of brotherly and sisterly love, without distinction, and kindness to members of the animal kingdom. And when perfection is sought ("Bodhisattva"), it is a quest for enlightenment that culminates in a combination of wisdom and compassion. Kenneth K. Inada states this reality in a perfected being as follows:

> An all-knowing person must necessarily be an all-loving person, and an all-loving person must necessarily be an all-knowing person. This fact shows that intelligence and practice ideally must coincide at all times . . . an intelligent act is not only intensive but also extensive . . . it goes beyond individualist (limited) designs. In fact, the act . . . must always be open for the involvement of others.[49]

In this characterization of an ideal or perfected self as a condition for moral knowledge, the ability to love all creatures is viewed as necessary to all knowledge. Loving impartiality is the perfection of our capacity to know; however, loving impartiality is not attained by oneself but with the involvement of others. We shall come back to that point later.

Charles Reynolds has formulated an "Ideal Participant" theory of moral cognition that he regards as a Christian version of the connection between being an all-loving and all-knowing person: God is a transcendent person who is both all-loving and "omniscient with respect to all relevant facts."[50] To show how love more concretely guides our knowledge of what is right, Reynolds draws upon what parents and future parents wish for their own children and what those who do not have children wish for the children of their friends. Based on the transcultural empirical research of Tamara Dembo, the most common wishes are for "health," "economic security," "knowledge" or "intelligence," and "happy marriage" (or "loving and being loved").[51] Reynolds regards these as the sorts of things individuals naturally wish for those they love. They are clues to what God loves and to the content of that love. These wishes presuppose a wish for the continued existence of these children.

Clearly individuals can and do exhibit the kinds of emotions characteristic of parents, expressed in the wish that the self and others exist and in the empathic sharing of the grief and joy of others. Loving all in these ways, the self included, is loving impartiality. Is there evidence of direct appeals to such emotions in the context of trying to correct moral perceptions and judgments?

Consider a rather poignant and powerful example. The events described in this example took place at the time the United States was at war in Vietnam and was bombing Laos. I ask the reader to compare the response of the USAID refugee relief chief in Cambodia with those of two Laotian refugee-survivors of the bombing of villages in Laos. The official says:

> Sure, some of the villages get bombed, there's no other way to fight a war out here. . . . All refugees talk about the bombing. They don't like [it]. But even if you found an example in which it was proven conclusively that houses were bombed, so what?

The two Laotian refugee-survivors say:

> The village woman was a person of good character. . . . She died in the middle of the forest by the cow she tended . . . in misfortune with unsurpassed sadness. : . . The airplanes truly killed the people at a time when they knew nothing about what was going on. . . . When you see this, how do you feel about your own brothers and sisters and relatives? Would you not be angry and concerned? Compare our hearts with yours.

> In the year 1967, my village built shelters in the forest . . . holes . . . to which we could flee. But there were two brothers who went out to cut wood in the forest. The airplanes shot them and both brothers died. Their mother and father had just these two sons and were in the same hole with me. I think with much pity about this old father and mother who were like crazy people because their children had died.[52]

Notice that both Laotians are very emotionally aroused and sad at the deaths they witnessed and could not prevent; notice also their clear expectations that parental, sisterly, and brotherly love do and will evoke emotions of deep regret at the death of any human being, whether American or Laotian. The one Laotian directly seeks to move anyone implicated in these killings, and any future such killing, to imagine that actual and potential victims are brothers and sisters and relatives; he expects that imagining oneself thus related to someone does not allow one to kill or condone killing them; he expects also that the love we bear brothers, sisters, and kinfolk is appropriately applied to all other innocent persons—Laotians included. In short, these Laotians both exhibit and try to elicit in those who will listen the loving impartiality that embraces all persons in a universal community with the love we have for ourselves, for our own lives, and for the lives of those we love dearly.

These Laotians were able to perceive how wrong it is to kill harmless people, threatening no one, because their capacity for impartial love was vividly awakened; they were vividly imagining the loss of the victims and the grief their deaths cause and should cause for all who know of them. But the USAID official is so emotionally distanced from these victims that he does not even recognize the moral facts expressed by refugees with whom he seems to have conversed. When he speaks of refugees who "talk about the bombing," he asserts only that "they don't like it." The refugees I quoted do not simply dislike the bombings; they have an intense dislike or aversion to the bombings that they believe is shared or should be shared by every decent human being who can imagine their children, brothers, or sisters as the victims; they believe that this aversion will stop any decent human being from dropping bombs on innocent human beings. Unless and until the USAID official sees any loss of Laotian lives as he would the loss in similar circumstances of his own life and of persons he dearly loves, he is not experiencing these bombings as the Laotians are. With respect to the morality of these bombing raids, he is quite removed from two of the ideal conditions for distinguishing right from wrong: namely loving impartiality, and what loving impartiality illumines, namely a vivid imagination of what is happening to the people being bombed. And, he is not grieving with those who grieve.

But something else is at work. The USAID official evinces a loyalty to a national cause being pursued through war, and what he regards as necessary to win that war has his endorsement. In the bombing of Laotian villages, he sanctions actions he would condemn in his local police force. He may wish others to exist and he may be capable of empathy, but love of country thwarts him from loving all in these ways.

And so we revisit that vexing reality of our times: though a soldier can be tried for crimes against humanity for killing a single unarmed citizen of any state, friendly or hostile, nations employ conventional weapons and target atomic weapons that knowingly kill or will kill these same unarmed persons. Nations sanction what at the level of individual behavior is murder or premeditated murder, as the case may be. Is this inevitable? Is loving impartiality an ideal for individuals but not for nations? Is love for one's nation and one's fellow citizens always and necessarily a distortion of loving impartiality?

But these questions raised about nations are questions, as noted earlier in this chapter, that have been raised regarding all of our attachments to particular groups. It is not enough to discuss our attachments to ourselves insofar as the self is connected to communities through those parental kinds of emotions that unite us in empathy and connect us to the requisites of community in the support of spawning, nurturing, and protecting human lives. Self-love of this kind is a necessary ingredient for actualizing loving impartiality. But we are connected to others and to communities in ways that require a fuller, richer description of the emotions that inform loving impartiality. Human beings are members of various human associations. Among these are nations to be sure, and also more local political jurisdictions. But the variety of human associations goes far beyond explicitly governmental groupings: religious, cultural, professional, political, educational, recreational, charitable, economic, and ethnic associations and institutions abound, especially in democratic countries. The self has many loyalties or "loves." To love oneself is to love the many associations to which that self is loyal and with which that self is identified.

So far, self-love has been examined as to its affirmation of individual human life and its capacity for empathy with other human beings. Loving impartiality cannot be attained without these. Now it is necessary to examine the love each self bears to particular groups and to see how those emotional attachments can contribute to loving impartiality. We know that these attachments can stand in the way of achieving loving impartiality. But we know also, in discussing Polanyi earlier, that moral insight can come from consciousness-raising groups.

Loving impartiality, described as an all-loving self, describes an ideal orientation or relation of the self to others such that all human beings belong to one inclusive community. Loving impartiality, described as love for community, describes that all-inclusive community in its ideal relations to less than inclusive communities.

We turn now to consider the relation of love for communities to loving impartiality.

Love of Communities and Loving Impartiality

The idea that the ideal of a more inclusive community is a corrective for distorted moral cognition is not new. H. R. Niebuhr contends that theists and nontheists alike will, in pursuing a responsible way of life, "interpret all events and their reactions as occurrences in universe."[53] And he depicts this universe as a universal community inclusive of all beings and being.

Recall that portion of Robert Jay Lifton's study of Vietnam veterans, mentioned in chapter 7 which describes this very experience of interpreting one's action as taking place in the whole universe of being.[54] The Vietnam veterans in question were experiencing profound psychological disturbances, including enormous guilt over their involvement in situations in which innocent civilians were killed. Lifton mentions two recurring images present in the struggle of these veterans with their guilt. The first was that their transgressions caused "a wound in the order of being"; the second was an image of "a world beyond the transgression itself." This image of a world beyond meant to these veterans that in order "to transcend the conditions of the transgressions (the atrocity-producing situation) one had to open oneself up to the larger 'order of being' one had injured."[55] In fact, these veterans spoke of psychiatrists and chaplains who sought to assuage their guilt over the killing of innocent civilians—including aged individuals and children—as representing to them a "counterfeit universe." They were angry at those chaplains and psychiatrists because these veterans experienced their guilt as enabling them to feel human again.

A universal community made up of all of humanity receives explicit recognition in the laws of land warfare: Intentionally killing an innocent, unarmed individual is a crime against humanity. Nations are not the last court of appeal for judging what is just and unjust and what rights should be deemed universal. The concept of a universal human community is embodied as well in the United Nations, finding expression in its charter and in its universal declarations of human rights. An "all-loving" perspective toward human beings as human beings is by no means confined to the Christian and Buddhist examples noted above.

What we have found, then, is that the positive, all-embracing regard for human beings as "companions in being" is experienced in moral reflection, enacted into international law, and institutionalized on a global scale. What may not be so evident is that these examples all describe perceptions and concepts that were not attained by individuals working in isolation: the veterans were engaged in group therapy or rap sessions; the laws of land warfare involved the efforts of many in concert, and the same may be said of the published works of the United Nations. These groups are examples, again, however imperfect, of the ideal Inada describes above: to achieve knowledge an act designed to do that must be open to the involvement of others. To be all-loving means also that one has positive regard, not only for the lives, well-being, and freedom of all individuals and groups but also for their perceptions and knowledge. Stating this same point in a somewhat different way, to be all-loving means that all individuals and groups are recognized as having the potential to serve as representatives of that universal community—that inclusive human community already in each of us but yet to be realized.

But so far I am still describing loving impartiality as a particular kind of perspective informed by a positive affect for all human beings as companions in being and as sources of moral instruction and correction, whether as individuals or communities. I have described loving impartiality as an ideal to which communities, as well as individuals, have expressed loyalty. But is not loyalty to an all-inclusive community precisely at odds with loyalty to any particular community, any of which is less than all-inclusive? Am I not, after all, forced to agree with Roderick Firth and Reinhold Niebuhr that attachments to particular communities, even those, perhaps especially those, aspiring to represent the universal community of humankind, are partial rather than impartial?

Loyalty to particular communities, whatever their professed ideals, cannot by itself constitute loving impartiality; nor can any particular community be anything more than a partial, imperfect representative of an all-inclusive community. Is it possible, then, for loyalty to a particular community also to be loyalty to all of humankind?

I will argue that the following ideal social conditions are expressions of loving impartiality, permitting love of particular communities to be also love for the whole human community: (1) actualization of the moral requisites of community; (2) freedom of association; (3) institutionalized loyal opposition; (4) universal support for intentional moral communities.

1. Actualization of the Moral Requisites of Community

As the reader will recall from chapter 5 certain inhibitions and proclivities are logically and functionally necessary for there to be human agents and communities. To some it may seem paradoxical to identify moral behavior as an ideal condition for knowing what is moral. Someone may well wonder how what is moral can be actualized unless, and until, what is moral is known. But that quandary arises only if it were true that everything identifiably moral results, or has resulted, from human reflection and decision making. That, however, is not true. I can act in ways that only later are perceived to be moral or immoral by me or by others. More to the point, however, is the fact that there are certain naturally occurring inhibitions and proclivities that we can discover to be moral only because they are already occurring. And equally important is the fact that these inhibitions and proclivities are required for making discoveries of any kind. The discovery of truth is contingent upon the love of truth and truth telling itself, truth telling to oneself and to others.

In a sense, it should not be necessary to state such obvious points were it not the case that the nature of these functions of morality and their existence as natural phenomena are covered over by our current tendencies to exclude all that is moral from the realm of the factual. I have previously indicated in chapter 7 how this is done and why I take it to be a distortion of reality.

Ideally, these moral requisites of community would be perfectly and completely actualized in any community of which it could truthfully be said that its institutions embodied and exhibited the loving impartiality requisite to knowing right from wrong. In fact, of course, we are not acquainted with any such known community. That fact does make it difficult to attain knowledge of what is moral. The fact that individuals engaged in scholarly endeavors, including scientific endeavors, can and do cheat is a simple example of rendering difficult the pursuit of knowledge. Inequalities of power, among individuals and groups, is a more complicated example of how institutionalized impartiality is rendered difficult to achieve within a community. This will be discussed more fully below.

It should be observed that the actualization of the moral requisites of community is a practical description of loving impartiality as a social reality characterizing an institution, community, or nation. Actualizing the moral requisites of community is necessary but not sufficient for actualizing loving impartiality. Freedom of association is also necessary.

2. Freedom of Association

As we have mentioned again above, Polanyi invokes democratic institutions and societies as essential for the discovery and accumulation of knowledge and for sorting out what is true from what is false. He was led to this, at least in part, by his observations of how totalitarian governments not only suppress truth but also distort it and perpetrate falsehoods. But he does not tell us how such ideals are to be sustained and how false views of them are to be corrected. He does not identify explicitly those conditions on which moral knowledge depends. Freedom of association is one of those conditions.

The most powerful case for freedom of association known to me is one made by the religious and social ethicist James Luther Adams, presently professor emeritus at Harvard. Adams has made a lifetime study of what made the rise of Hitler and Nazism possible in Germany. A key thing that Hitler did after seizing power was

to abolish, or attempt to abolish, all organizations that would not submit to control. The middle organizations—for example, the universities, the churches, and voluntary associations—were so lacking in political concern that they created a space into which a powerful charismatic leader could march with his Brown Shirts. . . . This toboggan slide into totalitarianism was accelerated by the compliance of governmental structures, provincial and local, including the secondary school system. Considering this broad range of compliance,

> we may define the totalitarian society as one lacking effective mediating structures that protect the self-determination of individuals and groups.[56]

Adams then observes that in the absence of effective mediating structures, Nazism had the power to cause worldwide suffering and death, including the holocaust. Adams is not indulging in over- simplification, however, for he notes as well the horrors wrought by democracies, despite freedom of association within them—horrors such as Dresden, Hiroshima, and Nagasaki. I view such behavior as a reminder, if a reminder is needed, that societies do not fully actualize the moral requisites of community and that freedom of association, however necessary for moral insight, does not suffice by itself to achieve such insight and actions in accord with it. I will take up the bombing of cities below. Mediating structures are required, Adams contends, because without them, the people governed in a specific jurisdiction are not effective either as consenting or dissenting powers. Mediating structures are also indispensable to realizing and maintaining a separation of powers in any democratic society.[57]

There are mediating structures of a governmental nature, such as states, counties, cities, towns, and the like, all within a more comprehensive national jurisdiction. In the nongovernmental sphere groupings abound, including those of a commercial, industrial, educational, artistic, professional, recreational, or philanthropic nature. The more a government seeks to abolish, control, or otherwise render ineffective associations people voluntarily form in these spheres, the more totalitarian that regime becomes. This applies also to groupings such as families and churches. Families, insofar as one is born into them, are not totally voluntary. Churches in modern democracies are, however, as Adams observes, viewed as voluntary, even though in their frequent ties to families they do contain some involuntary elements. In any event, families and churches are important mediating structures that a totalitarian government seeks to render ineffective as sources of social power, that is, as sources of influence and/or of resisting influence in the public sphere. They are part of the dispersal and separation of powers essential to the freedom and power of individuals, a freedom and power obtained through participation in groups. Adams makes this point most succinctly when he says, "Power must be both distributed and shared if tyranny or domination is to be held in check."[58] Or again, when he characterizes the democratic society as "an association of associations."[59]

Freedom of association is, then, for Adams, a functional requisite of actualizing a democratic society and state. This means that a democratic society embodies separate and widely dispersed powers in its institutions and groupings. Voluntary associations, which are not creatures of the state, provide a means for individuals to participate in social decisions that affect public policy; at the same time, such associations, when in conflict with the state, provide for the institutionalization of dissent. Adams sums up the vital role of free associations for saving democracy from totalitarianism:

> The voluntary association has become the characteristic and indispensable institution of a democratic pluralistic polity—in contrast to an authoritarian or overintegrated (totalitarian) polity. Inevitably, associations compete with each other for support.... The availability of a variety of voluntary associations make it possible for an individual to cooperate in concert with others of similar mind on a particular issue, and yet to participate also in other associations bringing together people quite unwilling to support the particular concern of the former group. This is the organizational meaning of pluralism.... Here we see the multiple relatedness of the individual in an open society.[60]

Adams, like Polanyi, is concerned to distinguish democracy from totalitarianism. Polanyi focuses on the necessity of democratic institutions and ideals for the attainment of truth in general and of scientific knowledge in particular: The quest for truth is not possible within a totalitarian jurisdiction in which the very ideal of truth is denied and suppressed. Adams focuses on the social conditions necessary to sustain democratic institutions that embody democratic ideals and render those ideals socially operative: Within a totalitarian jurisdiction, these social conditions are absent or effectively weakened by state suppression and control. When these social conditions are absent or sufficiently suppressed, the rights of individuals and groups are violated so that the free and tolerant discourse and communication necessary to scientific and moral knowledge is not a social reality. And when that is true, the very bearers of knowledge, individuals and groups, are at risk of imprisonment, exile, or even death. Adams sees voluntary associations as centers of power to help prevent such governmental policies. Indeed, as he has noted, "voluntary associations often serve as watchdogs exposing the government as a violator of the law (also as refusing to enforce the law)."[61]

A major reason for the attention Adams gives to the necessity of empowering people through the free formation of groups is that governments are capable of being corrupt and unjust as well as being the embodiment of transcendent ideals and the guarantors of justice. And governmental power will be abused if there is no countervailing power strong enough to prevent or correct such abuse. Freedom of association permits the constant creation of groups with power to influence and/or resist public policies. This makes it possible for the voices of those who are not in power to be heard by those who are. Indeed, under some expressions of power, it may not be possible for those so inclined to ignore such voices. This kind of thing happened when women organized to win the vote and more recently to achieve standing in social roles and work from which they had been largely excluded. African Americans have also benefited from the formation of voluntary associations, such as the NAACP, the Southern Christian Leadership Conference, and many others.[62] The exercise of these powers affect what is perceived or noticed and what is actually knowable because what is hidden comes to light. The importance of a pluralistic expression of such power is that it moves a given society toward the inclusiveness of perceivers and perceptions entailed by the ideal of loving impartiality. This would not happen without the freedom that empowers the perceivers and perceptions excluded from what is publicly known to penetrate the barriers that exclude them from the public arena.

Freedom of association is, then, a necessary social condition for creating and sustaining democratic institutions and ideals. These institutions, in turn, fuel the discovery of what is true, and fuel as well corrective processes for sorting out truth from falsity, processes that include a widening and deepening of the empathy characteristic of loving impartiality. But actualizing the freedom to form groups, though necessary for actualizing impartiality, is not sufficient for that purpose. Opposing groups, however voluntary their membership, may seek to destroy one another; groups can and do arise that take as their purpose to isolate, subordinate, or even destroy a given group. Indeed, the constant tendency toward the suppression of voluntary associations is based on the fear that they undermine the authority of any governing power. This fear is present in the aversion for free associations expressed by Hobbes. As Adams remarks, "For Thomas Hobbes free associations were 'worms in the entrails of the sovereign,' necessarily to be 'wormed.'"[63]

This fear of Hobbes persists. The fear was, and is, that nongovernmental groups and diverse parties within government that oppose official government behavior and existing laws and/or policies are unloyal to that government, and that such alleged disloyalty, wittingly or unwittingly, undermines the ability of the government in question to govern and maintain order. Throughout history, this fear of the freedom to organize and express dissent has served governments as a rationale for stifling freedom of association and diversity of thought. Recently, one need look no further than mainland China and other still-existing one-party national governments for brutal behavioral and verbal expressions of this rationale. The freedom to organize dissent will be seen as a threat to a society and a government that lack the concept of a "loyal opposition." This concept, and the underlying rationale for it, sanctions not only freedom of association but also a multiparty system and a separation of powers among the major branches of government. And so we turn to consider another necessary, though not sufficient, ideal condition for actualizing loving impartiality and hence, of moral cognition, namely institutionalized loyal opposition.

3. Institutionalized Loyal Opposition

The reader will recall from the discussion in chapter 1 that Hobbes depends upon a powerful government, speaking with one voice, to create order and the conditions necessary for justice by enforcing compliance with the "social contract" on which sovereignty is based. Without a unified and powerful assertion of force, individuals pursue their own self-interest. Groups only represent a more powerful and unstable force for disorder and conflict with no natural interest in the larger society and its well-being. Calvin, in sharp contrast, is convinced that human beings are possessed of natural impulses to be moral, to form communities, and to know the moral requisites for forming and sustaining communities. At the same time, Calvin is equally convinced that human beings are possessed of willful impulses to be immoral and to fail to perceive and act upon the moral requisites of community. This makes for some moral conflict, as well as harmony, within individuals and among individuals and groups. Calvin, therefore, believes that governments can and do aid people in being moral and actualizing justice; but, at the same time, he believes that lesser officials, "the lower magistrates," have a moral responsibility to resist "higher magistrates" whenever their actions are unjust and to replace them when necessary.[64] Governments and their various branches are to share a loyalty to justice. But loyalty to justice may wane among those wielding power and it is necessary to separate powers in such a way that opposition to injustices can predictably take place.

But Calvin's advocacy of resistance to injustice is quite limited insofar as it does not apply to the people who are enjoined to obey even unjust rulers. Calvin does make a narrowly applicable exception: Rulers are not to be obeyed if doing so means that God will be disobeyed; rulers are also subject to God's will.[65] Calvin planted significant seeds that others nurtured. Calvinistic theory developed what Reinhold Niebuhr calls "a living relation with democratic justice," and, relative to other political theories, "came closest to a full comprehension of all the complexities of political justice."[66]

Calvin believed that rulers "had a covenant with God to rule justly and the people had a covenant with God to obey."[67] But Calvin did not see implied in this a covenant between the ruler and the people. What the early Calvinists did was

> to insist that this covenant was triangular, between the ruler, the people, and God; that it was a covenant of justice; and that if the ruler broke it by injustice, the people were absolved of obedience. Thus justice, rather than mere order and peace, become the criterion for government; and democratic criticism became the instrument of justice.[68]

These early Calvinists retained Calvin's concept of "lower magistrates," or "ephors." Resistance to injustice was also the responsibility of these elected representatives of the people.[69] But what was the reasoning behind the early Calvinists' extension of the idea of a "loyal opposition?"

To begin with, these early Calvinists, like Calvin, viewed human beings as naturally social, inclined to form associations.[70] Furthermore, human beings have a knowledge of what is just and are inclined to act on this knowledge. The purpose of all human associations is to fulfill vocations of actualizing piety toward God and just relations toward one's neighbors, other human beings. Governments are human associations with these same purposes but with delegated power and authority to aid all associations to achieve justice. The powers of government include the power to punish perpetrators of injustices, as well as to enact regulations (laws) that would help prevent injustices. Since all human beings and their associations seek piety and justice and have the knowledge to judge what is unjust, they can and should seek to rectify any situations in which governments act unjustly. Furthermore, the power of government should not be used to suppress freedom of association because the purpose of these associations is to cultivate piety and justice.

But if people are inclined to be just, why are governments needed to aid them? And if governments are expected to provide such aid, why is it necessary to have a predictable source of resistance to governmental authority and power within governmental structures as such? Because people are sinful is the answer Calvin and the early Calvinists gave to both questions. People have enough moral knowledge and moral proclivities to form and sustain associations and communities. But they also have many desires and appetites that bring them into conflict with others and with themselves as moral beings. To provide sanctions or punishments to prevent or rectify injustices, a government is one association authorized to use force. Government officials, however, are also capable of immoral desires, including the wielding of force on behalf of selfish desires rather than on behalf of justice. Indeed, power is sometimes sought for its own sake. Human beings are also sinful in the sense that they have limited knowledge. The human tendency to abuse power, to use it excessively or for purposes other than as an aid to justice in the whole community, means that there should be people within and outside of government with power enough to resist a given governmental abuse or an abusive government.

You have in early Calvinism a clear rationale for the development of multiparty democracies and the specific notion of a loyal opposition. Human beings share a common loyalty to justice and associations formed to actualize it; human beings have limited knowledge and inclinations in conflict with justice, and corrective associations are required to resist these.

Some readers may object to this preoccupation with Calvin and

Calvinists. Certainly I would agree with Reinhold Niebuhr when, after praising the Calvinists for their understanding of the complexities of democratic justice, he notes the rightful place in any history of democracy "for many secular, as well as religious, movements." But he also sees certain tendencies in secular movements toward "libertarianism in their reaction to the evils of government" or tendencies "to base their democratic theories upon the idea of the goodness of human nature; and consequently to underestimate the perils of anarchy, while they directed their attention to the perils of tyranny."[71] The point I wish to stress is that only certain theological or philosophical views taken of human nature will provide a rationale for "loyal opposition," both in the form of multiparty systems of government and in the form of freely organized dissent by those governed. Calvinists do provide such a rationale, one that actually functioned in history and in democratic constitutions.[72] That is not to say, however, that the Calvinists have the only possible rationale. Nor is it to claim that the early Calvinist theory of associations should be uncritically accepted.

Calvin and Calvinists did not, certainly from the perspective of its critics past and present, fully enough appreciate nor consistently act upon what their own notion of loyal opposition implied. They recognized that the existence of sin meant that some groups might require curbing in the name of justice.[73] This is not the place to rehearse some of the behavior of Calvin and Calvinists for which they have been understandably criticized and still continue to be.[74]

Calvinist theories of association were being formed both as goads to resistance and as justifications for it. They were espoused by leaders and members of groups dissenting from religious and political forms of domination.[75] In Calvinist theory, it is predictable that Eastern Europeans should call for an end to single-party forms of government and for the punishment of evil in high places. As I have been writing this very chapter, East Germany, Hungary, Rumania, and Czechoslovakia have taken up the twin cause of freedom of association, multiparty systems of government, and of recognition of the loyalty of their opposition, a loyalty to human rights and to their nations or people. Poland's break with one-party rule came earlier.

In all of these instances, underground associations surfaced, among them religious organizations. Symbolic of this surfacing of suppressed power were the immediate religious celebrations in Rumania as services were held, bells were rung, and Christmas was everywhere, almost as though atheistic suppressions had never happened or had influenced no one. In Poland, the church was a constant and open force for change; in East Germany its role became more visible as a safe haven for demonstrators. As James Luther Adams has so carefully documented, both the Jewish and Christian traditions have provided reasons for explicitly challenging the ultimacy of particular governments and for challenging particular violations of justice or abuses of power.[76] Institutionalized loyal opposition needs no elaborate defense as a social condition for moral cognition. The correctives for the gross violations of human rights are once again being formed out of human associations that constitute a loyal opposition and that call for the regularization of such loyal opposition. It is interesting to note the common concern that people who have so long had freedom of association and loyal dissent repressed will neither know what a democracy is nor know how to form one. This is a powerful if inadvertent expression of the role freedom of association and institutionalized dissent have in shaping the moral perceptions essential to the protection of human rights.

I have mentioned religious organizations at this juncture, however, to turn attention to the role of intentional moral communities that plant the seeds and nurture the growth of the ideals of democratic justice. Though necessary for attaining loving impartiality, institutionalizing loyal opposition is unobtainable without some basis for cultivating common loyalties among those individuals and groups who otherwise differ, or stand to differ, from one another in a range of ways and circumstances. The ideal social condition for such common loyalties is, I wish to contend, universal support for intentional moral communities.

4. *Universal Support for Intentional Moral Communities*

So far, in speaking of a loyal opposition, the social context for the term *loyal* has been largely confined to a given society and its governing bodies. The loyalty shared by parties opposing one another or a government in power has been largely described as a loyalty to justice. In chapters 10 and 11, I will offer a more detailed account of justice and its relation to the moral requisites of community. For my present purposes it is sufficient to say that this loyalty to justice presupposes that people generally share the inhibitions and proclivities that constitute what I am calling the moral bonds of community as described in chapter 5.

But it will not suffice to think of this loyalty to justice as an allegiance to justice within and for a particular society. The commitment to justice cannot be confined in this way if it is to be an expression of loving impartiality and a necessary condition for moral cognition. Each nation in the world is one particular association among others. Mutual instruction among the nations, which is a key element of what is achieved by loving impartiality, is a communal activity, a common venture. The ideal condition for that is a community in which all human beings and their associations are included. As we have noted before, the existence of such a community is presupposed or implied by universally asserting human rights at the United Nations, and by defining and punishing crimes against humanity at Nuremberg, for example.

But what social conditions are necessary to generate, nurture, and envision such an all-inclusive community and its perspective on justice among nations and for all of humanity? No one organization like the United Nations and no group of nations like those sitting in judgment of others at Nuremberg can claim to be such an ideal community nor claim fully to embody its perspective. And so we are brought back to the question as to when it is, and how it is, that loyalty to a particular community can also constitute loyalty to all of humankind? Loyalty to all of humankind is practiced and fostered in intentional moral communities and in those human groups and communities whenever and to whatever degree they function as intentional moral communities.

First of all, then, what is an intentional moral community? It is a human association: self-consciously pursuing moral instruction as an end in itself; striving to discover, interpret, and teach the requisites of human communities and individual self-fulfillment; and judging its effects from the perspective of what a totally inclusive human community would look like and how in such a community each of its members would relate to one another, to their own capacities as individuals, to one another's communities, and to the powers perceived to make all of these relations realistic human aspirations. One can find some of these defining characteristics of an intentional moral community in a great many human associations. It is less often the case that human associations self-consciously aim at all of these goals and do so as an explicitly valued end in itself. Certain groups formed for attaining particular social goals through political action may not be concerned with moral instruction as such but may rather seek sufficient political power through electing certain individuals, for example, to achieve those social goals by a majority vote in the United States Congress.

Communities founded on the basis of religious faith tend to be intentional moral communities, committed as they are to the cultivation of religious piety and the moral development of individuals and communities. Indeed, religious communities specifically institutionalize moral instruction. Churches, synagogues, mosques, temples, and other centers of worship and learning such as monasteries and colleges exist to teach individuals, groups, and communities what is moral and to move them toward actualizing what are visualized as moral goals for all human beings. Such religious communities generate moral exemplars; moral exhortation, both oral and written; moral education, both oral and written; moral activism, ranging from setting an example to organized efforts at social change; and a moral vision, a realm of perfect justice and peace. Such a realm is described in Jewish and Christian traditions, for example, as the "kingdom of God."[77] Interpretations of what this realm will be like, how and when it will come about, and to what extent it is this-worldly and other-worldly are much debated within religious communities.[78] Indeed, these differing interpretations are often tied to the formation and nurture of divisions within communities of faith. H. Richard Niebuhr provides an explicit study of the notion of the "kingdom of God" in religions and cultural development in the United States and of its relation to "denominationalism."[79] The fact that there are many different religious communities points to a basic limitation of all human associations: whatever their commitments to notions of the equal worth of all human beings, every particular religious community excludes individuals, however advertently or inadvertently.[80] That is true also of groups that are determined to invite members from every group and nation on the globe. Nevertheless, judging themselves from the perspective of a universal community provides a running critique of particular communities of faith, as it does of particular governments and of all human institutions as well.[81]

There are those in the United States who are inclined to focus on the family as the locus of moral instruction and character development. The family cannot actually be or become the only locus for moral instruction in any society larger than a given family unit. Human interactions will exhibit the moral requisites of community or they cannot even take place as exchanges of information and as cooperative actions. These exhibits of morality "model" moral behavior and help shape the young and all other participants in human associations. No human association is devoid of moral instruction, for good or ill, however unintended it may be. One can only marvel at debates in the United States as to whether morality should be taught in the public schools. Simple actions such as intervening to stop a fight or inaction in the face of one are powerful moral messages. Furthermore, it is impossible to teach the history of the United States and to understand its contemporary democratic structures without describing the religious and moral beliefs embodied in them.

What is even more surprising is the attempt to exclude public schools from the realm of intentional moral communities. Ironically, public schools in the United States have never more uniformly, in principle, stood so directly for inclusive human communities; people of all races and ethnic groups, both male and female, are to have equal standing in our society, throughout its social, political, and economic institutions. That is a powerful attempt to teach a particular vision of what shape the entire community of human beings is supposed to take in its particular human associations. Would it weaken this commitment to racial and gender justice to acknowledge its moral character? Would this commitment be weakened by including in the various curricula concrete ways in which justice is sought and the intellectual and motivational bases for doing so, as embodied in a variety of religious and nonreligious associations both historically and contemporaneously? I am, of course, suggesting not only the need for such curricula but also arguing that moral cognition is benefited by the actual existing institutions that would be the subject matter of such more self-conscious moral instruction. Such instruction would not constitute indoctrination, provided that the rich diversity of religious and nonreligious examples of intentional moral communities were to be presented and described. This would apply to movements as well. Certainly groups within the feminist movement, some religious, some nonreligious, have functioned as intentional moral communities, as we already observed from Ruth Smith's account of her experiences. That would be true of the Southern Christian Leadership Conference and probably also of some other civil rights organizations.[82]

The tenor of my remarks about public education should be kept in context. I have no interest in any attempt at imposing my own views. I am only interested in stimulating the discussions and organizations, some of which already exist, to try to work out more self-conscious ways to encourage moral instruction and morally responsible behavior within public school settings.

What is meant by universal support of intentional moral communities and why is that a necessary ideal? In the United States, and many other countries as well, religious communities are tax-exempt. This is one significant expression of the ideal that governments and the societies being governed should, at the very least, not make it difficult for voluntary endeavors to form and sustain intentional moral communities. At least indirectly, governments recognize the worth to the society of using the money raised by intentional moral communities—these embrace nonprofit educational institutions and organizations as well—for the purposes they freely deem to be morally beneficial to their members, to their larger society, and to the global community. There are societies in which governments give financial assistance to religious organizations. Educational institutions in the United States are not only tax-exempt but in a number of ways receive tax dollars, at the very least aid for students. Some of these institutions have religious affiliations.

But why should such support be universal? Recall that the ideal of loving impartiality entails as one of its key elements the quest for mutual instruction of individuals and groups, by individuals and groups. There is no way to limit the value of every possible source of cognitive input. The limits to knowledge are practical: no human being has the time and powers to benefit from what could be learned from every other human being, this despite the fact that some decisions, such as any decision to order a massive nuclear attack or to permit the globe's forests to be cut without environmental regulation, would, or certainly could, adversely affect every human being, the decision-makers as well. The ideal of mutual instruction asks us at least to find ways to enlarge our vision of how all of humanity is or could be affected by what we say or do. There does not seem to be any way to argue that somewhere there is a human being capable of making moral choices who could be declared exempt from any responsibility for what happens when intentional moral communities are suppressed or left unprotected from forces that undermine or destroy them.

Of course, there are those who see no good coming from explicitly religious communities and who object to any larger societal support for them, such as exemption from taxation. What I am suggesting to those who have such views is simply that they have the same privileges to aim at mutual instruction within the human community, organizing in ways congenial to them for this purpose. If, however, they are not willing to be judged by a vision of an inclusive human community, that does pose some problems. I want to illustrate that now. The illustration I offer is not one in which there is evidence of any self-conscious attempt to avoid the perspective of humanity as a community. The inattention to such a perspective, however, has the same effect.

Remember the question I raised earlier about the distortions of moral cognition associated with loyalty to one's own nation. I posed it earlier in connection with the response of a USAID official to the bombing and killing of innocent Cambodians by the United States. Recall what he said, "Sure, some of the villages get bombed, there's no other way to fight a war out here. . . ." This official was in a position to know that the killing of innocent individuals was no hypothetical by-product of such bombing; the very refugees he was assisting were coming from such villages in Laos with explicit stories of the deaths of individuals, young and old alike, who had no part in the war. This USAID official is no isolated individual. Not only do nations generally condone attacks on civilians, but the general tendency of twentieth-century moral reasoning is against absolute prohibitions of every kind. Indeed, Michael Walzer has provided us with a poignant example.[83] I read his impassioned defense of just conduct in war with intense interest and found his arguments impressive until, near the end of his book, he contemplates the possibility of defeat for the country that has been behaving justly. At that point he posits the very exception to strict justice that is the functioning policy of most, if not all, modern nations: you do what you have to do to win. There is no other way to fight a war. And once this idea is part of policy, you can and do justify killing innocent persons in order to prevent *risking* the possibility of defeat or in order to hasten victory. In sharp contrast, I have been arguing that one innocent victim, deliberately targeted as in this case, is too much. Walzer began his book in support of this view as the correct one for international policy, but he ends up providing an instance in which this view is properly to be regarded as "unrealistic" and not sufficiently in the national interest. I turn to Walzer's argument.

Walzer argues for the necessity, in supreme emergencies, to use unjust means to defend a democratic nation against a tyrannical, totalitarian regime. He contends that the victory of Nazi Germany in World War II would have had such terrible consequences that early in the war, in 1940, Britain was justified in bombing the very centers of German cities, knowing with certainty that many unarmed civilians would be killed, including individuals too young or too old to aid the German war effort. There is, and was, no question about the injustice of these means; many of the British declared their opposition to this deviation from aiming at military targets.

There are questions, however, as to whether there was a supreme emergency, whether there was no alternative to bombing city centers, and whether bombing cities produced the expected results. Walzer's arguments simply state official calculations that the war was being lost at the time; that British bombers were the only offensive weapon available at the time; that bombing was so inaccurate in the early raids that only one-third of the attacking forces dropped bombs within five miles of the intended target; and that demoralizing the German population would be the result, the only one immediately obtainable. The expected result, however, has been challenged in retrospect. Indeed, it could have been challenged prospectively, since the bombing of British cities increased resistance. Furthermore, one could anticipate what later proved true also: that many city residents not at the time in the war effort were forced into it by the bombings. Many needed new employment and new places to live. Besides, they now had much to fear from the British and being part of a defensive effort now made sense. Everything considered, it is not clear whether the early offensive against the cities shortened or prolonged the war. Walzer does not condone the continued bombings of civilian targets as bombing became more accurate.

Was there, nevertheless, a supreme emergency? How could one know? It might have been possible to use the bombers where there were reasonable opportunities to damage military targets, and otherwise calculate that Germany's many fronts, improved British technology, and new allied participation would prove as effective as they turned out to be. In 1940, all of this was speculation, including the claim that bombing the centers of cities was the one effective thing to do.

So where does this uncertainty leave us? First of all, it is very important to determine how one ought to behave if in fact a supreme emergency exists, and whether the conventions of just conduct in war must, of necessity, be violated. Walzer says that in a supreme emergency survival takes precedence over human rights. He explicitly rejects the view that the convention holds and "rights are strictly respected whatever the consequences"; he accepts, instead, the view that "the convention is overridden, but only in the face of an imminent catastrophe." On the face of it, what he says sounds eminently reasonable, but is it? I have a serious problem with his formulation.

If indeed the survival of a whole nation with its democratic traditions is at stake, the actions taken to try to assure its survival should surely be described as efforts to protect human beings, hence, as efforts to protect and further human rights. Anyone or any group responsible for imminently threatening the very lives of another individual or group is by any definition someone or some group quite immediately causally connected to the violent means that pose an imminent threat of extinction or defeat. Such individuals or groups are not morally innocent and the use of force against them is just, not unjust.

Suppose, however, that Germany had the express aim of exterminating the British people—all of them. Suppose also that the Germans had succeeded in landing a large army on English soil. Suppose, furthermore, that the tactic of the German army was to capture one village, town, and city after another, killing a high percentage of each of the populations but always keeping some of the English people with them in the battle zones, their supply depots, and military installations. This they do because they have at the time only one potent British offensive weapon to fear, namely bombers. If these bombers constituted in fact, for argument's sake, the only possible way to halt the German advance or even drive the Germans off the island entirely, the use of them would certainly be condoned by Walzer. But tragic as their use would be, the situation is not a total break with the convention of using only just means. The German army would be the intended target; any innocent civilians killed would be unintended though somewhat predictable victims. (One could imagine that some of these desperate people in the war zone might escape or be killed in such attempts.) I am not certain, but I think that Walzer would regard bombing the German army under these circumstances as within the confines of just means. Be that as it may, it is, by hypothesis, a supreme emergency. To justify the bombing that would very likely kill some innocent civilians would not only be a matter of doing what is necessary for the survival of the British people; it would also have to be done for the sake of preventing further killings of innocent human beings. In short, the bombings can only be justified on the basis of saving innocent lives and on the basis that the innocent lives being killed by the means used cannot be saved, if at all, by any other means.

The example I have contrived is rather extreme, but it brings out our responsibility always to act on behalf of human rights, and in this extreme emergency, to do what is least evil; to do nothing would be extreme abandonment of the requisites of community. Although it does not immediately involve the survival of a whole community, attacking terrorists who hold innocent people hostage at the point when they have demonstrated their resolve to kill those hostages by killing some is a case of the same kind of least evil act. One acts in a way that definitely threatens the lives of one's own citizens, in the only way remaining to save some or all of them. Again, however, there is no abandonment of a policy of absolute commitment to the protection of innocent lives.

Walzer has an understandable concern that those who stop at nothing be stopped. I share his concern. His mode of reasoning about it, however, is such that it allows for calculations of expediency to override a strict policy of intending the protecting of human rights. What I have argued is that the mode of reasoning does make a difference in specific cases. Inadvertently, Walzer's mode of reasoning allows love for a particular community to take precedence over love for the requisites of community. From the perspective that the right includes all human beings under the jurisdiction of the moral requisites of community, it is not the survival of the nation that is the aim but rather the persistence of any nation's efforts to protect all innocent lives. That changes the perspective from which necessity is judged. You do what is necessary and possible to prevent the loss of any innocent individual's life. That means also that a given nation does everything possible to preserve that commitment as a basic premise for all of its policies. In short, every possible effort is made to avoid crimes against humanity. Air forces should be held to the same standard as obtains for soldiers on foot. That they have not always been reveals how far the world has come from the very simple and clear standards that underlie laws against murder. The moral meaning of "self-defense" has been extended beyond recognition on behalf of national security. These distortions are being addressed at present by some church bodies as exemplified in the way in which American Catholic bishops are altering their church's position with regard to the stockpiling and possible use of nuclear weaponry.[84]

I have now completed an analysis of loving impartiality as an ideal set of conditions for informing and correcting moral cognition. This account is an extensive departure from any of our more recognizable, standard portraits of impartiality, such as those found in ideal observer theories. In chapter 9, I wish to indicate what other ideal conditions are essential to moral knowledge. To illustrate something of what constitutes moral knowledge, the moral requisites of community will be further articulated and some selected social policy questions will be examined in chapters 9, 10, and 11.

I conclude now with a brief summary of the major elements that compose loving impartiality:

A. Self-love as an all-loving perspective informed by: (1) wishing oneself and the other to exist and live; (2) an empathetic willingness to grieve and rejoice with others, which makes it possible to vividly imagine how it is for oneself and others to be on the receiving end of some contemplated action or interaction.
B. Love of particular communities as an all-loving perspective informed by: (1) actualization of the moral requisites of community; (2) freedom of association; (3) institutionalized loyal opposition; and (4) universal support for intentional moral communities.

NINE

Moral Knowledge
Ideal Companionship

I remind the reader that chapter 8 began with a description of Firth's Ideal Observer theory. In Firth's theory, certain characteristics of an ideal observer are alleged to identify the conditions that define true moral judgments as follows: "*X* is right," means "*X* would be approved by an ideal observer who is omniscient, omnipercipient, disinterested, dispassionate, and otherwise a normal human being." Firth's conception of impartiality as disinterestedness and dispassionateness has the effect of omitting from moral cognition self-love and the self's love for particular communities. For reasons fully discussed in chapter 8, self-love and love for communities are necessary for perceiving moral demands and doing so with as much veridicality as our limited perceptual and empathic powers allow. The ideal of impartiality, what I am calling *loving impartiality,* is attained by one who is *all-loving.*

What then is the full theory of moral cognition I am proposing? Is it attained by simply substituting loving impartiality for disinterestedness and dispassionateness, and otherwise leaving the Ideal Observer's other characteristics intact? Given what loving impartiality is and what it implies, this is not possible. Firth's Ideal Observer theory needs to be reformulated significantly. For one thing, the ideal conditions for moral cognition are no longer to be construed as descriptive of an observer. And on that point, I will begin.

Ideal Companionship: Empathy and Observation

It is quite understandable that Firth would refer to the ideal conditions for moral cognition as characteristics of an observer. Observing is something that can be done with relative detachment. Indeed, given Firth's notion of impartiality, detachment from particular interests and passions is precisely what is ideally necessary in order to distinguish between truth and falsity with respect to our moral judgments. Observation is also an apt way to characterize the gathering of nonmoral facts, granting the usual assumptions, shared by Firth, that such facts are best discovered by someone impartial in the sense of being free from the biases attributed to particular interests and passions. Facts are, in this view, regarded as value-free or neutral.

The standpoint of a detached observer is consistently maintained with respect to vividly imagining how all others are affected by an action being assessed by Firth's omnipercipient observer. It is on the basis of the observer's omniscience, that is, knowledge of all the nonmoral facts, that such a complete visualization of effects is attained.

In his discussion of omnipercipience, Firth calls attention to certain facts about moral perception that might have led him to consider love as a necessary trait of the ideal observer. He notes, for example, "Some have suggested that our failure to treat strangers like brothers is in large part a result of our inability to imagine the joys and sorrows of strangers as vividly as those of our siblings."[1] The ability to imagine the joys and sorrows of all, as we do those of family members, is characteristic of loving impartiality as depicted in chapter 8. Although it is not for Firth a logical error to attribute virtues such as love and compassion to an ideal observer, the possession of these virtues does not, in Firth's view, make anyone a better moral judge:

> The value of love and compassion to a judge, considered solely as a judge, seems to be in the qualities of knowledge

and disinterestedness which are so closely related to them; and these two qualities, as we have seen, can be independently attributed to an ideal observer.[2]

I think Firth is correct in arguing that one who has complete knowledge of nonmoral facts, has general interests, and is otherwise normal will have the ability to vividly imagine how it is for strangers as well as for family members. It is in principle, however, possible for such an individual to be indifferent to the joys and sorrows imagined unless that individual is possessed of two characteristics or proclivities: (1) the wish that the self and others exist; and (2) the willingness and ability to rejoice and grieve with the self and others. Without these abilities and proclivities an individual may be indifferent to the fate and the joys or sorrows of themselves and others and hence fail to experience as morally required an action that is morally required. Hence, moral judgment will be impaired or incorrect. I am taking the view that these empathic interests and passions are part of being lovingly impartial, that is, all-loving.

Someone might reply that individuals who are normal have the capacity to develop these characteristics. I cannot and would not disagree. But this is not an argument available to Firth. He expressly rules out the necessity of love and considers self-love as distortive of moral judgments. But Firth's appeal to normality does mean that an ideal observer is not like the devil described by C. S. Lewis, namely, superb in the knowledge needed to judge what is right and wrong, while judging that the "wrong" ought to be done.[3] Firth has also ruled out wishing someone ill by depriving an ideal moral judge of the influence of such emotions as hatred and jealousy as depicted in his concept of dispassionateness. As far as I can ascertain, however, an ideal observer as depicted by Firth could suffer from a kind of detached indifference that would not allow for predictably experiencing moral demands with accuracy.

Let me illustrate that by returning to a previous discussion. Recall the example of someone observing that Sally, a three-year-old, is about to be pushed off a bridge high enough to result in death should she fall from it. We can anticipate as morally wrong any intentional attempt to bring about Sally's death. But what does this assume? Certainly some desire that Sally live rather than die, and some empathic response, such as the anticipated sorrow at her death, not only within Sally's family and among her friends but also within the bystander witnessing the attempt on her life. Such a bystander is not an observer only, certainly not a detached one. Rather, such a bystander is an ideal companion, one inclined to protect Sally from death and harm as far as possible. The intensity of the wish for life for oneself and Sally, and the empathic anticipation of joy at her rescue and of grief at the failure to do so, will be matched by the intensity of the effort to save her and of the wrong felt that anyone would seek her death. In a case like this, a total stranger to Sally would normally be a companion to her in much the same way as her parents and closest friends would be. In chapter 8, actualization of the moral bonds of community was depicted as one condition requisite for attaining loving impartiality. Those moral bonds include both the proclivity to nurture and protect life, as well as the inhibitions against killing oneself and other human beings. These natural proclivities and inhibitions attach the bystander to Sally in the ways already described above and help make a companion out of a seemingly unattached stranger.

The reader will note that I have begun to describe the ideal conditions for moral cognition as something characteristic of an ideal companion rather than an ideal observer. Some of the reasons for this should already be evident. Moral demands engage those human abilities and propensities that connect us to other persons in positive, life-affirming, and empathic ways. These relations to ourselves and others are not those of someone who is engaged solely in making observations, though being observant is a vital part of any experience of moral requiredness and of obtaining the data on which a true moral judgment can be made. Rather, a good companion is someone who is not a threat to our very lives and well-being, and who is willing to share our joys and sorrows, as friends and parents are expected to do. Of course, friends and parents can be ideal companions, but it is not necessary to be a friend, that is, a close, well-known companion, or a parent to be an ideal companion in the two senses specified above as characteristic of "good companionship." Being a companion also covers the kinds of relationships that can obtain in being members and/or associates in various groups, institutions, and communities. No one term says everything about being an ideal moral judge, but being an ideal companion comes much closer, I would venture, than being an ideal observer.[4]

Strictly speaking, the ideal conditions for moral cognition do not only describe a state of being and a set of characteristics descriptive of an individual. It is more accurate to speak of these conditions as descriptive of a state of being or state of affairs, namely of "ideal companionship." As we noted in chapter 8, loving impartiality is a whole set of conditions for moral cognition that include not only the individual's membership in groups but also the very nature of such groups. Democratic structures and institutions, for example, are ideally necessary for moral perceptiveness, whether on the part of individuals or groups. In short, the ideal conditions for moral cognition constitute a whole state of being or a whole state of affairs best described as "ideal companionship."

So far the description of ideal companionship has been confined largely to a discussion of loving impartiality. What about the other ideal conditions for moral cognition that Firth identified as characteristics of an ideal observer? I refer to omniscience, omnipercipience, and being otherwise normal as a human being. These remain relevant but require reformulation.

Certainly, as already noted in chapter 8, knowledge of nonmoral facts or reality are necessary to obtaining truth with regard to what is morally right or wrong. Firth argues that, logically, no limit can be placed on the amount of such knowledge ideally necessary, and hence, omniscience is the ideal.[5] Ideal companionship, however, is being defined in a way that recognizes the limits of human intellect and the limits of human willingness to do and to see what is right ("sin"). The quest for truth takes place in that kind of structure.

And so, moral knowledge, like all other kinds of knowledge, has some degree of uncertainty built into it. The "fact," for example, that the atom is the smallest bit of matter, something I was taught as a student, is no longer regarded as a "fact." Human knowledge has to be content with being "sufficient" for the action, purposes, and theories that draw upon what comes to be regarded as true of reality, that is, as "factual." The "logic" of obtaining knowledge has to describe a process that includes conditions rendered necessary and relevant to that process precisely because the human intellect is limited and the will and ability to do and to see what is right is limited. Hence, we described in chapter 8 the necessity of democratic institutional structures and organizations and of intentional moral communities. These help us sufficiently to actualize the moral requisites of community, so that the process of gathering and verifying knowledge is rendered sufficiently devoid of self-deception and of infidelity to the truth and truth telling. All of this has been discussed in chapter 8. The point to be made now is that *sufficient* knowledge of reality, not omniscience, characterizes what I am calling "ideal companionship."

This same point applies to "omnipercipience." Ideal companionship is to be characterized as including being able to imagine vividly how it is for everyone who would be affected by an action or policy being contemplated. Sufficient perceptivity is what is ideally required. Whereas Firth contended that this ability to imagine how it is for others followed from what is known about nonmoral facts and from our general interests and passions as human beings, something more is involved. Attaining sufficient perceptivity follows also from taking a positive interest in one's own life and that of all others, and from an empathic willingness to rejoice and grieve within oneself and with others.

At this juncture, Firth's ideal observer and ideal companionship have been compared to all of the ideal observer's characteristics except that of being "otherwise normal." But the special characteristics of ideal companionship have not yet been fully identified.

There is an ideal condition for moral cognition not explicitly identified and analyzed by Firth. I refer to the element of power.

Ideal Companionship: Sufficient Power

One of the questions I did not ask Roderick Firth while he was still alive but now wish I had is why he did not take up omnipotence as a possible trait of the ideal observer. Perhaps he took the view, an understandable one, that omniscience and omnipercipience as traits can be achieved and possessed only by an individual with the requisite power. Why, then, should it be necessary to state the obvious?

I think it is necessary because in the absence of a discussion of power, the distinct impression is created that the powers individuals normally bring to moral judgments, such as the powers of observation, intellect, and imagination, if present to the degree necessary, will generate sufficient knowledge and sufficient perceptivity. But the powers of an individual human being are not sufficient for perfecting moral cognition. As we noted in chapter 8, knowledge, including scientific knowledge, is only attained within a communal context. Indeed, knowledge is not possible in a totalitarian society in which power can be used to suppress truth or to enforce theories that serve to enhance the power of those who govern. Nothing less than the power of groups, collectivities, and institutions to seek truth is essential to knowledge.

So far we have been speaking about the power needed to be sufficiently knowledgeable and sufficiently perceptive. Consider also what is requisite to being an all-loving individual. Individuals are male or female and members of racial and ethnic groups. To be all-loving is to have the powers of empathy that cover the whole range of human selfhood and experience. It is not necessary to open the current debates about the distinctiveness of the experience of being a man or woman, black or white, and the like. The point is that the conditions characteristic of ideal companionship must not be limited by lack of power to enter into the full range of human experiences.

Singling out the ideal of sufficient power calls attention to the way in which the uneven distribution of power within a community distorts the level of awareness necessary to perceive clearly and correctly what is morally required of us as companions within particular communities and in our relations to one another as members of the whole human community. Individuals and groups whose rights are not actualized, and who at the same time lack sufficient power to influence or otherwise participate in their larger societies and their political structures, have experiences and knowledge needed by those with power; being devoid of the input of those unjustly deprived of rights tends to perpetuate the moral ignorance that helps perpetuate the injustices in question.[6] And so the moral knowledge of an individual or particular community is dependent upon not only the amount of power a given individual or community possesses, but also the relative power of other individuals and communities. It is with good reason that power is said to be corrupting and absolute power, absolutely corrupting. Inequalities of power that allow for, or demand, the suppression of individuals and groups with distinct moral perspectives distort moral perception and hence also moral actions and public policy.

Sufficient power, then, within the context of depicting the ideal conditions for discovering what is morally true, refers to the power necessary to be all-loving; it refers to the power to gain the knowledge, imagination, and empathy characteristic of ideal companionship.[7]

Ideal Companionship: Exhibiting Otherwise Normal Human Characteristics

The reader will recall that the ideal conditions for moral cognition are discovered by examining the procedures by means of which individuals or groups attempt to decide moral questions, to resolve doubts about moral decisions they have made, or to reduce disagreements about moral decisions between or among individuals or groups. But, as Firth rightly notes, the meaning of ethical statements is not completely accounted for by an analysis of such ideal conditions. The reason for this is that

> Most of us, indeed, can be said to have a conception of an ideal observer only in the sense that the characteristics of such a person are implicit in the procedures by which we compare and evaluate moral judges, and it seems doubtful, therefore, that an ideal observer can be said to lack any of the determinable properties of human beings.[8]

What Firth is saying about an ideal observer at this point is what I wish to say about ideal companionship; those who may be said to be ideal companions, except for the ideal characteristics specified above, do not, to borrow Firth's expression, lack any of the determinable properties of human beings.

Firth believes that "the determinate properties of an ideal observer, however, except for the ideal characteristics...are apparently not capable of precise definition."[9] With this I would also agree. I do, like Firth, acknowledge that being human implies that the meaning of ethical statements are in some respects ambiguous, and I agree with Firth that such ambiguity does not invalidate his thesis "that ethical statements are statements about an ideal observer and his ethically-significant reaction."[10] My quarrel with Firth has to do with his specific description of an ideal moral judge and of such a judge's ethically significant reactions. For reasons discussed above, I regard it as more appropriate to speak of "ideal companionship" to designate the ideal conditions for moral cognition rather than of what characterizes an ideal observer.

But something more needs to be clarified. To speak, as Firth does, of the "determinable properties" of human beings is in some respects misleading. Human relations cannot be fully described as properties of individuals but as shared realities. Friendship, for example, connects two or more individuals and is not adequately described as a "property" of each of these individuals; but friendship is characteristic of human beings, not just friendliness as an individual "property." Friendliness among friends is also a mutually shared characteristic of the friendship relation itself and the interactions elicited by such a relation. It would be more accurate to say that "otherwise normal" means that except for certain ideal characteristics, ideal companions do not lack the determinable properties and relations characteristic of human beings.

When one speaks of "ideal characteristics," one is speaking about human traits or relations that are possessed to an extreme degree, to a degree not attainable by human beings. Thus, for example, human beings are capable of feeling and exhibiting love in the form of positive affection for themselves and others, but the ideal of being all-loving is beyond reach. Stated as an ideal, however, being all-loving, that is, loving impartiality, renders explicit what is more often implicit in human striving to perceive and do what is right. Once explicitly identified, loving impartiality can function as a goal and guide to moral correction and development.

As I have depicted it, loving impartiality includes in it a love of self and of others expressed as a wish that the self and others exist. As already noted above, this human proclivity to wish ourselves and others to exist makes sense out of the humane impulse to perceive and act on a moral demand to protect someone like three-year-old Sally from being killed. But how shall we understand this wish that Sally exist if we change her circumstances and find ourselves confronted with a Sally who is terminally ill and suffering what she reports as, and what looks to be, unbearable pain? Has the inclusion of a wish to live imported into our notion of the ideal self a particular view of what is right? I raise this question because there are those who would say that under those circumstances it is reasonable, some would say morally justifiable, to wish for Sally's death and to wish that it come sooner rather than later. And if it is reasonable to wish for one's own death and that of others in such circumstances, does that imply that the wish that the self and others exist cannot be treated as an element in the cognitive ideal to be all-loving? Furthermore, if it is, for some, morally justifiable to wish to end Sally's life, does that mean that making the wish that she live a cognitive ideal is at the same time to make it a moral ideal, a moral ideal that stands in opposition to mercy killing?

In chapter 4 we discovered that Gewirth's justification of suicide rested on his conception of what constitutes the ideal expression of human freedom, which for Gewirth is a fundamental moral right: What he regarded as impartially rational turns out to appear to be so because a certain expression of freedom is depicted as rational. In turn, is what I am regarding as impartial, albeit lovingly so, a moral ideal that implies the irrationality of what Gewirth regards as rational, namely, ending life under certain circumstances? Isn't it reasonable that some people would when terminally ill and in unbearable pain experience a wish that they die? Or to put it another way, does the theory of ideal companionship imply that such wishes are necessarily unreasonable or irrational?

Ideal Companionship and the Wish That the Self and Others Exist

To begin with, it is important to indicate that the wish that the self and others exist is a natural phenomenon. Although I will argue that the desire that the self and others live is also a moral ideal, the fact that such a desire is present in human beings does not by itself establish or justify it as a moral ideal. The desire to die, to kill, or to be killed are all desires that occur as natural phenomena as well. It is as a fact of life that the wish that the self and others live enters into moral cognition and the quest to know what is right. Whether that fact is also a moral ideal comes as a result of moral deliberation, moral deliberation that includes, as we have seen, much more in its compass than the fact that humans wish themselves and others to live.

The quest for moral knowledge, indeed any knowledge, must of necessity begin with a positive desire that the self and others exist. To begin instead with the desire that the self and others die is to take away any incentive to know anything, and if acted upon, is to put an end to the discovery and accumulation of knowledge itself. Knowing, logically and actually, requires a knower, indeed a whole community of knowers.

But if moral deliberation begins with the wish that the self and others exist, it would seem to imply that the question as to the rightness and wrongness of suicide and euthanasia has already been decided. Why deliberate? Clearly more is at stake in moral cognition than the wish that the self and others exist. There is also present in moral deliberation the human propensity to grieve and rejoice with ourselves and others. This proclivity means that we are susceptible to feelings of empathy, toward ourselves and others, whenever we and others suffer. Empathy toward one who is suffering inclines the one who has such empathy to wish that such suffering end. And if it appears that such suffering can only end if the life of the sufferer is ended, suicide, assisting in suicide, and euthanasia become subjects of genuine cognitive deliberation, the outcome of which cannot be predicted simply on the basis that people naturally wish themselves and others to live.

One reason, then, that the natural wish that the self and others live does not by itself decide moral questions is that all of the cognitive ideals, and the natural processes inherent in their actualization, are engaged in moral perception and reflection. Out of empathy for Sally's suffering, for example, her parents with the concurrence of the family's physician, may set in motion extreme comfort measures, such as high dosages of pain relief of such a magnitude that life-sustaining measures are compromised and Sally's life will almost certainly be shortened. Her parents can, in such circumstances, retain the wish that Sally live, but when, as specified above, pain relief becomes the primary aim of their interventions on her behalf, their wish that she live cannot at the same time be expressed in the form of doing everything that promises to sustain her life as long as possible. The wish that she exist is left to express itself as grief, once she dies, that she is no longer with them: They miss her. Provided her death is clearly inevitable with or without extreme pain relief, grief that she died is compatible, morally, logically, and psychologically, with their relief that whatever suffering remained in her dying moments or days, if any, has definitely ended.

Another reason that the wish that the self and others exist does not by itself decide social questions is that the lives of individuals can come into conflict. If, for example, someone about to kill Sally can, by hypothesis, be prevented from doing so only by police shooting to kill from a distance, the ideal of loving all, of wishing all to exist, can only serve to protect Sally's life but it cannot at the same time equally protect the life of her assailant.[11] The moral decision is bent in that direction by the failure of the assailant to observe the moral requisites of community and Sally's innocence of any such break in the bonds that tie the police to her. Of course, the ideal of loving impartiality does guide the police to disarm and not kill an assailant when the circumstances permit trying to save Sally's life in that way. The same applies to captured soldiers in war. Once they are disarmed, their lives are to be protected, as are those who are arrested by the police in the act of disobeying the law.

So far then, I have been illustrating how the wish that the self and others live can and does function as a guide to moral cognition without invalidating the ideal companionship theory by including in it elements that are supposed to serve to help decide what is morally right or wrong but that are actually moral biases. Indeed, the moral status of wishing the self and others to exist as a moral ideal, as a virtue, has to be argued. To argue that case requires also a discussion of how to understand the wish to die and its implications for moral decision making, particularly in circumstances in which the wish that the self, or anyone else, live tends to wane, or at least by all appearances to disappear altogether. The fact that the wish to die cannot reasonably function as an ideal to guide the quest for knowledge generally does not by itself rule out the possibility that it can or should be what guides decisions in some circumstances, especially those in which the life prospects of individuals are certainly near an end or severely and irreversibly curtailed.

I turn, therefore, to a consideration of the wish to die. The focus will be on certain situations in which this wish is evoked in which such a wish is generally regarded as understandable and regarded by some as a guide, sometimes as the best guide, to what is morally right. I refer to certain events around severe illnesses that prompt some people to favor suicide, assisted suicide, or euthanasia. In taking up the wish to die as a natural phenomenon occurring within the context of life-threatening and life-compromising illnesses, I intend to address how the wish to die functions within the ideal companionship theory.

Ideal Companionship and the Wish to Die

The wish that the self and others live is among the specified characteristics of an ideal companion. What about the wish to die? Is any act prompted and guided by the wish to die, by definition regarded as morally wrong, given the defining characteristics of ideal companionship? The answer is no: The reason is that the moral status of the wish to die depends upon what perceptions and judgments result from all of the characteristics of ideal companionship, and these include not only the specified ideal characteristics but whatever else is characteristic of human beings as such: An ideal companion, except for characteristics specified as ideal, is "otherwise normal." This means that the moral status of the wish to die, and of acts carrying out this wish, depends not only on the ways in which empathy relate to the wish that the self and others live but on the ways in which the wish to die normally relate to the wish to live normally, both in general and in situations in which the wish to die could plausibly be expected to be stronger than the wish to live.

Suicide is one action that can be undertaken to realize the wish to die. Individuals may be said to have committed suicide if, and only if, they have intentionally terminated their own lives. In his discussion of when a decision to commit suicide is rational from the point of view of someone contemplating it, the philosopher Richard B. Brandt precisely takes up the factors that affect the relative strength of the wish to die and the wish to live. Normally, he regards it as reasonable that someone who takes a dim view of life on a given day considers that life may be better in days to come. That is a strong possibility, given how grim today is, for one driven to despair of life altogether. Brandt does believe, however, that there are circumstances in which it is clear beyond any reasonable doubt that death has become preferable to life and that it will be until the end, and then "the rational thing is to act promptly."[12] By "act" Brandt means commit suicide. "Let us not," he says, "pursue the question of whether it is rational for a person with a painful terminal illness to commit suicide; it is."[13]

Suicides among the terminally ill are relatively rare, for one reason because many are in hospitals and do not have the means or opportunity to end their lives. In 1975, before the present desire for having physicians assist in suicides and engage in euthanasia, Brandt turns to what he regards as a more practical problem, namely when it is that suicides, for reasons other than painful terminal physical illness, are rational.[14]

Brandt comes to the conclusion that individuals may rationally and rightly decide to terminate their own lives. Furthermore, Brandt believes others have a moral obligation to help if help is needed. He notes, "A patient's physician has a special obligation, from which any talk about the Hippocratic oath does not absolve him."[15]

From Brandt's perspective, there is no question that circumstances arise for individuals in which it is reasonable to expect them to wish to die, and beyond that, reasonable as well to carry out that wish by ending their lives. They should do this on the basis of a careful assessment of their own welfare.

Peter Sainsbury, a physician doing research in clinical psychiatry in England, takes a view of suicide in stark contrast with that of Brandt. After citing considerable research, Sainsbury makes the following observations:

It has therefore become our point of view that suicide falls squarely within the realm of community medicine and psychiatry; and prevention will depend on the capacity of the medical, psychiatric, and welfare personnel, and on the willingness of the public health administrators to organize the social and psychiatric services in the light of the facts now available. The view that healthy people kill themselves, and justifiably so, if circumstances are sufficiently adverse, or that the individual should be "free" to decide his own fate is not tenable to us; the protection of the suicidal is as much a medical and community responsibility as any other cause of death against which prophylactic and therapeutic measures are available.[16]

Instead of the special obligation to aid individuals in committing suicide urged by Brandt, Sainsbury emphasizes: "The doctor needs to be made aware of suicide as a preventable cause of death early in his career."[17] Also, psychiatrists are urged to take steps to educate general practitioners so that they come to accept suicide prevention "as a medical responsibility" and "become aware of the need to collaborate with the psychiatric services in dealing with the problem."[18]

Historically, the view of Sainsbury mirrors popular opinion as it began to develop in the nineteenth century and into the twentieth. Citing English literature, George Rosen observes:

By the early nineteenth century suicide was being considered less in moral and theological terms and increasingly as a social and medical problem. Indeed, by the beginning of the twentieth century, even though disapproving of suicide, popular opinion had generally come to view such acts as deviations from normality. . . . By the twentieth century, in the conventional wisdom of the middle class, suicide was more significant socially as a disgrace rather than as a sin, and could conventionally be glossed over by attributing it to mental aberration.[19]

Investigations of suicide as a social and medical phenomenon took place, beginning in the first half of the nineteenth century, most prominently in France but also in Great Britain, in the German language area of central Europe, and in the United States.[20] Rosen concludes his historical account of such research with sociological studies that point to Durkheim's conclusion, stated in 1897, that "suicide will not be widely prevalent in a society that is well integrated politically, economically, and socially."[21]

Introducing Durkheim adds a third perspective on suicide: Brandt depicts it as a decision of an individual that can be made freely and rationally for the benefit of that individual; Sainsbury depicts it as an irrational individual act, brought on by medically preventable causes; and Durkheim depicts it as an act of an alienated individual, who under the right social conditions, would be highly unlikely, statistically, to commit suicide. Both Sainsbury and Durkheim are asserting that when the wish that the self live is overwhelmed enough to lead an individual to commit suicide, the individual cannot be described as "normal." For Sainsbury, something has gone wrong with the individual's relation to the self, and so also the relation to others; for Durkheim, something has gone wrong with the individual's relation to others, and also the relation to the self. Brandt, however, asserts that the individual's wish to live can be viewed as senseless or futile, in dire circumstances, certainly when the individual is painfully and terminally ill, for example; whether the wish to live or the wish to die should prevail in an individual's life is a matter for that individual to calculate, considering which is most beneficial as a basis for action.

Although Rosen is correct to notice that suicide came to be understood largely in the language of medicine and the social sciences rather than the language of morality and theology, it is moral and theological or metaphysical differences that divide people on how to assess and understand suicide and how individuals and societies ought to relate to those who commit suicide. If, as in Calvin, human beings are naturally social selves who nevertheless realize their nature with communal support, Durkheim's focus makes sense. If, as in Hobbes, individuals naturally seek to preserve their own lives, Sainsbury's focus makes sense. If, as in Bentham and Mill, individuals naturally seek to avoid pain and gain pleasure for themselves, and their wish that the self and others live is contingent on the ratio of pleasure to pain resulting from acting on such a wish, Brandt's focus makes sense. As the reader will recall, for Calvin, the right to life is based on a natural responsibility to live and nurture life; for Hobbes, the right to life is a natural right; for Bentham and Mill, the right to life is a calculated right; and for Brandt, this is a calculated right you claim if you wish it.

In the current debates over the morality and rationality of suicide, assisting in a suicide and euthanasia, these three traditions are in conflict. They differ with respect to the moral and legal status individuals and communities should grant to an individual's wish to die and to acts designed to realize that wish. They differ, at least in large part, because of their differing theological anthropologies or metaphysical assumptions about human nature. These three major traditions and their anthropological assumptions are clearly represented within the majority and dissenting opinions of the Massachusetts Supreme Judicial Court in the Brophy case.[22] Before presenting the opinion of the court in question, some description of the case is in order.

Paul Brophy, a firefighter in his midforties, was diagnosed as being in a semivegetative state from April of 1983 and at the time of the decision in September of 1986. All therapeutic medical interventions were being withheld and Brophy was breathing on his own. His care could best be described as aimed at "comfort only" and it was excellent. He was free of bed sores, for example. Food and water were being given through a G-tube and it was not creating any adverse side effects. Medical experts testified that Brophy was not imminently dying and that he could live for a number of years, perhaps more than twenty or so. The majority, four of seven justices, were convinced that a lower court correctly understood Brophy's comments to others earlier in his life as a wish on his part to be allowed to die under these circumstances. He had, for example, once said that he did not wish to live if he were to be in a situation like that of Karen Ann Quinlan.

State Interests and Conflicting Views of the Wish to Die: The Brophy Decision

The Majority Opinion: The Wish to Die as the Basis of a State-Implemented Right to Die

Writing for the majority (four of seven justices), Judge Liacos framed the question before the Massachusetts Supreme Judicial Court as follows: Is there a state interest to implement Brophy's wish not to live in his present circumstances? Liacos is willing to assert a state interest in carrying out Brophy's wish to die on behalf of what he regards as Brophy's right to self-determination. This right, according to Liacos, has deep roots in the history of the United States. To make his argument, he quotes John Stuart Mill:

> [T]he only purpose for which power can be rightfully exercised over any member of a civilized community, against his will, is to prevent harm to others. His own good, either physical or moral, is not a significant warrant. He cannot rightfully be compelled to do or forbear because it will be better for him to do so, because it will make him happier, because in the opinion of others to do so would be wise or even right. [23]

Liacos feels compelled to offer additional reasons for depicting Brophy's wish, and the state's interest in carrying it out, as a reasonable choice to die a natural death rather than to be the subject of life-sustaining care. He considers Brophy to be in a situation in which efforts to sustain life are in conflict with medicine's obligation to relieve suffering. In what sense, however, can Brophy be considered to be suffering? He argues that Brophy is in some kind of twilight zone in which "the body lives in some fashion but the brain (or a significant part of it) does not."[24] On this very point, he cites another court case in which medical procedures used to sustain life in such circumstances are said to be "accurately described as a means of prolonging the dying process rather than a means of continuing life."[25] And he also cites other sources that speak of such continuation of medical intervention as "protracted agony" and the choice to forego it as "a right to die with dignity."[26] In short, Liacos is contending that individuals should be free to assert a right to reject life-sustaining medical interventions under certain circumstances.

Within the majority opinion, as delivered by Liacos, no inalienable right to life, under the protection of the state, is asserted on behalf of Brophy. Rather, a right not to be interfered with is set forth, a private sphere in which the value of one's life may be calculated by the individual. Effectively, the state has no interest in protecting a life that is not desired. It is interesting to note that Justice Stevens of the United States Supreme Court is explicit about this in his dissenting opinion in the Nancy Cruzan decision: "A State that seeks to demonstrate its commitment to life may do so by aiding those who are actively struggling for life and health."[27] Liacos sees no struggle for life in Brophy, and Stevens sees none in Cruzan. Nor do they regard such a struggle as something individuals in their circumstances would wish to carry on. And, so, a state need have no compelling interest in each individual life, for the right to life is not inalienable and it may understandably be wished away.

Implicitly, Liacos and Stevens have rejected the Hobbesian notion that individuals strive to preserve their own lives, and that this striving is a constant and permanent part of their nature as human beings. Whatever Liacos and Stevens would ultimately claim regarding the relative strengths of the wish to live and the wish to die as natural phenomena, they can definitely envisage some circumstances in which some actions based on the wish to die should not only be tolerated by the state but protected as an individual right. In the Brophy decision, the weight given to the wish to die was challenged.

Justice Lynch's Dissenting Opinion: The Wish to Live as the Basis for a State-Protected Natural Right to Life

Among the three dissenting judges, Lynch is the one who invokes Hobbes in his opinion. It is not surprising, therefore, that Lynch says: "My principal objection is that the State's interest in the preservation of life has not been given appropriate weight."[28] And, Lynch adds, "the majority nullify, if only in part, the law against suicide."[29] For Lynch, the state's interest in the preservation of life is an interest in preserving the particular patient's life and in preserving the sanctity of all human life. "Maintaining the sanctity of life," says Lynch, "may well be the reason society invests the State with sovereign authority."[30] Lynch mentions both Hobbes and Locke as sources for this view.

Since, for Hobbes, the drive to preserve one's own life is a powerful and natural one for everyone, he argued that the right to life is natural, and it is a claim no rational individual would surrender to a sovereign. Indeed, the legitimacy of governments rests on their actual ability to protect human life. To commit suicide, from a Hobbesian perspective, is irrational and efforts should be made to prevent it. Lynch does explicitly see the state's interest in the prevention of suicide as that of "the prevention of irrational self-destruction."[31] Not all refusal of treatment is to be regarded as an instance of such irrational self-destruction. But in Brophy's case, what is being refused is not burdensome and invasive, and its refusal will be the reason he dies; and so there is reason to invoke the state's interest in preventing what can be seen as a suicide. For the sake of caution, Lynch would favor preserving Brophy's life, insofar as the provision of food and water is involved.

Lynch, however, is not expressing his opinion in a purely Hobbesian way. He speaks of a state interest in preserving the *sanctity* of all life. This puts one in mind of the Declaration of Independence, in which the self-evident and inalienable right to life is bestowed on the individual by the Creator. How consistently Hobbesian Lynch is in his thinking is not something one can glean from what he says in his dissenting opinion. What is clear is that

individuals have a definite right to life and to the state's protection
of that right, including also protection against irrational destruction by individuals of their own lives. In Hobbes, the theological
basis for this affirmation is a doctrine of human nature, one that
depicts individuals as seeking their own preservation. No one can
be expected to regard it as reasonable to ask or require anyone to
relinquish the right to preserve one's own life. Nor is it reasonable
that anyone would wish to relinquish that right. Indeed, it is not
even possible to take away a right that belongs to individuals by
their very nature, hence inalienable. In this tradition, rights, not
responsibilities, are primary. But a third tradition was represented
in that Brophy decision in which responsibilities are primary.

Justice Nolan's Dissenting Opinion: The Preservation of One's Own Life as a Natural Responsibility

Justice Nolan feels compelled not only to dissent but also to
write a separate opinion. Though, like Lynch, he asserts a state interest in protecting Brophy's life and all of life; and though, like
Lynch, he views removing food and water in this case as the proximate cause of death, he wishes to delineate what he regards as the
basis of United States laws:

> I can think of nothing more degrading to the human person
> than the balance the court struck today in favor of death
> against life. It is but another triumph for the forces of secular
> humanism (modern paganism) which have now succeeded in
> imposing their anti-life principles at both ends of life's spec-
> trum. Pro dolar.[32]

Nolan explicitly evokes a religious and theological difference between his perspective on life and that of the majority. He wishes to
put that theological quarrel into the record.

As Nolan is aware, modern "paganism," as he refers to it, thinks
of itself as secular. But that does not mask its affinity with its

ancient expressions that were religious rivals of Christianity and Judaism. Before Greece embraced Christianity, Greek physicians did administer poisons. This was true despite the fact that the Hippocratic Oath, an ancient Greek document, prohibited giving poisons.[33] That oath did win out, but it did so as Christians embraced it and Christianity came to supplant ancient Greek and Roman religions and cultures.[34]

Nolan's reasoning and the language he uses are drawn from the Roman Catholic tradition. He notes that the principle of double effect does not apply to Brophy's situation. In Nolan's view, since the G-tube was in place, food and water were not at that point a medical intervention. To deny Brophy food and water is therefore to intend death rather than comfort as such. Nolan does accept the withdrawal of all burdensome medical interventions, in Brophy's case, for the sake of comfort, but not for the sake of death, even if the decision to avoid all burdensome treatments may have the unintended effect of shortening life. But Brophy's death will be due to starvation; and in approving his death, Nolan contends that the court is approving euthanasia and suicide. And, says Nolan, "Suicide is direct self-destruction and is intrinsically evil. No set of circumstances can make it moral."[35] Although Nolan does not speak of rights in his opinion, there is no doubt about his rejection of any "right" to commit suicide or to request euthanasia. Asserting such "rights," and also legalizing them, would be to ignore the moral obligation to avoid actions aimed at killing oneself or having oneself killed.

Although Nolan's specific opinions on the Brophy case are not those of all professing Christians, his view of human nature is very much a part of both the Jewish and Christian traditions. I refer especially to the natural proclivities to refrain from killing and to protect and nurture life, which are expressions of the sociality of human nature. But in this day and age, it is not possible to take for granted that those who profess to be Jewish or Christian will reflect the doctrine of human nature that has dominated the theology of these traditions; they will not necessarily find the foundation for human rights in those natural responsibilities that are an expression of our social nature and render possible and actual our communal life and individual life itself. Of course, one could argue that to the extent that professing Christians and Jews affirm perspectives found in Hobbes or Mill, then, to that extent, these perspectives are in some sense part of Christian and Jewish traditions.

Be that as it may, the analysis of three different doctrines of human nature found in written opinions of Massachusetts Supreme Court justices regarding Paul Brophy serves to illustrate how assumptions about human nature, implicit or explicit, significantly shape reactions to the wish to die and actions designed to actualize such a wish. From this analysis we learn that the theory of ideal companionship does not by definition indicate whether suicide, assisting in a suicide, and euthanasia are right or wrong: The theory of ideal companionship does not provide a definition of "otherwise normal" and does not, therefore, indicate, for example, whether human nature is such that suicide, based on a wish to die, is within the range of normality or reasonable behavior in some circumstances, or whether it is rather always to be viewed as abnormal or irrational in some sense. At least in part, then, nonmoral facts about human motivation, conscious and unconscious, are what we debate when we debate about the rightness or wrongness of directly aiming at securing our own deaths.

We learn something else from the Brophy decision. Despite their conflicting views of human nature and of when the wish to die becomes a wish to commit suicide, the justices of the Massachusetts Supreme Judicial Court all share the concern not to let a wish to die undercut legal support for the wish that the self and others live. All of them are resolved to keep in place the state's interest in preventing suicide and in preserving life. The majority retain the wish to live as their cognitive ideal by interpreting Brophy's wish as a wish to be free of medical interventions that prolong his dying, and by interpreting his death as a result of his inability to swallow and hence obtain food and water without invasive medical intervention. As we have seen, the dissenting judges object to honoring a wish that, since food and water are involved and death is not imminent, is, in effect, honoring a wish to die: Honoring such a wish should be interpreted as a failure to prevent suicide and preserve life. All the same, all of the justices are agreed that the wish to be free of all other burdensome medical interventions, in Brophy's circumstances, does not compromise the court's interest in preventing suicide and preserving life.

Because the Brophy court did not debate whether the state should prevent suicide and preserve life, it is not surprising that some of the ideal conditions for moral cognition were not exemplified in the written opinions of the court. The reader will recall the significant implications of the requisites of community and love of community for questions about our responsibilities to preserve our lives and those of others. A thorough discussion of policy with regard to suicide, assisting in a suicide, and euthanasia would include these elements of loving impartiality as a cognitive ideal. The question as to whether a policy of assisting in a suicide and permitting euthanasia is justifiable will be discussed below, immediately after completing our account of moral cognition.

What, then, is still missing from our account of the ideal conditions for moral cognition? There are certain beliefs that must be in place and functioning if the whole moral enterprise is to be sustained. For that to happen, these beliefs must also be beliefs of what is true of reality, that is, of our world and of ourselves as human beings. That was the subject of chapter 6.

In chapter 6, we examined three functioning beliefs that in any individual may be completely below the threshold of awareness, or to various degrees consciously acknowledged. These beliefs are logically and functionally necessary to account for actually occurring moral behavior, which without such beliefs cannot be expected to take place. They take the form of three kinds of faith, or confidence: (1) that a cosmic moral power exists; (2) that goodness is more powerful than evil; and (3) that morally responsible behavior is in some way ultimately vindicated. As with other ideal conditions for moral cognition, the degree to which such confidence can and needs to be expressed cannot be stated with certainty. What we can know as human beings is that our moral life and its structure persist even though there are conscious doubts expressed in various communities concerning any one or more of the three types of confidence in the power of morality. For purposes of describing the ideal conditions of moral cognition, therefore, we can do no better than assert the necessity of a sufficient degree of confidence in the practicality of making moral choices in the senses specified above. Ideally, sufficient confidence is functionally required that moral choices are sustainable over time, and that they are not futile. In short, that moral choices are believed to be genuine options for human beings is an ideal condition for moral cognition.

It is now possible to summarize what constitute the ideal conditions for moral cognition. These ideal conditions identify conditions individuals and/or groups would have to actualize, as well as processes they would have to follow—conditions that define when moral rightness or wrongness is being correctly perceived and judged. These ideal conditions include the following: (1) sufficient knowledge of nonmoral facts or reality; (2) sufficient perceptivity to imagine how it is for all those affected by any actions being contemplated; (3) loving impartiality (as described in chapter 8); (4) sufficient power and confidence in the power of morality (as described in chapter 6); and (5) otherwise normal human tendencies. These ideal conditions may be said to characterize a state of being and state of affairs called "ideal companionship."

As already indicated above, the wish to die and how to respond to it pose special questions, not only for human rights and responsibilities but also for the ideal conditions for moral cognition. To clarify these, I wish now to take up the debates around physician-assisted suicide.

Physician-Assisted Suicide

As I write, there is a concerted effort to legalize physician-assisted suicide. Although a voter initiative for that purpose was rejected by 54 percent of the voters in Washington state in November 1991, supporters of physician-assisted suicide in California succeeded in placing a similar initiative, called the "Terminal Illness, Assistance in Dying, Initiative Statute," on the ballot for the November 1992 elections. This initiative was also defeated by 54 percent of the voters.

Physicians have also begun to press for physician-assisted suicide. A committee of twelve physicians, making recommendations regarding the care of what they called "hopelessly ill patients," included physician-assisted suicide among the kinds of care that should be offered: ten of the twelve physicians took the view "that it is not immoral for a physician to assist in the rational suicide of a terminally ill person."[36] These physicians made it very clear that what they were approving was physician-assisted suicide, that is, the provision by a physician of the means by which patients can end their own lives. They do not equate assisting in a suicide with the recommendations they have made to provide patients with maximal pain relief and flexibly adjusted efforts to minimize suffering. They do not equate actions aimed at comfort, even when such actions have the effect of shortening life, with actions aimed at ending life. And so they issue a call for wide and open discussion of assisted suicide.

Such a discussion cannot be advanced by dwelling on highly questionable instances, such as those generated by Dr. Jack Kevorkian and his highly publicized "suicide machine."[37] It is better to examine a carefully documented case, published by the physician involved. I refer to the case of Diane, described as "A Case of Individualized Decision Making" by Timothy E. Quill, M.D.[38] Quill presents a clear and plausible rationale for his actions. I will begin by examining his rationale.

A Rationale for Physician-Assisted Suicide

Quill's patient, Diane, was diagnosed as having acute myelomonocytic leukemia. The odds she was given of surviving painful and prolonged treatment were 25 percent. Though these odds are debated, the outcome without treatment is not: certain death within days or weeks, or at most a few months. Diane believed strongly that she would suffer terribly from treatment and that the treatment would be unsuccessful. She did not wish to be treated for leukemia. Quill's response to this desire constitutes the first of three significant reasons he has to assist his patient to commit suicide.

The Right to Choose Death

Quill has for a long time advocated active and informed choices by patients of treatment or nontreatment. By themselves these choices need not be made with the intention of ending one's life. Patients may refuse treatment they regard as unduly burdensome and of little or no compensating benefit, everything considered. Quill notes also, however, that he has long advocated "a patient's right to die with as much control and dignity as possible."[39] If one is to do so, then the choices being favored extend beyond the refusal of treatment to the employment of necessary and sufficient means to die when and how one wishes. Many refer to this respect for the choices of patients as respect for autonomy. Indeed, autonomy has been widely depicted as a moral principle.[40] But does it encompass a choice to take one's own life, which is, after all, paradoxically a choice to end all further choices? Quill addresses this question.

The Rationality of Aiming at One's Own Death

Although Quill, as well as Diane's family, had reservations about Diane's refusal to accept treatment, he arranged hospice care for her and made every effort to persuade her to remain in it. Again she refused, expressing a wish instead to "take her life in the least painful way possible." Quill defends this choice as follows: "Knowing of her desire for independence and her decision to stay in control, I thought this request made perfect sense."[41] Quill speaks of checking the rationality of his patient by having conversations to ensure that her judgment was not colored by despair and that all other alternatives had been found wanting. For Quill, taking one's life can be reasonable, and the physician is the one to confirm that it is so for a given patient who, as in this case, will soon die and who no longer wishes to continue the comfort treatment she is receiving. But Quill offers further reasons to involve the physician in facilitating suicide.

Extending the Range of Help

In Quill's own words, "Diane taught me about the range of help I can provide if I know people and if I allow them to say what they really want."[42] Quill is explicit about the kind of help his patient needs because she has chosen suicide: (1) assuring that the suicide will be effective so that the lingering death feared by Diane would not occur; (2) avoiding a violent death and its adverse effects on the patient's family; (3) providing the requisite information, calling her attention to the Hemlock Society; (4) prescribing and indicating the dosages of barbiturates needed to commit suicide; and (5) comforting her family. To help the family and Diane still further, Quill does not inform the medical examiner that a suicide has taken place, giving as the cause of death acute leukemia. Although, as Quill asserts, he gave Diane and her family the best care possible, he is not certain that the law, society, and the medical profession would agree. Therefore, he protects Diane's and his own family from autopsies, investigations, and any possible criminal charges.

In being "helpful" to Diane and her family in all these ways, Quill is consenting to her suicide. Why ought he to affirm and lend support to her decision to commit suicide? Because, Quill argues, people do suffer in the process of dying. Controlling and lessening suffering is not the same as ending it. Diane decides the time has come to end her life precisely at the point at which, as Quill describes it, "Diane's immediate future held what she feared the most—increasing discomfort, dependence, and hard choices between pain and sedation."[43] In short, Quill, like Diane, considers it reasonable and justifiable to avoid choosing between pain and sedation, even if that means choosing to end one's own life or assisting someone to kill herself. Quill is not satisfied to have the physician's role be that of lessening suffering; the physician's role should be extended to include assistance in the elimination of suffering.

As the reader can see, the case I have been discussing strongly supports physician-assisted suicide. Indeed, I believe Quill is a conscientious physician. I do not intend to question his motives. I do intend to question the rightness of physicians assisting in suicides. Nothing less than the future of medicine and our social fabric is at stake.

A Rationale against Physician-Assisted Suicide. As we have seen, the decision by a physician to aid a patient to commit suicide implies moral approval for such aid and for the act it assists. This moral approval changes the nature of the relationship between physicians and their patients and how they behave toward one another. These changes are morally substantial because as I shall argue, several important moral requisites of community are thereby violated and moral cognition is severely undermined. And the violations of these moral responsibilities are violations of human rights.

Advocacy for Life is Undermined or Lost

Given Quill's convictions regarding the right to choose death, not only is he willing to support Diane's refusal of a 25 percent chance to escape a certain death, but he helps her family overcome their reluctance to accept her refusal. In effect, those most able to give Diane strong reasons to wish to extend her life are all encouraged to accept what is perceived to be her wish to die. One stout advocate for Diane's life might have made a difference. Even so, the affirmation of an individual's life even when, and especially when, she is deemed to be dying is and has been one of the most significant ways in which physicians have eased dying for the incurable and brought healing for others. And the affirmation of each individual patient's life has been one of the most significant ways in which physicians have contributed to sustaining the inhibitions against taking human life and sustaining the proclivities to nurture life, health, and spiritual growth.

Advocacy for Pain Relief Is Undermined or Lost

Once the choice to take one's life is perceived as justifiable, the need for meticulous efforts to relieve pain and alleviate suffering is simply not there, or at least not as pressing. Al Jonsen recognizes this unfortunate implication of physician-assisted suicide: "If pain can be ended by the death of the patient, why persist in the careful titration of medicine and emotional support that relieves pain and, at the same time, supports life."[44] One of medicine's greatest advances, pain relief, is put in jeopardy by any shift to physician-assisted suicide as an accepted practice. One of medicine's greatest moral responsibilities, empathic nurturing care, is also put in jeopardy by this shift in relating to patients who are suffering.

Preventing Suicide Is Severely Compromised

Included in the rationale in favor of physician-assisted suicide is the notion that the patient has a right not only to refuse treatment but also to die. If physicians are being enjoined to extend their care for patients by ensuring death for those patients who choose it, when and under what circumstances are such choices to be honored? The moral boundaries limiting the justification for therapy, however difficult to determine at times, involve assessments of the harms and benefits of using that therapy as compared with not using it. When, for example, death is certain without therapy and a complete cure virtually certain *with* therapy, physicians have a basis for working hard to gain acceptance for that therapy, even to the point of seeking a court order or treating without consent under emergency conditions. But what if the patient expresses a preference for death and requests assistance? If choosing death is an individual right, then others have an obligation to secure death for the bearer of that right or at least an obligation not to prevent the quest for death, and any assistance necessary to secure it. Once

Kevorkian's willingness to assist in a suicide was well known, individuals came to him who were not terminally ill. To argue that he could have and should have refused to assist them is to argue that physicians are only obligated to assist terminally ill patients.

But that argument means that the circumstances that justify physician-assisted suicide are not those determined solely by the express wishes of patients. Indeed, Quill clearly wants to limit his assistance to those suicides he deems to be rational. And despite what he says about his commitment to the right of patients to choose death, his express actions and thoughts reveal a commitment as well to making a judgment, as a physician, as to whether Diane's suicide is rational. After all, as a physician he is aware that medicine generally tries to prevent death by suicide. And that, for him, is a dilemma that bears scrutiny.

To begin with, there are physicians who are convinced, by their own research and that of others, that those who kill themselves are suffering in ways that can be and should be prevented. Peter Sainsbury, a director of clinical psychiatric research already cited above, does not regard anyone who commits suicide as "healthy."[45] Sainsbury urges that doctors be educated in medical schools and in their careers to be aware of suicide as a preventable cause of death. Whereas Quill refers his patient to the Hemlock Society, Sainsbury is working toward easy access to psychiatrists by all health care personnel and by lay organizations, explicitly mentioning the Samaritans. As the reader may know, the Samaritans are as dedicated to preventing suicide as the Hemlock Society is to helping individuals commit suicide readily and painlessly.

A recent psychiatric study specifically notes the growth of movements such as the Voluntary Euthanasia Society in the United Kingdom and the Hemlock Society in California. The study notes that these organizations believe that those who have painful, disfiguring, or disabling terminal diseases should be encouraged and assisted in viewing suicide as a rational solution. These authors cite studies indicating that the numbers of suicides increase as a result of publicity and cite further studies that suicides are almost always associated with mental disorders. They doubt that the additional number of suicides stimulated by publicity will be rational. Furthermore, they regard depression as underdiagnosed and inadequately treated. With all of this in mind, they studied terminally ill patients who were competent and willing to give consent, and who experienced pain, severe disfigurement, and/or severe disability. They summarize their findings as follows: "Among 44 terminally ill patients, the majority (N = 34) had never wished death to come early. Of the remainder, three were or had been suicidal and seven more had desired early death. All the patients who had desired death were found to be suffering from clinical depressive illness."[46] For obvious reasons this study did not use "suicidal thinking" as a criterion for diagnosing depression. Despite the small sample, the study coupled with all previous research calls into serious question the rationality of suicide.

Preventing suicide is also a total communal effort, an effort not confined to the medical profession but highly influenced by it. Beyond the medical research that strongly suggests that people who profess a desire to commit suicide are not functioning rationally, there is a whole body of research that views suicide as a social problem with social causes. I refer again to research that pointed toward Durkheim's assessment that "suicide will not be widely prevalent in a society that is well integrated politically, economically, and socially."[47] When physicians like Quill weigh in against the constraints society places upon suicide and assisting in it, they may, from a communal perspective, be viewed as a threat to the social fabric and the human relationships that help integrate, or hold together, our society. The nurture and protection of human life, especially of those individuals whose hold on it may for various reasons be tenuous, is at the very core of what is required to sustain communities, families, friendships, and human cooperation. We are literally here at one another's mercy. Quill would have us reinterpret mercy in a way that undermines this axiom of our very existence.

But Quill and others may protest. What physician-assisted suicide proposes to accomplish is limited to those individuals who *choose* to kill themselves at the very end of their lives, under very limited and special circumstances. Something more needs to be said about the assumption that these suicides can and will be limited and voluntary.

Informed Choice Does Not Serve as a Limiting Condition for Physician-Assisted Suicide

As we have observed, what Quill and others propose is that physicians assist only in decisions to end one's life when physicians judge such decisions to be rational. The judgment that a particular suicide is rational, or rationally justifiable, is a judgment that under certain circumstances it makes sense to take the view that it is better to die than to live. This judgment is a logical extension of judgments constantly made by medical professionals: (1) that their interventions be more beneficial than harmful; and (2) that they make every effort to prevent, avoid, and/or remove what is harmful to their patients. If a patient is perceived to be suffering unduly, and if the physician who perceives this can conceive of no preferable way to relieve that suffering, it would be best that the patient die. This is a rationale not only for honoring a request to help assure a patient's death but also a rationale for assuming that given certain circumstances, as judged by the physician, death is what a patient would and/or should want, whether or not a desire for it is being expressed. In short, this rationale for physician-assisted suicide is also at once a rationale for euthanasia, voluntary and involuntary.

A carefully documented government study of the practice of physician-assisted suicide and euthanasia in the Netherlands offers evidence for the actual conditions under which physicians provide for the death of their patients.[48] In the Netherlands, euthanasia is officially under the strict mandate that it be persistently requested by the patient. Yet, in addition to 2,300 instances of active voluntary euthanasia and 400 cases of physician-assisted suicide annually, there were 1,000 annual instances of active *involuntary* euthanasia. And there were 13,511 annual cases that qualify as cases of active involuntary euthanasia but were not called that in the government report. I refer to 4,941 instances of giving morphine in excessive doses with the intent of inducing death and 8,570 instances of withholding or withdrawing life-prolonging interventions with the intent of causing death, and doing so in all of these instances without the consent of the patients involved.[49] If the reader does not wish to classify these as involuntary euthanasia, these are, in any event, deaths aimed at by the actions of physicians in the absence of any request by their patients that they act with the patient's death as their aim. In 14 percent of the cases of involuntary euthanasia, the patients were fully competent, and in 45 percent of the cases in which the lives of hospital patients were terminated without their consent, families were not informed.[50]

How could it happen that physicians would act to assure death for their patients without their consent in violation of official guidelines and the law? Among the most frequently cited reasons were: "low quality of life," "no prospect of improvement," and "the family could not take it anymore."[51] In short, the physicians judged that it was best that the patient die when they made that judgment, not later. Patient requests do not limit the extent to which physicians assure the death of their patients; understandably, they only act in this way when they judge it is right so to act. Dutch physicians now account for 11.3 percent of all deaths in their country through their practice of involuntary euthanasia.[52]

As Quill presents it, the case of helping Diane commit suicide seems benign and very much an individual instance of meeting a patient's wishes. I trust that the reader is amply aware, for some of the reasons suggested, what a profound change in the role of physicians and of the foundations of our society is at stake in what Quill has done and advocates. Even if we grant that Quill made some reasonable assumptions about Diane's actual wishes, her wishes were not tested by making certain that someone in the situation was permitted, or if necessary, assigned the role of a persistent advocate for her life and treatment in the first instance, and for comfort care in the second instance. When Quill relinquishes this role for himself, and then also persuades the family to abandon this role as well, two very important components of the requisites of community are left without a defender: the inhibition against taking human life, one's own included; and the proclivity to nurture. In this case, nurture would consist either in treatment if consented to or offering comfort while life lasts, including the affirmation of the preciousness of individual life in its last days. This has been the role of physicians in the West, in accord with the ethical traditions embodied in the Hippocratic Oath for at least twenty-four centuries.

If the reader believes it would have been an interference in Diane's freedom for Quill to stay within that tradition, then I have failed somehow to convey sufficiently how much Diane as a free moral agent is, or can be, influenced by the affirmation of her wish to die at her own hands by both her physician and family. Diane may well have wished to have assurances that her family and friends be spared any burdensome, prolonged bedside care and nurture. She has the power to speed the beginning of their new lives without her, and she has this power even if no one is willing to help her. But it was Quill's decision to move toward a situation in which any reasons she might still have had to live and die a natural death were no longer encouraged. In short, there is no way to remove moral suasion in Diane's case. It is there in the path Quill chose; it is there as an alternative path when physicians retain their roles as advocates for life, even when comfort treatment is the most appropriate way to express it by reason of the patient's terminal condition and wishes.

But it is important to place Quill's actions in a larger context. We have done that by pointing to what is happening in the Netherlands as a result of giving official approval to physician-assisted suicide and euthanasia, mercy killing. When physicians depart from their role of advocating life and nurture of the fatally ill, they often do not honor the patient's right to be treated as a moral equal, which includes the right of refusal or consent to whatever the physician advocates. Another requisite of community is thereby violated. Justice requires that individuals relate to one another as moral equals, as human companions who share the inhibitions and proclivities that actualize the moral bonds of community. The presumption of moral equality and the freedom to participate in communal structures is only lost, at least temporarily, by those who break one of these moral bonds, for example, by intentionally killing someone under circumstances the community deems criminal and punishable. Freedom is in fact one of the significant issues in moving toward legally permitting physicians to be free to kill intentionally, or to help someone kill themselves. If physicians are free to kill intentionally, or assist someone to kill themselves, will some die who never even participated in the decisions that led to their deaths? The answer from the Netherlands is "Yes." Furthermore, whenever there are mistakes in diagnoses and prognoses, there will be people who are killed or kill themselves who would not have chosen to do so had they had the correct information. Mistakes happen. These will always be fatal whenever physicians are permitted to kill or assist in a suicide.

But there are already those who, having accepted the policy of voluntary euthanasia and physician-assisted suicide in the Netherlands, express no alarm over the clear evidence that involuntary euthanasia occurs, no alarm over the predictable errors in medical judgments that occur, and no alarm that competent individuals had no voice in their own fate.[53] For them, the role of physicians has already been redefined, and physicians in the Netherlands are simply doing what they always do, acting on their own best professional judgment. The last point raises an important question as to what it means to be a "professional" and make "professional" judgments. Quill's behavior and the current practices in the Netherlands should also be examined from that larger perspective.

What It Means to Be a Professional Is Undermined or Lost

In a previous study, I found fairly widespread agreement on at least three defining characteristics of professions generally: (1) special or unique competence in special tasks and services; (2) a professional-client relationship; and (3) general or social competence in professional and community tasks and services.[54] Physicians who actively aid their patients to commit suicide significantly change what is regarded as professional in all three of these aspects of being a professional. I will argue that these changes in what it means to be a professional are so serious that they are not morally justifiable.

Some have pointed to the medical profession as a profession par excellence because of its reliance on the sciences and highly developed technologies and technical skills.[55] Be that as it may, physicians certainly receive specialized training and education in medical schools, and they receive additional training and education on the job. Certainly they possess highly refined knowledge in making diagnoses and prognoses, and various specialists, such as neurosurgeons and surgeons generally, possess highly refined skills and techniques. These constitute unique competencies and allow them to engage in unique tasks and services for the benefit of individuals and communities. Because of all this, a high degree of self-governance and self-evaluation is not only permitted but is also necessary because of the qualifications needed to set standards of competence. Continuing education and membership in medical societies, including highly specialized associations, are deemed essential to sustaining a sufficient degree of professional responsibility.

Consider now some of Quill's most salient judgments in treating his patient Diane. It was well within his professional competence and responsibilities to diagnose Diane's illness; inform her of the efficacy, risks, and effects of available therapy; and inform her as well of the prognoses associated with therapy and with foregoing it. There is no specialized knowledge, however, as to whether Diane should pass up a 25 percent chance at a cure. One could argue, therefore, that Quill does the one best thing open to him as a professional, which is to find out whether or not Diane wants to seek a cure and whether she understands fully the implications of all of her options, including the seriousness of delaying treatment as she is asked to think about it carefully. But Quill does not leave it at that. He says that he "gradually understood the decision from her perspective and became convinced that it was the right decision for her."[56] This I find puzzling. Quill does not tell us what it is that convinced him. If the chance of that cure had been a little or much higher would he have been convinced? What chance of a cure would lead Quill to see a patient's perspective as wrong for them?

There is a lot at stake here for Quill as a professional; when, if ever, should he fail to try to save a patient's life when he has a chance to do so by curing or reversing a condition that would otherwise lead to that patient's death? I say "try" because any medical intervention is morally and legally bound to obtain a patient's consent or a court order when that is appropriate morally and legally. But instead of remaining an advocate for Diane's life, he adopts her perspective as right for her—a perspective that includes her fatalistic belief that she would die during treatment and lose her opportunity to live some more outside of a hospital, however briefly. The point I wish to make does not hinge on the correctness or incorrectness of Quill's opinion as to what is right for Diane. Rather, Quill's opinion on this is not one he can base on his knowledge and skills as a physician. Indeed, the very difficult moral decision Diane faces is one for her to make. Choosing between some brief but predictable normal life outside of a hospital and a painful treatment that may lead to her death at any time is extremely difficult, if not impossible, to second guess. In such a case, a 25 percent chance at life is also a 75 percent chance to experience a painful death; painful, because adequate pain relief could, sometimes, compromise treatment. There is no scientific and no clear moral basis for taking sides. Quill, therefore, has no grounds, in this respect, as a professional, to give up his general advocacy for what he can do to cure and save Diane's life. Above all, Quill as a physician has no medical or moral basis for making judgments about the circumstances in which Diane, or any of his other patients, would or should prefer death to life. In fact, I wish now to argue that the responsibilities of the physician to advocate the preciousness of individual lives, even when those individuals can only be comforted, should be an ethical hallmark of the physician-patient relation.

Medicine, like all of the professions, involves a professional-client relation. This is true also in the typical hospital situations in which a team of health care providers relate to any given patient. Trust is an extremely important aspect of the physician-patient relation. The life and well-being of patients are highly dependent on the knowledge and skills of physicians, but no less so on their trustworthiness. Truthfulness is essential to trustworthiness. But what about a faithful, unwavering affirmation of each individual patient's life? What the study of physicians in the Netherlands reveals is that once physicians start making judgments as to when life should end for a given patient, it is not only the worthwhileness of living while seriously ill that is questioned, but also the commitment to treating patients and family members as morally responsible individuals, as moral equals of the physicians. And so some competent patients, and in other instances family members, were not informed of the physicians' decisions and actions deliberately to end life. These are serious breaches in honoring the human rights not to be deceived, not to be the victim of an intentional homicidal project, and not to be robbed of one's basic equality as a moral being, responsible for one's life, one's relationships to others, and one's relationship to the universal community of humanity and of being itself.

Quill apparently remains truthful to Diane and her family. His relationship to them, however, does become problematic. He creates a context, step by step, in which it is difficult, if not impossible, for Diane and the family to take up a sustained advocacy for Diane's therapy, in the first instance, and for Diane's life-extending comfort care, in the second instance. Diane is surely in a difficult position should she surface with a change of heart as the whole process moves toward her express wish to take her own life. Be that as it may, Quill has helped to create and sustain a situation in which no one predictably assures Diane all along the way that her continued existence is precious and welcome despite her illness, and despite her strong desire to avoid the kind of nurture she would need from continuing in comfort-only hospice treatment. It is all too easy for any of us to feel that we are a burden to others when illness makes us completely, or almost completely, dependent on the aid of others. The hallmark of the medical profession has been, and should continue to be, that the physician removes that burden by rendering aid while life lasts, even if that aid, in the end, is in the form of comfort only. This satisfies the two-fold requirements of justice: not to cause evil and to nurture. (We shall have more on this in chapters 10 and 11.) To consider oneself and one's life a burden to others is to suffer, and physicians should not, however inadvertently, cause such suffering.

Although Quill did not, as he presents the case, deceive Diane and her family, he did deceive the medical examiners and the larger community by failing to report the immediate reason for Diane's death. Although he had good intentions, this action, as well as his assistance in a suicide, needs to be examined from the standpoint of how professionals, and he as a physician, should be related to their larger communities.

Although as I have tried to show, Quill and other physicians cannot claim that their special professional expertise extends to decisions as to how each individual should weigh their priorities and special responsibilities while gravely ill, physicians do share in the moral responsibilities that serve to make communities possible. In short, like all members of the human community, they should honor human rights. Human beings have a right not to be made innocent victims of an intentional homicidal project; they have a right to be nurtured in their dependence and interdependence on others for the necessities of life and self-development; they have a right to be treated as equally worthy members of the human community; and they have a right to be regarded as morally responsible decision-makers unless and until their incompetence, or their violations of the rights of others, requires some lesser degree of freedom, or even punishment, as the case may be.

As professionals, physicians have a special responsibility not to undermine or violate these rights. It is a special responsibility because of the power physicians have by reason of their knowledge, skills, and communal standing, and by reason of the extreme vulnerability of their clients when they are ill, or fearful that they may be. Physicians by their actions can strengthen or weaken the extent to which a given community avoids killing, suicide, and failures in nurturing or caring for one another. Physicians, by their actions, can and do directly affect death rates and standards of care in their communities.

Patients also share in these responsibilities to strengthen, rather than undermine, the requisites of community. They can strengthen our inhibitions against killing and our proclivities to nurture by the manner in which they choose, or strive, to live while gravely ill or dying. We know that published accounts of choices to take one's own life spark imitative behavior. We know also how inspirational are the accounts and direct experiences of individuals who find meaning and purpose in their lives in the face of inevitably fatal illness, and in living while dying. Those who live with comfort treatment also symbolize the preciousness of life and nurture. If physicians come to regard their responsibilities to aid people to live as meaningfully and comfortably as possible, as optional when illnesses are serious, some patients will not know whom to entrust with their lives and to whom to turn for assurances of their worth. Will not the high standards we rightfully set for informed choices with regard to medical treatment demand that if assistance in a suicide and/or mercy killing are accepted options, that individuals be told this before they submit to treatment? And will there be settings for seriously ill individuals who desire treatment in a setting in which physician-assisted suicide and euthanasia are not practiced? If a community views the demand for physician-assisted suicide and/or mercy killing as human rights, then the community has the responsibility to provide personnel and institutions for honoring them. Granting physicians individual immunity from these practices will not grant them immunity from the responsibility to make individuals aware of their rights and to help them be in touch with those who honor those rights. Medicine's responsibility to save and nurture life will be hopelessly compromised by providing optional assistance in killing oneself and having oneself killed.

In a democratic society, the policies of whether or not assistance in a suicide and/or euthanasia are legally permissible will quite justly be decided by members of the community and their lawmakers. I have argued against the legalization of physician involvement in helping individuals to commit suicide or have themselves killed. I have suggested, as well, some reasons why individuals should not seek to make rights out of their desires for suicide and/or euthanasia. The very moral foundations of our communal life are at stake.

Diane could have committed suicide without Quill's help. I would not encourage her to do so. And I am contending that Quill and physicians generally should not engage in actions or make judgments that encourage her to do so. I am also contending that communities not move toward laws that encourage her to do so.

Laws that would establish a right to physician assistance for committing suicide, and hence, a responsibility for physicians to provide such assistance, create a serious problem for moral cognition. Both the government and the community within its jurisdiction will have compromised the possibility of achieving loving impartiality within the community and among its members. For loving impartiality is (1) a form of self-love informed in part by wishing oneself and the other to exist; and (2) a love of particular communities informed by the actualization of the moral requisites of community. Loving impartiality is not compromised by permitting Diane, and those in similar circumstances, to refuse life-threatening burdensome treatment, even when such treatment is the only chance significantly to increase her life span. She requires the freedom to assess her moral responsibilities to herself and others. But to enact a policy that permits physicians to go beyond their competence by affirming a patient's wish to die, or by presuming that they know when others have such a wish, involves the state in an official sanction of the wish to die on the part of individuals and physicians. When that happens, as it has in the Netherlands, the presumption of the wish to live is severely compromised. We have already documented the results of such a change in the context for moral cognition. Many patients are involuntarily killed because they are presumed to have wished to die, given their circumstances, without being asked; in some cases patients are not asked, even when they are competent to express their wishes. In the Netherlands, the state is not only failing to protect the lives and freedom of its citizens adequately, but it is also undermining virtue. I refer to the virtue of improving one's moral character by improving one's adherence to and understanding of the ideals of moral cognition.

The responsibility to nurture moral development, and as part of that, to nurture individual and communal improvements in moral cognition, has not yet been explicitly discussed. Nurture will be more thoroughly discussed in chapters 10 and 11. We turn now to consider how rights are related to justice.

PART III

Justice Reconceptualized

Justice, Rights, and Nurturing Life, Health, and Self-Development

TEN

The Nature and Bases of Rights
Justice, Nurture, and Divorce in Western Law

In her most recent book, *Rights Talk: The Impoverishment of Political Discourse*, Mary Ann Glendon, a professor of law at Harvard University, has presented a fascinating comparison of rights talk in the United States of America with rights talk in European liberal democracies.[1] She notes, as I have, the influences of Hobbes and Mill, influences much stronger in the United States than in Europe: Classical and religious traditions have retained more influence in Europe than in the United States. Hence, when she notes differences between United States and European conceptions of rights, these include some of the following characteristics of American rights talk: "its legalistic character, its exaggerated absoluteness, its hyperindividualism, its insularity, its silence with respect to personal, civic, and collective responsibilities."[2] These are rather stunning and significant inadequacies. She stresses especially the many unfortunate implications of what she calls "a near-aphasia concerning responsibilities" that "makes it seem legitimate to accept the benefits of living in a democratic social welfare republic without assuming the corresponding personal and civic obligations."[3]

This strong tendency to disconnect rights from responsibilities has serious practical and theoretical consequences. In accord with the rights theory I have been developing, rights are not and cannot be actualized unless individuals, groups, and social institutions are willing and able to act responsibly. By acting responsibly, I mean acting to maintain the moral bonds of community. Understanding responsibilities as the basis for rights in no way diminishes a strong concern for human rights. On the contrary, communities committed to honoring human rights are communities in which its members are committed to meeting their moral responsibilities to one another and to other communities. The reader should know that Glendon's criticism of American rights talk is motivated by a desire to strengthen what she regards as America's already strong rights tradition. And she also sees that strengthening rights is dependent on strengthening the connections, conceptually and behaviorally, between rights and responsibilities.

In this chapter I wish to pull together, clarify, and apply a theory of rights rooted in and derived from our most fundamental human responsibilities. It is a theory that stoutly defends individual rights, but not the kind of isolated individualism that disconnects individuals from one another and from their communities by disconnecting them from their responsibilities to sustain and cultivate the moral bonds of community. The chapter will discuss (1) how justice identifies the relation between rights and responsibilities; (2) rights as just expectations and claims; (3) justice and rights as practical necessities; (4) nurture as a requirement of justice and hence a right and responsibility; and (5) what nurture as a right implies for current divorce laws in the West and their picture of marriage.

Justice: Identifying the Relation between Rights and Responsibilities

John Stuart Mill has stated most clearly the basic relation between justice and rights: "Justice implies something which is not only right to do, and wrong not to do, but which some person can claim from us as his moral right."[4] And what is this "something" that can be claimed as a moral right? Mill specifies this by indicating what kind of obligation (I would say responsibility) justice is:

Justice is the name for certain classes of moral rules which concern the essentials of human well-being more nearly, and are therefore of more absolute obligation than any other rules for the guidance of life; and the notion we have found to be the essence of the idea of justice, that of a right residing in an individual, testifies to this more binding obligation.[5]

In these two passages, Mill gives us his explication of justice in its longstanding generic sense: Justice is the name for what is our due, what we owe one another, what we can claim from one another as human beings. For Mill, rights are claims that are made in accord with justice: What is claimed is some obligation from some individual, group, or institution. For Mill, justice is the name for those moral rules (obligations) to which rights lay claim. Justice, then, using now my own language, is itself a moral responsibility: (1) to honor rights that correctly claim one or another of our various moral responsibilities; and (2) to claim from other individuals, groups, or institutions only those actions for which they can be held morally responsible.

The meaning of justice requires further clarification and development. For one thing, Mill characterizes rights as claims. I believe it is important to understand how individuals can be said to be bearers of rights, inalienable rights. To have rights, I shall argue, does not require bearers of rights to claim them, though justice may sometimes require it. Nor does an individual have to be capable of making claims, or have the capacity to function as a moral agent in order to have rights. This is true not only of legal rights but also of moral rights. For reasons that should become apparent it is also important to distinguish Mill's "moral rules" from what I refer to as moral responsibilities.

Before I proceed, two brief comments are called for. First, I am aware that the notion of justice has been used in quite a number of ways as the literature on justice amply attests.[6] Second, justice also refers to special responsibilities: distributive justice to allocations of goods, retributive justice to the occasions for societal applications of punishment. My present focus is on justice in its generic sense and how justice in its generic sense is linked to rights. What is said about justice in this regard will shape how distributive and retributive questions and policies are perceived and evaluated from a moral perspective.

Rights as Just Expectations and Claims

Mill is on the right track when he views justice as "the name for certain classes of moral rules that concern the essentials of human well-being." Certainly the moral bonds of community, the moral responsibilities that make communities possible and sustainable are "essentials of human well-being." Yes, but they are more than that: The moral bonds of community include what is essential for there to be human beings who can experience well-being. They include procreation and nurture as well as the avoidance of killing. They include, in other words, specific kinds of human bonds, such as those of parents to children. These bonds are not best described as moral rules but rather as morally significant relations or moral responsibilities.[7]

It is clear that Mill does not think of moral rules as bonds that connect individuals and groups to one another. If he did, he would not characterize the "essence of the idea of justice" as "that of a right residing in an individual." Rather what resides in individuals are inhibitions and proclivities requisite for communal life and human life itself, which are the basis for morally significant relations. Since these ways of relating, these moral responsibilities, are characteristic of individual human beings, what also resides in individuals, groups, and institutions are expectations that moral responsibilities will be met. Students and teachers enter classrooms with the expectation of truthful, nonviolent communication and sharing of knowledge and experiences. When this doesn't happen, expectations are not met. The failure to meet such expectations is a violation of rights. What resides in individuals, then, are the moral responsibilities that bring individuals into being and sustain their cooperation. Given that such moral responsibilities reside in individuals, the expectations that people will act on such responsibilities also reside in individuals. These expectations are rights. They do not need to be claimed, that is, asserted, to exist as rights.

"To expect" is at once "to consider reasonable, due, or necessary" and to consider bound in duty or obligated, according to *Webster's Ninth New Collegiate Dictionary.* A right, then, is first and foremost a just expectation, that is, a state of being characterized by ties of mutually expected responsibilities to one another, as individuals and as members of groups and institutions. This state of expecting responsible behavior of ourselves and others need not always be conscious or self-conscious. When, for example, we attend a town meeting or college lecture in a relatively stable community we do not usually consciously consider the fact that we go unarmed and that we do not expect violence against us. The moral structure, acting on the requisites of community—our moral responsibilities as human beings—can create and sustain communal forces that are as relied upon in the daily activities of a community as is the force of gravity, and no more reflected upon. The fabric of a community is tightly woven together by individuals, groups, and institutions as they act responsibly and in this way create and maintain a network of connected patterns of mutual, just expectations. Violations of these expectations tear at this fabric. Should someone come to a town meeting or college lecture and shoot at someone, this would clearly be a violation of the just expectations of those attending: It is a violation of our human right to life. It is at the same time one individual's failure to act responsibly, to maintain the natural inhibition against killing. In situations like this, individuals and public officials are likely to make a just claim, to assert their rights against the errant individual, and should that happen the individual in question will be subject to punishment, at the very least to temporary loss of freedom.

We see from this example that rights as just expectations have a continuous existence, characterizing human beings by reason of their moral ties to one another. Such expectations form the basis for rights as just claims, as demands that some individuals, groups, or institutions meet their moral responsibility to act justly, to honor these expectations, in situations where this is not happening. Rights held inalienably are just expectations; rights demanded are just claims.

That rights are continuous, that individuals are and can be bearers of rights and endowed with them, rests on the natural occurrence of the inhibitions and proclivities characteristic of human beings, those that comprise the requisites of community identified in chapter 5. Human beings and institutions are at once characterized by a capacity to be morally responsible and by expectations based on this capacity. Without the possibility to act justly, to act in accord with the requisites of community, no expectation tied to such acts would exist and no demand for such acts would make sense or be met. Justice, then, is the name for all those moral responsibilities that are requisites of community and that human beings can expect and claim from one another.

The reader may be wondering about the assertion that we are continuous bearers of rights insofar as we are continuously expecting moral responsibilities to be acted on. Surely it is obvious that at least some, perhaps many, of our actions and ties to others are not morally significant, and certainly not requisites of community. Although that is undoubtedly true, it is equally true that some of our ties to others do have continuous moral significance. Among the requisites of community identified in chapter 5 are certain inhibitions that assist human beings to avoid certain injustices or violations of human rights. I refer to inhibitions such as those about killing, stealing, lying, and promise breaking, including infidelity within one's marital covenant. In short, our moral responsibilities to avoid causing evil are continuously honored even while we sleep. Indeed, the moral philosopher Bernard Gert argues that all moral rules should be formulated as rules that call upon individuals not to cause evil precisely because such rules can clearly be exacted of us, and continuously so.[8]

But Gert, like Mill, is not explicitly concerned with procreation, nurture, and providing for one's parents, either as requisites of there being moral agents and communities, or as moral responsibilities. These responsibilities clearly suggest that life will not go on if human beings simply avoid causing evil in the ways cited above. We need to examine why these moral responsibilities should be included among the expectation and claims of justice.

Justice and Rights as Practical Necessities: Moral Requisites of Communities

Having characterized the moral rules named by justice as those that "concern the essentials of human well-being more nearly" and as "therefore of more absolute obligation than any other rules for the guidance of life," Mill goes on:

> They have also the peculiarity, that they are the main element in determining the whole of social feelings of mankind. It is their observance which alone preserves peace among human beings: if obedience to them were not the rule, and disobedience the exception, every one would see in every one else an enemy, against whom he must be perpetually guarding himself.[9]

As we noted in chapter 2, there are rules that forbid human beings to hurt one another: observing these prohibitions reveals the fitness of an individual "to exist as one of the fellowship of human beings."[10] Among these prohibitions the most stringent forbid acts of wrongful aggression, or wrongful exercise of power over others; the next most stringent prohibitions forbid wrongfully withholding from others what is their due, as in failing to render good for good.

All of us as human beings have rights to be secure from violations of these prohibitions. Security is something "no human being can possibly do without: on it we depend for all our immunity from evil, and for the whole value of all and every good, beyond the passing moment."[11]

We can see from these last two paragraphs just how close Mill comes to affirming a theory of justice and rights based on what I have called the moral requisites of community. But there are some critical differences between Mill's theory and mine. When Mill poses the question as to why anyone is morally bound to honor human rights, his answer is, "I can give him no other reason than general utility."[12] And the highest utility attaches to the claims of justice that, for the reasons already examined, are joint human efforts to make "safe for us the very groundwork of our existence."[13] This last statement sounds very much like what I proposed in chapter 5, but again, the differences are highly significant. It is important to explain briefly why the term *utility* is one I would avoid, and to explain how I see the relation of moral responsibilities and rights to the "groundwork of our existence."

There is no question that justice is the basis for security and making safe the groundwork of our existence. Mill is correct on this point. But justice refers to moral responsibilities and rights that make possible, as well as render safe, our human communities; justice is community forming as well as community sustaining. Justice not only comprises inhibitions (restraints) against causing evil, responsibilities not to hurt others, but also comprises proclivities (actions) to procreate and nurture. These inhibitions and proclivities are both necessary to restrain, prevent, and remove evils, but they are also necessary for individuals to exist at all, and to exist safely and freely. Justice is necessary not only to make safe communities, the groundwork of our existence, but also to initiate and secure the very existence and persistence of communities without which individuals can neither exist nor come into being.

Without procreation and nurture no one comes to be and persists. Procreation and nurture are social acts requiring the cooperation of more than one individual, and the cooperation of others complying with the inhibitions and proclivities characteristic of justice. No individual and no couple can stand alone to assure the sustenance of life. No one is immune from illness and fatigue, to cite only one of the obvious reasons for interdependence. Nurture, as I understand it, is as essential to protecting life and the right to it as the prohibition against killing; it is essential also to physical, moral, and spiritual development, and the rights to these.

So far, then, it is evident that Mill and I differ in the way in which we discover what justice requires of us. And this difference leads me to add procreation and nurture to the moral responsibilities encompassed by justice. Whereas Mill tries to discover the rules "essential to well-being," rules that involve our security and fitness for human fellowship, I try to discover the requisites of community.

Furthermore, as we noted earlier, if you ask Mill why we should honor human rights, he appeals to "general utility." There is no question that the requisites of community have very high utility, since they make possible our very existence and our freedom to pursue our various goals. But the identification of these highly practical human relationships is guided not by asking what has utility for our pursuits, but rather by asking what is functionally and logically necessary for our existence and for our pursuits.

What if Mill replied, as he could, that he would be willing to acknowledge the high utility of the human relationships that make community possible. After all, he might be willing to add that he has recognized that individuals should be educated; indeed he has argued that the government should require education for all and that a prime purpose of education is to develop and facilitate the social feelings and abilities that increase participation in society and its institutions. What is more, he observes: "The fact itself of causing the existence of a human being is one of the most responsible actions in the range of human life."[14] He also takes the view that some parental responsibilities can justifiably be legally required. Given his doctrine, however, that each of us naturally pursues our own happiness (utility), there is, for Mill, no necessary and no natural predictable relation between utility and nurture. (I shall not repeat the criticism of Mill's doctrine of psychological egoistic hedonism offered in chapter 2.)

Nurture: A Responsibility, Right, and Requirement of Justice

Nurture is a natural proclivity. It is exhibited in the procreating units of the mammalian species. Among humans, the provision of shelter, nourishment, discipline, and education for their offspring is much more extensive and prolonged than among other mammalian species. Bringing a human being into the world brings with it all the aforementioned responsibilities to nurture. Communities expect couples who procreate to nurture, and there are laws against the neglect and abuse of children, as well as laws requiring child support. Communities are also prepared to share in the nurture of children. The commitment is worldwide, as the United Nations' "Universal Declaration of Human Rights" attests. Among the rights communities are expected to honor and secure are rights to education and to a standard of living adequate for the health and well-being of oneself and one's family, including food, clothing, housing, medical care, and necessary social services. Motherhood and childhood are entitled to special care and assistance, and all children are entitled to this same social protection, whether born in or out of wedlock.

Nurture, as I am using the term, is clearly understood in some respects as a requirement of justice worldwide. There are explicitly acknowledged rights to nourishment, shelter, health care, and necessary social services. These rights are to be realized through ensuring an adequate standard of living for individuals and their families. The right to education is to be compulsory and free, at least through the elementary school level. Although the right to education as the United Nations articulated it is portrayed as a communal, governmental responsibility, the other rights, as well as preschool education, presuppose responsible parents. But how well are communities and governments encouraging and fostering responsible parenthood? And how well are children being educated outside of the home to become responsible parents?[15]

In 1948, when the United Nations approved its *Universal Dec-*

laration of Human Rights, Article 16 spoke of the right of men and women to marry and found a family. The third paragraph of Article 16 declared: "The family is the natural and fundamental group unit of society and is entitled to protection by society and the State." Some kinds of protection have already been mentioned: freedom to marry and have a family; a standard of living adequate for sustaining the lives and health of families; and free education, at least at the elementary level. In Article 26, on the right of all to an education, the freedom and responsibility to educate their children is at least partially protected: "Parents have a prior right to choose the kind of education that shall be given to their children."

I view this as a partially protected freedom because parents may not have the resources to opt for what is not publicly provided. Still, affirming the right to choose suggests attention by the community and the State to what will make parental choice a real possibility. In the United States, for example, parents have the option to educate their children themselves within their own homes, provided that they meet certain curricular and other requirements set by their state. In this case, however, there are also economic constraints, particularly while the children are young and require close supervision by a parent who might otherwise be earning wages.

But the United Nations' *Universal Declaration of Human Rights* does not expressly address the responsibilities parents have to educate their children morally and assist them to develop a good moral character. The inhibitions and proclivities that actualize the moral requisites of community can be strengthened through giving instruction, by being an example, and by rewarding positive development. Development of the personal characteristics congenial to the realization of the ideals of ideal companionship can be strengthened by similar parental efforts. Food, shelter, clothing, and health care do not suffice to sustain and protect the lives and well-being of children, or, for that matter, adults. Life and well-being depend also on developing and exhibiting the inhibitions and proclivities that make communities possible. Insufficient self-love and lack of empathic understanding of others threaten life and well-being, whether through substance abuse, violent or hateful behavior, or other violations of human rights and one's own self-hood. Nor can freedom be achieved in any of these ways. Having brought children into existence, parents who make no effort to improve their moral development are abandoning them in a highly significant and potentially lethal way. And, the effort to aid and instruct children cannot be accomplished unless parents also accept the responsibility continuously to improve their own moral development.

The responsibilities to improve one's own moral character, and to aid others in doing so, are not only parental responsibilities but responsibilities for everyone. For W. D. Ross, improving one's own moral character is one of the two "duties of self-improvement." He describes these as improving "our own condition in respect of virtue or of intelligence."[16] (I take it that Ross means by "intelligence" what we would more likely refer to as "intellectual abilities.") These same two duties to improve ourselves obtain in our relations to others "whose condition we can make better in respect of virtue or of intelligence."[17]

In Plato's *Apology*, Socrates finds it incredible that he, or anyone else for that matter, should be accused of knowingly corrupting young people. To corrupt others would be to subject oneself to the wrongdoing of those one has corrupted. Why would anyone be so foolish? Socrates recognizes that our lives, our freedom, and our well-being depend on whether others meet their moral responsibilities. Since human beings are capable of doing wrong as well as doing what is right, the formation and sustenance of communities require, among other activities, that individuals cultivate the inhibitions and proclivities that actualize and maintain the moral bonds of community. Nurturing moral development in ourselves and others are therefore also moral requisites of community. Individuals, families, and social institutions have responsibilities to work on behalf of virtue.

A word is in order about virtues. Virtues are traits of character and dispositions. For example, the inhibition against lying and the proclivity to tell the truth, when viewed as traits of an individual, can be described as honesty, a moral virtue. Honesty refers to a disposition to avoid lying and to tell the truth. An individual's moral "character" consists of a whole set of more or less permanent virtues to the extent that it is "good," and consists of a whole set of more or less permanent vices, to the extent that it is "evil." Moral virtues are dispositions to act in accord with the moral requisites of community; vices are the dispositions to violate these moral requisites.

Since the moral requisites of community are actualized by certain inhibitions and proclivities, one could describe these as virtues or dispositions. There are some who are inclined to think that the whole of morality is concerned with virtue and character.[18] But it would be a serious error to try to encompass all of the moral life by reference to virtues, or traits of character, or even an entire way of life. These are, to be sure, important aspects of morality. The moral bonds of community, however, are morally significant relations between and among individuals, and between and among groups and social institutions. What happens to these relationships and within them has moral significance. When, for example, an individual sets the record straight about a neighbor who has been falsely accused of a crime, this is the morally right relationship to that neighbor and to the community and its institutions. The act helps to sustain the moral bonds of community. The act may not be particularly virtuous, if in this case, the individual has been truthful only for ulterior motives.

Motives are also traits of character regarded as morally praiseworthy and blameworthy. Of particular importance to attaining a good character is the desire to be responsible, to do what is right, to be morally conscientious. Moral conscientiousness would include also the desire to improve one's cognitive abilities to perceive what is right and what is wrong. Striving for the traits and circumstances that constitute ideal companionship and the conditions constitutive of ideal companionship would be virtuous. Indeed, such a quest has been viewed as a whole way of life, having as its purpose the reign of justice on earth, or from certain religious perspectives, the reign of God on earth. Also from a religious perspective, some would say that human efforts alone will not usher in a universal community characterized by justice and peace.[19] Nevertheless, to be the kind of person who works toward such a community, and who assists others to do likewise, is to be morally virtuous, a person of good character.

Returning now to the United Nations' description of the right to a free education, we note some partial concern for moral education. Mentioned in Article 26 is that education should be directed "to the strengthening of respect for human rights and fundamental freedoms," and to the promotion of "understanding, tolerance, and friendship among all nations, racial, or religious groups, and shall further the activities of the United Nations for the maintenance of peace." It is not exactly clear what kind of curriculum is implied by these goals for education, but the goals are such that they can only be achieved by some degree of moral development in those who are being educated. But simply to say that parents have a prior right to choose the kind of education their children will receive does not, as we noted earlier, specifically acknowledge parental responsibilities for the moral development of their children, not even with respect to the United Nations' moral goals for education for their children. Presumably, parents are free to choose an education for their children that does not seek the moral goals of concern to the United Nations. I do not think the United Nations had this in mind. Whenever rights are articulated without a rationale, however, and without reference to the responsibilities on which they are based, we are left without significant guidance as to how such rights are to be actualized and honored. Furthermore, the moral goals the United Nations does mention do not reach to the most fundamental moral responsibilities that require cultivation if those goals are to be realized. With so much education going on outside of family circles, educators, more than ever before, have responsibilities to teach and model the moral requisites of community. Nor should parental responsibilities to do likewise be taken for granted. The dispositions of all human beings include tendencies toward the neglect of responsibilities as well as tendencies toward causing evil. And so, in the traditions Calvin represents, governments are viewed as necessary to restrain individuals and groups from evil and to enforce justice, the actualization of human rights and responsibilities. Education is necessary but not sufficient for the moral development of individuals and communities; laws and their enforcement are also necessary. And, we remind the reader, so are intentional moral communities and the freedom and responsibility to form and maintain them.

So far, then, I have depicted nurture as an individual, parental, and communal responsibility: (1) to provide the necessities of life for oneself and others, including care while ill; (2) to educate oneself and others morally and intellectually; (3) to cultivate one's own moral development; and (4) to aid others to develop morally. All of these modes of nurture serve to protect, sustain, and enrich human lives, our own, and those of others. At the same time, these are ways in which individual and group freedom is increased and enhanced, adding to the protection given to human freedom by the natural inhibitions and legal restraints against causing evil. But our account of the various forms nurture takes as a moral responsibility is not yet complete. Nurture also includes responsibilities: (1) to prevent and avoid illness, injuries, life-threatening situations, and violations of human rights generally; and (2) to save or rescue ourselves and others from these same situations and violations. These are also individual, parental, and communal responsibilities. These responsibilities of nurture as related to health care and the "duty to rescue" will occupy us in chapter 11. For the remainder of this chapter, I wish to focus on the responsibility and right to nurture as they apply to divorce laws. Presently, the nurture of children is undermined by them.

Rights and Responsibilities to Nurture in Western Divorce Laws

Glendon describes in considerable detail what she calls "the lone rights-bearer" found in American law and legal discourse.[20] The right that epitomizes this emphasis on rights as belonging to or characteristic of separated, independent individuals, is the "right to be let alone." In 1890, Samuel D. Warren and Louis D. Brandeis wrote, in an influential article, "Gradually the scope of these legal rights [to life, liberty, and property] broadened; and now the right to life has come to mean the right to enjoy life—the right to be let alone."[21] In 1928, Louis Brandeis, a United States Supreme Court Justice, called the right to be let alone "the most comprehensive of rights and the right most valued by civilized men."[22]

Viewing individuals as rights-bearers is not uniquely American. It occurs in modern legal systems more generally but with important qualifications. In German Basic Law, for example, the individual's social dimension is made explicit. The right of individuals to the free development of their personalities is limited by the "rights of others," "the constitutional order," and the "moral code." Courts are required to give all of these various rights weight in their decisions.[23] Summarizing the similarities and differences obtaining between American and European legal systems, Glendon notes:

> The hallmark of modernity in law is, as Sir Henry Maine pointed out in 1861, that, "The individual is steadily substituted for the Family as the unit of which civil laws take account." What distinguished American law is not its "individualism," but its view of what the individual is. The comparative perspective suggests that our image of the lone rights-bearer has predisposed us to an unnecessarily isolating version of privacy.[24]

As Glendon also observes, nowhere else is the separation of individuals from each other as "pronounced as in the rights discourse of the United States, where 'liberty,' and 'equality' did not rub shoulders with 'fraternity,' and where, at the end of the nineteenth century, the essence of the right to life would be reconceptualized as the 'right to be let alone.'"[25]

When Glendon asks where this idea of individuals as isolated rights-bearers originates and why it is so much more strongly held in the United States, she refers to the dominance within seventeenth and eighteenth century philosophy of depictions of humans as solitary creatures in a state of nature. This is a departure from ancient philosophies, what we know about protohuman hominids, and life in simple societies. Glendon briefly summarizes such accounts in Hobbes, Locke, Kant, and Adam Smith. Though varying, these philosophers had little to say about family life or what women might have been doing in a state of nature. And, says Glendon, "their generic images of 'man' as a radically free and independent individual necessarily implied the rejection of many traditional views of what was 'natural' in the relations between the sexes and between parents and children."[26] They treated the dependency of children as a quickly passing phase and paid little attention to the circumstances of mothers. Yet Hobbes saw children as under the power, or Rousseau as under the care, of others until they could fend for themselves. Though Rousseau saw the family as a "natural" society, he described family relations in the state of nature as "instinctive" and "fleeting." Locke, concerned to undercut attempts to justify monarchy by appeals to a supposedly benevolent "natural" dominion of parents over their children, attacked the family.[27] "Thus," says Glendon, "at the very heart of the modern tradition of natural right, there was a repudiation of the idea of the human person as 'naturally' situated within and constituted through relationships of care and dependency."[28]

Glendon is correct to stress that the ideas of Hobbes and Mill influenced American law much more than continental European law.[29] One reason for this is the persistence in Europe of older images of human individuality. These include Aristotle's contention that human beings are political, that is, social, animals. Aristotle asserts that a man "who is in need of nothing through being

self-sufficient is either a beast or a god."[30] Another, older image is
that of Jewish and Christian affirmations of human beings made in
the image and likeness of a loving Creator. But as Glendon recognizes, the differences between American and continental European
legal systems is a matter of degree. As we have seen in earlier chapters and will observe again a little later, the various concepts of the
individual are being debated in law and in the larger public arena.

As already indicated, one of the important areas affected by the
growth of individualism in Western law is that of familial relations.
Western divorce laws have permitted an increase in suffering for
children and custodial parents. Legal support for nurture has
greatly declined.

Between 1969 and 1985, divorce law in almost every Western
country was, in Glendon's words, "profoundly altered."[31] In the
mostly Catholic countries of Italy and Spain, civil divorce was introduced, and in Portugal divorce was extended to include Catholic marriages. "The chief common characteristics of all these
changes," according to Glendon, were the recognition or expansion of nonfault grounds for divorce, and the acceptance or simplification of divorce by mutual consent."[32] When in 1969, California
became the first Western jurisdiction to eliminate fault grounds for
divorce, some believed that this would be what would happen in
other places.

Glendon sampled twenty countries to study divorce law in the
West. Most of them did not eliminate fault grounds for divorce but
rather added a nonfault ground: Among them are mutual consent,
separation, or marriage breakdown. Usually these statutes hedge
in the breakdown or separation grounds by safeguards for dependents and by waiting periods. In some of these compromise statutes, the courts retain some power to deny a unilateral nonfault
divorce if the dissolution of the marriage would result in severe
hardship or unfairness for a nonconsenting spouse who is not at
fault. The following table summarizes Glendon's findings.

Grounds for Divorce in Nineteen Countries

Mixed Fault and Nonfault Grounds			Nonfault Grounds Only	
Required waiting period of more than 1 year for contested unilateral nonfault divorce	Required waiting period of 1 year or less for contested unilateral nonfault divorce	Mutual consent required for nonfault divorce	Judicial discretion to deny contested unilateral divorce	No judicial discretion to deny divorce
Austria (1978)	Canada (1968–86)	U.S. (2 states)	Netherlands (1971)	Finland (1987)
Belgium[a] (1974–82)	Switzerland[a] (1907)		W. Germany (1976)	Sweden (1973)
Denmark (1969)	United States (22 states)			United States (18 states and D.C.)
England[a] (1969)				
France[a] (1975)				
Greece (1983)				
Iceland[a] (1921)				
Italy (1970–87)				
Luxembourg[a] (1975–78)				
Norway (1918)				
Portugal (1975–77)				
Spain (1981)				
United States (8 states)				

Note: Reprinted by permission from Mary Ann Glendon, *Abortion and Divorce in Western Law: American Failures, European Challenges* (Cambridge: Harvard University Press, 1978), 68.

This table classifies countries according to two criteria: the extent to which their divorce statutes have (1) abandoned the fault principle and (2) accepted the possibility of divorce by one spouse who opposes the divorce and has committed no marital "fault." The dates of the most recent major changes relating to the grounds of divorce are in parentheses. Countries vary, of course, in the extent to which these ideas are put into practice by the courts, the cost of implementing statutory rights, the opportunities offered for tactical delay, and so on. Ireland, which allows no divorce, is not included in the table.

[a]In these systems of mixed grounds, the court has discretion to deny a divorce sought by one spouse against a nonconsenting partner who has committed no "fault" in the technical sense of the divorce laws.

Once again America is among the countries marked by an extremely individualistic approach, accepting in effect an individual right to divorce. As Glendon points out:

> Sweden and nineteen American jurisdictions have accepted the idea that each spouse has a right to divorce. Canada since 1986 and twenty-two American states are very close to this position, because the breakdown ground in their statutes is available after a waiting period of a year or less, and the courts have no discretion to deny a divorce on hardship grounds. [33]

What sets these countries apart from the other countries in Glendon's sample is that "the forms of divorce they have adopted have altered the legal definition of marriage itself by making it a relationship terminable at will" and that by one spouse's will. [34]

Although the countries sampled differ in the extent to which they provide for the financial needs of children and their custodial parents after a divorce, it is nevertheless the case that in all of these countries, custodial parents bear the major economic burdens that result from divorce. Also, children's situations are worsened financially, and as we shall document shortly, in other ways as well.

Within the American and English systems, in which judges have almost complete discretion in divorce settlements, Glendon reports:

> The expense of raising children after divorce falls disproportionately heavily on the custodial parent, who in the great majority of the cases is the mother. Study after study has shown that after divorce, noncustodial parents typically enjoy a higher standard of living than that of the custodial parent and dependent children, and indeed often higher than they themselves had before the divorce. [35]

This means that the mother's earnings and public assistance are more important than support payments for meeting the needs of children. And that is a problem for women in both England and the United States and throughout the West: "In England and the United States, a typical unemployed female head of household lives on half of the net average production worker's wage, while the French, Swedish, or West German counterpart lives on 67 to 94 percent of what an average production worker earns in those countries."[36] And inadequate as it is, child support is often unpaid in the United States. Efforts have been stepped up to enforce payments, but these efforts are also opposed by civil libertarians concerned about the privacy rights of support debtors should there be employees' wage deductions and federal help in tracing support debtors. But the amounts awarded for child support in the United States are too low, usually less than noncustodial parents can afford and less than half of the costs necessary to raise a child at some nominally decent level.[37] Judges are reluctant to burden absent fathers, have little concern for reducing the costs of the AFDC program, and tend greatly to underestimate what it costs to raise a child.[38]

The United States endorses spousal independence and self-sufficiency as do the Nordic countries but without their commitment to assure it by public or private means. Lacking in the United States are features one finds in the Nordic and continental legal systems: careful judicial supervision of the financial arrangements for children; mechanisms to ensure that child support is adequate; efficient ways to collect child support; a system of advancing support up to fixed amounts in cases of default.[39] Given the lack of a generous public assistance to families, Glendon concludes that the United States, more than any of the other countries examined, "has accepted the idea of no-fault, no-responsibility divorce."[40]

So far, this account of changes in divorce law has been focused on the economic deprivations divorce brings to children and their custodial parents, largely women. This unfairness is not totally compensated even by legal systems that expend a great deal of effort to glean adequate spousal support payments and to make up for the loss of it in direct assistance. This is true because divorce is associated with a number of serious problems encountered by children. Studies exist that children of divorced parents are significantly more at risk than children of intact two-parent families for the following adversities:

◆ Behavior problems[41]
◆ Suicide[42]
◆ Unhappiness[43]
◆ Problems in social development[44]
◆ Lower self-esteem[45]
◆ Setbacks in and diminution of academic performance[46]
◆ Dropping out of school[47]
◆ Loss of grandparents[48]
◆ More distanced familial relations with stepparents and stepgrand parents[49]
◆ Increased problems in adulthood[50]

This list of specific studies of the children who have experienced a divorce (mostly American studies) is by no means complete. I am only concerned to illustrate that it is completely unrealistic to individualize decisions to divorce. Each individual is deciding for others, not just themselves, especially in a legal system in which their responsibilities for others are not required of them. Individuals who walk away from their spouses, or their spouse and children, exercise enormous unilateral power, breaking off relationships with all the hurt and changed circumstances that ensue from such a shattering of relationships. In the American legal system, those offended against are virtually powerless to prevent or restrain such irresponsible spousal behavior, and powerless to exact some shared responsibility for, at the very least, material necessities.

The rights of children to be aided, to be supported, can be actualized to a very high degree by law and law enforcement. That has been demonstrated in countries like Sweden and in certain counties of Michigan.[51] Furthermore, Glendon takes the view of law she finds in the anthropologist Clifford Geertz, namely that law interprets our culture to ourselves and sums up and reinforces our ideals. Given this interpretive and constitutive function of law, "changing the law so as to eliminate a duty where one has long existed cannot help but have some effect on behavior and attitudes. . . . American divorce law in practice seems to be saying to parents, especially mothers, that it is not safe to devote oneself primarily or exclusively to raising children."[52]

In view of the extreme disadvantages experienced by children and custodial parents within the existing structures of American legal practices, Glendon proposes the following: (1) Separate divorces that involve children from those that do not; (2) for the largest single category, divorces involving children, make the welfare of children the first priority of the financial arrangements and create mechanisms to assure these are adequate and fair; and (3) change the tax laws so that the individuals paying support for children will gain some tax advantages.[53]

Although these are, I believe, very helpful suggestions, Glendon is aware that there are philosophical struggles being fought out in American communities and beyond. Which views will prevail have a significant bearing on the degree to which responsibilities to nurture will be actualized and encouraged by a community's laws. According to Glendon, the American story about marriage as it is told in the law and in popular literature has these ingredients: (1) Marriage is a relationship with the primary purpose of fulfillment for the individual spouses; (2) if this function ceases, no one should be blamed and either spouse may terminate it, if they wish; (3) each spouse should be self-sufficient, but if this is not possible, property division and temporary maintenance should be arranged; (4) children appear in the story only faintly, at best in the background as "shadowy characters."[54] Glendon follows this story by noting that other stories do exist in American culture. These depict marriage as a lifelong relationship, for better or for worse, persisting in sickness and in poverty. These are stories as well that stress that parenthood is an awesome commitment, and that one should be prepared to take on responsibilities and see them through.[55] But for the most part, these stories are absent from American law. In the cultural discussions of marriage and family life, Glendon tells us: "American law has weighed in heavily on the side of individual self-fulfillment. It tells us that if a marriage no longer suits our needs . . . we can choose to sever the relationship."[56]

Underlying these competing stories Glendon has so aptly summarized are competing conceptions of what is natural and what rights are associated with our natural inhibitions and proclivities. Hobbes, as the reader will recall, depicts individual human beings as naturally solitary, seeking pleasure and avoiding pain for themselves, and driven by the desire for self-preservation. Social relations and communities only come into being by agreement and contract. Being married and having children are not natural relations. What sustains them are the pleasures they yield and whatever force laws are able to exert. In the Hobbesian view, whatever force laws exert is experienced as an arbitrary imposition on the individual's natural inclinations, particularly when the marital relation and/or children bring the individual pain. One can readily see that someone who has internalized the Hobbesian concept of the self and its purposes would favor a legal system in which the individual is not required to nurture and aid others and can at will sever relationships with a spouse and children. Since failure to nurture and render aid is natural to one concerned with self preservation, and severing pleasureless or painful relations equally natural, why should any blame be attached to any of these practices. In this Hobbesian view, self-fulfillment is not naturally connected to rendering aid, to being married, and to having and nurturing children.

Now drop the drive for self-preservation but retain the quest for pleasure and avoiding pain. Then add a powerful drive to be "let alone," to live one's own life as one sees fit, and you have the essential concept of the self found in Bentham and Mill. In this view, self-fulfillment is also not naturally connected to rendering aid; to marital relations; and to having, raising, and nurturing children—it is not even naturally connected to preserving one's own life. Self-fulfillment, at its core, is doing what one wants with one's own life. I wish to be fair to Mill. He very much sought to make a case for educating individuals to be social, to participate in their communities, and to meet their responsibilities to educate and financially support their children. But, as we have indicated previously, Mill's appeal to utility, grounded as it is in the egoist desire for pleasure, does not provide a sufficient basis for the socially responsible self Mill admires. Mill has severed the natural association between pleasure and responsibility and so has to find ways to tie them together, but from individuals not necessarily naturally inclined to derive pleasure from being responsible.

In this book, I have endeavored to tell a different story about self-fulfillment. As individuals we are naturally guided in our behavior by inhibitions and proclivities. These same inhibitions and proclivities are community forming and community sustaining. Indeed, these inhibitions and proclivities are requisites of communal life, forming and maintaining what I have called the moral bonds of community. These moral bonds are formed and maintained by inhibitions against causing evil, that is, against destroying individuals and/or human relations, and proclivities to procreate and nurture ourselves and others. Nurture includes proclivities to aid and protect ourselves and others, to develop morally and help others develop morally, and to prevent and remove evil. Human beings have other inclinations as well which have the potential to overcome the inhibitions and proclivities that are constitutive of the moral bonds of community.

And so human communities have to cope with the destruction of the moral bonds through actions such as killing, stealing, lying, unfaithfulness in one's relations, and the like. These predictable behaviors are one of the major reasons for governments, laws, and enforcement agencies. The combination of the potential for doing what is right and knowing what that is, and of the potential for doing wrong, intentionally or out of ignorance, argues for a democratic form of government with more than a one-party system and involving a separation of powers; this same combination argues for education concerned with the development of moral character, for freedom of association, and in particular, for communal support for freely formed and maintained intentional moral communities. Intentional moral communities cultivate the kind of self-fulfillment contained in the story of this book.

Self-fulfillment is achieved through the development of one's potential as a unique individual to contribute to the formation and sustenance of the moral bonds of community and democratic institutions that make their free formation and sustenance possible. Self-fulfillment is the development of one's capacity to be lovingly impartial and live in just and peaceful relations with the whole human community, and with the powers in and beyond this world. From this vantage point, the problem is not that American law, and increasingly Western law, elevates individual self-fulfillment as its goal. Rather, the problem is that these laws tend at present to be informed by a view of self-fulfillment that puts the self at odds with moral responsibility, and with what makes for justice and harmonious human relations in our communal life.

The picture of self-fulfillment I have tried to paint is one in which the self in its most basic inhibitions and proclivities is in harmony with the needs and requirements of communal life. These same inhibitions and proclivities actualize the moral responsibilities that make human rights a reality in this world. Let us now, in chapter 11, examine the struggle to actualize human rights in legal approaches to the "duty to rescue," and in the policy debates over access to health care. In these two instances, the struggle involves not only competing visions of self-fulfillment but also competing visions of communal life.

ELEVEN

Justice and Nurture
Rescue and Health Care as Rights and Responsibilities

In chapter 10, I described nurture as an individual, parental, and communal responsibility. Nurture is a demand of justice; a responsibility justly expected and justly claimed, and hence, a moral right. Nurture as a right, responsibility, and requisite of both self-fulfillment and communal life can be effectively neglected, or even overwhelmed in laws and practices guided by a view of the individual as a self-sufficient, "lone rights-bearer." Contemporary divorce laws in Europe and especially in America illustrate how the neglect of nurture as a right and responsibility strain marital and familial relations, to the detriment particularly of custodial parents and their children.

But there is more that needs to be said about nurture. Nurture and communal responsibilities include responsibilities (1) to save and rescue human life; (2) to prevent and avoid illness, injuries, and violations of human rights generally.

It is not difficult to give examples of communal efforts to actualize the responsibilities mentioned under (2) above: individuals, families, and schools provide education designed to help individuals and communities stay healthy and safe; communities provide police and fire protection and safety regulations, as well as criminal justice systems and laws against violations of human rights; governments locally and nationally carry out public health measures, ranging from provisions for clean air, water, and food products, and occupational safety, to the funding of education and research to enhance all of these individual, familial, and communal efforts to prevent illness, injuries, threats to life, and violations of human rights generally. However strong or weak, there is widespread recognition of these responsibilities as requisites of communal life.

I do not plan to take up the myriad concerns that these vital modes of nurture represent. A rich and abundant literature exists on all of these subjects. For the purposes of this book, I wish only to indicate that these various efforts to prevent the harms mentioned are to be regarded as responsibilities to nurture, and as responsibilities, individuals, families, and communities expect and may justly claim from one another. These include expectations at the international level from organizations like the World Health Organization and the World Court, and from international law and treaties, such as those to protect the environment.

Nurture, in the form of rescuing or saving people from starvation, torture, and the ravages of war or natural disasters, is also practiced at an international level. The International Red Cross, the United Nations, various human rights organizations, and various agencies representing a whole range of religious organizations and traditions worldwide exist to save human lives. And many of the organizations that have prevention as a mandate are also devoted to rescuing lives, such as police and fire-fighting personnel, national defense forces, health care workers, and the like. Indeed, as I first began this chapter in the summer of 1992, a great many voluntary and governmental relief efforts were being carried out on a massive scale. These included responses to hurricane damage in the United States and aid to sick and starving people in Somalia and territories in the former Yugoslavia.

It is important to note that those being assisted in Somalia and the former Yugoslavia are victims of serious violations of human rights. These violations have been perpetrated, not only by individuals acting on their own but also by armed groups, including members of armies that should be protecting the individual lives of unarmed individuals and ensuring the safety of the communities they are attacking. In short, while the proclivity to nurture, to save and protect lives, is ever at work, so is the tendency to cause evil, to kill and to leave lives unprotected. From Calvin's perspective, both the proclivity to nurture and the proclivity to cause evil are to be anticipated. As already discussed in previous chapters, our will and ability to act justly make democracy possible, and our will and ability to act unjustly make democracy necessary.

But democratic institutions and governments as such do not necessarily explicitly affirm and support the very proclivities that make communities and democratic structures possible. Rescue is not uniformly and clearly viewed as an individual right and as a responsibility individuals, family members, and communities can and should expect of one another, and exact from one another when necessary. There are conceptions of rights and of human proclivities that tend to weaken, or even repudiate, rescue as a human right. This bears some scrutiny.

Rescue: A Responsibility and a Right

Michael Tooley, a philosopher, is convinced that there is a moral responsibility to save lives, and that it is as serious a responsibility as the responsibility to refrain from killing.[1] In trying to explain why there is a tendency to think of refraining from killing as a stricter responsibility, he calls attention to the energy and time required by positive actions to render aid or rescue someone. What this means, says Tooley, is "that in deciding what to do a person has to take into account his own right to do what he wants with his life and not only the other person's right to life."[2]

Notice what Tooley is doing to rescue as a right. Although he has included rescue within the right to life, the responsibility to rescue has been weakened, if not vitiated entirely. Tooley does not say that the responsibility to rescue has to take into account other moral responsibilities, such as the responsibility not to lose one's own life taking foolish risks to save someone. A potential rescuer also has a right to life. What Tooley is saying instead is that potential rescuers have a right to do what they want with their lives.

Tooley does not qualify the responsibility to rescue in the way in which all responsibilities have to be qualified: responsibilities do sometimes come into conflict with one another. And as already noted, the right to life of a would-be rescuer may be on the line in some of the situations calling for rescue.

By citing a *right* to do what one wants with one's life as a possible reason to deny life-saving aid to someone, Tooley advertently, or inadvertently, leaves open the question as to whether governments have the responsibility, or even the right, legally, to exact rescue as a responsibility and to punish failures to do so under some circumstances. Whatever Tooley's own view may be in this respect, there is no question, as noted in chapter 10, that "the right to be let alone" has found its way into American courts, and it does serve to deny that anyone has a responsibility to rescue strangers. As we shall see, even kinfolk are treated as strangers within American courts.

Mary Ann Glendon, a legal scholar already referred to in chapter 10, explicitly discusses how American law deals with the "duty to rescue" in her book *Rights Talk* in a chapter concerned with "The Missing Language of Responsibility."[3] It turns out that the language of responsibility is notably absent from American court decisions that involve the "duty to rescue." As she observes:

> In a long line of decisions in American courts, bystanders
> consistently have been exempted from any duty to toss a
> rope to a drowning person, to warn the unsuspecting of an
> impending assault, or to summon medical assistance for some-
> one bleeding to death at the scene of an accident. In one
> well-known case, the operators of a boat-rental service sat on
> the shore of a lake on the Fourth of July and watched as an
> inebriated customer slowly lost his grip on his overturned
> canoe and drowned. A unanimous Supreme Judicial Court
> confirmed that the defendants were not obliged to heed the
> drowning man's screams for help.[4]

Although the Fourth of July case occurred in 1928, Glendon points out that the rule such a case stands for is "still firmly established." In 1980, for example, "it was held that an aunt had no duty to warn her eleven-year-old nephew that the seat on a power mower was loose."[5] Furthermore, she quotes from the standard textbook used to educate future lawyers:

> The law has persistently refused to impose on a stranger the moral obligation of common humanity to go to the aid of another human being who is in danger, even if the other is in danger of losing his life.[6]

> The text continues by giving examples such as that of an expert swimmer who is not required to do anything as he sits on the dock, smokes, and watches the man drown, adding that no one is required to "bind up the wounds of a stranger . . . or to prevent a neighbor's child from hammering on a dangerous explosive . . . or even to cry a warning to one who is walking into the jaws of a dangerous machine."[7]

In the United States, this kind of instruction is not insignificant. A large proportion of public officials have had legal training, and one of the lessons they have been expected to learn is to disassociate their notions of morality from what is legal or illegal. Although this rule as applied in rescue cases currently has many critics, it shows real staying power. It is also being applied in cases in which local government officials have not been held responsible for failures on the part of the police, social workers, and the like, to help people in danger.[8] Indeed, Glendon is concerned that the language being used in court decisions gives "the impression that the United States Constitution somehow embodies a no-duty-to-rescue rule writ large" while failing to stress that the Constitution permits governments, federal and state, to act affirmatively on behalf of those within their jurisdictions.[9]

Readers should not rest secure in the thought that the responsibility to rescue is safe from the influence of what the law may do and say. An American study provides data to support the notion that being aware of a legal duty to rescue does affect people's perceptions of that responsibility.[10] Subjects were asked to evaluate the morality of the conduct of an individual who saw someone drowning and did nothing to help. A group of subjects who were told that assistance in the situation in question was a legal requirement judged the inaction more severely than the group that was told that no such legal responsibility exists. We know also from Lawrence Kohlberg's research that there is a strong tendency to equate what is moral with what is legal and/or customary.[11]

In continental European legal systems, the responsibility to rescue involves one's civic duties, not one's private rights. Criminal sanctions, fines, are exacted from those who fail to rescue. The responsibility imposed is a moral minimum, requiring only those measures that do not involve significant costs or risks, measures such as summoning the proper authorities. The fines are low enough to emphasize the mainly hortatory purpose of the laws on rescue. Summarizing the European emphasis on the law as a teacher and enforcer of moral standards, Glendon observes:

> Continental European commentators take it for granted that making the failure to rescue at least a *public* wrong will operate to encourage compliance with certain basic duties attaching to good citizenship. As a leading French legal scholar put it, the rescue laws serve as reminders that we are members of society and ought to act responsibly.[12]

In European law, we do observe an explicit enforcement of the responsibility to rescue and, hence, in effect, a moral and legal right of the individual to be rescued. Note that there is growing uneasiness in the United States over the no-duty-to-rescue rule. Some courts have expanded what is meant by a "special relationship" and some states require motorists, and in some cases, bystanders, to provide reports on traffic accidents that involve them, or that they have witnessed, as the case may be. Also, all American jurisdictions now have "Good Samaritan" laws that grant immunity from civil liability to individuals who unintentionally cause harm when voluntarily aiding an endangered individual. Furthermore, when the state of Vermont passed such a law in 1967, it established a general duty to assist someone in peril, and penalties for failing to do so in certain circumstances. Minnesota has such a statute as well. As Glendon observes, after reporting these exceptions, "there is nothing alien to American values in making failure to come to the aid of an endangered person a criminal offense."[13] But as we have already noted earlier, the rule against rescue is strongly entrenched in American law and has spread to cases that involve the responsibilities of governments and government officials, even those who have rescue among their responsibilities. Glendon is gently commending a move toward the European approach represented by the laws in Vermont and Minnesota. Everything I have said so far about the requisites of community and loving impartiality leads me to agree with Glendon. I should add the idea, cited above, of the French legal scholar, André Tunc, that individuals need to be reminded by way of rescue laws that we are members of communities and ought to act responsibly.[14] This need for legal reminders and sanctions is realistic, in part, because individuals sometimes have desires that if acted upon, cause evil or allow evil to happen. Governments, in Calvin's view, restrain people from acting on evil desires and remind them of their responsibilities. If and when laws enforce and teach what are the requisites of community, the laws themselves function as requisites of community, or at least, as essential support for their more predictable actualization. This is particularly true for communities encompassing a great diversity of traditions and groups. For in such circumstances, laws help assure that rights will exist for all individuals and groups, whatever their differences.

The responsibility to nurture is, then, among other things, a responsibility to aid or secure aid for those whose lives are threatened. Illness is one of the significant ways in which human life and well-being are put at risk. Does nurture also embrace an individual and communal responsibility to assist those who are ill, and to live in a way that promotes our health and the health of others? Nurturing our lives and those of others, as I have argued earlier, does express itself in these ways. As indicated earlier as well, parents nurture their children by means of efforts to prevent illness and to provide for care when they are ill. Serious failures in such nurture are serious threats to the very lives and well-being of their children, and if serious enough, can result in legal charges of neglect. But what about such nurture for those beyond the reaches of our immediate familial circles? Is there a right to health care? Does the responsibility to nurture extend to health care? Is there a communal responsibility to provide health care for all?

Health care in the United States and generally has been discussed as a question of justice, particularly as a question of distributive justice. Nurture, to the best of my knowledge, has not been an explicit part of the recent debates over universal access to health, at least not in the philosophical literature. But nurture, I contend in chapter 10, is a requirement of justice. I do view nurture as a moral requisite of community, a moral bond connecting us to one another in our communities. I will now offer reasons for universal access to health care that are shaped by our responsibilities and rights to nurture.

Health Care: Responsibilities and Rights to Nurture

Nurturing health and life is what health professionals, public health law, and parents do. How inclusive and extensive should such nurture be? To respond to these questions, I have chosen to focus on proposals for some kind of national health insurance (hereafter, NHI) being debated extensively as I have been working on this chapter. Some hope that some proposal like those I will now examine will be in place soon, perhaps before the present analysis is published. Such predictions are part of the history of these debates over health care. I regard the longstanding impasse in this debate to be the result of, in large measure, what is said or mostly implied about justice and human rights within the proposals themselves, as well as in the debates over them. Nurture as a concept is not found in these discussions.

NHI in some form has been proposed for the United States for more than seventy-five years. Rashi Fein, a political economist at Harvard, who has carefully documented the debates, finds the staying power of NHI quite remarkable. One can, he says, draw two quite opposite conclusions from this: "that, since the conception of NHI has survived for three-quarters of a century, it can't be all bad; or that since it has not been enacted over such a span of time, it must be fatally flawed."[15] What will be apparent in the discussion that follows is that NHI persists as an understandable reaction to concerns about justice and rights. Enactment will remain elusive, or so I contend, so long as the reasons for a right to health care and a communal responsibility to secure that right are not formulated in ways that are extensively persuasive to the populace and their public officials. Policies that are not sufficiently democratic and just as formulated and implemented will continue to prove troublesome even if enacted. I wish to make suggestions in the direction of a more democratic and just approach. That, at least, is my hope.

I will analyze four actual policy proposals for NHI in the United States that are and will be taken seriously in the political arena. Such an analysis will clarify and render explicit the conceptions of justice largely implicit in these policy proposals. Applying the theory of justice I have developed so far, I will indicate what I find less than satisfactory in the proposals that will provide, at the same time, some suggestions for reformulating the rationale for NHI, indicating what rights and responsibilities attach to provisions of health care and why I think it is a communal and individual responsibility to provide access to health care for everyone on the basis of their need for it.

These proposals are not explicitly or primarily proposals to enact a particular view of justice. Rather, they are explicitly and primarily policy proposals for a particular form of NHI. Assessing how just a policy is involves more than identifying the concept of justice that informs and shapes it. To be persuasive, a policy proposal is compelled to meet at least four kinds of possible objections to its acceptance, enactment, and implementation: (1) that it is on the face of it unjust or unfair; (2) that the existing policy, or a policy other than the one being proposed is more just, or at least no less just than what is being proposed; (3) that whatever the merit of the policy being proposed, it cannot succeed, or the chance that it will is very remote; (4) that the proposal is, for whatever reason, cognitively flawed or provides no predictable or reliable process for avoiding serious cognitive errors.

In summary, our ethical assessment will evaluate four concrete proposals of NHI from the perspective of: (1) what justice demands; (2) whether each is in any sense necessary, given the alternatives, actual or possible; (3) how likely each is to succeed; and (4) how cognitively sound each is. These are not arbitrary considerations for evaluation; they all occur within the debate over NHI.[16] Each will be classified and defined in use rather than now, in advance. I should define the term *policy*, however: a goal, or set of goals with specified means to that goal or set of goals.

1. "National Health Program for the United States: A Physician's Proposal"[17]

This proposal (hereafter called Plan 1) is put forward by "Physicians for a National Health Program." It is written by a committee, co-chaired by David Himmelstein (M.D.) and Steffie Woolhandler (M.D., M.P.H.). The authors have provided a concise summary as follows:

We propose a national health program that would (1) fully cover everyone under a single comprehensive insurance program; (2) pay hospitals and nursing homes a total (global) amount to cover all operating expenses; (3) fund capital costs through separate appropriations; (4) pay for physician services and ambulatory services in any of three ways: through fee-for-service payments with a simple fee schedule and mandatory acceptance of the national health program payment for a service or procedure (assignment), through global budgets for hospitals and clinics employing salaried physicians, or on a per capita basis (capitation); (5) be funded, at least initially, from the same sources as at present, but with all payments disbursed from a single pool; and (6) contain costs through savings in billing and bureaucracy, improved health planning, and the ability of the national health program, as the single payer for services, to establish overall spending limits.[18]

What Justice Demands

Himmelstein and Woolhandler (hereafter H&W) are calling upon the national government to adopt their program as an alternative to the present health care system. Why? Because they view the present system as "failing" in the following ways: (1) many people in need are denied access to health care; (2) increasing expense, inefficiencies, and a growing bureaucracy; (3) pressures that threaten the traditions of medical practice in the form of cost control measures, competition, and the quest for profit; (4) fear of financial ruin in patients already suffering.

That health care should be allocated in accordance with need is one widely held conception of justice as applied to health care.[19] To argue that governments should mandate a program that assures such an allocation is to treat such needs as the basis for a right of access to the health care appropriate to meet those needs as they arise. This, in turn, implies that a community, through its governing bodies, has a strict responsibility to provide the resources necessary to make such access possible.

H&W's concern for those who suffer illness does not end with their strictly medical needs: The cost of care for those uninsured and underinsured can be a financial disaster. Prospectively, this can frighten some people from seeking access or continuing in care; retrospectively, this can leave someone completely poverty stricken. The authors are not explicit about it, but they seem to be invoking a community's more general social mandate to enlist government aid for all those who are too poor to meet their basic needs for food, shelter, and the like.

The costs and inefficiencies of the present health care system, as well as the lack of insurance or sufficient money for millions of patients, are unjust for health care providers. The standards of care are compromised by providing less care for the uninsured, avoiding some procedures, consultations, and costly medications. The use of diagnosis-related groups (DRGs) to cut costs places physicians between the demands of administrators for early discharge and the needs of elderly patients who cannot receive care at home. The authors mention also the concern for the bottom line in health maintenance organizations (HMOs) and the general lack of ensuring basic services in public health, such as prenatal care and immunizations for everyone. Again, the authors are mounting a moral argument that the medical profession cannot give the care they ought to give. The resulting unmet needs of patients and the inequalities in the treatment when it is offered, that is, substandard care for the uninsured and the underinsured elderly, are conditions that communities have a responsibility to rectify. One can infer from the authors that it is a matter of right that health care providers be able to practice medicine with a clear conscience.

So far we have noted that the costliness of medical care is cited as playing a role in unjustly denying care to some, either by denying access or by providing less than what is best or needed. This is what some have called price-rationing.[20] H&W, however, are also concerned to stop the escalating costs of medicine relative to the total goods and services available to the U.S. economy and U.S. government: "The total expenditure would be set at the same proportion of the GNP as health costs represented in the year preceding."[21] They expect that existing injustices will be rectified without an additional proportion of GNP, provided that the national government is the single payer of costs and requires all health services and health care providers to stay within the budgets allocated. The authors anticipate that costs will be reduced by this change in administration and by enacting incentives to reduce "excessive care."[22] Missing from their account are reasons for thinking that the present proportions of health expenditures are justified. Nevertheless, this cap on expenditures suggested by the authors is put forward as a responsibility of the national government and, as such, rests on an implicit conception of how the nation's resources ought to be justly allocated.

Necessity

H&W do not consider other proposals to change the U.S. health care system. Their plan is presented as the solution to injustices in the present system. Their alternative to the present system is not compared to other alternatives, except to note favorably its resemblance to Canada's national insurance policy. H&W do note, without elaboration, "Patchwork reforms succeed only in exchanging old problems for new ones."[23] The alternative is their comprehensive national health program in which:

> Everyone is included in a single public plan covering all
> medically necessary services, including acute, rehabilitative,
> long-term, and home care; mental health services; dental ser-
> vices; occupational health care; prescription drugs and medical
> supplies; and preventive and public health measures.[24]

Chance of Success

H&W are aware that their proposal will be judged as to whether the goals of the program can be achieved and whether it will gain sufficient support, socially and politically, to be adopted and tested for its efficacy.

H&W believe that they have provided for meeting the medical needs of those individuals presently without access to care because they have a federally mandated and funded program for universal coverage, and this coverage is comprehensive, as noted above, and does not erect the present financial barriers to vital care through patient copayments and deductibles. These barriers are eliminated.

H&W cite the Canadian system of health care as evidence that comprehensive coverage and the removal of copayments and deductibles do not drive up the cost of health care. For this to be true it is necessary to have global prospective budgets, to sort out necessary from unnecessary care, and to cut administrative costs by insisting on the government as the single payer. Canada is an example of keeping down costs with global prospective budgets and with government as the single payer.[25] And to top it off, H&W propose a cap on federal spending that would of necessity keep costs down.

But can their proposal become policy for the U.S. government? One reason they give us is that almost every public opinion poll over the past thirty years has shown that most Americans and 56 percent of physicians presently support a universal, comprehensive, publicly administered national health program."[26] The authors invite physician acceptance by proposing flexibility on the method of paying for services, whether by fees, salaries, or capitation. In favoring state and local administration of health services, fears of a distanced bureaucracy are considerably laid to rest. The authors do not make this point explicitly, however. Also, patients would have a free choice of providers, reducing that form of opposition as well.

Cognitive Processes
"We are physicians active in the full range of medical endeavors."[27] In this and the next two paragraphs, H&W describe their experiences in the U.S. health care system and the problems and solutions they envisage as a result. They anchor their proposal by appealing to their credentials and expertise, but they do not rest their whole case on their own authority and expertise.

In addition to calling for accountability to the electorate at both the federal and state level, the authors suggest local participation in planning and evaluating medical services: "Boards of experts and the community representatives would determine which services were unnecessary or ineffective, and these would be excluded from coverage."[28] There is, then, a commitment to a public dialogue and to forums for its implementation. At the same time, it should not be overlooked that the authors advocate a cap on federal spending. This sets a definite limit to public deliberations and their latitude in influencing those global budgets and their allocations to states and local communities.

2. "Health Insurance for the Nation's Poor"[29]

We turn now to a much more modest proposal for NHI offered by Uwe E. Reinhardt, a professor of political economy at Princeton University. Reinhardt's reasons for advocating what H&W above might wish to call "patchwork reform" will serve to call into question a number of the arguments H&W use to defend their plan.

Reinhardt's plan (Plan 2) has the following essential features: (1) federal fail-safe insurance for any American who does not have adequate private health insurance coverage; (2) nonemergency care from a limited number of local health maintenance organizations (HMOs); (3) HMOs bidding competitively for the right to serve federally insured patients; (4) the quality of care externally monitored and patients able to vote with their feet; (5) emergency care available from the nearest provider and that care adequately compensated; (6) financing of the federal program based on ability to pay. The proposed fail-safe program would absorb Medicaid.[30]

What Justice Demands

Like the authors of Plan 1, Reinhardt begins to build his case for his federal program by pointing to the increasing number of uninsured individuals in the United States. But the problem of unmet medical needs is not simply the numbers involved. Until the early 1980s, the uninsured could obtain relief for truly serious conditions from neighborhood hospitals. But this situation is not now sustainable: the present predilection for prospective compensation, competitively set, not only destroys the hidden tax base but also puts the health of the poor at risk. This new situation poses the question as to whether people are willing to be taxed to assure that the health needs of the poor are met; it poses as well the question as to "whether, at long last, all of America's poor ought to be granted some basic entitlement to health care."[31]

Reinhardt makes it very clear that he is talking about the demands of justice. He believes that no one can imagine that the situation now pertaining, or the one pertaining in the early eighties, can be called "an egalitarian distribution of health services."[32] To nail down his contention, he reports two examples during 1985: one, an accident victim lay unconscious in a Florida hospital that has no neurosurgeon while two larger hospitals with neurosurgeons refuse to accept him because there is no assurance that the bill will be paid; and two, a comatose three-year-old girl is refused by two hospitals in South Carolina because her family has no health insurance; a hospital one hundred miles away finally admits her.

Reinhardt shares the concern of the authors of Plan 1 for preserving the freedom of physicians to practice medicine in accord with their "professional code of ethics," free from the threats to their economic security and the detailed monitoring by external lay boards, which would be their lot if medical care were left totally to the free market.

Necessity

The reasons for changing from the present U.S. health care system and adopting Reinhardt's proposal focus, as we have seen, on the unmet needs and health risks of the poor and those otherwise uninsured or underinsured. And these unmet needs and health risks will keep escalating unless, and until, his proposed remedy is adopted.

But unlike the authors of Plan 1, Reinhardt takes account of alternatives to his plan. Though he favors an NHI scheme of the sort suggested in Plan 1, he rejects it because it is not a "viable policy option," that is, it is not a plan that stands a "reasonable chance of being legislated and implemented."[33] He argues that "devising a viable policy option for the nation's poor" would be off to "a solid start if it were to accept as a more or less permanent policy parameter that this country is unlikely ever to implement in practice the lofty egalitarian precepts it professes during public debate on health policy."[34] Reinhardt believes that efforts to help the poor have been stymied by protestations that the poor have the best of health care. The best is so expensive that often nothing has been done. Thus, Reinhardt expects Plan 1 to fail; he has hope for Plan 2. His plan is an "improvement" over what obtains now, since it "would be an honest two-tiered health care system that would grant the poor dignified access to a humanely endowed bottom tier."[35]

Reinhardt also regards two other possible policies as not viable: policies that mandate employer-provided insurance and policies that rely on a free market.

Chance of Success

Although Reinhardt's major focus is on the likelihood that a given plan to provide health care for the poor will or will not be adopted, he also attends to the likelihood that a given plan will attain the goals it sets for itself.

Reinhardt's argument that plans such as Plan 1 will not become national policy is based on his assessment of "realistic policy parameters."[36] To be viable, a policy must stay within such policy parameters. He defines a policy parameter as "a cultural, political, economic, or administrative constraint so immovable within the time frame of the proposed policy as to approximate a state of nature."[37] The most important policy parameters constraining public policy on indigent care are: (1) the national ethos; (2) the legislative process; and (3) fiscal constraints.[38]

The National Ethos. Americans think of themselves as egalitarian. This does apply to economic opportunity, as far as Reinhardt is concerned, but offering greater economic opportunity than other countries does not imply an egalitarian distribution of basic human services. Rather, Reinhardt maintains, a belief in equal opportunities to advance economically is likely to lead one "to favor an inegalitarian distribution of economic privilege, because ignorance and poverty are then viewed as products primarily of sloth rather than of bad luck."[39]

Reinhardt does not view the inegalitarian distribution of health services as maliciously intended. If these services were less expensive, they would undoubtedly be shared by the well-to-do. But it is very difficult to move the well-to-do toward sacrificing some of the freedom of choice and superior amenities now enjoyed, given the societal view that success and poverty primarily result from free choice rather than mere good or bad fortune respectively. Reinhardt offers the following argument to support this unwillingness to guarantee strictly egalitarian access to all of the health care available:

> The regulatory structures that must be erected to enforce
> socialization of a commodity inevitably blunt the innovative
> edge of the system that produces the commodity. Thus...
> enforcement of greater equality in the distribution of human
> services would come at the expense of technical progress in
> the production and delivery of these services.[40]

Based on international comparisons, Reinhardt finds that argument persuasive. Plan 1 is vulnerable to this argument on at least two counts: (1) it would keep federal spending constant relative to the GNP; (2) it would create boards to specify what constitutes "unnecessary care." In the first instance, innovation may be reduced by lack of funding. In the second instance, innovation may be stymied because its "necessity" is uncertain, or not perceived. The problem of money is not so acute whenever the GNP experiences substantial increases. But the regulatory problem remains, and H&W have not explicitly offered reasons to expect that their plan, once implemented, is immune to such problems. That means that those who benefit from American medical care at present have a reason to fear some of the changes suggested in Plan 1 because the overall quality of medical care and its delivery are very likely subject to decline.

H&W do have a reply to this last appeal to fear of change among Americans. As noted above, they cite public opinion polls as evidence that the majority of Americans support a program like Plan 1, including the Canadian program. But Reinhardt is not moved by that survey data.

The Legislative Process. Even if there were to be a survey that would convince legislative representatives that the American public favors an egalitarian distribution of health care, Reinhardt contends that legislative action to bring about such a distribution would still not be possible. Reinhardt singles out the moneyed interests of three groups: trade unions, trade associations of health care providers, and health insurers. Although these groups do not have the power to dictate public health policy, each of them has been able to persuade Congress to veto legislative proposals the interest group opposes. Reinhardt draws from that fact the following very strong implications about what it would take to render viable a health program for the nation's poor: It "must not detract perceptibly from the bottom lines of health care providers and insurers, and . . . its chance for implementation is enhanced if it adds to these bottom lines."[41] Furthermore, this policy parameter is "virtually immutable even in the longer run."[42]

If Reinhardt is correct about the power of insurers, "Plan 1" can in no way be considered a viable policy option: "Plan 1" calls for phasing out all private health insurance. Canada did abolish private insurance, indicating that it can be done, but the U.S. government will have to reckon with larger, more powerful insurers and large groups that may not be ready to exchange what they have for what may yield them less.

Fiscal Constraints. Reinhardt takes note of the federal government's quest to reduce its deficits and to do so without raising taxes. Because of this, he does not expect a significant contribution from the federal government toward solving the problems of the

uninsured any time within the next several years other than to ignore hidden taxes upon business. An example of that would be to
mandate employer-paid health insurance. Reinhardt was certainly
right to anticipate proposals of that kind. In 1989, several have
been submitted for scrutiny, including one in the Senate and
House.[43] We will be examining one of those proposals below.[44]

Although mandating private business firms to provide health insurance for all employees may be one of the only viable ways to
help the uninsured in the near future, Reinhardt is critical of any
policy that relies on hidden taxes, which are "invariably unfair and
inefficient."[45] For example, businesses have to pass on the cost of
mandated health insurance to their customers; failing that, they
would have to try to reduce wages. Reducing wages, if successful,
would constitute a regressive tax on employees. Those in the lower
wage brackets could be seriously impoverished by this.

Reinhardt believes that a major advantage of his proposal within
the American context is that it does not call for a full-fledged national health insurance program. Through appropriate calibration
of the tax rate on adjusted gross income, most Americans could be
motivated to seek private insurance. Also, his plan sufficiently
compensates health care providers for care of the poor. His plan
respects the "bottom lines" of providers and private insurers and
significant policy parameters; thus no one has egalitarianism forced
on them.

What about the cost of Reinhardt's program, given his own
warnings regarding financial constraints? Taxes would be based on
ability to pay, and the taxes would be low for those with insurance. Reinhardt suggests that additional money could be raised by
levies on the consumption of alcohol and tobacco and by a health
care tax on gasoline, a major toxic pollutant. One might also remove a major remaining tax shelter and no longer exclude
employer-paid health insurance premiums from taxable income.
This last suggestion invites opposition from trade unions and private insurers. Reinhardt wonders, however, how long this nation
can justify subsidizing health insurance even for upper-income
business executives while appealing to budgetary constraints as a

justification for excluding millions of poor families from basic health insurance coverage. In this case, Reinhardt sees the current tax subsidy to private health insurance as "neither equitable nor economically efficient."[46]

Cognitive Processes

It is not surprising to find Reinhardt relying at times on the authority of economists. Indeed, the whole plan is the product of an expert policy analyst, taking into account the economic and political factors that shape policy and largely determine what policies are adopted and implemented. Reinhardt is sensitive to the situations of health care providers and of those in need of health care. He is not, however, explicitly concerned to increase their ability and power to help define their needs, rights, and responsibilities, or increase their participation in deciding how the health care system could best respond to these. As noted, the authors of Plan 1 also did not move much in this direction. Plans 1 and 2, therefore, do not meet the expectations expressed in the principles by which the American Public Health Association (APHA) judges any proposal designed to provide "National Health Care." Several of these principles are concerned with the improvement of cognitive processes: consumer and provider participation in ongoing planning and evaluation for the sake of improving the delivery of health services; education and training of health workers; and consumer education as to their rights and responsibilities.[47] We shall have more to say about cognitive processes later.

3. "A Consumer-Choice Health Plan for the 1990s: Universal Health Insurance in a System Designed to Promote Quality and Economy"[48]

Suppose someone were to agree with Reinhardt that there are constraints within the United States such that a national insurance proposal like Plan 1, and the Canadian plan so similar to it are not viable and will not be enacted, certainly not in the foreseeable future. Suppose also that this same individual, or collection of indi-

viduals, were to agree with Reinhardt that everyone now uninsured or otherwise barred financially from health care should be
insured in order to provide them access to health care. Would such
agreement lead to an endorsement of Plan 2, or of a plan essentially
indistinguishable from it? No, it would not. The evidence for such
an assertion is not difficult to discover. The "Consumer-Choice
Health Plan for the 1990s" (Plan 3) put forward by Alain
Enthoven and Richard Kronick (E&K) differs from Plan 2, but the
reasons for proposing it include those shared by Reinhardt as indicated above. Plan 3 represents an attempt to formulate a politically
viable and socially acceptable system of universal health care coverage, and yet in ways that still invite debate.

Briefly summarized, Plan 3 has the following major elements:
(1) "Everyone not now covered by an existing public program
would be enabled to buy affordable subsidized coverage, either
through their employers, in the case of full-time employees, or
through 'public sponsors,' in the case of the self-employed and all
others";[49] (2) employers are required to provide private insurance
for all full-time employees and their dependents not otherwise
covered; (3) the State provides subsidized private insurance for all
others, including employees of small businesses (fewer than 25 employees); (4) all plans include at least the basic benefits packages of
the HMO Act, subject to tighter definitions and restrictions as
deemed necessary to control costs; (5) there is no premium for
those with incomes below the poverty level and a sliding scale for
those with incomes up to 150 percent of the poverty level; (6) consumers otherwise pay 20 percent of the average premiums, and employers or the public sponsor, as the case may be, 80 percent, and
no more that 8 per cent of the payroll for small businesses; and (7)
all deductibles and coinsurance are limited to 100 percent of the annual premium.

What Justice Demands

Like the authors of both plans 1 and 2, E&K are concerned
about the number of Americans who have "no financial protection
from medical expenses." As they go on to say: "The present fi-

nancing system is inflationary, unfair, and wasteful."[50] These negative features are also increasing, not abating. The inflationary trend contributes to "deficits in the public sector, threatening the solvency of some industrial companies, and creating heavy burdens for many people."[51] E&K take note of further unfairness: close to two-thirds of all uninsured people are above the poverty level and more than two-thirds of uninsured adults are employed. When such persons are seriously ill, the cost of their care is largely borne by taxpayers, insured persons, or both. From this, the authors conclude that "voluntarily or involuntarily, some people are taking a free ride. Those who can do so ought to contribute their fair share to their coverage and be insured."[52] What is more, these authors (as did Reinhardt) point to recent cost-cutting measures by governments and employers, which are drying up hospital resources for providing uncompensated care and have led some hospitals to close their emergency rooms.

Waste in giving health care is, in a number of ways, a by-product of the financial barriers to care. The uninsured, for example, obtain much of their primary care in the outpatient departments and emergency rooms of public hospitals rather than in the less expensive physicians' offices. Postponing care and lack of preventive care, such as prenatal care, lead to more costly, serious illnesses and to illnesses that could have been avoided. Additional inefficiencies that drive up costs contribute to situations in which the personal savings of the uninsured are depleted.[53]

The demands of justice, then, are the basis for what E&K call the "two main goals" of their proposal: (1) "financial protection from health care expenses for all"; (2) promotion of cost consciousness.[54]

Necessity

If you ask E&K why it is necessary to change the present health care system, they would cite the demands of justice discussed above:

We cherish efficiency and fairness, but we have a system that is neither efficient nor fair. Very few Americans believe that

other Americans should be deprived of needed care or subjected to extreme financial hardship because of an inability to
pay.[55]

They go on to indicate that the American community lacks institutions to correct such inefficiency and unfairness. This proposal is
the remedy for what is lacking.

But what about other proposals now being put forward that
purport to overcome the inefficiencies and unfairnesses with which
E&K are concerned? Why should Plan 3 be adopted? Why not
other contenders, such as plans 1 and 2? In a word, theirs is the
necessary plan because none of the others will work. Their plan
has a reasonable chance to be adopted and to meet its goals; all
others will fail in one or both of these ways.

Chance of Success

One of the major reasons E&K have for believing that their plan
is more likely to be adopted than any of the others is that it is a
"proposal for incremental change," a change "compatible with
American cultural preferences."[56] Like Reinhardt, they do not
think Americans will sacrifice what they already have in the quality
of care for socialized medicine, as in Britain. Nor do they expect
existing health care systems to go out of business quietly and without a struggle. Like Reinhardt, they regard HMOs as partially successful in increasing efficiency and maintaining quality. Their plan,
like Reinhardt's, creates incentives for increasing reliance on
HMOs. But it does so differently.

E&K do not explicitly discuss Reinhardt's proposal. One could
expect them, however, to take issue with Reinhardt's suggestion of
a broad-based tax to pay for extending and absorbing Medicaid.
By doing this, Reinhardt takes a step, however large or small, toward a more federally controlled health care system. And that,
E&K contend, is something Americans oppose, favoring as they
do "limited government and decentralization."[57] One suspects that
the authors favor such a view of democratic justice. Explicitly,

however, the authors contend that these values, and the reluctance to permit governments to redistribute income in any radical way, predispose Americans toward their proposal, since it relies on the reform of incentives in the private sector and encourages those kinds of health care systems already achieving some level of efficiency.

E&K believe that the state as a public sponsor of health insurance can achieve economies of scale, so that smaller, and even middle-sized, employers would be able to purchase insurance at lower rates, with the states acting as brokers. The states also can achieve greater administrative economies by using the agencies that currently obtain coverage for public employees. Moreover, through the use of public sponsors, everyone can be covered at more reasonable rates.

E&K's plan raises money for these public sponsors by having every individual or family above the poverty line, and every employer, contribute some money to the federal government to be used to support the state-administered public sponsors. Employers would only be tax exempt for their 80 percent contribution, and this too would help finance the public sponsors. This provision contrasts with a Massachusetts proposal for mandating employer-provided health insurance that cannot use federal tax laws to generate the funds to assure health care for everyone.[58]

E&K realize that their proposal would mean that the minimum wage would, in effect, be raised by 8 percent. They suggest ways in which this effect could be mitigated.[59] No plan to extend health coverage can be achieved without some regulation and tax support; the authors regard their proposal as a "realistic compromise," "disturbing" economic decision making less than other policies being suggested.[60]

Cognitive Processes

Once again, the perspective is that of bringing some kind of expert advice into the arena of public policy. In this case the expertise is in the sphere of business and commerce. The cognitive enterprise is one of assessing how to provide incentives to cut the costs of health care while extending the population being covered, with as little disruption of existing businesses, and as little growth of government structures and control, as possible. As we have seen, the method of justifying this approach is to point to its congruence with American values and to the power of vested financial interests to oppose radical departures from them. The moral reasons for holding these values as such are not directly addressed.

The authors do make some explicit provisions for critical and widespread scrutiny of how well their plan, once implemented, actually accomplishes its goals. For one thing, the states that have the money to contract affordable insurance for those presently uninsured are accountable to the consumers, who are also voters. Furthermore, E&K consider it a public good to monitor the health care system. There should be assessments of technology and of outcomes so that providers, sponsors, and consumers will all be well informed.[61] The data should also help in "yielding efficient, high quality care."[62]

But as we noted with respect to Reinhardt's proposal, E&K do not meet the criteria of the American Public Health Association for improving critical reflection on health care: consumers and providers should participate in the planning and evaluation; health workers should be trained and educated; and consumers should be educated as to their rights and responsibilities. These concerns are evident in the proposals put forward by Rashi Fein to which we now turn.

4. Toward a National Health Policy Based on Rights to Equity and Cost Control.

Rashi Fein has provided a book-length analysis that admirably illuminates some of the reasons that detailed proposals of the kind we have been discussing so far have consistently failed to become public policy in the United States.[63] For seventy-five years, the debate over NHI has been framed largely by experts, increasingly economists, and carried on by experts, without the necessary mass education and wide participation of the public. Furthermore, the debate has not yet sufficiently clarified what kind of community we are and intend to be; more specifically, the case for health care as a right has not been made, and hence the case for the government's responsibility for guaranteeing universal access to health care has also not yet been made. In this context, Fein amply documents the way in which details of various plans have drawn fire from proponents of alternative detailed plans, always in sufficient numbers to defeat all past legislative NHI efforts.

In the light of his research and careful reflection, Fein has two very basic suggestions to make. First of all, instead of making detailed proposals, we should sketch out and debate the principles that should guide a national health care policy. That debate should not be carried on in simply narrow circles but in the wide arena of public education, with broad public participation. In addition, since Fein expects neither an immediate consensus nor immediate action, he sets out an agenda for what can and ought to be done while the debate over NHI takes place. (So far, as this book goes to press, the current administration in Washington has not heeded Fein's call for an open, public debate before formulating and presenting a plan.)

What Justice Demands

Fein's appeal to justice is explicit. Health care is a right. There are, for Fein, two parts to this right.

First, there is the right of citizens to have money and resources allocated in ways that square with their perceptions of the benefits of health care and of the benefits that might come from using some of that money and resources in other ways. This right is similar to what we expect from our community "in areas such as national defense, highways, education, fire and police protection."[64] All of these require budget decisions.

Second, the right to health care is a right to an equitable distribution of care, a distribution that "reflects medical need and the costs and benefits of care rather than individual income, wealth, political power, or social status."[65] This right is similar to what we expect "in areas such as access to education, parks, and a basic level of sustenance."[66] All of these require allocation decisions. Fein observes that health care, left to market forces, would yield results at variance with the values espoused on behalf of education, the values that move us to offset the consequences of inequalities in incomes. At the same time, equity would not serve us well if the health sector were to be expanded to the detriment of the needs for housing, food, or education.

And so, health care comprises two rights, one to cost-control and the other to equity. Both are necessary. "To achieve them," Fein contends:

> requires a structure that can address both macro and micro health policy, that can determine the citizenry's perceptions and translate them into an effective program, that enables us to make collective decisions. Such a structure operates at various levels. It is called government.[67]

Fein has another reason for invoking government to address medical care. In the marketplace, people vote with dollars and some have more votes than others. However imperfect, the democratic method can more reasonably be expected to meet the health needs of the total population.

And what tasks do these rights to cost-control and equity exact of government? "A universal health insurance program with budget control," says Fein.[68] The government need not produce health care, only concern itself with the amount produced. The government need not operate the delivery system, only hold its agents accountable. The government need not make medical or clinical decisions, only provide incentives and a framework to assist those decisions to reflect medical needs. Achieving equity will increase individual choice insofar as such choices are presently constrained by limited means.

For Fein, to ask what justice demands of us, to ask what we owe one another, is to ask what kind of community we aspire to be in our relations to one another, particularly when some among us are ill or otherwise in need. Competition, as in the free market, should not be the only way in which we relate to one another. Health care should not be allowed to become "just another industry." Fein says, "It is useful to have parts of our society and economy organized in ways that strengthen our solidarity with others, our charitable instincts, our sense of cooperation."[69] The task of government is to encourage those impulses without which equity cannot be achieved. At the very end of his book, Fein clearly names those impulses. Whether we will actualize a more equitable system of health care, something we can and should do,

> depends upon whether enough of us care enough to work at translating concepts of decency, humaneness, cooperation, universality, and justice into actions that would protect all members of the American family. At stake is not only our health care system but the very nature of our society.[70]

Necessity

As Fein sees our current situation, the American public has no sense of a national crisis that would compel immediate and comprehensive action:

> America is willing to wring its collective hands about the costs of medical care, but is not yet prepared to act effectively to control them; . . . it is willing to talk about the need for equity, but not prepared to legislate its enhancement.[71]

Fein does think, however, that NHI will come to be seen as necessary to achieve equitable cost containment. This will come about as price rationing and inequities grow and the middle class is increasingly more affected. Fein gives a detailed account of the forces that will lead to the congressional enactment of NHI.[72]

But if the time for NHI is not yet ripe, what imperatives are there to act now and what actions do they call for? Two kinds of activity should take place. First, since some kind of national, comprehensive, and budgeted system of health care is inevitable, and since detailed schemes keep being defeated, the principles on which NHI can be formulated should now be debated.

But this will take time, and there are people who will suffer if nothing else is done. There are specific changes in the present health care system that will help reduce such suffering. What these should be is guided and rendered imperative by the right to equity and cost-containment in health care. What follows is a summary of Fein's agenda for immediate public involvement in efforts to improve our health care system:

1. Unite with others who see the federal budget as a social document expressing our values.
2. Question the distribution of expenditures and the tax burden;
3. Support the simplification of Medicare's financing, benefit, and payment mechanisms, rejecting means-testing and vouchers for private insurance;
4. Reduce benefit disparities in Medicaid;
5. Provide long-term care—both programs;
6. Extend health insurance coverage;
7. Retain funding for public health, nutrition, and other prevention programs;
8. Help institutions helping the most sick and needy;
9. Encourage competition, such as HMOs;
10. Monitor performance;
11. Become more knowledgeable and more involved, more discerning about pronouncements by professionals, and more able to differentiate analysis and value judgments.[73]

So far as the debate over principles is concerned, Fein's suggestions for framing the NHI debate are embodied in discussions of what will succeed and what will facilitate the most informed decision making.

Chance of Success

Fein argues that health care must be a right both to equity and to cost-containment:

> In the past much of the support for NHI derived from its equity component while much of the opposition was based on the potential for cost increases. Today those who would emphasize equity and those who would emphasize cost control should recognize they need each other. Only if both goals are sought can a sustainable program be erected.[74]

These two goals should be viewed as subject to two constraints: what will be congruent with American experience and attitudes; and what will reasonably mesh with existing ways of financing health care and with the institutions now in place. The current four-hundred-billion-dollar industry is no accident. What is ruled out is a national health service as well as an unbridled free market. A socialized system is too distant from American perspectives; a free market does not take into account what the government now does to support medical care, research, and education.

The reader will recall that all the plans presented in this chapter are working within these constraints. What this admittedly small sample of proposals is able to illustrate, however, is that the responses to these constraints are far from uniform. Plans 1 and 3, for example, differ sharply with respect to the necessity for retaining private health insurance: Plan 1 abolishes private insurance; Plan 3 has government make use of it very largely. Plan 2 includes suggestions that could move in the direction of Plan 1; Fein is much more inclined to leave this matter flexible in the hands of individual states.

Fein emphasizes the advantages of a state-administered rather than federally administered health care system. This, he believes, will help make cost-containment more of a reality and more subject to the needs and oversight of the voters. This could also result in more attention to calibrating premiums on the basis of ability to pay. Nevertheless, the federal government should be involved to make certain that everyone is insured, that benefits are equal, that mobility across states is taken care of, and that financial assistance to states is provided. Although federal assistance could vary, it should be predetermined, not based on the past expenditures of the state. Obviously, these suggestions encourage cost-containment. Federal assistance is also important to help prevent discrimination and to emphasize prevention with respect to what benefits should be available. Everyone agrees that preventing illness, and catching illnesses in their earlier stages, is cost-effective as well as humane. Federal assistance should not be an imposed state burden; states are closer to the people for fine tuning, and allocation criteria can be more nearly determined by those who will live with them.

Fein, like E&K, recognizes how deeply American is the idea of cost-sharing. Like the authors of Plans 1 and 2 he is also aware of how unfair it can be. In the end, he believes the success of any plan depends upon allowing for some measure of cost-sharing. He suggests that unfairness be reduced by the use of tax credits.

Fein agrees with all the other authors that simply mandating employer-provided insurance will not meet the goals of universal and comprehensive health care. Some of the uninsured and under-insured are not predictably cared for in this way.

Cognitive Processes

As the reader has observed, a constant and consistent theme in Fein's proposals is that of participation by the public. He favors a major role for state governments largely because they are much more subject to knowledgeable input and control by citizens and their organizations. Although he does not specify how to accomplish it, Fein urges that the debate over NHI not be left to various experts but that it be expanded to include the public much more, a public that should be provided a greater degree of knowledge about what is at stake. Here he is resonating to similar principles espoused by the APHA mentioned previously. All three of the other proposals discussed above can be faulted for giving insufficient, explicit attention to these principles. Fein is concerned to empower individuals within a heightened democratic process and by means of a benefit package that poses no barrier to preventing illnesses and treatment of illnesses in their earliest stages. These principles are also shared by the APHA.[75]

It should not be overlooked that, from Fein's perspective, the underlying question posed by a debate over health care is the question of what kind of community we are and ought to be. That question itself invites wide public participation in all aspects of health care, the conceptualization of it as well.

A Concluding Assessment: Increasing Justice in Health Care Policy

We have examined four concrete proposals for NHI in the United States. All four proposals contain elements found in debates now going on and likely to continue among lawmakers and prospective lawmakers in the United States. They are plans that stay within the broad working parameters of U. S. health care policy. None accept a totally free market system; each finds a role for the federal government but not one as extensive and powerful as in Britain's national health service. All agree that there should be universal access to health care and that the current situation is not acceptable. Fein documents the problems that prompt the press toward NHI: thirty-seven million Americans, in early 1987, were without any private or public health insurance; prices for health insurance have been rising at between one-and-a-half and two times the rate of the consumer price index.[76] Given the increasingly high cost of health care, the fact that two-thirds of uninsured individuals are employed will not guarantee that any of these employed individuals or their dependents will be able to afford the health care they need when they need it.

As our analysis amply demonstrates, however, despite what these plans have in common in seeking NHI, they clearly have reasons to criticize one another's plans, and to work against plans other than their own. Fein, however, sees how this rush to detailed plans, crafted by experts, contributes to a stalemate in a debate not sufficiently carried on in the public arena. Indeed, Fein has implicitly made a case for increasing the extent to which policy decisions are carried on in a cognitive context more nearly approximating the conditions for "ideal companionship," particularly "loving impartiality." Fein advocates a more democratic process for formulating and debating the principles that make the case for NHI and what it should entail. Also the policy that is adopted should be highly subject to local citizen and state input and control, even if that means variation in policies across states. He does expect federal help financially and other assurances of fairness in coverage across the country, whatever plans may be locally adopted. The American Public Health Association, as noted earlier, adds concretely to improving moral cognition and democratic justice by suggesting that national health policies include: consumer and provider participation in ongoing planning and evaluation for the sake of improving the delivery of health services; education and training of health workers; and consumer education as to their rights and responsibilities.[77] Fein does explicitly speak of this last point, pleading for more education on the issues for everyone so that expert opinion can be more critically evaluated by the general public.

Both the APHA and Rashi Fein do much more than the other advocates for NHI herein examined to identify and work for policies and processes that would improve the conditions essential to attaining moral insight and knowledge. But the debate over NHI, I now wish to argue, has not yet sufficiently addressed nor adequately characterized health care as a right and a responsibility of individuals and communities. Since Fein does explicitly depict health care as a right and also as a communal responsibility, I will compare relevant aspects of his account with that of my own.

Justice and the Right to Life

I agree with Fein: What we do about health care reflects what kind of community we are; and what we think ought to be done about health care reflects what kind of community we think we ought to be.

As I indicated in chapter 5, there are certain moral responsibilities that are requisites of community. Among these are the responsibilities to protect existing human life by the avoidance of killing and by the provision of care and nurture essential to the existence, sustenance, and development of human life. The right to life is the just expectation and claim to having one's life protected in the ways indicated immediately above. Furthermore, this right to life is one every individual can justly expect and claim from their communities and ultimately from the whole human community, as exemplified in United Nations' documents and as called for by the standard of loving impartiality. It is a requisite of community that no human being fall outside of the moral responsibilities to protect life: The right to life is equally a right for each individual.

Health care is one of the important ways in which lives are saved and nurtured. Indeed, twentieth-century medicine is much more of a factor in saving and nurturing lives than in any of the previous centuries for well-known reasons that require no elaboration here. Yet this heightened lifesaving ability of medicine has not yet been adequately recognized in public policy. Many areas in which life is clearly seen to be on the line are covered by laws and government regulations: sanitation; clean water and more lately clean air; pure food, free of known contaminants and more lately, cleansing land of its contaminants; and cleanliness in hospitals, restaurants, and other establishments, as well as many other ways to reduce bacterial infections. Some of these governmental protections of life have long been enforced, such as the pasteurization of milk and treatment of drinking water. The legislative and enforcement records may be imperfect, but the achievements in preventing deaths are well documented in standard histories of public health. In many areas of public health, then, the protection of life has achieved the status of a legally enforced right through legislation and regulatory agencies of federal, state, and local governments. It is time to do the same for saving and nurturing health and life in the delivery of medical care.

Recall that Fein views health care as a twofold right, one to equity and the other to cost-control. The right to equity is the right to a distribution based on medical need and the costs and benefits of care, not income, wealth, political power, or social status. He then compares this right to what is expected in the way of access to education, parks, and a basic level of sustenance.[78] In mentioning a right to a "basic level of sustenance," Fein is invoking the government's protection of individual lives. It is the right to cost-control, however, that he compares with what we expect from our community in such areas as national defense and fire and police protection.[79] These are explicitly governmental services for protecting human lives. It is true that these items all require budget decisions, as Fein indicates. All of these services, however, should be and generally are equitably distributed. In fact, the decisions about how much money is to be spent in each of these areas depends very much, among other things, on whether enough money has been allocated to protect all of the lives in the communities being served. From the point of view of justice as I am using the term, the right to health care is a right of each individual to have the same access to the best possible medical efforts to save, sustain, and nurture life that the community can afford and knows how to provide. The right to life should be regarded as equally a right for all members of a community. That is the presumption that guides, or should guide, what is spent for armed services, police forces, and fire departments. The right to health care should be budgeted on the same presumption as these other life-protecting communal services; and these services are intended for whole communities and everyone in them.

The clear link between the right to health care and the right to life makes the need for NHI very urgent. Those who are uninsured or underinsured are at a heightened risk of death. Their equal right to life is not being honored by the community and its governing bodies. Fein may be correct in observing that the provision of health care is not yet perceived as a crisis and will not be until more people come under the squeeze of its high costs. But the failure of a wealthy society to save lives that can be saved by assuring access to its excellent health care facilities is, in the view of justice I have been presenting, a moral crisis, that is, a preventable violation of human rights, the fundamental right to life.

Justice is threatened also by the way in which cost-control is being discussed in these proposals. The concern with high costs is legitimate but the cuts should not be aimed at reducing care that genuinely meets medical needs. Furthermore, in the short run at least, to equalize the right to life will require more money, not less. There are ways, however, to save money without cutting care. I will note some of these shortly below.

Justice and Equality

Reinhardt is among those who flatly and explicitly see no prospect in the United States that the majority now enjoying access to health care would be willing to pay the price to grant others access to that same high quality of care. His solution is to accept, at least for the foreseeable future, a two-tiered system that is expressly less than equitable. Enthoven and Kronick effectively support a similar set of what they call "basic benefits" for publicly sponsored insurance and add that these should be subject to restrictions deemed necessary to control costs.

This concern to keep the costs of medical care down by reducing the amount and kind of care available is all too common.[80] In a well-known text in biomedical ethics, Tom Beauchamp and James Childress speak of guaranteeing everyone "a decent minimum" in health care, without trying to specify what that would be.[81] Still others are advocating the rationing of certain services for individuals beyond a certain age.[82] And so in the name of comprehensive heath care, we have "experts" ready to introduce age discrimination into the health care sector of our communities as a matter of public policy. An equal, individual right to life is not their primary focus, to say the least. In Britain, we can observe "universally provided" government services saving money by failing to provide certain services to individuals beyond a certain age.[83] In all of the instances of cost cutting described so far, the tie between a medical service, such as a physician and the individual patient, with a medical need determined by a physician, has been replaced by a calculus of the "greatest good for the greatest number." What is deemed "good" in this calculus, for people like Reinhardt and E&K, are their own interpretations of dominant American interests and preferences.

This last point applies to H&W's suggestions that the budget for health care expenditures be capped and tied to its percentage of GNP, and that budgets be prospectively set. Within their proposal they candidly discuss how to go about deciding which services, for the sake of reducing costs, should be considered "unnecessary." Once again, these decisions are not those of an individual physician determining whether or not an individual patient requires care. It is again overall utility that sets limits on available care. In Canada, a country that uses the kind of prospectively limited global budgets recommended by H&W, services are beginning to be curtailed and there are increased waiting periods for the care available.[84] And, what is more, given this situation, individuals with sufficient money come to the United States for care when necessary. Again, saving money is done at the expense of care.

But what about the questions being raised about rising costs, and the possibility that vital services and goods other than health care will shrink unduly unless health care costs are frozen or reduced? Such problems should indeed be addressed. If we take as the primary responsibility of health policy, however, that it aim at preventing preventable deaths and nurturing lives, how money is allocated should, at this point, be addressed very differently.

To begin with, the tendency is to view the limits to be placed upon health care as a trade-off among a variety of public goods and services, all of them vital and worthy.[85] Americans, however, are willing to make sacrifices when they see their individual and collective lives at stake. They do so by transfers of wealth from one sphere to another. Consider the enormous transfer of money for national defense throughout the cold war; research and education are also boosted whenever they are assimilated to national defense as they sometimes have been. Consider also how some of our money is spent in the so-called private sector. We refer to the private sector as "so-called" because all of the money in it is money obtained from others in both the private and public sectors of various communities, our own included. We spend enormous amounts for recreation, for the salaries of entertainers and executives, for goods we can never use because they are so numerous, and for products injurious to our health that directly drive up the amount of illness and the costs of care, such as drugs, alcohol, and tobacco to name a few. Individuals and communities have a responsibility to make every effort to reduce the consumption and easy availability of drugs, alcohol, and tobacco, and to create incentives to live in a responsibly healthy way. It should not be overlooked that being married helps protect individuals from self-destructive habits, ill health, and even premature death, as some recent studies reveal.[86] Nor should the significance of intentional moral communities be overlooked in this regard. The responsibility to nurture human life should move individuals and communities to allocate a greater share of their resources for disease prevention and health care and to create disincentives to make frivolous and harmful expenditures.

But the willingness to transfer money from the private to the public sector to help guarantee universal access to medical care depends also on responsible use of the health care system. The purpose for access to medical care is to obtain a diagnosis, a prognosis, and treatment, if needed and efficacious, and only if needed and efficacious. It is important to support an ethical and economic climate in which physicians are rewarded for avoiding interventions that are not medically indicated, as well as avoiding excessive diagnostic procedures. In these respects, the legal climate should also support technically sound medicine, rather than medical practices driven by fear of being sued. The cost of malpractice insurance is another cost that requires cutting. (Note the policy mentioned below.)

The same ethical climate that encourages physicians to deal honestly with medical need should encourage as well honesty in relating to patients. Patients should have enough information to assess the known risks and benefits of any suggested treatment. Their needs are not only medical, and patients may sometimes exercise moral responsibility by refusing rather than accepting treatment deemed by physicians to be medically beneficial. For example, a medical treatment may carry a high risk of immediate death or a lifelong disability, whereas refusing it may allow an individual a reasonable chance to complete some worthy vocational or familial goal. There should be respect for responsible patient choices. It is particularly important that patients who are irreversibly and imminently dying have the freedom to make choices for aggressive pain management or comfort-only treatment, of the sort available through hospice care. Morally responsible care can be very expensive, but it can also, as a matter of routine, reduce expenses. Irresponsible care is clearly costly and wasteful by definition. One should not only think about the limits of resources to offer care; the need for care is also limited by morally and technically responsible decisions by patients and caregivers alike. As already indicated earlier, the need for the use of medical resources is limited to the extent that individuals and communities encourage and practice healthy ways of living, working, and interacting. Crime, which has not been mentioned yet, is a large medical expense, not to mention an expense that affects the amount of public money available for medical care. Our emergency care is stretched to its limits, at times, by victims of crimes.

With the focus on protecting lives and health for everyone alike, there are other ways to reduce health care costs by cutting expenditures for practices that drive up costs and do not increase the quality and accessibility of health care. C. Everett Koop, the former surgeon general, who now heads the Koop Institute at Dartmouth Medical School, has some suggestions.[87] One is to provide tax credits as an incentive to insurance companies to implement more efficient administrative systems. The estimated savings are one hundred billion dollars. Another suggestion, designed to save two hundred billion dollars, is to undertake outcome research to test the effectiveness of costly high technology or surgical procedures, as compared with less costly conventional or nonsurgical treatments. Still another suggestion is to change malpractice litigation to binding mediation in order to save some forty to seventy billion dollars a year. I do not know how Koop has computed the amount of money his proposals would take out of the health care bill, but they should help make equal access to existing health care more affordable. In short, his cuts are not at the expense of an equal right to nurture.

The possibility of bringing down the expense of drugs is well illustrated by what happened in the case of AZT, a treatment for patients testing positive for the AIDS virus and/or suffering from AIDS. Pressure from these patients and the accompanying publicity combined to persuade the manufacturer to reduce significantly the price of the drug. Public scrutiny of costs is another path to some reductions in health care expenditures without compromising care. In the case of AZT, the scrutiny led to making more care more widely available to those in need. In Canada, federal regulation means that Canadians pay 32 percent less than American consumers do for the very same drugs.[88]

Of course there are temporary situations of scarcity in medicine that are unavoidable. I have in mind the development and testing of new drugs and technologies. During the early period of experimentation, whether with new drugs, technologies, or other therapies, availability is limited in the face of uncertainties. Also, medical facilities can be scarce resources because of emergencies or demographic changes that outpace perceptions of a community's needs. How, in these various circumstances, it is possible to honor the principle of an equal right to life has been very thoroughly and very competently discussed elsewhere.[89]

The quality of care and reduction of costs can be, and is already to some extent, also achieved through an increased use of primary care, or family, physicians. In some HMOs, access to specialists, whose fees are higher, is screened by primary care physicians. Indeed, Koop (mentioned above) would have the federal government use some of its present expenditures in medical schools to help make primary care a more attractive option for medical students.

What I have been illustrating so far is how a theory of rights grounded in and actualized by the moral requisites of community views health care as one of the significant ways in which individuals and communities meet their moral responsibilities to rescue, protect, and otherwise nurture human life. Nurture extends as well to relieving pain and suffering, and restoring or improving bodily and mental functions. When a community provides universal, comprehensive health care, that community is doing what one would hope and expect from each of us, namely rendering the aid needed to a family member, next-door neighbor, or stranger who is injured, distressed, or falls ill before our very eyes. Seeing health care as nurture keeps the focus on the interpersonal character of health care and on the natural proclivities underlying such care. To speak of providing a "decent minimum" of such care, or of rationing it, removes the whole discussion of health care from this elemental human propensity to offer whatever assistance is possible and needed to relieve the suffering, or save the life of a fellow human being. What we do for each individual who needs our help is a test of what we do with our humanity.

Justice and Government's Responsibilities and Role

I have been contending that the case for universal access to health care rests on the responsibilities individuals and communities have to save, protect, and nurture life. These are requisites of individual agency and of communal life, itself a requisite of the existence and freedom of individual agents. These are especially requisites for the life and functioning of all individuals. Nurture and refraining from killing are equally responsibilities and rights for all. To assure equality of these basic rights, access to health care is a necessity.

The assurance that access to health care is universal within a given political jurisdiction becomes a responsibility of government in a situation such as the present one in the United States in which some individuals, including those who are gainfully employed, are priced out of the market for insurance, as are some employers. If the amount and quality of care is tied to ability to pay, as it increasingly is according to H&W and others, then treatment is not equally tied to need. Some individuals will be disabled or die for lack of funds, however hard they work and however responsibly they conduct their lives. When this happens, sick individuals have not been secured in their basic rights.

When medical costs were much more reasonable, the costs of those who could pay little or nothing were passed on to others. But now, this practice of passing on costs to those with insurance is driving up already escalating costs of insurance so much that a greater number of individuals cannot meet the increased cost of health insurance. Fein, then, rightly asserts that the right to health care, including as it does some right to cost-control, can only be achieved by

> a structure that can address both macro and micro health
> policy, that can determine the citizenry's perceptions and
> translate them into an effective program, that enables us to
> make collective decisions. Such a structure operates at various
> levels. It is called government.[90]

I will not repeat the numerous avenues open to governments—to reduce costs in the health sector without reducing the quality of care, and to reduce the amount of care necessary, through incentives to practice sound medicine and healthy living and disincentives for practices that undermine sound medicine and healthy living. Government is needed for reducing costs in these ways also, because both patients, actual and potential, and health care providers need the same kind of help to do what is responsible in the health sector as they need to drive automobiles responsibly. I need not belabor the regulations, incentives, disincentives and oversight of our driving that help assure safety on the roads and hence our rights to life and freedom. Individuals, left to themselves, are not always responsible, nor can they protect themselves against irresponsible drivers left free to do as they please, even if no one intended anyone's death. These realities apply to health habits and professional behavior as well. Libertarian concepts of justice simply will not lead to policies that assure that our fundamental rights to life and freedom will be equally secure insofar as these depend on health care. For a detailed exposition of the libertarian position on this, and for an excellent critique of it, I refer the reader to a fine essay by Allen Buchanan.[91]

Rashi Fein offers another reason for governmental involvement in seeking to make health care equally accessible to all of its citizens. Fein shares my concern for how we are and should be related to another. Competition, as it occurs in the market, is not the only kind of relation communities should engage in and cultivate. Clearly it is not a helpful or charitable way to relate to someone who is ill. Fein takes the view, "It is useful to have parts of our society and economy organized in ways that strengthen our solidarity with others, our charitable instincts, our sense of cooperation."[92] Encouraging such impulses, without which "equity" (I would say "equality") cannot be achieved, is a task of government. From my point of view, the responsibility of government Fein is calling attention to is nothing less than strengthening and maintaining the moral bonds of community. In the case of health care, what is being strengthened and maintained is the proclivity to nurture one another. Instead of speaking of doing this as merely "useful," I have argued for it as a practical necessity of our common life, a matter of strict justice.

This appeal of Fein's to "charitable instincts" and my uncritical acceptance of such an appeal invite opposition from certain quarters. By involving government in the encouragement of our proclivities to be charitable and by implication, sanctioning government interference in our proclivities to fail to be charitable, Fein and I are approving of "enforced beneficence." Fein and I, some would argue, should distinguish justice and beneficence, that is, charitable impulses, and action based on such. "No one," says

Mill, "has a moral right to our generosity or beneficence, because we are not morally bound to practice those virtues toward any given individual."[93] What is Mill asserting? If he is right, does that mean that government should not be in the health care field in the ways that Fein and I are suggesting? Are Fein and I advocating a violation of what constitutes a right to be free of certain kinds of government interference?

Justice and Beneficence

Beneficence has come to take on a rather broad meaning in philosophy. One need look no further than William K. Frankena's introduction to moral philosophy, a popular text, long in print.[94] According to Frankena, the principle of beneficence says at least four things:

1. One ought not to inflict evil or harm (what is bad).
2. One ought to prevent evil or harm.
3. One ought to remove evil.
4. One ought to do or promote good.[95]

Frankena regards these four "principles," using his term for the moment, as different, parts of the principle of beneficence. W. D. Ross is among those who distinguish beneficence from what he calls the duties of "not injuring others," his version of (1) above.[96] These duties not to injure others he summarizes as the duty of nonmaleficence. Ross regards this duty as the most stringent of all duties. Frankena also sees the moral injunction not to inflict evil or harm as the most weighty part of beneficence as he understands it.

But these affirmations of what moral responsibilities are the most stringent do not stand up to scrutiny in actual, concrete situations. Terms like nonmaleficence and beneficence are far too abstract to allow for generalizations about their relative weightiness.

Consider the judgment by a physician that a particular individual has appendicitis and a white count high enough to warrant immediate surgical intervention. The warrant for surgery can be described as follows: the individual with appendicitis is at risk of a ruptured appendix and possible death, a risk that can be averted by removing the appendix; surgical removal of the appendix entails a much lower risk of death. A decision for surgery is a decision that means the physician will injure the patient, even inflict death in rare cases; it is a decision to cause evil or harm, certainly injury with a risk of death. At the same time, it is a decision to prevent what is perceived as certain death, if there is no intervention, and possible death if surgery is delayed too long. This is a decision to prevent an evil, death, and also to remove one, namely the pain of appendicitis. In this case, the prevention and removal of evil are interrelated in such a way that both are more stringent than the general moral responsibility not to injure, or even to refrain from an act that will risk, however slightly, killing someone.

If you ask Mill whether there is a moral responsibility to such lifesaving surgery, he would clearly answer "yes." As he says, "to save a life it may not only be allowable but a duty... to kidnap, and compel to officiate, the only qualified medical practitioner."[97] These lifesaving actions Mill regards as just, insofar as the responsibility to save life is more stringent than the responsibility to refrain from what he would otherwise regard as unjust, namely interference in the freedom of the physician. In this instance, there is a just claim to the prevention of an evil, death, and to the removal of what would cause it, claims more stringent than the claim of the physician to be left alone, or to be free of the coercion of others. If Mill were using beneficence in Frankena's sense, he would not say that no one has a right to beneficence. Obviously, Mill views at least some instances of removing and preventing an evil, such as saving a life, as instances of justice and not of beneficence.

At this point, one might be tempted to guess that Mill equates beneficence with doing good. But that is not totally accurate because some actions, such as rendering good for good, are not, for Mill, counted as beneficent, but rather as just: "Good for good is also one of the dictates of justice."[98] The failure to return benefits one accepts when those benefits are needed is a real hurt, "a disappointment of expectation," a very great evil present in "such highly immoral acts as a breach of friendship and a breach of promise."[99] Such intense disappointments of expectation, such great hurts, are precisely characteristic of the sentiments aroused by violations of justice. In Mill's words,

> The principle, therefore, of giving to each what they deserve—that is good for good, as well as evil for evil—is not only included within the idea of justice as we have defined it, but is a proper object of that intensity of sentiment which places the Just, in human estimation, above the simply Expedient.[100]

Our discussion of Mill has so far revealed that Frankena's very general characterizations of beneficence, and its four principal parts as he sees them, are general and indefinite enough to include, in all four instances, what for Mill are demands for justice. Refraining from evil, preventing and removing evil, and doing good, in returning good for good, can all refer to specific moral rules (Mill's term) that are rules of justice. Individuals expect that others will act in accord with these rules, and failure to meet such expectations are "hurts" and violations of rights, that is, violations of what is our due as individuals. As Mill notes above, such rules specify duties that are not simply expedient because they can be exacted from others as one exacts a debt. That is the distinctive mark of justice; justice is a name for duties (Mill's term) that individuals have a right to exact from others. That is not true of "beneficence" as Mill uses the term. What then does Mill mean by beneficence?

Mill views beneficence as a virtue. Beneficence as a virtue is not something owed to any given individual. Those who posit that humanity generally has a right to all the good we can do for it are forced to include beneficence in the category of justice. This happens because the basis for exacting from anyone a duty to benefit humanity is that of treating what is exacted as a debt, or as a repayment for what society does for us, which is a case of gratitude.

And, argues Mill, both indebtedness and gratitude are instances of justice. In short, Mill's argument is that if what you call beneficence can be claimed as a right, it is another instance of justice, not beneficence.[101]

Mill uses the terms *generosity* and *charity* as synonyms for beneficence. For Mill there are no moral responsibilities to be generous or charitable. We find parallel notions in contemporary moral philosophy. Frankena treats kindness as a personality trait that aids individuals in being moral but he does not hold people morally responsible for being kind.[102] Similarly, Bernard Gert regards concern or care for others as a moral ideal, not something that is morally required of anyone. Indeed, on the way to designating concern for others as a moral ideal, he rejects any attempt to make love and compassion moral requirements. Gert summarizes his distinction between what is morally demanded and what is properly an ideal as follows:

> "Live and let live" is probably the best statement of what the moral rules demand. Do not interfere with others; do not cause them any evil. If one wishes to go beyond the moral rules to moral ideals, one can change it to "Live and help live."[103]

Even preventing and removing evils are regarded as moral ideals, not moral rules. Moral rules forbid causing evil.[104]

Gert's way of linking what is morally required to prohibitions against causing evil is very similar to Mill's way of identifying what is morally required and justly claimed as a right. Recall that Mill uses *justice* to refer to moral rules "which forbid mankind to hurt one another (in wrongful interference with each other's freedom)."[105] And justice is, at this point, again distinguished from beneficence. Mill recognizes an interest in trying to inculcate "the duty of positive beneficence" but to a far lesser degree because "a person may possibly not need the benefits of others; but he always needs that they would not do him hurt."[106] But whereas Gert portrays various acts aimed at benefiting others, such as caring and removing and preventing evil, as moral ideals, Mill speaks of the "duty" of beneficence. Mill does say saving a human life, whether called an act of beneficence or justice, is an act that an individual "may rightfully be compelled to perform."[107] Clearly, then, Mill sees saving a life as a matter of justice and not as a moral ideal.

What then are we to conclude as to the relationship between justice and beneficence? Despite Frankena's careful differentiation of the concept of beneficence, it remains too abstract to be helpful as a guide to action. A brief account of Mill's rules of justice reveals that every one of the four principles Frankena identifies as parts of the principle of beneficence are stated in ways that include what Mill considers to be specific rules of justice. Gert treats caring and much of what passes as beneficence in the philosophical literature not as moral responsibilities individuals can justly expect and exact from one another, but as moral ideals.

I agree with Mill that moral responsibilities (which he calls duties or moral rules) we have incurred, such as a promise, a friendship, receipt of a benefit, and the responsibility to save a life or prevent a death, are all encompassed by *justice* as I am using the term. All of these relationships are, other things being equal, requisites of community. (I add "other things being equal" because I have stated these in the form of specific moral responsibilities, and in cases when any one of these specific moral responsibilities conflict with another, the most weighty one in the circumstances should prevail.)[108]

But what is the relationship of government to "beneficence" as "kindness" or charitable inclinations—that is, as virtues? Certainly it would be difficult, and I agree with Mill, a mistake, to take the view that any individual or group, including a government, has a just claim to everything that could reasonably be called an impulse toward, or an act of, generosity or charity. There are actions, however, that Mill himself places within the sphere of justice that are expressions of what may be and are described as charitable proclivities. What I have been designating as actions and policies of nurturing are precisely such charitable proclivities. Nurture, as one of the requisites of community, not only may be expected and exacted of us, but ought to be whenever failures in nurture would risk or incur preventable deaths, disabilities, and suffering. Governments, therefore, have a responsibility to protect, whenever necessary, an equal right to nurture. But why is it necessary to encourage these specific impulses to nurture, which are charitable impulses, to help someone with a medical need? Because there are obstacles in the way of having and acting on these impulses, high costs among them. And it is also true, as our scrutiny of Calvin has reminded us, that human beings have evil and purely self-serving impulses alongside their generous ones. One purpose of government is to provide, as necessary, incentives for generosity and disincentives for forms of egoistic impulses that are destructive of the moral bonds of community.

When Fein calls for governmental assistance consisting of incentives to incline citizens toward charitable, bonding, and cooperative activities, I would not simply call this "useful" as he does; I would say that incentives of this kind, where human life and suffering are at stake, are necessary for carrying out those requisites of community and nurture, which are demands of justice.

Therefore, I would qualify Mill's view of beneficence and reject Gert's assertion that the demand to "live and help live" goes beyond the demands of what he calls the "moral rules" and I call our moral responsibilities. Some help one another as a matter of justice. Banding together to see one another through illnesses and other threats to life is exactly the kind of aid we expect of one another. Given the costs of care and the scope of our community, a country the size of the United States, governments are there to help us do this collectively by giving our fair share of aid, that is, by giving aid in accord with our capacity to share relative to others. By ourselves, at any given time, some of us could not pay for even one hospital stay, though gainfully employed. Together, sharing our resources, we can be part of what it takes.

In the essay mentioned above, Buchanan presents a tentative defense of providing universal access to at least a "decent minimum" of health care by enforcing beneficence.[109] I will not rehearse his arguments for this. His major reason for exploring this possibility as a possibly necessary policy is that all of the major theories of justice, all theories of distributive justice, are flawed and unable to make convincing cases for universal access to health care. He acknowledges what I have already aired above, that "beneficence" is a vague concept and is unable to offer sufficient guidance for health care policy. With that I agree. I have dropped the concept of beneficence for the concept of nurture, which does call for specific kinds of moral responsibilities from individuals and communities, from patients and health care providers, and from governments.

Although Buchanan considers beneficence to be a vague notion, he does not question that its demands, including generosity, are not demands of justice. As the reader is aware, I have argued against this by arguing that some expressions of generosity are encompassed by the responsibility to act justly.

But do any of Buchanan's criticisms of major theories of justice apply to the one I am advocating? He would regard my theory as egalitarian, given its commitment to equality of access and of treatment as medically indicated. He would have the following complaint against the form it takes: If the level of health care to which everyone is entitled is set as high as is technically possible, then such a commitment would unacceptably strain social resources, and the loss of opportunities to meet needs other than health care would be too great.[110]

If by "technically possible," Buchanan refers not only to the best medicine we have to offer but also to what is strictly medically indicated and efficacious with respect to a specifically diagnosed ailment, then "technically possible" sets some limits to care. If Buchanan thinks we know that these limits to providing healthcare are not sufficient, given all the resources needed by our community, it is still incumbent on him to consider all of the cost-cutting measures that I have discussed above that do not compromise treating people in accord with their medical need. There is nothing in Buchanan's essay about the many forms of resource constraint and reallocation an egalitarian can uncompromisingly sanction and advocate. Before we give up the simple humanitarian goal of treating everyone as we would wish to be treated, namely as one having the option to seek and obtain the available efficacious medical treatment for a treatable medical ailment, I find no convincing reason why cost-cutting measures that do not compromise the quality and availability of health care should not first be rigorously pursued. The efforts would also generate considerable knowledge we do not now possess as to what we can and cannot do in the way of health care because of what actual care for everyone costs.

Justice and the Ideal Conditions for Moral Cognition. There is still another set of reasons to involve government in assuring equal access to health care. It is a matter of democratic justice. It is, in other words, a matter of enabling citizens to participate meaningfully in their community and communities. Health care is surely a vital part of communal life and its benefits. There is no need to repeat the concrete suggestions to facilitate democracy, those found in Fein and those I added. A very interesting aspect of creating universal access to health care is that doing so enhances the ideal conditions for moral cognition, for a whole community and for each of its individual members. Let me briefly explain how.

As the reader recalls from chapters 8 and 9, loving impartiality is one of the ideal conditions for moral cognition. Among its components are wishing that the self and others exist, and empathy, the will and capacity to grieve and rejoice with the self and others. It takes little imagination to realize that increased opportunities to choose health care, for oneself and others, are also increased opportunities to actualize loving impartiality. Loving impartiality, as love for all members of the human community, is also rendered more attainable when avenues to give and receive medial care are based on the needs we have as human beings and not on the contingencies of good or bad fortune—or on our economic status, race, gender, ethnic origins, or religious identities. Loving impartiality is expressed when we aid and are aided as human beings in need.

I have not approached the discussion of universal access to health care in one of the typical ways, that is, by considering and criticizing competing theories of justice. One reason for this is that I have been concerned to offer a constructive theory as an alternative to theories that have been found wanting by their critics. The cogency of the criticisms of existing theories is a second reason for omitting yet another appraisal of them. For such an appraisal, I refer the reader again to the excellent essay by Buchanan.[111]

Among the theories of justice evaluated by Buchanan is the very impressive work of the philosopher John Rawls.[112] His theory can be interpreted, as well as used, to make a case for some kind of right to health care. But as Buchanan indicates, the Rawlsian conception of justice and the theories that draw upon it are inadequate for guidance on the content of this right and how weighty access to health care is relative to access to other social goods. But Buchanan does not take up the issue of moral cognition. He does not ask whether a specific theory of impartiality is implicated in the possible adequacy or inadequacy of a theory of justice as applied to health care. Rawls and the other theorists work with a notion of impartiality quite different from impartiality as I have depicted it. Like Firth, whose view was aired in chapters 8 and 9, Rawls is a major defender of impartiality as disinterestedness.

Rawls uses an ingenious device or thought experiment as a means to set out the conditions that are requisite for an impartial perspective. He has us imagine ourselves as in an "original position" of free and equal individuals choosing what principles of justice ought to obtain in the society in which we will be members with a desire to pursue certain goods as part of our rational plans for our lives. We do so behind a "veil of ignorance," not knowing what position we will have relative to others in that future society. The assumption is that we are "mutually disinterested" as we decide what principles of justice will govern our lives and the distribution of the goods we seek. Being mutually disinterested means that each individual choosing principles of justice is not taking an interest in any other individual making these same choices: "Mutual disinterest" assumes that the parties deliberating for "mutual advantage" are not bound by "any prior moral ties to each other." These same parties do have a knowledge of the moderate scarcity that makes social cooperation both "possible and necessary."[113] Such disinterestedness and scarcity are the "natural circumstances of society" to which Rawls refers when he states, "An account of our considered moral judgments should draw upon the natural circumstances of society."[114]

By now it should be evident that there is a profound difference between what Rawls and I take to be the "natural circumstances of society" from which to draw an account of what we perceive and judge to be morally just. What makes social cooperation possible is not scarcity but the very moral bonds of community from which Rawls would have us disconnected. What makes cooperation necessary is not only scarcity but also natural proclivities toward egoistic, nonaltruistic striving and causing evil. Furthermore, the possibility of perceiving what justice demands of us in the form of requisites of community, our moral responsibilities and rights, rest on an all-loving perspective informed by wishing the self and others to exist; empathy, the willingness and capacity to grieve and rejoice with the self and others; and a love of community that puts itself under the scrutiny of the community that includes all human beings and being itself. These natural proclivities and the inhibitions against causing evil affirm as a first principle of justice maximum protection of life, compatible with equal protection for all. This is not a repudiation of maximum liberty compatible with like liberty for all, the first principle Rawls derives from his conditions for moral cognition. Rather, the protection of life is the aspect of justice on which the actualization of all other aspects of justice, including liberty, depend. With the weight on saving, protecting, procreating, and nurturing life to make communities and all rights and benefits actual for human beings, health care as a vital part of the equal protection of life takes on a clear priority over many other goods and benefits. It has a rationale similar to and as powerful as the rationale for national security, public health law, fire and police protection, and other community services, local and national. All of that has already been discussed previously. I will not belabor the concreteness of what can be said about health care policy from the perspective of loving impartiality. That, too, has already received attention. Providing health care for one another in our communities is at the very heart of the just, nurturing relations on which the inception, sustenance, and future of any community depend. Indifference to the fate and well-being of our companions in being underlies injustice, not justice. Even to perceive the needs of others, medical and otherwise, requires empathy and a wish that they live. Those same proclivities are springs of moving us to nurture, to justice.

It would take me too far afield to respond in detail to Rawls. The differences I have examined serve the limited purpose of undergirding the right to health care as I understand it, and of clarifying further the nature of the theory of justice I have but begun to develop in this book. It is time now for some concluding observations on the nature, limits, and some of the implications of the account of human rights I have been commending.

Epilogue

When I began this book several years ago, I thought that the considerable literature on human rights would provide strong cognitive support for natural rights, particularly the rights to life and liberty. That proved to be wrong. Strauss and MacIntyre, each in their own way, convinced me that something was wrong with modern and contemporary conceptions of rights; each considers earlier conceptions of our moral life more promising sources for efforts to overcome the erosion of humanity's moral structures, rights and all. Gilligan points to the tragic ways in which contemporary individualistic conceptions of rights separate individuals from one another, and from their impulses to engage in and sustain caring relationships and communities. My task changed from a comprehensive study of contemporary theories of rights to an earnest effort to find out what was undermining our confidence in our possession of natural rights, and why theories of rights could promote ways of thinking destructive of our most precious ties to one another as human beings. That led to nothing less than developing a theory of my own as to how best to conceptualize and cognitively support universal natural rights. During this whole period, I was urged on by the gross violations of human rights being perpetuated around the world: terrorist activities, armed conflicts, riots, disregard of gravely ill individuals lacking care, laws that virtually ignore the rights of children and custodial parents, increased acceptance of self-destructive behavior. Many of these violations I began to address explicitly, as the basis for doing so became ever clearer.

Examining the contrast between Hobbes, ushering in the modern era, and Calvin, a bridge between the medieval and modern eras, proved illuminating: Hobbes repudiates the previous consensus represented in Calvin, that human beings are naturally social animals and that communal life is rooted in and sustained by the human proclivity to be morally responsible. Hobbes portrays human beings as naturally egoistic, self-interested, and self-preserving. That notion of natural egoism is expressly embraced in the highly influential works of Bentham and Mill: to be free of interference from others is natural; to be socially responsible requires coercion and education, even sacrifice. This sharp conflict between the interests of individuals and those of others and of society pervades contemporary thought.

Recently I read one of the most extreme expressions of our disconnectedness from one another in yet another contemporary work on human rights. Judith Thomson, a moral philosopher at MIT, says, "If your mother kills you, it is not your father's claims she infringes."[1] Thomson thinks it obvious that only the one killed has sustained a violation of rights. She does not think of the mother's act as a mortal blow to a deep and precious bond between a child and its father. Indeed, she precisely does not base rights on human relationships but on individual claims.

But not only are rights based on human relationships; they have no reality apart from them and apart from the moral responsibilities that make human relationships possible. That is the thesis I defend in this book. It was discovered by asking not only how an individual comes to have rights to life and liberty but also how an individual comes to be an agent and to be protected at all. To come to be and to be protected is only possible through procreation, nurture, and refraining from killing and harm. These natural proclivities and inhibitions are necessary for individual agents to be and persist, and at the same time, they are among the proclivities and inhibitions that are necessary for communities to be and to persist. Relationships that are logically and functionally requisites of communities are at the same time the very caring relations that connect us to one another in friendships; in families; in economic, recreational, political, artistic, professional, and religious associations; and in promise-keeping covenants that make trade, treaties, and constitutional democracies a human possibility. We are naturally social, however self-serving we may also be.

Many of our contemporary views of what constitute knowledge have also separated individuals, groups, cultures, and nations from one another. There are theories that take our moral perceptions and judgments out of the realm of knowledge, relegating them to spheres of subjectivity, privacy, and unique historical and cultural traditions. In my classes I find that students have come to view their decisions as ever more personal and individual. In exams, I have asked students to examine the major arguments that have and could be given to defend and to oppose participation in a bombing mission that would knowingly kill innocent civilians. I asked them also to come to a definite conclusion as to what they would and should do, giving reasons for what they would do and morally justify. One student began his answer by calling this a very personal decision and because of that he would talk to no one before deciding. Not surprisingly, he was also not impressed by what ethicists have had to say. This is another instance of being disconnected—in this case, from other individuals, traditions, and scholarship, all of which are potentially sources of knowledge, as well as sources of companionship at a time of difficulty and possible agony. After all, it is not easy for someone to disobey the command of a superior officer; but neither is killing innocent individuals a matter of indifference.

In responding to this aspect of our present ethos and to theories that subjectivize and relativize what we deem to be moral, I was more concerned to offer a theory of moral cognition than to spend time criticizing theories I found unacceptable. First I addressed the untenable separation of our moral responses from our perceptions, and hence from factual reality. Moral requiredness is a perceptual experience and is the basis on which we distinguish moral facts from nonmoral facts. I found no evidence for taking moral perceptions and judgments out of the realm of facts, once certain dogmas are not allowed to stand in the way of investigation.

Verifying the truth of our moral claims also necessitated some hopefully constructive innovation. Leading and widely accepted philosophical conceptions of impartiality separate us from self-love, and from our love for others and our communities. This makes no sense to me, because these emotions are necessary to reveal what we need to know in order to perceive our moral responsibilities to one another. And so, I speak of "loving impartiality" as an ideal condition for moral cognition, an all-loving perspective we can only approximate. Polanyi, and certain feminist insights, helped me see that knowledge is a communal enterprise.

Jacob Bronowski is another scientist who asserts, as I have in this book, that *all knowledge* "has been built up communally."[2] What enables any fact to be verified is one of the moral requisites of community—truth telling. As Bronowski puts it, "There is a social nexus which alone makes verification possible. This nexus is held together by the obligation to tell the truth."[3] And because of this, it follows for Bronowski that "positivist and analyst methods" imply the social axiom that "We OUGHT to act in such a way that what IS true can be verified to be so."[4] Bronowski's thinking on knowledge appears to square with what I have come to affirm: Only if we can *know* and *do* what is moral, can we know anything at all. And we do have the proclivities and inhibitions that activate the moral responsibilities and human relations that actualize our communities and individual rights. And we have the faith (confidence), functionally or self-consciously, religiously or nonreligiously, that the powers in us and beyond us are sufficient to overcome evil and render moral behavior practical. Or at least, so I contend.

The existence of evil makes democracy and democratic institutions necessary; the existence of morally responsible behaviors makes democracy possible. I have argued, as have many others, that the pursuit of knowledge requires a democratic polity and the virtues that sustain its structures. Freedom of association and loyal opposition are key elements. I have added to the ideal conditions for moral cognition universal support for intentional moral communities, such as churches, synagogues, and temples, in which individuals discipline themselves to cultivate morality, and to view themselves from an inclusive perspective, all of humanity and reality. Individuals and groups need a setting in which to confess their errors and to recognize the indispensability of humility in our individual and communal lives.

The book concludes with justice as the name for all those moral responsibilities, those moral bonds of community that we can expect from others, and if need be, claim from others as rights. I found the concept of beneficence to be excessively vague and unhelpful. Instead, nurture, a set of moral responsibilities, requisite of community, a demand of justice, more concretely than beneficence elicits what can guide us in areas such as physician-assisted suicide, divorce law, laws governing rescue, and health care policy. That is what I have endeavored to illustrate. In all of these areas, it as also clear that human rights are only rendered actual by ensuring that individuals and communities meet the responsibilities on which our very lives and liberties to act depend.

It should go without saying that I have provided no more than a beginning of a theory of justice, the development of which surely requires further illumination from a rich and abundant literature on the subject far beyond what I have cited. It is also true that some very significant human rights have not even been mentioned let alone explicated. A notable one is the right to property, which rests on the inhibition against stealing, a requisite of community that I all too briefly identify and illustrate. This important right is one I do wish to study. Property surely entails a whole plethora of significant ways in which human beings are connected to nature and to one another.[5] And property is also a source of conflict as well.

The ancient Hebrew prophet Micah expresses so elegantly and concisely what this book wants to convey:

What does the Lord require of you but to do justice, and to love kindness, and to walk humbly with your God. (Mic. 6:8, NRSV)

Some among us will see this as an admonition emanating from what is required of us solely by reason of our humanity. Some of us, like myself, will see this admonition as emanating from our humanity but as it is shaped, informed, and empowered by a Divine Being. But all of us can know and do what is just and kind. That at least is what I have been contending.

Notes

Introduction

1. Alasdair MacIntyre, *After Virtue* (Notre Dame, Ind.: University of Notre Dame Press, 1981), 2.

2. Cited in Hans Küng, *Does God Exist?: An Answer for Today* (Garden City, N.Y.: Doubleday, 1980), 692–93.

3. Alasdair MacIntyre, *After Virtue*, 5.

4. See, for example, Karen Lebacqz, *Justice in an Unjust World* (Minneapolis: Augsburg, 1987).

5. G. E. M. Anscombe, *Ethics, Religion and Politics* (Minneapolis: University of Minnesota, 1981), 33.

6. Ibid., 42.

7. Leo Strauss, *Natural Right and History* (Chicago: University of Chicago Press, 1953).

8. Ibid., 251.

9. Ibid., 243.

10. Ibid., 225.

11. Carol Gilligan, *In a Different Voice: Psychological Theory and Women's Development* (Cambridge: Harvard University Press, 1982), 164 and 156.

12. Ibid., 160.

13. Ibid., 125.

14. Ibid.

15. Ibid., 123.

16. Ibid., 124.

17. Ibid.

18. Ibid., 154.

19. Ibid., 155.

20. Alan Gewirth, *Human Rights: Essays on Justification and Applications* (Chicago: University of Chicago Press, 1982), 8.

21. Michael Tooley, "A Defense of Abortion and Infanticide," in Joel Feinberg, ed., *The Problem of Abortion* (Belmont, Calif.: Wadsworth Publishing Co., 1973), 51–91.

Chapter 1. Rights: A Historic Break with the Past

1. Leo Strauss, *Natural Right and History* (Chicago: University of Chicago, 1953), 182.

2. See, for example, Max Weber, *The Protestant Ethic and the Spirit of Capitalism*, trans. T. Parsons (New York: Harper & Row, 1958); Max L. Stackhouse, *Creeds, Society, and Human Rights: A Study in Three Cultures* (Grand Rapids, Mich.: Eerdmans, 1984); Jane Dempsey Douglass, *Women, Freedom and Calvin* (Philadelphia: Westminster Press, 1985).

3. Strauss, *Natural Right and History*, 166.

4. Ibid.

5. Ibid., 168.

6. Ibid., 166.

7. Ibid., 169.

8. Thomas Hobbes, *Leviathan* (1651; reprint, Indianapolis, Ind.: Bobbs-Merrill, 1958), chapters 13 and 17.

9. Ibid., chap. 13, 107–8; chap. 17, 141–42; chap. 13, 108; and chap. 17, 139–40.

10. Strauss, *Natural Right and History*, 189.

11. Calvin, *Institutes of the Christian Religion*, ed. John T. McNeill (Philadelphia: The Westminster Press, 1960), Book II, chap. VII, 1. (See especially footnote 1 on p. 348 and Book IV, chap. XX, 14.)

12. Ibid., IV, XX, 14–16.

13. Ibid., II, VIII, 1 and 2; and II, VIII, 11.

14. Ibid., II, VIII, 39; III, VII, 6; and IV, XX, 12.

15. James L. Adams, "The Law of Nature: Some General Considerations," and "The Law of Nature in Greco-Roman Thought," *Journal of Religion* 25, no. 2 (April 1945), 88–96 and 97–118.

16. Calvin, *Institutes*, IV, XX, 15 & 16.

17. Ibid., II, II, 22; and IV, XX, 16.

18. Ibid., II, II, 12–13; and IV, XX, 16.

19. Ibid., II, II, 13 and 17; and III, VII, 7.

20. Ibid., IV, X, 8; and II, II, 13.

21. Ibid., II, VIII, 39–40.

22. Ibid., II, II, 14–16; and I, XVI, 1.

23. Ibid., I, XVI, 8–9; and I, XVII, 2–9. There is considerable debate over Calvin's understanding of predestination. Nevertheless, Calvin, whether consistently or inconsistently, considers persons responsible for their choices.

24. Ibid., IV, XX, 1–10.

25. Strauss, *Natural Right and History,* 144.

26. Ibid., 144–45.

27. Calvin, *Institutes,* IV, XX, 31.

28. Ibid., IV, XX, 1–3; and II, VIII, 10–11.

29. Ibid., IV, XX, 16.

30. Ibid., II, VII, 6–9; and II, VII, 12–13.

31. Ibid., II, VIII, 45–46.

32. André Biéler, *The Social Humanism of Calvin* (Richmond, Va.: John Knox Press, 1964), 54–58.

33. Calvin, *Institutes,* III, VII, 7.

34. Hobbes, *Leviathan,* Part III, chap. 43.

35. Ibid., Part I, chap. 13, 107–9, and Part II, chap. 29, 253.

36. Calvin, *Institutes,* IV, XX, 11–12.

37. Hobbes, *Leviathan,* Part II, chap. 18, 144–45.

38. Ibid., Part II, chap. 21.

39. Ibid., Part II, chap. 18.

40. Ibid., Part II, chap. 21, 176–80.

41. David Brion Davis, *The Problem of Slavery in Western Culture* (Ithaca, N.Y.: Cornell University Press, 1966).

42. See, for example, Lisa Sowle Cahill, *Between the Sexes: Foundations for a Christian Ethics of Sexuality* (Philadelphia: Fortress Press, 1985), 46–56.

Chapter 2. From Natural Rights to Utility

1. Jeremy Bentham, *An Introduction to the Principles of Morals and Legislation* (1823; reprint, Garden City, N.Y.: Doubleday, 1961).

Bentham's work ends with an explicit criticism of the *Declaration of Independence.*

2. President's Commission for the Study of Ethical Problems in Medicine and Biomedical and Behavioral Research, *Deciding to Forego Life-Sustaining Treatment: Ethical, Medical, and Legal Issues in Treatment Decisions* (Washington, D.C.: U.S. Government Printing Office, 1983).

3. Ibid. Bentham's first chapter begins with that assertion.

4. Jeremy Bentham, "Anarchical Fallacies," in Frederick A. Olafson, ed., *Society, Law, and Morality* (Englewood Cliffs, N.J.: Prentice-Hall, 1961), 345.

5. Ibid., 347.

6. Ibid., 349.

7. Ibid., 353.

8. K. B. Smellie, *Great Britain Since 1688* (Ann Arbor: University of Michigan Press, 1962), 230.

9. John Stuart Mill, "Utilitarianism," in Marshall Cohen, ed., *The Philosophy of John Stuart Mill* (New York: Random House, 1961), chapter 4, 362–70.

10. Ibid., 384.

11. Ibid., 385.

12. Ibid.

13. Ibid., 386.

14. Ibid., 380.

15. Ibid., 391.

16. Ibid., 393.

17. Ibid., 391.

18. Ibid.

19. Ibid., 396.

20. Ibid.

21. Ibid., "On Liberty," 197.

22. Ibid., 200.

23. Ibid., 197.

24. Ibid., 198.

25. Ibid.

26. Ibid., 304.

27. Gerald Dworkin, "Paternalism," *The Monist* 56, no. 1 (January 1972): 64–84.

28. President's Commission for the Study of Ethical Problems in Med-

icine and Biomedical and Behavioral Research, *Deciding to Forego Life-Sustaining Treatment: Ethical, Medical, and Legal Issues in Treatment Decisions,* 26–27.

29. Ibid., 26–27.

30. Ibid., 33.

31. Ibid., 36.

32. Ibid., 79.

33. Ibid., 207.

34. Ibid., 206.

35. Ibid., 24.

36. Ibid., 36.

37. Ibid., 135.

38. Ibid., Table 1, p. 218.

39. Ibid., 208.

40. Ibid., 43.

41. Mill, "Utilitarianism," 363.

42. Ibid., 364.

43. I will not repeat the many criticisms made of this Benthamite calculus adopted by Mill as well. See, for example, W. D. Ross, *The Right and The Good,* (London: Oxford University Press, 1930); David Lyons, *Forms and Limits of Utilitarianism* (London: Oxford University Press, 1965); Arthur J. Dyck, *On Human Care* (Nashville, Tenn.: Abingdon, 1977); and J. J. C. Smart and Bernard Williams, *Utilitarianism For and Against* (New York: Cambridge University Press, 1973). See also Russell Hardin, *Morality within the Limits of Reason* (Chicago: University of Chicago Press, 1988) for a utilitarian critique of the Benthamite calculus.

Chapter 3. From Natural Rights to Class Consciousness

1. Friedrich Engels, *Herr Eugen Dühring's Revolution in Science,* chapters 9 and 10, in Frederick Olafson, ed., *Society, Law, and Morality* (Englewood Cliffs, N.J.: Prentice-Hall, 1961), 271 [1878 edition, Emile Burns, tr.].

2. Ibid.

3. Ibid.

4. Olafson, *Society, Law, and Morality,* 253. Olafson, without comment, simply credits Engels with working out "the Marxist view of morality and science . . . in some detail."

5. Eugene Kamenka, *Marxism and Ethics* (New York: St. Martin's Press, 1969), 1–7. In these pages, Kamenka argues that Marx cannot really be interpreted as accepting the views of Engels on ethics since they were too obviously inconsistent with and much more explicitly stated than his own.

6. Engels, *Herr Eugen Dühring's Revolution in Science*, 271.

7. Ibid., 270.

8. Ibid., 271.

9. Ibid.

10. Ibid., 272.

11. Ibid., 273.

12. Ibid., 274.

13. Ibid.

14. Ibid., 275.

15. Ibid.

16. Ibid., 271.

17. Ibid.

18. Kamenka, *Marxism and Ethics*, 5.

19. Ibid.

20. Karl Popper, *The Open Society and Its Enemies*, chapter 22 in ed., *Society, Law, and Morality*, 291.

21. Ibid.

22. Karl Marx and Friedrich Engels, *Manifesto of the Communist Party*, in Robert C. Tucker, ed., *The Marx-Engels Reader* (New York: W. W. Norton, 1978), 491.

23. Ibid.

24. Ibid., 500.

25. Kamenka, *Marxism and Ethics*, 9.

26. Ibid., 16.

27. Marx, *Economics-Philosophical Manuscripts* (1844), cited in Kamenka, *Marxism and Ethics*, 18.

28. Marx, *German Ideology* (1939 edition), cited in Kamenka, *Marxism and Ethics*, 23.

29. Kamenka, *Marxism and Ethics*, 29.

30. Ibid., 55.

31. Ibid., 57.

32. Ibid., 45.

33. Ibid., 58.

34. Aleksander I. Solzhenitsyn, *The Gulag Archipelago* (New York: Harper & Row, 1973), 308–9.

35. Ashley Montagu, "Foreword" (no pagination), Petr Kropotkin, *Mutual Aid: A Factor of Evolution* (1914; reprint, Boston: Extending Horizons Books, n.d.).

36. Ibid.

37. Milovan Djilas, *The New Class: An Analysis of the Communist System* (New York: Praeger, 1962), 32–33; 106–7.

38. Ibid., 27–28.

39. Ibid., 29–30; 33–37.

40. Ibid., 44–46; 68–69; 78; 88–89.

41. Ibid., 163.

42. Kamenka, *Marxism and Ethics*, 24.

43. Leo Strauss, *Natural Right and History* (Chicago: University of Chicago Press, 1953), 317.

Chapter 4. Natural Rights: Autonomy versus Interdependence

1. Max L. Stackhouse, *Creeds, Society, and Human Rights: A Study in Three Cultures* (Grand Rapids, Mich.: William B. Eerdmans Publishing Company, 1984).

2. "Preamble," *Universal Declaration of Human Rights*. The complete document is reproduced in Stackhouse, *Creeds, Society, and Human Rights*, Appendix II, 286–94.

3. Ibid.

4. Ibid., Article 1.

5. Alasdair MacIntyre, *After Virtue* (Notre Dame, Ind.: University of Notre Dame Press, 1981), 67.

6. Ibid.

7. Ibid.

8. Ibid.

9. Ibid., 67–68.

10. Ibid., 68.

11. Ibid., 244.

12. Alan Gewirth, *Human Rights: Essays on Justification and Applications* (Chicago: University of Chicago Press, 1982).

13. Ibid., 7.

14. Ibid., 1.

15. Like Kant, Gewirth is in search of "categorical imperatives."

16. Gewirth, *Human Rights,* 1. At this point, Gewirth uses the language of Mill, whose influence will also occur in the discussions of moral agency that follow.

17. Ibid., 2.

18. Ibid., 3.

19. Ibid.

20. Ibid.

21. Ibid., 2.

22. Ibid., 4.

23. Ibid., 4–5.

24. Ibid., 5.

25. Ibid.

26. Alan Gewirth, *Reason and Morality* (Chicago: University of Chicago Press, 1978), 211–12.

27. Ibid., 213–17. Gewirth implicitly uses just-war criteria to make his case.

28. Ibid., 219.

29. Gewirth, *Human Rights,* 233.

30. Gewirth, *Reason and Morality,* 140–44.

31. Gewirth, *Human Rights,* 233.

32. Ibid., 196.

33. Ibid., 181–96.

34. Gewirth, *Reason and Morality,* 217–30.

35. Ibid., 229.

36. Ibid., 271.

37. Ibid.

38. Ibid.

39. Ibid., 256.

40. Ibid.

41. Ibid.

42. Ibid., 119–25 and 140–45.

43. Ibid., 294–99.

44. Ibid., 136–37.

45. Ibid., 264–65.

46. Alan Gewirth, *Human Rights,* 5.

47. Immanuel Kant, *Lectures on Ethics* (New York: Harper & Row, 1983), 148.

48. Ibid., 153.

49. Ibid., 150.

50. Ibid., 152.

51. This is very well argued in criticism of Gewirth by Franklin Gamwell, *Beyond Preference: Liberal Theories of Independent Associations* (Chicago: University of Chicago Press, 1984), 54–66.

52. MacIntyre, *After Virtue*, 65.

Chapter 5. Moral Bonds as Requisites of Community

1. There is nothing particularly moral, right or wrong, about agreeing to paint a house for someone who wishes to change its color. Yet, the agreement to do it sets up a morally significant relation between the two contracting parties. Such a contractual relation may be a very temporary community, although a person who does a good job may become someone who will be called upon again, or even become a friend.

2. As indicated by the example in note 1, affiliative relations contain a moral element. The painter who agrees to come and does all that was promised creates a moral relation, and the one who does not keep promises creates an "immoral" relation, or a break in what was a morally created relation. A collection of individuals, like an audience for a play, are not as such communities, although they are latently communally related insofar as they do not harm one another and so function as part of the community of human beings. Such collectivities are likely to be connected as members of a larger community, such as a town or a region within a larger political unit.

3. See, for example, John Rawls, *A Theory of Justice* (Cambridge: Harvard University Press, 1971); and Robert Veatch, *A Theory of Medical Ethics* (New York: Basic Books, 1981).

4. Ibid.

5. The story of John Darsee at Harvard is contained in a report written by an ad hoc committee chaired by Richard S. Ross, M.D., of Johns Hopkins School of Medicine and reprinted in full in an article entitled "Medical School Dean Releases Report on Falsification of Research Data," *Harvard University Gazette* 77, no. 20, (29 January 1982). See also Arnold S. Relman, "Lessons from the Darsee Affair," *New England Journal of Medicine* 308, no. 23 (June 9, 1983): 1415–17.

6. This point is well made by a scientist and also by a moral theologian respectively. See Jacob Bronowski, *Science and Human Values* (New York: Harper & Bros., 1965); and H. Richard Niebuhr, *Radical Monotheism and Western Culture* (New York: Harper & Bros., 1960).

7. That is the major difficulty I have with the argument by Robert Veatch, *A Theory of Medical Ethics*, that human beings agree to the avoidance of killing on the basis of a contract. Rather, human beings have the inhibitions about killing and lying characteristically sufficient to permit agreement that killing and fraud be punishable offenses, and sufficient to draw up rules and invent institutions to do so fairly.

8. Barton McLain Griffin, *The History of Alton* (Somersworth, N.H.: New Hampshire Publishing Co., 1960, 1965), 19.

9. Ibid.

10. Ibid.

11. Ibid.

12. Ibid. Why the author uses capital letters for the expression "to form a community" I do not know; only a few isolated words are capitalized in this history.

13. Petr Kropotkin, *Mutual Aid: A Factor of Evolution* (Boston: Porter Sargent Publishers). No date is given for this reissue of Kropotkin's book, originally published in London, England, in 1902.

14. See, for example, Jon Levinson, *Sinai and Zion* (San Francisco: Harper & Row, 1987); and Walter Harrelson, *The Ten Commandments and Human Rights* (Philadelphia: Fortress Press, 1980). Harrelson understands rights in much the way I am developing in this book. As he says in his preface, "One's obligations to others are in fact the realities that the others have a right to expect."

15. Alasdair MacIntyre, *After Virtue* (Notre Dame, Ind.: Notre Dame Press, 1981).

16. See Arthur Dyck, *On Human Care* (Nashville, Tenn.: Abingdon, 1977), 53, for Piaget's distinction between constitutive rules and constituted rules.

17. Walter Harrelson, *The Ten Commandments and Human Rights*, interprets the injunction to honor one's parents as a responsibility to provide for one's parents when they no longer are able to provide for themselves. The anguish of those who cannot care for their parents or who must relinquish their care to others, for example, a nursing home of some

kind, witnesses to the strong bond between parent and child, and the strength of the proclivity to honor one's parents through nurturing them when they need it.

Chapter 6. Requisites of Morality, Freedom, and Community

1. James M. Gustafson, *Ethics from a Theocentric Perspective*, vol. 1, *Theology and Ethics* (Chicago: University of Chicago Press, 1981), 129–36. Gustafson has given an excellent account of the religious affections such as gratitude.

2. Imanuel Kant, *Fundamental Principles of the Metaphysic of Ethics* (London: Longmans, Green, 1955), 46–48.

3. Edward O. Wilson, *On Human Nature* (New York: Bantam, 1979), 216.

4. Edward O. Wilson, *Biophilia* (Cambridge: Harvard University, 1984).

5. Ibid., 121.

6. Ibid., 145.

7. Ibid., 140.

8. Ibid., 140.

9. Wilson, *On Human Nature*, 210.

10. This part of the story is in the received biblical text (Job 42:7–17) shared by Jews and Christians. There are biblical scholars, however, who see this ending as part of a "prose framework" made up of chapters 1 and 2 as prologue to the story in chapters 3–37, and as epilogue in chapters 38–42. See, for example, Jon Levinson, *Creation and the Persistence of Evil* (San Francisco: Harper & Row, 1988), 153–56.

11. Ronald M. Green, *Religious Reason* (New York: Oxford University Press, 1978). Green has expanded the scope of his study in his more recent work, *Religion and Moral Reason* (New York: Oxford University Press, 1988).

Chapter 7. Moral Knowledge: Experiential Bases of Responsibilities and Rights

1. G. P. Adams, "The Basis of Objective Judgments in Ethics," *International Journal of Ethics* 37, no. 2 (January 1927): 134–35.

2. Bertrand Russell, *Human Society in Ethics and Politics* (New York: New American Library, 1962), 19.

3. Ibid.

4. Alan Gewirth, *Human Rights: Essays on Justification and Applications* (Chicago: University of Chicago Press, 1982), 233.

5. Gordon Allport, *Becoming* (New Haven: Yale University Press, 1955), 73.

6. Solomon Asch, *Social Psychology* (Englewood Cliffs: Prentice-Hall, 1952).

7. Ibid.

8. Richard S. Ross et al., "Medical School Dean Releases Report on Falsification of Research Data," *Harvard University Gazette* 77, no. 20 (29 January 1982). This article contains a full report of John Darsee's fraudulent research released by an ad hoc committee chaired by Dr. Ross, Dean of the Faculty and Vice Chairman for Medicine at the Johns Hopkins School of Medicine. See also, Arnold S. Relman, "Lessons From the Darsee Affair," *NEJM* 308 (1983), 1415–17.

9. W. D. Ross, *The Right and the Good* (Oxford University Press, 1930), 40–41.

10. Ibid., 32–33.

11. Wolfgang Köhler, *The Place of Value in a World of Facts* (New York: Meridian, 1959), 84–85.

12. F. H. Allport, *Theories of Perception and the Concept of Structure* (New York: John Wiley & Sons, 1955), 118.

13. Kurt Lewin, *A Dynamic Theory of Personality* (New York: McGraw-Hill, 1935). On pages 243–44, Lewin reviews this research by Zeigarnik.

14. Maurice Mandelbaum, *The Phenomenology of Moral Experience* (Glenco: The Free Press, 1955).

15. Fritz Heider, *The Psychology of Interpersonal Relations* (New York: John Wiley & Sons, 1958).

16. Ibid., 219.

17. Ibid.

18. Asch, *Social Psychology,* 355.

19. H. Richard Neibuhr, *The Responsible Self* (New York: Harper & Row, 1963), 74.

20. Ibid., 75.

21. Ibid., 76.

22. Ibid., 76–77.

23. Ibid., 87.

24. Ibid., 89.

25. Robert Jay Lifton, *Home from the War* (New York: Simon & Schuster, 1973).

26. Ibid., 36–37.

27. Ibid., 103–4.

Chapter 8. Moral Knowledge: Loving Impartiality

1. Gordon Allport, *Becoming* (New Haven: Yale University Press, 1955), 73.

2. These are discussed in H. Richard Niebuhr, *The Responsible Self* (New York: Harper & Row, 1963), 74–77. See also Richard B. Brandt, *Ethical Theory* (Englewood Cliffs, N.J.: Prentice-Hall, 1959), chapters 7 and 10, for additional, more refined theories of this kind.

3. Roderick Firth, "Ethical Absolutism and the Ideal Observer," *Philosophy and Phenomenological Research* 12, no. 2 (March 1952), 317–45.

4. Ibid., 321.

5. Ibid.

6. Ibid.

7. Ibid., 325–29.

8. See, for example, William K. Frankena, *Ethics*, 2d ed. (Englewood Cliffs, N.J.: Prentice-Hall, 1973), 110–14.

9. Roderick Firth, "Ethical Absolutism," 338.

10. Ibid., 340.

11. Reinhold Niebuhr, *Moral Man and Immoral Society: A Study in Ethics and Politics* (New York: Charles Scribner's Sons, 1932).

12. Joseph Butler, *Butler's Works*, ed. Samuel Halifax, vol. 2, *Sermons* (Oxford: Oxford University Press, 1850).

13. Ibid., 150–51.

14. Ibid., 151.

15. Robert Jay Lifton, *Home from the War* (New York: Simon & Schuster, 1973).

16. Ibid., 346.

17. Ibid., 347.

18. Ibid.

19. Ibid., 350.

20. Ibid., 35–71. See also Lifton's references in note 9, page 452.

21. Ruth Smith, "Feminism and the Moral Subject," in *Women's Consciousness, Women's Conscience,* ed. Barbara Hikert Andolsen, Christine E. Gudorf, and Mary D. Pellauer (New York: Harper & Row, 1987). For a similar point, see Preston Williams, "Impartiality, Racism, and Sexism," in *The Annual of the Society of Christian Ethics,* ed. Larry L. Rasmussen (Dallas: The Society of Christian Ethics, 1983), 147–59.

22. Smith, "Feminism and the Moral Subject," 242.

23. Ibid.

24. Michael Polanyi, *Science, Faith, and Society* (1946; reprint, Chicago: University of Chicago Press, 1964).

25. Ibid., 30.

26. Ibid., 33.

27. Ibid., 41.

28. Ibid., 49.

29. Ibid., 56.

30. Ibid., 71.

31. Ibid., 73.

32. Ibid., 77.

33. Ibid. Polanyi argues that "both Bolshevik and Fascist actions were based on theories of unlimited violence."

34. Ibid., 78.

35. Ibid., 80.

36. Ibid., 84.

37. Karen Lebacqz, *Justice in an Unjust World* (Minneapolis: Augsburg, 1987). Lebacqz describes the epistemological significance of a whole range of excluded groups around the globe and argues that their insights are necessary to see injustice for what it is. A brilliant analysis of heightened perceptions of racial injustice is given in Martin Luther King, Jr., *Where Do We Go From Here: Chaos or Community?* (New York: Harper & Row, 1967).

38. Alan Gewirth, *Human Rights: Essays on Justification and Applications* (Chicago: University of Chicago Press, 1982), 128.

39. Ibid.

40. Ibid.

41. Ibid., 132.

42. Ibid., 135.

43. Ibid., 138.

44. Aristotle, *Nicomacheon Ethics*, Book IX, chapter 4.

45. Ibid., Book IX, chapters 4 and 9.

46. Ibid., Book IX, chapter 10.

47. Ibid., Book IX, chapter 7.

48. Quotations are from *The Holy Bible*, New Revised Standard Version (Nashville, Tenn.: Thomas Nelson Publishers, 1989).

49. Kenneth K. Inada, "The Buddhist Perspective on Human Rights," in Arlene Swidler, ed., *Human Rights in Religious Traditions* (New York: Pilgrim Press, 1982), 75.

50. Charles Reynolds, "Elements of a Decision Procedure for Christian Social Ethics," *Harvard Theological Review* 65, no. 4 (October 1972): 510.

51. Ibid., 513–14.

52. Robert Jay Lifton, *Home from the War* (New York: Simon & Schuster, 1973), 351–52.

53. H. Richard Niebuhr, *The Responsible Self* (New York: Harper & Row, 1963), 87.

54. Jay Lifton, *Home from the War*, 103–4.

55. Ibid.

56. James Luther Adams, "Mediating Structures and the Separation of Powers," in *Voluntary Associations: Socio-Cultural Analyses and Theological Interpretations*, ed. J. Ronald Engel (Chicago: Exploration Press, 1986), 217.

57. Ibid., 218.

58. Ibid., 225.

59. Ibid.

60. Ibid., "Voluntary Associations," 252–53.

61. Ibid., 253. I am presupposing that democratic institutions rest on the participation of a voting citizenry. See the definition of democracy in Michael Perry, *The Constitution, the Courts, and Human Rights* (New Haven: Yale University Press, 1982), 3–4.

62. C. Eric Lincoln, *The Negro Pilgrimage in America* (New York: Bantam Books, 1967).

63. Adams, *Voluntary Associations*, 251.

64. Calvin, *Institutes of the Christian Religion*, John T. McNeill, ed. (Philadelphia: Westminster Press, 1960), Book IV, chapter XX, 31, 1518–19.

65. Ibid., 1520–21.

66. Reinhold Niebuhr, *The Nature and Destiny of Man: A Christian Interpretation*, vol. 2, *Human Destiny* (New York: Charles Scribner's Sons, 1941), 281.

67. Ibid., 282.

68. Ibid., 282–83.

69. Ibid., 281. I am speaking of "early Calvinists" in the references cited here and at note 35, whereas Niebuhr calls these thinkers "later Calvinists." In doing so, I have chosen to follow Frederick S. Carney, "Associational Thought In Early Calvinism," in D. B. Robertson, ed., *Voluntary Associations: A Study of Groups in Free Societies* (Richmond, Va.: John Knox Press, 1966), 39–53.

70. Ibid.

71. Reinhold Niebuhr, *Human Destiny*, 283–84.

72. George H. Williams, "The Religious Background of the Idea of a Loyal Opposition," in Robertson, *Voluntary Associations*, 55–89.

73. Carney, "Associational Thought In Early Calvinism," 43–50.

74. See, for example, William J. Bowsma, *John Calvin: A Sixteenth-Century Portrait* (New York: Oxford University Press, 1988); and Jane Dempsey Douglass, *Women, Freedom and Calvin* (Philadelphia: Westminster Press, 1985).

75. Carney, "Associational Thought In Early Calvinism," 39–53.

76. Adams, "Mediating Structures and the Separation of Powers," 222–35.

77. J. L. Houlden, "The Kingdom of God," in James F. Childress and John Macquarrie, eds., *The Westminster Dictionary of Christian Ethics* (Philadelphia: Westminster Press, 1986).

78. Niebuhr, *The Nature and Destiny of Man*, 2:244–86, provides an example of asserting the necessity of keeping a tension between efforts to establish a Kingdom of God and the unattainable ideals by which such efforts should be judged.

79. H. Richard Niebuhr, *The Kingdom of God in America* (New York: Harper & Brothers, 1937).

80. H. Richard Niebuhr, *The Social Sources of Denominationalism* (New York: Henry Holt, 1929).

81. This is powerfully represented in certain black theologians and social critics such as Martin Luther King, Jr., *Where Do We Go From Here: Chaos or Community?* (New York: Harper & Row, 1967); and Alexan-

der Crummel. See Charles Reynolds and Riggins J. Earle Jr., "Alexander Crummel's Transformation of Bishop Butler's Ethics," *Journal of Religious Ethics* 6, no. 2 (Fall 1978): 221–39.

82. Lincoln, *The Negro Pilgrimage in America*, 141–48, documents some of the organizations formed in the civil rights movements, some of which had the marks of intentional moral communities.

83. Michael Walzer, *Just and Unjust Wars: A Moral Argument with Historical Illustrations* (New York: Basic Books, 1977).

84. *The Challenge of Peace*. The United Methodists in the United States also issued a letter on these problems, *In Defense of Creation*. In an excellent critique of the latter, Paul Ramsey compares both letters. Paul Ramsey, *Speak Up for Just War or Pacifism* (University Park, Pa.: Pennsylvania State University Press, 1988).

Chapter 9. Moral Knowledge: Ideal Companionship

1. Roderick Firth, "Ethical Absolutism and the Ideal Observer," *Philosophy and Phenomenological Research* 12, no. 3 (March 1952): 335.

2. Ibid., 341.

3. C. S. Lewis, *Screwtape Letters* (New York: Macmillan, 1967).

4. For some of the same reasons, H. Richard Niebuhr depicts an ideal moral judge as a "companion in being" and Charles Reynolds as an "Ideal Participant." See H. Richard Niebuhr, *The Responsible Self* (New York: Harper & Row, 1963); and Charles H. Reynolds, "Elements of a Decision Procedure for Christian Social Ethics," *Harvard Theological Review* 65, no. 4 (October 1972): 509–30.

5. The necessity of "omniscience" as compared with "all the relevant knowledge" was debated in the literature. See R. B. Brandt, "The Definition of an 'Ideal Observer' Theory in Ethics," and Roderick Firth, "A Reply to Professor Brandt," *Philosophy and Phenomenological Research* 15 (1955): 407–13 and 414–21. See also Reynolds, "Elements of a Decision Procedure for Christian Social Ethics," for a discussion of "omniscience."

6. Karen Lebacqz, *Justice in an Unjust World* (Minneapolis: Augsburg, 1987). In this work, Lebacqz explicitly argues the deficiency in moral cognition that results when the voices of the relatively powerless are absent from deliberations about what is justly owed these same deprived individuals and groups.

7. Reynolds, "Elements of a Decision Procedure for Christian Social Ethics," discusses the issue of power and posits "supreme power" as characteristic of an "Ideal Participant."

8. Firth, "Ethical Absolutism and the Ideal Observer," 344.

9. Ibid., 344–45.

10. Ibid., 345.

11. There are those who accept as their moral ideal an absolute prohibition against killing even under such circumstances. See, for example, John H. Yoder, "What Would You Do If...? An Exercise in Situation Ethics," *The Journal of Religious Ethics* 2, no. 2 (Fall 1974), 81–105. No explicit claim is made that this is an ethic that is generally shared or that it ought to be.

12. Richard B. Brandt, "The Morality and Rationality of Suicide," in Seymour Perlin, ed., *A Handbook for the Study of Suicide* (New York: Oxford University Press, 1975), 70.

13. Ibid.

14. For documentation of the press for physician-assisted suicide, see William Reichel, N. K. O'Connor, and Arthur J. Dyck, "Euthanasia and Assisted Suicide: How Should Physicians Respond?" *American Family Physician* 46, no. 3 (September 1992): 689–91.

15. Brandt, "The Morality and Rationality of Suicide," 73.

16. Peter Sainsbury, "Community Psychiatry," in Perlin, *A Handbook for the Study of Suicide,* 173.

17. Ibid., 177.

18. Ibid.

19. George Rosen, "History," in Perlin, *A Handbook for the Study of Suicide,* 22.

20. Ibid., 22–26.

21. Ibid., 26.

22. Massachusetts Supreme Judicial Court, *Patricia E. Brophy v. New England Sinai Hospital, Inc.* (1986).

23. Ibid. Liacos cites Mill, "On Liberty," from *In re Caulk,* 125 N.H. 226, 236 (1984).

24. Ibid. Liacos refers to *Barber v. Superior Court for Los Angeles County,* 147 Cal. App. 3rd 1006, 1014 (Ct. App. 1983).

25. Ibid. Liacos cites *John F. Kennedy Memorial Hosp. Inc. v. Bludworth,* 452 So 2d 921, 923 (Fla. 1984).

26. Ibid. Liacos cites *Matter of Conroy,* 98 N.J. 343 (1985).

27. Supreme Court of the United States, *Cruzan v. Director, Missouri Dept. of Health* (1990) Stevens, J. dissenting.

28. Massachusetts Supreme Judicial Court, *Patricia E. Brophy v. New England Sinai Hospital, Inc.*, Lynch, J. dissenting.

29. Ibid.

30. Ibid.

31. Ibid.

32. Ibid., Nolan, J. dissenting.

33. This disparity between Greek medical practices and the injunctions of the Hippocratic Oath has led some scholars to regard the oath as Pythagorean and not Hippocratic. See the original claim to this effect by Ludwig Edelstein, "The Professional Ethics of the Greek Physician," *Bulletin of the History of Medicine* 30 (1956): 392–418.

34. "The Hippocratic Oath" and "From the Oath According to Hippocrates in So Far as a Christian May Swear It" are reprinted in Stanley J. Reiser, William J. Curran, and Arthur J. Dyck, eds., *Ethics in Medicine* (Cambridge: MIT Press, 1977), 5 and 10. A recent book traces the encounter of Hippocrates with both the pagans and Christians: Owsei Tomkin, *Hippocrates in a World of Pagans and Christians* (Baltimore: Johns Hopkins University Press, 1991).

35. Massachusetts Supreme Judicial Court, Nolan, J. dissenting.

36. S. H. Wanzer et al., "The Physician's Responsibility Toward Hopelessly Ill Patients: A Second Look," *New England Journal of Medicine* 320 (1989): 844–49.

37. For example, on the front page, an article by Richard A. Knox, "Igniting a deadly debate," *Boston Sunday Globe* (27 October 1991), describes Kevorkian as the "suicide doctor" and documents his activities at the time.

38. Timothy Quill, "Death and Dignity: A Case of Individualized Decision Making," *New England Journal of Medicine* 324, no. 10 (March 7, 1991): 691–94.

39. Ibid., 692.

40. Tom L. Beauchamp and James F. Childress, *Principles of Biomedical Ethics* (New York: Oxford University Press, 1989).

41. Timothy Quill, "Death and Dignity," 693.

42. Ibid., 694.

43. Ibid., 693.

44. Al Jonsen, "Letter to the Washington State Medical Association in

response to Initiative 119," in Ron Hamel, ed., *Active Euthanasia, Religion and the Public Debate* (Chicago: The Park Ridge Center, 1991), 104.

45. Peter Sainsbury, "Community Psychiatry," in Perlin, ed., *A Handbook for the Study of Suicide,* 173.

46. J. H. Brown et al., "Is it Normal for Terminally Ill Patients to Desire Death?" *American Journal of Psychiatry* 143, no. 2 (February 1986): 208.

47. G. Rosen, "History," in Perlin, ed. *A Handbook for the Study of Suicide,* 26.

48. R. Fenigsen, "The Report of the Dutch Governmental Committee on Euthanasia," *Issues in Law and Medicine* 7, no. 3 (Winter 1991): 339–44.

49. Ibid., 340–41.

50. Ibid., 343.

51. Ibid., 343.

52. Ibid., 341.

53. P. J. van der Mass et al., "Euthanasia and Other Medical Decisions Concerning the End of Life," *Lancet* 338 (1991): 669–74.

54. Arthur J. Dyck, "Ethical Bases of the Military Profession," *Parameters* 10, no. 1 (March 1980): 39–46.

55. Eliot Freidson, *Profession of Medicine* (New York: Dodd, Mead, 1970).

56. Quill, "Death and Dignity," 692.

Chapter 10. The Nature and Bases of Rights: Justice, Nurture, and Divorce in Western Law

1. Mary Ann Glendon, *Rights Talk: The Impoverishment of Political Discourse* (New York: The Free Press, 1991).

2. Ibid., x.

3. Ibid., xi.

4. John Stuart Mill, "Utilitarianism," in Marshall Cohen, ed., *The Philosophy of John Stuart Mill* (New York: Random House, 1961), 380.

5. Ibid., 391.

6. See, for example, the excellent analysis by Douglas Sturm, "The Prism of Justice: *E Pluribus Unum?*" *The Annual of the Society of Christian Ethics,* ed. Thomas W. Ogletree (Dallas: The Society of Christian

Ethics, 1981), 1–28. In addition, see Karen Lebacqz, *Six Theories of Justice* (Minneapolis: Augsburg, 1986).

7. W. D. Ross, *The Right and The Good* (Oxford University Press, 1930) also uses the expression "morally significant relations" to describe the nature of moral duties. He regards these as "intuitions" and does not think of them as functional, observable, and logically inferable requisites of community, taking the form of naturally occurring inhibitions and proclivities.

8. Bernard Gert, *Morality: A New Justification of the Moral Rules* (New York: Oxford University Press, 1988).

9. Mill, "Utilitarianism," 392.

10. Ibid.

11. Ibid., 385.

12. Ibid.

13. Ibid.

14. Mill, "On Liberty," 310.

15. A key institution in providing assistance to parental efforts in moral education is the school. Currently there is much debate about introducing curricular materials designed to educate students about their sexual behavior, especially preventing the spread of AIDS and teenage pregnancy. Some groups involved in parenting produce books and pamphlets for adolescents on sex, birth control, and AIDS that offer a highly individualistic conception of values; a tendency to portray values as individual preferences; a strong tendency to view sexual behavior and behavior generally as private rather than as social and of communal significance; a strong, usually indirect, tendency to dissuade youth from viewing parents and adults as role models; and little material on the purposes of family formation and of the other major institutions of communal life. It is not difficult to understand why many parents voice deep concerns about the potentially adverse effects of introducing sex education into public schools. In response, the Joseph P. Kennedy, Jr., Foundation has developed a curriculum that intends to address some of the serious behavioral choices faced by teenagers today. The curriculum is intended to foster growth in morally responsible behavior by connecting youths to their families, other adults, and their communities. The Community of Caring is a program of values education that is aimed at preventing teen pregnancy and other destructive behaviors, grounded in the universally ac-

cepted ethical values of caring, responsibility, trust, and respect for self, others, and the family. In two out of three school systems, according to a recent study by The Center for Health Policy Studies, Community of Caring students reported stronger values in terms of helping others, attention to personal health, stronger relationships within the family and lasting peer relationships. In one Community of Caring school, 42% more students reported stronger values than the control school. For information on the Community of Caring School Program, write to: Eunice Kennedy Shriver, Community of Caring, Inc., 1350 New York Ave, Suite 500, Washington, DC 20005.

16. W. D. Ross, *The Right and The Good*, 21.

17. Ibid.

18. See, for example, Stanley Hauerwas, *Character and the Christian Life: A Study in Theological Ethics* (San Antonio: Trinity University Press, 1975). The claim in this book is made on behalf of the Christian's moral life.

19. Reinhold Niebuhr, *The Nature and Destiny of Man* (New York: Charles Scribner's Sons, 1941), vol. 2, chap. 9.

20. Mary Ann Glendon, *Rights Talk*, 47.

21. Ibid.

22. Ibid., 55.

23. Ibid., 63.

24. Ibid., 67.

25. Ibid., 47–48.

26. Ibid., 69.

27. Ibid., 69–70.

28. Ibid., 70.

29. Ibid., 70–75.

30. Ibid., 70.

31. Mary Ann Glendon, *Abortion and Divorce in Western Law: American Failures, European Challenges* (Cambridge: Harvard University Press, 1987), 66.

32. Ibid., 67.

33. Ibid., 69.

34. Ibid., 81.

35. Ibid., 86.

36. Ibid., 90.

37. Ibid., 87.

38. Ibid.

39. Ibid., 83–91.

40. Ibid., 105.

41. Michael Fendrich, Virginia Werner, and Myrna Weissman, "Family Risk Factors, Parental Depression, and Psychopathology in Offspring," *Developmental Psychology* 26, no. 1 (January 1990): 40–50; and Carolyn Webster-Stratton, "The Relationship of Marital Support, Conflict, and Divorce to Parent Perceptions, Behaviors, and Childhood Conduct Problems," *Journal of Marriage and the Family* 51, no. 2 (May 1989): 416–30.

42. Steven Stack, "The Effects of Divorce on Suicide in Denmark, 1961–1980," *The Sociological Quarterly* 31, no. 3 (Fall 1990): 361–68." See also Ira Wasserman, "The Impact of Divorce on Suicide in the United States, 1970–1983," *Family Perspective* 24 (1990): 61–68.

43. Thomas S. Parish, "Evaluations of Family by Youth: Do They Vary as a Function of Family Structure, Gender, and Birth Order?" *Adolescence* 25, no. 98 (Summer 1990): 354–56.

44. Ibid.

45. John Beer, "Relationship of Divorce to Self-Concept, Self-Esteem, and Grade Point Average of Fifth- and Sixth-Grade School Children," *Psychological Reports* 65, no. 3 (December 1989): 1379–83.

46. Lise M. C. Bisnaires et al., "Factors Associated with Academic Achievement in Children Following Parental Separation," *American Journal of Orthopsychiatry* 60, no. 1 (January 1990): 67–76; and Steven Kaye, "The Impact of Divorce on Children's Academic Performance," *Journal of Divorce* 12, no. 2–3 (1989): 283–98.

47. Gary Sandefur et al., "Race and Ethnicity, Family Structure, and High School Graduation," Institute for Research on Poverty, Discussion Paper No. 893-89, University of Wisconsin–Madison (August 1989).

48. Andrew Cherlin and Frank Furstenberg, Jr., *The New American Grandparent: A Place in the Family, A Life Apart*: (New York: Basic Books, 1986); and Janet Finch and Jennifer Mason, "Divorce, Remarriage and Family Obligations," *Sociological Review* 38, no. 2 (May 1990): 231–34.

49. Ibid.

50. Bryon Rodgers, "Adult Affective Disorders and Early Environ-

ment," *British Journal of Psychiatry* 157 (October 1990): 539–50.

51. Mary Ann Glendon, *Abortion and Divorce in Western Law*, 110–11.

52. Ibid., 111.

53. Ibid., 102.

54. Ibid., 108.

55. See, for example, Lisa Sowle Cahill, *Between the Sexes: Foundations for a Christian Ethics of Sexuality* (New York: Paulist Press, 1985); David M. Feldman, *Birth Control in Jewish Law* (New York: New York University Press, 1968); and James M. Gustafson, *Ethics from a Theocentric Perspective*, vol. 2 (Chicago: University of Chicago Press, 1984).

56. Glendon, *Abortion and Divorce in Western Law*, 108.

Chapter 11. Justice and Nurture: Rescue and Health Care as Rights and Responsibilities

1. Michael Tooley, "A Defense of Abortion and Infanticide," in Joel Feinberg, ed., *The Problem of Abortion* (Belmont, Calif.: Wadsworth Publishing Co., 1973), 55–91.

2. Ibid., 85.

3. Mary Ann Glendon, *Rights Talk: The Impoverishment of Political Discourse* (New York: The Free Press, 1991), 76–108.

4. Ibid., 79.

5. Ibid., 80.

6. Ibid.

7. Ibid.

8. Ibid., 89–98.

9. Ibid., 97.

10. Ibid., 88.

11. Lawrence Kohlberg, *The Philosophy of Moral Development* (San Francisco: Harper & Row, 1981).

12. Glendon, *Rights Talk*, 84–85.

13. Ibid., 88.

14. Ibid., 85.

15. Rashi Fein, *Medical Care Medical Costs: The Search for a Health Insurance Policy* (Cambridge: Harvard University Press, 1989), 34.

16. Some readers may have recognized that these criteria are abridged adaptations of criteria used within just-war theory.

17. David Himmelstein and Steffie Woolhandler, "A National Health Program for the United States: A Physician's Proposal," *NEJM* 320 no. 2 (12 January 1989): 102–8.

18. Ibid., 102.

19. Gene Outka, "Social Justice and Equal Access to Health Care," *JRE* 2, no. 1 (Spring 1974): 11–32.

20. Larry Churchill, *Rationing Health Care in America: Perceptions and Principles of Justice* (Notre Dame, Ind.: University of Notre Dame, 1987).

21. Himmelstein and Woolhandler, "A National Health Program for the United States," 105.

22. Ibid., 102.

23. Ibid.

24. Ibid., 103.

25. Ibid.

26. Ibid., 107.

27. Ibid., 102.

28. Ibid., 103.

29. Uwe E. Reinhardt, "Health Insurance for the Nation's Poor," *Health Affairs* Spring 1987: 101–12.

30. Ibid., 108–9.

31. Ibid.

32. Ibid.

33. Ibid., 102.

34. Ibid., 104.

35. Ibid.

36. Ibid., 103.

37. Ibid.

38. Ibid.

39. Ibid.

40. Ibid., 104.

41. Ibid., 105.

42. Ibid.

43. Edward Kennedy and Henry Waxman, S768 and HR1845.

44. The proposal by Enthoven and Kronick (see note 48) has mandating employer-paid insurance as one important feature.

45. Reinhardt, "Health Insurance for the Nation's Poor," 107.

46. Ibid., 110.

47. *The Nation's Health,* March 1990, 11.

48. Alain Enthoven and Richard Kronick, "A Consumer-Choice Health Plan for the 1990s: Universal Health Insurance in a System Designed to Promote Quality and Economy," *NEJM* (First of Two Parts) 320, no. 1 (5 January 1989): 29–37; (Second of Two Parts) 320, no. 2 (12 January 1989): 94–101.

49. Ibid., 31.

50. Ibid., 29.

51. Ibid.

52. Ibid., 30.

53. Ibid.

54. Ibid., 31.

55. Ibid., 30.

56. Ibid., 31.

57. Ibid., 101.

58. Chapter 23 of the Acts of 1988 signed into law by the Governor [of Massachusetts], 21 April 1988.

59. Enthoven and Kronick, "A Consumer-Choice Health Plan for the 1990s," 97.

60. Ibid.

61. Ibid., 35.

62. Ibid.

63. Fein, *Medical Care Medical Costs.*

64. Ibid., 194.

65. Ibid., 194–95.

66. Ibid., 195.

67. Ibid.

68. Ibid., 196.

69. Ibid., 192.

70. Ibid., 222.

71. Ibid., 216.

72. Ibid., 216–20.

73. Ibid., 220–22.

74. Ibid., 215.

75. *The Nation's Health,* March 1990, 11.

76. Fein, *Medical Care Medical Costs,* xi.

77. *The Nation's Health,* March 1990, 11.

78. Fein, *Medical Care Medical Costs,* 194-95.

79. Ibid., 194.

80. See, for example, John Kilner, *Who Lives? Who Dies?: Ethical Criteria in Patient Selection* (New Haven: Yale University Press, 1990), especially the section on "Ability to Pay," 175-91.

81. Tom L. Beauchamp and James F. Childress, *Principles of Biomedical Ethics* (New York: Oxford University Press, 1989).

82. Daniel Callahan, *Setting Limits: Medical Goals in an Aging Society* (New York: Simon & Schuster, 1987); Norman Daniels, *Am I My Parents' Keeper* (New York: Oxford University Press, 1988).

83. Henry Aaron and William B. Schwartz, "Rationing Health Care: The Choice Before Us," *Science* 247 (26 January 1990): 416-22.

84. B. Brown, "How Canada's Health System Works," *Business and Health*, July 1989, 28-30; Adam L. Linton, "The Canadian Health Care System: A Canadian Physician's Perspective," *NEJM* 322, no. 3 (18 January 1990): 197-99.

85. This is a very important way of thinking that entered into the current legislation enacted by the state of Oregon. That legislation cuts some services to Medicaid recipients.

86. Charlotte A. Schoeborn and Barbara F. Wilson, "Are Married People Healthier? Health Characteristics of Married and Unmarried U.S. Men and Women," presented at the American Public Health Association, 15 November 1988; Yuaureng Hu and Noreen Goldman, "Morality Differentials by Marital Status: An International Comparison," *Demography* 27 (1990): 233-50; Lorraine T. Midanik, Arthur L. Klatsky, and Mary Anne Armstrong, "Changes in Drinking Behaviors: Demographic, Psychological, and Biomedical Factors," *The International Journal of the Addictions* 25 (1990), 599-619.

87. Paula Tracy, "Koop Blasts Hillary's Task Force," *New Hampshire Sunday News*, Manchester, N.H., 28 March 1993. Koop opposes the secrecy with which the task force is working. His suggestions to them were contained in a letter that had not been answered at the time of his article.

88. Fran Pollner, "Battling the High Cost of Drugs," *Harvard Health Letter*, vol. 18, no. 9, July 1993, 9-12.

89. Kilner, *Who Lives? Who Dies?*

90. Fein, *Medical Care Medical Costs*, 195.

91. Allen Buchanan, "Health Care Delivery and Resource Allocation," in R. M. Veatch, ed., *Medical Ethics* (Boston: Jones and Bartlett Publishers, 1989), 291-327.

92. Fein, *Medical Care Medical Costs*, 192. In an excellent work, Michael Walzer, *Spheres of Justice: A Defence of Pluralism and Equality* (New York: Basic Books, 1983) argues that it is not simply useful but just to organize some spheres of society to facilitate cooperation rather than competition.

93. John Stuart Mill, "Utilitarianism" in Marshall Cohen, ed., *The Philosophy of John Stuart Mill* (New York: Random House, 1961), 380.

94. William K. Frankena, *Ethics*, 2d ed. (Englewood Cliffs, N.J.: Prentice-Hall, 1973). The first edition was published in 1963.

95. Ibid., 47.

96. W. D. Ross, *The Right and The Good* (London: Oxford University Press, 1930), 21.

97. Mill, "Utilitarianism," 397.

98. Ibid., 393.

99. Ibid.

100. Ibid.

101. Ibid., 378–81.

102. Frankena, *Ethics*, 70–71.

103. Bernard Gert, *Morality: A New Justification of the Moral Rules* (New York: Oxford University Press, 1988), 177.

104. Ibid., 157. Gert summarizes the moral rules on this page. The duties to obey law and to do one's duty are morally required insofar as violations of these rules would violate one or another of the moral rules and so would cause evil.

105. Mill, "Utilitarianism," 391–92.

106. Ibid., 392.

107. Mill, "On Liberty," in Cohen, ed., *The Philosophy of John Stuart Mill*, 198.

108. I am using "other things being equal" in the same way that W. D. Ross uses the expression *prima facie* in the second chapter of *The Right and the Good*.

109. Buchanan, "Health Care Delivery and Resource Allocation."

110. Ibid., 318–19. Buchanan's other arguments against egalitarianism are directed at versions of it that I am not espousing.

111. Ibid.

112. John Rawls, *A Theory of Justice* (Cambridge: Harvard University Press, 1971).

113. Ibid., 126–30.
114. Ibid., 438.

Epilogue

1. Judith Jarvis Thomson, *The Realm of Rights* (Cambridge: Harvard University Press, 1990), 289.
2. Jacob Bronowski, *Science and Human Values* (New York: Harper & Row, 1965), 57.
3. Ibid., 58.
4. Ibid.
5. One of the areas in which property rights function prominently is that of business. It is heartening to read an account, just published as I go to press, of a business that self-consciously bases decisions upon the responsibility to nurture the moral bonds of community and the environment. I refer to the book by Tom Chappell, President of Tom's of Maine, *The Soul of a Business: Managing for Profit and the Common Good* (New York: Bantam Books, 1993).

Bibliography

Aaron, Henry, and William B. Schwartz. "Rationing Health Care: The Choice Before Us." *Science* 247 (26 January 1990): 416–22.

Adams, G. P. "The Basics of Objective Judgements in Ethics." *International Journal of Ethics* 37, no. 2 (January 1927): 128–37.

Adams, James Luther. "The Law of Nature: Some General Considerations," and "The Law of Nature in Greco-Roman Thought." *Journal of Religion* 25, no. 2 (April 1945): 88–96 and 97–118.

———. "Mediating Structures and the Separation of Powers" and "Voluntary Associations." In *Voluntary Associations: Socio-Cultural Analyses and Theological Interpretations,* edited by J. Ronald Engel. Chicago: Exploration Press, 1986.

Allport, F. H. *Theories of Perception and the Concept of Structure.* New York: John Wiley & Sons, 1955.

Allport, Gordon. *Becoming.* New Haven: Yale University Press, 1955.

Anscombe, G. E. M. *Ethics, Religion, and Politics.* Minneapolis: University of Minnesota Press, 1981.

Aristole. *Nichomachean Ethics.* Book IX, chapter 4.

Asch, Solomon. *Social Psychology.* Englewood Cliffs, N.J.: Prentice-Hall, 1952.

Beauchamp, T. L., and J. F. Childress. *Principles of Biomedical Ethics.* New York: Oxford University Press, 1989.

Beer, John. "Relationship of Divorce to Self-Concept, Self-Esteem, and Grade Point Average of Fifth- and Sixth-Grade School Children." *Psychological Reports* 65, no. 3 (December 1989): 1379–83.

Bentham, Jeremy. *An Introduction to the Principles of Morals and Legislation.* 1823. Reprint. Garden City: Doubleday, 1961.

———. "Anarchical Fallacies." In *Society, Law, and Morality,* edited by Frederick A. Olafson. Englewood Cliffs, N.J.: Prentice-Hall, 1961.

The Holy Bible. New Revised Standard Version. Nashville: Thomas Nelson Publishers, 1989.

Biéler, André. *The Social Humanism of Calvin* Richmond, Va.: John Knox Press, 1964.

Bisnaires, Lise M. C., et al. "Factors Associated with Academic Achievement in Children Following Parental Separation." *American Journal of Orthopsychiatry* 60, no. 1 (January 1990): 67–76.

Bowsma, William J. *John Calvin: A Sixteenth-Century Portrait.* New York: Oxford University Press, 1988.

Brandt, Richard B. *Ethical Theory.* Englewood Cliffs, N.J.: Prentice-Hall, 1959.

———. "The Definition of an 'Ideal Observer' Theory in Ethics." *Philosophy and Phenomenological Research* 15 (1955): 407–13.

———. "The Morality and Rationality of Suicide." In *A Handbook for the Study of Suicide,* edited by Seymour Perlin. New York: Oxford University Press, 1975.

Bronowski, Jacob. *Science and Human Values.* New York: Harper & Bros., 1965.

Brown, B. "How Canada's Health System Works." *Business and Health* July 1989: 28–30.

Brown, J. H., et al. "Is It Normal for Terminally Ill Patients to Desire Death?" *American Journal of Psychiatry* 143, no. 2 (February 1986): 208–11.

Buchanan, Allen. "Health Care Delivery and Resource Allocation." In *Medical Ethics,* edited by R. M. Veatch. Boston: Jones and Bartlett, 1989.

Butler, Joseph. *Butler's Works.* Edited by Samuel Halifax. Vol. 2, *Sermons.* Oxford: Oxford University Press, 1850.

Cahill, Lisa Sowle. *Between the Sexes: Foundations for a Christian Ethic of Sexuality.* Philadelphia: Fortress Press, 1985.

Callahan, Daniel. *Setting Limits: Medical Goals in an Aging Society.* New York: Simon & Schuster, 1987.

Calvin, Jean. *Institutes of the Christian Religion.* Edited by John T. McNeil. Philadelphia: Westminster Press, 1966.

Carney, Frederick S. "Associational Thought in Early Calvinism." In

Voluntary Associations: A Study of Groups in Free Societies, edited by D. B. Robertson. Richmond: John Knox Press, 1966.

Chappell, Tom. *The Soul of a Business: Managing for Profit and the Common Good*. New York: Bantam Books, 1993.

Cherlin, Andrew, and Frank Furstenberg, Jr. *The New American Grandparent: A Place in the Family, A Life Apart*. New York: Basic Books, 1966.

Churchill, Larry. *Rationing Health Care in America: Perceptions and Principles of Justice*. Notre Dame, Ind.: University of Notre Dame Press, 1967.

Daniels, Norman. *Am I My Parents' Keeper?* New York: Oxford University Press, 1988.

Davis, David Brion. *The Problem of Slavery in Western Culture*. Ithaca: Cornell University Press, 1966.

Douglass, Jane Dempsey. *Women, Freedom, and Calvin*. Philadelphia, Westminster Press, 1985.

Dworkin, Gerald. "Paternalism." *The Monist* 56, no. 1 (January 1972): 64–84.

Dyck, Arthur. *On Human Care*. Nashville, Tenn.: Abingdon, 1977.

———. "Ethical Bases of the Military Profession." *Parameters* 10, no. 1 (March 1980): 39–46

Edelstein, Ludwig. "The Professional Ethics of the Greek Physician." *Bulletin of the History of Medicine* 30, no. 5 (September–October 1956): 392–418.

Engels, Friedrich. *Herr Eugen Duhring's Revolution in Science*, chapters 9 and 10. In *Society, Law, and Morality*, edited by Frederick Olafson. Translated by Emile Burns. 1878. Reprint. Englewood Cliffs, N.J.: Prentice-Hall, 1961.

Enthoven, Alain, and Richard Kronick. "A Consumer-Choice Health Plan for the 1990's: Universal Health Insurance in a System Designed to Promote Quality and Economy." Parts 1–2. *New England Journal of Medicine* 320, no. 1, 2 (5, 12 January 1989): 29–37, 94–101.

Fein, Rashi. *Medical Care, Medical Costs: The Search for a Health Insurance Policy*. Cambridge: Harvard University Press, 1969.

Feldman, David M. *Birth Control in Jewish Law*. New York: New York University Press, 1968.

Fendrich, Michael, Virginia Warner, and Myra Weissman. "Family Risk Factors, Parental Depression, and Psychopathology in Offspring." *Developmental Psychology* 26, no. 1 (January 1990): 40–50.

Fenigsen, R. "The Report of the Dutch Governmental Committee on Euthanasia." *Issues in Law and Medicine* 7, no. 3 (Winter 1991): 339–44.

Finch, Janet, and Jennifer Mason. "Divorce, Remarriage, and Family Obligations." *Sociological Review* 38, no. 2 (May 1990): 231–34.

Firth, Roderick. "Ethical Absolutism and the Ideal Observer." *Philosophy and Phenomenological Research* 12, no. 12 (March 1952): 317–45.

———. "A Reply to Professor Brandt." *Philosophy and Phenomenological Research* 15 (1955): 414–21.

Frankena, William K. *Ethics*. 2d ed. Englewood Cliffs, N.J.: Prentice-Hall, 1973.

Freidson, Eliot. *Profession of Medicine*. New York: Dodd, Mead, 1970.

Gamwell, Franklin. *Beyond Preference: Liberal Theories of Independent Associations*. Chicago: University of Chicago Press, 1984.

Gert, Bernard. *Morality: A New Justification of the Moral Rules*. New York: Oxford University Press, 1988.

Gewirth, Alan. *Human Rights: Essays on Justification and Applications*. Chicago: University of Chicago Press, 1982.

———. *Reason and Morality*. Chicago: University of Chicago Press, 1978.

Gilligan, Carol. *In A Different Voice: Psychological Theory and Women's Development*. Cambridge: Harvard University Press, 1982.

Glendon, Mary Ann. *Rights Talk: The Impoverishment of Political Discourse*. New York: The Free Press, 1991.

———. *Abortion and Divorce in Western Law: American Failures, European Challenges*. Cambridge: Harvard University Press, 1978.

Green, Ronald M. *Religious Reason*. New York: Oxford University Press, 1978.

———. *Religion and Moral Reason*. New York: Oxford University Press, 1988.

Griffin, Barton McLain. *The History of Alton*. Somersworth, N.H.: New Hampshire Publishing Co., 1965.

Gustafson, James M. *Ethics from a Theocentric Perspective*. 2 vols. Chicago: University of Chicago Press, 1981, 1984.

Hardin, Russell. *Morality Within the Limits of Reason.* Chicago: University of Chicago Press, 1988.

Harrelson, Walter. *The Ten Commandments and Human Rights.* Philadelphia: Fortress Press, 1980.

Hauerwas, Stanley. *Character and the Christian Life: A Study in Theological Ethics.* San Antonio, Tex.: Trinity University Press, 1975.

Heider, Fritz. *The Psychology of Interpersonal Relations.* New York: John Wiley & Sons, 1958.

Himmelstein, David, and Steffie Woolhandler. "A National Health Program for the United States: A Physician's Proposal." *New England Journal of Medicine* 320, no. 2 (12 January 1989): 102–8.

Hobbes, Thomas. *Leviathan.* 1651. Reprint. Indianapolis: Bobbs-Merrill, 1958.

Houlden, J. L. "The Kingdom of God." In *The Westminster Dictionary of Christian Ethics,* edited by James F. Childress and John Macquarrie. Philadelphia: Westminster Press, 1986.

Hu, Yuaureng, and Noreen Goldman. "Mortality Differentials by Marital Status: An International Comparison." *Demography* 27 (1990): 233–50.

Inada, Kenneth K. "The Buddhist Perspective on Human Rights." In *Human Rights in Religious Traditions,* edited by Arlene Swidler. New York: Pilgrim Press, 1982.

Jonsen, Al. "Letter to the Washington State Medical Association in Response to Initiative 119." In *Active Euthanasia, Religion, and the Public Debate,* edited by Ron Hamel. Chicago: The Park Ridge Center, 1991.

Kamenka, Eugene. *Marxism and Ethics.* New York: St. Martin's Press, 1969.

Kant, Immanuel. *Fundamental Principles of the Metaphysics of Ethics.* Extracts from *Critique of Practical Reason* (1788) and other works on the theory of ethics, translated by Thomas K. Abbott. London: Longmans, Green, 1955.

———. *Lectures on Ethics.* New York: Harper & Row, 1983.

Kaye, Steven. "The Impact of Divorce on Children's Academic Performance." *Journal of Divorce* 12, no. 2–3 (1989): 283–98.

Kilner, John. *Who Lives? Who Dies? Ethical Criteria in Patient Selection.* New Haven: Yale University Press, 1990.

King, Martin Luther, Jr. *Where Do We Go from Here: Chaos or Community?* New York: Harper & Row, 1967.

Knox, Richard A. "Igniting a Deadly Debate." *Boston Sunday Globe*, 27 October 1991, 1, 10.

Kohlberg, Lawrence. *The Philosophy of Moral Development.* San Francisco: Harper & Row, 1981.

Köhler, Wolfgang. *The Place of Value in a World of Facts.* New York: Meridian, 1959.

Kropotkin, Petr. *Mutual Aid: A Factor of Evolution.* London, 1902. Reprint. Boston: Porter Sargent Publishers, n.d.

Küng, Hans. *Does God Exist? An Answer for Today.* Garden City: Doubleday, 1980.

Lebacqz, Karen. *Justice in an Unjust World.* Minneapolis: Augsburg Publishing House, 1987.

———. *Six Theories of Justice.* Minneapolis: Augsburg Publishing House, 1986.

Levinson, Jon. *Creation and the Persistence of Evil.* San Francisco: Harper & Row, 1988.

———. *Sinai and Zion.* San Francisco: Harper & Row, 1987.

Lewin, Kurt. *A Dynamic Theory of Personality.* New York: McGraw-Hill, 1935.

Lewis, C. S. *Screwtape Letters.* New York: Macmillan, 1967.

Lifton, Robert J. *Home from the War.* New York: Simon & Schuster, 1973.

Lincoln, C. Eric. *The Negro Pilgrimage in America.* New York: Bantam Books, 1967.

Linton, Adam L. "The Canadian Health Care System: A Canadian Physician's Perspective." *New England Journal of Medicine* 322, no. 3 (January 18, 1990): 197–99.

Lyons, David. *Forms and Limits of Utilitarianism.* London: Oxford University Press, 1965.

MacIntyre, Alasdair. *After Virtue.* Notre Dame, Ind.: University of Notre Dame Press, 1981.

Mandelbaum, Maurice. *The Phenomenology of Moral Experience.* Glenco, Ill.: The Free Press, 1955.

Marx, Karl, and Friedrich Engels. *Manifesto of the Communist Party.* In *The Marx-Engels Reader,* edited by Robert C. Tucker. New York: W. W. Norton, 1978.

Midanik, Lorraine T., Arthur L. Klatsky, and Mary Anne Armstrong. "Changes in Drinking Behaviors: Demographic, Psychological, and Biomedical Factors." *The International Journal of the Addictions* 25 (1990): 599–619.

Mill, John Stuart. "Utilitarianism" and "On Liberty." In *The Philosophy of John Stuart Mill*, edited by Marshall Cohen. New York: Random House, 1961.

Montagu, Ashley. "Foreword," *Mutual Aid: A Factor of Evolution*, by Petr Kropotkin. 1914. Reprint. Boston: Extending Horizons Books, n.d.

Nation's Health, March 1990.

Niebuhr, H. Richard. *Radical Monotheism and Western Culture*. New York: Harper & Bros., 1960.

——. *The Responsible Self*. New York: Harper & Bros., 1963.

——. *The Kingdom of God in America*. New York: Harper & Bros., 1937.

——. *The Social Sources of Denominationalism*. New York: Henry Holt, 1929.

Niebuhr, Reinhold. *The Nature and Destiny of Man: A Christian Interpretation*. Vol. 2, *Human Destiny*. New York: Charles Scribner's Sons, 1941.

——. *Moral Man and Immoral Society: A Study in Ethics and Politics*. New York: Charles Scribner's Sons, 1932.

Olafson, Frederick, ed. *Society, Law, and Morality*. Englewood Cliffs, N.J.: Prentice-Hall, 1961.

Outka, Gene. "Social Justice and Equal Access to Health Care." *Journal of Religious Ethics* 2, no. 1 (Spring 1974): 11–32.

Parish, Thomas S. "Evalulations of Family by Youth: Do They Vary as a Function of Family Structure, Gender, and Birth Order?" *Adolescence* 25, no. 98 (Summer 1990): 354–56.

Perry, Michael. *The Constitution, the Courts, and Human Rights*. New Haven: Yale University Press, 1982.

Polanyi, Michael. *Science, Faith, and Society*. 1946. Reprint. Chicago: University of Chicago Press, 1964.

Pollner, Fran. "Battling the High Cost of Drugs." *Harvard Health Letter* 18, no. 9 (July 1993): 9–12.

Popper, Karl. "The Open Society and Its Enemies." In *Society, Law, and*

Morality, edited by Frederick Olafson. Englewood Cliffs, N.J.: Prentice-Hall, 1961.

President's Commission for the Study of Ethical Problems in Medicine and Biomedical and Behavioral Research. *Deciding to Forego Life-Sustaining Treatment: A Report on Ethical, Medical, and Legal Issues in Treatment Decisions.* Washington, D.C.: U.S. Government Printing Office, 1983.

Quill, Timothy. "Death and Dignity: A Case for Individualized Decision Making." *New England Journal of Medicine* 324, no. 10 (March 7, 1991): 691–94.

Ramsey, Paul. *Speak Up For Just War or Pacifism.* University Park: Pennsylvania State University Press, 1988.

Rawls, John. *A Theory of Justice.* Cambridge: Harvard University Press, 1971.

Reichel, William, N. K. O'Connor, and Arthur J. Dyck, "Euthanasia and Assisted Suicide: How Should Physicians Respond?" *American Family Physician* 46, no. 3 (September 1992).

Reinhardt, Uwe. "Health Insurance for the Nation's Poor." *Health Affairs* Spring 1987: 101–12.

Reiser, Stanley J., William J. Curran, and Arthur J. Dyck, eds. *Ethics in Medicine.* Cambridge: MIT Press, 1977.

Relman, Arnold. "Lessons from the Darsee Affair." *New England Journal of Medicine* 308, no. 23 (June 9, 1983): 1415–17.

Reynolds, Charles. "Elements of a Decision Procedure for Christian Social Ethics." *Harvard Theological Review* 65, no. 4 (October 1972): 509–30.

Reynolds, Charles, and J. Earle Riggins, Jr. "Alexander Crummel's Transformation of Bishop Butler's Ethics." *Journal of Religious Ethics* 6, no. 2 (Fall 1978): 221–39.

Rodgers, Bryon. "Adult Affective Disorders and Early Environment." *British Journal of Psychiatry* 57, no. 159 (October 1990): 539–50.

Rosen, George. "History." In *A Handbook for the Study of Suicide,* edited by Seymour Perlin. New York: Oxford University Press, 1975.

Ross, Richard S., M.D. "Medical School Dean Releases Report on Falsification of Research Data." *Harvard University Gazette,* 29 January 1982.

Ross, W. D. *The Right and the Good.* London: Oxford University Press, 1930.

Russell, Bertrand. *Human Society in Ethics and Politics.* 1952. Reprint. New York: New American Library, 1962.

Sainsbury, Peter. "Community Psychiatry." In *A Handbook for the Study of Suicide,* edited by Seymour Perlin. New York: Oxford University Press, 1975.

Sandefur, Gary, et al. "Race and Ethnicity, Family Structure, and High School Graduation," *Institute for Research on Poverty Discussion Paper No. 893–89.* University of Wisconsin–Madison, August 1989.

Schoeborn, Charlotte A., and Barbara F. Wilson. "Are Married People Healthier? Health Characteristics of Married and Unmarried U.S. Men and Women," presented at the American Public Health Association annual meeting, 15 November 1988.

Smart, J. J. C., and Bernard Williams. *Utilitarianism For and Against.* New York: Cambridge University Press, 1973.

Smellie, K. B. *Great Britain Since 1668.* Ann Arbor: University of Michigan Press, 1962.

Smith, Ruth. "Feminism and the Moral Subject." In *Women's Consciousness, Women's Conscience,* edited by Barbara Hikert Andolsen, Christine E. Gudorf, and Mary D. Pellauer. New York: Harper & Row, 1987.

Solzhenitsyn, Aleksandr I. *The Gulag Archipelago.* New York: Harper & Row, 1973.

Stack, Steven. "The Effects of Divorce on Suicide in Denmark, 1961–1980." *The Sociological Quarterly* 31, no. 3 (Fall 1990): 361–68.

Stackhouse, Max. *Creeds, Society, and Human Rights: A Study in Three Cultures.* Grand Rapids: Eerdmans, 1984.

Strauss, Leo. *Natural Right and History.* Chicago: University of Chicago Press, 1953.

Sturm, Douglas. "The Prism of Justice: *E Pluribus Unum?*" In *The Annual of the Society of Christian Ethics,* edited by Thomas Ogletree, 1–28. Dallas: The Society of Christian Ethics, 1981.

Thomson, Judith Jarvis. *The Realm of Rights.* Cambridge: Harvard University Press, 1990.

Tomkin, Owsel. *Hippocrates in a World of Pagans and Christians.* Baltimore: Johns Hopkins Press, 1991.

Tooley, Michael. "A Defense of Abortion and Infanticide." In *The Prob-*

lem of Abortion, edited by Joel Feinberg, 51–91. Belmont, Calif.: Wadsworth Publishing Co., 1973.

Tracy, Paula. "Koop Blasts Hillary's Task Force." *New Hampshire Sunday News.* Manchester, N.H., 28 March 1993.

Van der Mass, P. J., et al. "Euthanasia and Other Medical Decisions Concerning the End of Life." *Lancet* 338 (1991): 669–74.

Veatch, Robert. *A Theory of Medical Ethics.* New York: Basic Books, 1981.

Walzer. Michael. *Spheres of Justice: A Defense of Pluralism and Equality.* New York: Basic Books, 1983.

———. *Just and Unjust Wars: A Moral Argument with Historical Illustrations.* New York: Basic Books, 1977.

Wanzer, S. H., et al. "The Physician's Responsibility toward Hopelessly Ill Patients: A Second Look." *New England Journal of Medicine* 320, no. 13 (March 30, 1989): 844–49.

Wasserman, Ira. "The Impact of Divorce on Suicide in the United States, 1970–1983." *Family Perspective* 24 (1990): 61–68.

Weber, Max. *The Protestant Ethic and the Spirit of Capitalism.* Translated by T. Parsons. New York: Harper & Row, 1958.

Webster-Stratton, Carolyn. "The Relationship of Marital Support, Conflict, and Divorce to Parent Perceptions, Behaviors, and Childhood Conduct Problems." *Journal of Marriage and the Family* 51, no. 2 (May 1989): 416–30.

Williams, George H., "The Religious Background of the Idea of a Loyal Opposition." In *Voluntary Associations: A Study of Groups in Free Societies,* edited by D. B. Robertson. Richmond: John Knox Press, 1966.

Williams, Preston. "Impartiality, Racism, and Sexism." In *The Annual of the Society of Christian Ethics,* edited by Larry L. Rasmussen. Dallas: The Society of Christian Ethics, 1983.

Wilson, Edward O. *Biophilia.* Cambridge: Harvard University Press, 1984.

———. *On Human Nature.* New York: Bantam Books, 1979.

Yoder, John H. "What Would You Do If . . . ? An Exercise in Situation Ethics." *Journal of Religious Ethics* 2, no. 2 (Fall 1974): 81–106.

Index